# GRAINS OF SAND

## Melvyn Bragg's Cumbrian Novels

JOHN SHAPCOTT

**CHURNET VALLEY BOOKS**
1 King Street, Leek, Staffordshire. ST13 5NW  01538 399033 www.leekbooks.co.uk
© John Shapcott and Churnet Valley Books 2014
ISBN 9781904546979

# In Memory of Linda

Stay but till my Linda close
Her life begetting eye;
And let the whole world then dispose
Itself to live or die.

The cover is a painting by Sally Richardson

The Dedication is based on Robert Herrick's 'To Daisies, Not to Shut so Soon'.

# CONTENTS

# ACKNOWLEDGEMENTS

I would like to thank the dedicated band of readers who have commented on various chapters in draft form. The late Peter Preston was a particularly enthusiastic and helpful contributor in the project's early stages. Later he was joined by Nick Bentley, Leslie Powner, Pat Marshall and Katie Wales. These, together with colleagues in Keele University's English Department, have helped more than they can imagine. Pat Marshall bravely volunteered to proof-read the completed manuscript.

It has been my good fortune to communicate with two Lake District dwellers able to bring a personal touch to my questions about Melvyn Bragg's depiction of local customs. The late Margaret Armstrong, related to the Bragg family, provided me with copies of her personal archive of newspaper cuttings about Melvyn, together with her first impressions of some of his books. Linda and I also enjoyed her hospitality over afternoon tea at her home in Keswick. I was very fortunate to be in correspondence with the helpful and very knowledgeable Betty Marshall of Lamplugh who not only emailed me personal memories of the village but also sent me copies of *The Parish Church of Lamplugh* and *Lamplugh Church*, the first co-edited and the second written by her.

Jenny Graveson put her love of theatre to good use in tracking down old theatre programmes of *The Hired Man* and a copy of *Plays and Players* containing an informative two pages on the musical.

That distinguished critic of the rural novel, Glen Cavaliero, discussed Melvyn's novels with me at the 2011 Powys Society Conference in Llangollen, later posting me his published review of *The Silken Net*.

Michael Richardson of the Art Space Gallery, London, kindly sent me the gallery's 2014 catalogue for an exhibition of Julian Cooper's Lake District mountain paintings. I am especially indebted to Julian himself for making available for reproduction his dramatic 'Honister Crag' oil painting.

Kerry Wendt generously sent and allowed me to quote from her Ph.D. thesis on the epigraphic character.

I am indebted to Chris Sheppard and the staff at the Brotherton Library, University of Leeds, for making available a copy of Melvyn's unpublished novel, *Mirrors and Wire*, now part of the Library's voluminous Bragg Archive. And, of course, to Melvyn for allowing me to quote from this early youthful work.

It is thanks to a letter of introduction from Margaret Drabble that

I first got to know Melvyn. Margaret knew of my wish to write a critical study of his novels and suggested to her friend Melvyn that if we met we would be likely to find common ground. This is exactly what happened over a friendly breakfast meeting at which he gave his support to the project. We have met several times since then to discuss progress - Melvyn's only, and welcome, interference has been to treat Linda and me to lunch! His 'Afterword' offers a valuable insight into the novelist's take on autobiographical fiction.

Sadly, Linda died before the study was finished. During the dark nights that followed I was supported by friends, but in particular by Olly and Norman Heyes without whom it is doubtful whether this book would ever have been completed.

Linda was by my side as we explored various Cumbrian locations from Buttermere to Wigton, with me at all the meetings with Melvyn, found and copied old reviews of his novels, typed the first nine chapters of this book, read and discussed all the novels with me, and generally brought a sense of joy to the whole undertaking. There is a parting of lovers at the end of Melvyn's *Crossing the Lines*: '"I love you, you see," he said helplessly. "What'll I do without you?"'

## ABBREVIATIONS

The following are used for works by Melvyn Bragg cited in this book:

| | |
|---|---|
| WN | FOR WANT OF A NAIL |
| SI | THE SECOND INHERITANCE |
| WCW | WITHOUT A CITY WALL |
| HM | A HIRED MAN |
| PE | A PLACE IN ENGLAND |
| KC | KINGDOM COME |
| JL | JOSH LAWTON |
| SN | THE SILKEN NET |
| SE | SPEAK FOR ENGLAND |
| AM | AUTUMN MANOEUVRES |
| MB | THE MAID OF BUTTERMERE |
| TD | A TIME TO DANCE |
| SS | THE SEVENTH SEAL |
| SR | THE SOLDIER'S RETURN |
| SW | A SON OF WAR |
| CL | CROSSING THE LINES |
| RM | REMEMBER ME... |
| AE | THE ADVENTURE OF ENGLISH |
| BB | THE BOOK OF BOOKS |
| SB | THE SOUTH BANK SHOW |
| GM | GRACE AND MARY |

John Shapcott and Melvyn Bragg at the Keswick Literary Festival, 2011.

# PREFACE

Where to begin? Looking back it appears a happy coincidence that my first literary encounter with Melvyn Bragg, the Lake District, and Wigton was in another English region favoured by the Romantic Movement as a destination for tourists in search of the serene and the sublime amidst a rugged landscape. The date was Thursday 1 July 1976, and I was in a well-stocked independent bookshop in Truro, Cornwall, where Bragg's newly published *Speak for England* was on display. With a first degree in Sociology and Politics I was attracted by its promise of rescuing the neglected voices of the ordinary inhabitants of a Cumbrian town through an impressively wide range of transcribed interviews. And I was not to be disappointed. Here were uncensored first-person narratives detailing the changing fortunes of life through two World Wars and the decline of the British Empire as witnessed by those who endured rather than made history.

Two years later and I discovered Bragg the novelist appealing to my involvement in local politics - of which there is more to be said in Chapter 7 - with his publication of *Autumn Manoeuvres.* This book arrived through the post as one of the, then, New Fiction Society's choice of the best of new novels - other titles received included Graham Swift's *The Sweet Shop Owner* (1980), Thomas Keneally's *Confederates* (1979), and Iris Murdoch's *The Nice and the Good* (1968). The pace, energy and honesty of Bragg's political writing, married to the ideological construction of landscape, so impressed me that from then on I purchased each new Bragg novel upon publication. These novels became my introduction to the Lake District as a distinctive place within the United Kingdom, a region with its own jealously guarded and continuing sense of history, politics, culture and poetics.

Next came the experience of hearing Bragg speak at the Buxton Literary Festival in July 2010 about his sequence of semi-autobiographical novels culminating in *Remember Me...* (2008). Listening, I became convinced that his work owed a thematic debt to William Wordsworth whilst also being firmly in the tradition of Thomas Hardy and D.H. Lawrence, and that it represented an important contemporary strand in the survival and development of the English regional novel, composed of a mixture of autobiographical experiences, retrieved memories both personal and collective, and fictional inventiveness. Whilst I share, and will celebrate, Bragg's stress on a sense of place as paramount, I also intend for this study to point up the increasing appearance and influence of the autobiographical subject as the novels progress.

When explaining how he sees his work Bragg frequently cites William Blake's *Auguries of Innocence* poem, the opening quatrain of which reads:

> To see a World in a Grain of Sand
> And a Heaven in a Wild Flower,
> Hold Infinity in the palm of your hand
> And Eternity in an hour.
>
> (Blake, p.431)

In his 'Introduction' to *Speak for England* Bragg writes that '[t]o find the world in a grain of sand has been a sound method in science and art since men started looking for answers' (*SE* p.5), and true to this belief he has set nearly all his fiction in the Lake District and in his representative home town of Wigton. In the most recently published novel included in my study, *Grace and Mary* (2013), Bragg remains consistently true to his Blakean credo, asserting that the 'quest now was not only to find the truth in a grain of sand but to see all of life in a moment' (*GM*, p.46). Bragg's novels, from *For Want of a Nail* (1965) to *Grace and Mary* tend to read the Lakes, and the abutting town of Wigton, within the condition of England tradition, blending an acute awareness of political realities with the creation of an artistic imaginary that allows his commitment to regional identity to speak for the wider shores of cultural life in England. In this respect his work occupies an almost unique position in standing firm for a belief in the value of region, place, and the knowable community as celebrating the essentials of national identity and thereby the very notion of Englishness.

The range and quality of Bragg's fiction refutes contemporary obituaries on the death of the regional novel as a cultural force. In a *New Statesman* essay on the literary North (December 2013) the Dorothy Wordsworth biographer Frances

Wilson claims that, 'apart from Wordsworth, the sublimity of the landscape stems the flow of creativity' (p.54). My argument runs entirely contrary to her statement, and in demonstrating the wide range of genres encompassed by Bragg's novels - historical, political, Bildungsroman, Romantic, autobiographical, family saga, memoir, social documentary - shows the landscape of the Lakes in all its sublimity to be an ever-renewing source of creative imagination. As each novel is analysed in detail, the scale of Bragg's achievement as an imaginative and inventive writer of place across genres becomes evident.

Bragg's brand of proud regionalism does not stop short at the borders of Cumbria, but, rather, provides a model and means for relating to England as a whole. The threat of regional marginalisation remains a constant in an increasingly global world, and is met head-on in *Remember Me...* .The relevant passage is worth quoting at length because the conversation between the novel's literary hero, the now successful writer Joe Richardson and an American poet, Christina, helps define the parameters of the concerns that Bragg himself addresses as a provincial/regional novelist:

> As soon as they had secured a [pub] table in an empty corner, Christina struck.
>
> 'I read *A Chance Defeat* and I liked it,' she said in her level gravelly sexy New England accent. 'Tell me. Do you believe the English provincial novel carries guns any more? ... I mean when Hardy and Lawrence did their thing, Britain had an Empire and everybody listened. Everything that happens at the centre of an Empire is important both to those who want to join and those who want to beat it up. Even in the States we wanted to know what happened in Nottinghamshire and Wessex. Everything that mattered to you guys mattered to us guys. But will that wash any more?'
>
> 'If writing's any good,' he responded, rather feebly in tone and emphasis, 'then it doesn't matter where it's set, does it?'
>
> 'Not in theory,' she said crisply, 'I agree. And never in poetry. But the novel traditionally carries the news and

what's the news from the English provinces today?'...

'Same as usual,' said Joe, lighting up, 'same the whole world over, births, deaths and all that stuff in between.'

'I see what you're saying. And you're right, of course. But it seems to me that the novel has always tracked the power. I don't mean the political power necessarily although that counts. The best novelist alive could be in Finland but would anybody be as interested as by the best novelist in America or Russia? No, the power I'm talking about is where the heat is. And it seems to me that you've had great novelists over here and we have too - look at Faulkner, just look at Faulkner! - who have quarried the provinces but it's time to move on.'

'People still live there.'

'I know. Oh, I know.'

'Things happen. Life goes on.'

'Oh, I know. You're right.'...

'So what next? In your system. Of perpetually and opportunistically moving on to pastures new.'...

'Women writers - I know there have always been women writers but I mean self-consciously feminist writers - we are claiming more territory. The American Jews are riding high now. They're in the saddle. Next I think the blacks, in the States anyhow, they bring us news, and news we can trust because it's fiction. Faulkner still has the heat because of the blacks. Your old Empire, your Commonwealth has more and more writers demanding space for their experience. In the States the gays are gathering on the fringes and then there's genre writing. Crime's bigger than ever. I'm afraid the carnival's moved on from the English provinces.'

'Joe thinks you can find all human life in Wigton, don't you, Joe?'...

'Too royal,' Joe said. 'A man's a man for a' that. Rabbie Burns' working class poet, rare...'

(*RM*, pp.395-7)

All of these issues are dealt with in the novels I discuss, particularly the importance of the American novel and the recognition of voices from what were the Colonial fringes. The specific reference to Burns is a reminder of Bragg's democratic poetics as evidenced in his texts. In an essay titled 'The Possibilities of an Intelligent Regionalism in California' the American critic and poet Kenneth Rexroth makes the related point that regionally self-aware art produces informed and socially active democratic citizens. Further, reviewing Walt Whitman's *Leaves of Grass*, he is warmly appreciative of Whitman's readiness to 'find cosmogony under his heel' (quoted in Jason Arthur, p. 242), an American linking of the particular to the universal that redirects attention to Bragg's English Blakean approach to local place as a stimulus to universal experiences that reach beyond any supposed confines of region or the single self.

I have, by strictness of definition, limited my study to those novels which are set within Cumbria's present borders; *Remember Me...* is thus one of the books that I have omitted. The others are *The Nerve* (1971), *Love and Glory* (1983), *Crystal Rooms* (1992) and *Credo* (1996). The first four, whilst freeing their characters to roam in London, Europe and America, all include references to Cumbria and the Lakes, and all in the sense of an expressive yearning for a place of lost content. Much of *Credo*, Bragg's Dark Ages novel, is set in the ancient British Kingdom of Rheged (Cumbria) but its 757 pages traverse a wide geographical terrain from West to East, from Ireland to Northumbria.

In the course of writing this study I have also had the opportunity to access and read Bragg's early unpublished novel manuscript, *Mirrors and Wire* which is now a part of the Brotherton Library housed at Leeds University. Set mainly in Carlisle it offers only tentative clues to Bragg's future development as a regional novelist. There is, however, a moment in Chapter 10 that affords a glimpse of that immersion in the landscape as a force invested with the power to influence the human spirit that will become an integral part of future texts:

> ...the exhilaration they felt together in such a lovely spot
> swept into them as a still, pantheistic content - leading,
> as it led many pages of English poetry - to the deep

waters of rumination rather than the twinkling springs of gaiety. Perhaps it was the mountains; so mournfully, endlessly, immemorially, silently, contentedly, overwhelmingly Solemn; like cathedrals, prime ministers, tanks, diamond tiaras, good causes and wicked criminals, they were not to be found amusing.

(*MW*, p.62)

This passage apart, the manuscript is mainly interesting for the wide range of cultural references - for example, from Thelonius Monk to Gertrude Stein; from Woody Guthrie to James Joyce - giving an early indication of Bragg's ability to illuminate the provincial with a universally recognised cultural commentary, a skill which I will explore in some detail in later novels.

As regards breadth of cultural interest, Bragg has inherited the literary DNA of Arnold Bennett, whose wide-ranging enthusiasms - from journalism to literary fiction, from theatre to cinema, from painting to politics - find a ready echo in Bragg's multi-media engagements. Other commentators have remarked on Bragg's thematic indebtedness to Hardy and Lawrence - and I make my own references to these writers in the course of my study - but I am convinced of the case for positioning him as Bennett's literary heir. In particular, I will argue for the aesthetic twinning of Bragg's Wigton with Bennett's construction of Burslem, Stoke-on-Trent, as his Bursley, in the Five Towns novels and stories. Looking at Bennett's *The Old Wives' Tale* (1908) in his *The Epic Strain in the English Novel* (1958) E.M.W Tillyard recognises a 'successful rendering of a choric feeling ... Bennett reinforces that rendering by many vivid pictures of communal feeling and activity ... In fact, he supports his special choric theme by convincing you that life of all kinds was being transacted in the Five Towns. He gives us entry into a community. He also validates his choric theme by bringing to life the people who act it' (*Epic Strain*, p.185). Where Bennett's discerning eye discovers all of life in Bursley, so too does Bragg in Wigton.

Bragg's regional imagination is a crucial element in his art and it is this aspect of his writing that is at the heart of my study. His commitment to regionalism succeeds, in W.J. Keith's terms, in 'allowing a writer to focus on a specific ...and there find a manageable setting for a vision that may well extend beyond the regional' (*Regions of Imagination*, p.10). This recalls Hardy's comment that 'our magnificent heritage from the Greeks in dramatic literature found sufficient room for a large proportion of its action in an extent of their country not much larger than the half-dozen counties reunited under the old name of Wessex' ('General Preface', p.358). Bragg too reaches for Hellenic universality as he seeks to discover the history, beauty, energy, interest and significance in the provincial setting of Wigton and the region of the Lakes. It is a vision that is both affectionate and critical. My intention in what follows is to further critical assessment of a remarkable body of work whilst encouraging even more readers to share Bragg's great love for the landscape of the Lakes.

MELVYN BRAGG

For
Want of a
Nail

By the author of 'The Maid of Buttermere'

# ONE

# THEY'RE AW MUDDLED UP
## *FOR WANT OF A NAIL*

Looking back more with regret than in anger, the nostalgic glow of the 1960s now appears as one of those rare momentous decades in history when the flux of cultural and political movements glittered to deceive us into believing that all things were possible and that all change would be for the universal good. This era of hope was ushered in by a benign act of legal judgement in November 1960 permitting the publication of the first complete, unexpurgated edition of D.H. Lawrence's *Lady Chatterley's Lover*. It went on to embrace such diverse phenomena as, for example, the passing of the Abortion Bill and the Sexual Offences Bill, Theatre of the Absurd, the arrival of the birth control pill, the removal of stage censorship, Beatlemania, Vietnam protest demonstrations, an International Poetry Incarnation at the Albert Hall, and the unsettling innovations of postmodern literature. Melvyn Bragg arrived in London, at the epicentre of much of this heady atmosphere of change, in 1961, via Oxford University, to begin a career in broadcasting before becoming a published novelist in 1965.

*For Want of a Nail* is in many respects a typical first novel, drawing upon the author's boyhood memories of working class life in Cumbria, and creating a world of closely observed social realism through an exploration of the hero's maturing ego. The novel nevertheless partakes in the 1960s' breaching of privacy and discretion made possible by the publication of formerly banned underground classics by Lawrence and Henry Miller, and by the appearance of such works of cultural and psychological theory as R.D. Laing's *The Divided Self* (1960) in which Laing claims that 'our "normal" "adjusted" state is too often the abdication of ecstasy, the betrayal of our true potentialities ...' (*Divided Self*, p.12). Bragg's novel makes little comment on the politics of this new world, preferring to chart its arrival through the consciousness of an adolescent boy living on the geographical edge of cultural influence, and left very much to his own devices in attempting to interpret not only his own development but also that of his surrounding world. To an extent *For Want of a Nail* may be read as an exemplary fictional case-study for what

Richard Hoggart, in *The Uses of Literacy* (1957), calls 'the uprooted and the anxious' upwardly mobile child of the working-class:

> In part they have a sense of class which affects some in all groups. With them the sense of loss is increased precisely because they are emotionally uprooted from their class, often under the stimulus of a stronger critical intelligence or imagination, qualities which can lead them into an unusual self-consciousness (and make it easy for a sympathizer to dramatize their Angst). Involved with this may be a physical uprooting from their class through the medium of the scholarship system. A great many seem to me to be affected in this way.
>
> (*Literacy*, p.292)

Whilst Tom Graham, the main protagonist of Bragg's novel, makes the transition from a culturally and emotionally deprived working-class home to university, he does so cocooned from any sense of larger cultural, or political change - chewing gum but not Elvis Presley makes it on to the village hall dance floor, and news of Suez seems to have got mislaid before reaching the remoteness that is Tom's Cumbria. This apparent isolation from the mainstream of the nation's narrative separates Tom from Bragg, who further distances himself from his creation by presenting Tom's thoughts and utterances in free indirect discourse rather than by adopting the first-person narration of the typical Bildungsroman. Even so, there remain, as I will demonstrate, hints of an autobiographical self, as the fantasy prone youth sheds his illusions, innocence and inhibitions in negotiating what Hoggart refers to as the 'friction-point of two cultures' (*Literacy*, p.292).

Bragg undercuts what on the surface looks like becoming a totally successful escape from an unsatisfying environment - not only a divided and deeply unhappy family but also a Lake District described in uncharacteristically hostile and unsympathetic prose as a place of grey, cold and oppressively sullen skies - by removing Tom to London only to leave him in the novel's final pages totally isolated and feeling 'emptied, emptied, scoured. There was nothing to break his fall. Down and down through steady blackness' (*WN*, p.300). As he reluctantly gets out of bed Tom sees a crane framed in the window, a symbol of destruction which, as it swings into action, carries him back in his imagination to the countryside he had thought to escape, and reminding him of a 'great scaffolded tree which swings its long neck like branches in a wind' (*WN*, p.301). Tellingly, this reads as the despairing departing textual metaphor of an awakening novelist who finds himself in a state of suspended articulate hibernation, penning the half understood discontent of an angry young man. We sense Bragg's own thoughts and feelings animating a figure given to fantasy, morbidity and a psychologically disruptive level of excessive introspection. Whilst these traits - together with the surely not entirely coincidental fact of Tom and Bragg both being age 11+ in 1950 when the novel begins - may suggest an identification of author and central character, Bragg largely evades the strongly autobiographical bias often associated with a first novel.

The opening chapter introduces several key concepts which recur throughout Bragg's novels, not least the way in which the intimately experienced sense of place in and around Wigton, and towards High Ireby, plays a crucial role in the development of character. The brooding presence of the mountain referred to as 'The Saddle' is given its own geological biography and is brought into narrative play as something of a double-edged metaphor, representing both historical continuity as personified by the grandfather, Old Tom Paislow, and paradoxically the need to break free of community if creativity is to thrive. I have already suggested the power of the attraction of place upon personality when Tom's journey comes an imaginative full circle and the regional chain is concertinaed in the metaphor of the 'scaffolded tree'. Tom's identity has to be read in the context of his London bedroom as both prison and potential springboard to liberty, set alongside the deeply engrained knowledge of 'The Saddle'. His challenge will be to integrate these differently inflected aspects of personality. By way of contrast, his maternal grandfather, Old Tom Paislow, is at one with the mountain, its biospheric time history encompassing his own temporality: 'It pressed on top of "The Saddle". The whole of "The Saddle", Tom knew, pressed down on to crystals and fossils and ancient rocks and gases, hidden springs, caves, stalagmites and stalactites, and it moved and cracked and exploded inside itself so that, right at the bottom, there was coal. Thick black coal under his very feet' (*WN*, p.14).

Tom Paislow is rooted in his regional community by his time as an ex-miner whose knowledge of the '[t]hick black coal under his very feet' link him to the earth and what Keith Sagar expresses as 'the pattern of life, survival and dignity, generated by the conditions of mining life' ('Lawrence: Dramatist', p.157). He is further linked to the community by the ready use of dialect and the effect of its rhythm upon his behaviour, especially at times of tension. In the 1800 'Preface' to his *Lyrical Ballads* Wordsworth made the then poetically radical claim that he chose to use the 'plainer and more emphatic language' of the rural workers because 'such men hourly communicate with the best objects from which the best part of language is originally derived' and is therefore 'a more permanent and a far more philosophical language than that which is substituted for it by Poets' ('Preface', p.7). Bragg writes in *The Adventure of English* (2003) of how Wordsworth was reviled at first, and for many years, 'for daring to bring poetry from the voice of the people' but in the process 'kept English true to its original and tested self. He saved, celebrated and gave lasting literary energy to the ancient language of ordinary speech' (*AE*, p.229). It is worth noting, then, that at the outset of his writing career Bragg firmly positions himself as heir to Wordsworth's poetic programme, with a clearly demonstrated determination to maintain and celebrate a significant aspect of Cumbrian culture through the introduction of dialect as a defining aspect of that culture, and as a counter-balance to standardised English and its threat to regional linguistic individuality. There is, however, something of a paradox here inasmuch as Bragg's strong sense of a national narrative of Englishness - expressed openly and proudly in the documentary study *Speak For England* (1976) - is dependent in large measure on the successful integration of precisely those myriad regional local customs and speech patterns that taken *en masse* define a recognisable but diverse English national consciousness and culture. Whilst aesthetic and cultural approval of the regional may be read as patriotic and unitary, it is also open to interpretation as reflecting a more radical and recalcitrant centrifugal impulse to impede the imposition of politically centralised values.

Old Tom is representative of that resistant culture whose use of dialect is a recognisable marker of a known Cumbrian community but one which Bragg shows to be in retreat concurrently with his grandson's move from the knowable margins of a small self-sufficient community to the anomie of London. The novel's depiction of tension between acceptance and aspiration, between knowledge gained at first-hand by working the land and at one remove by reading, between the parochial and the national, suggests the fragility of long-accepted organically developed community cultural values in the face of modernity. Bragg's characterisation of the two Toms as the representatives of stasis and change exemplifies the debate about the definition of what constitutes legitimate culture, and Bragg's championing of Old Tom in order to write about seemingly small things in a large context is to popularise issues of contemporary national cultural/political debate from the regional margins. Raymond Williams concludes his definition of the term 'dialect' as being 'simply the way of speaking in a particular place' (*Keywords*, p.106). Its invocation in *For Want of a Nail* serves as an index of modernity, marking the social distance travelled by Tom from the standpoint of his grandfather. Old Tom's language is the age-old dialect of Cumbria, punctuated by a range of expletives expressing both a sense of social frustration and class defiance.[1] What becomes clear is that Bragg's fictional ancestry can be traced back through the use of dialect in a line running from James Kelman's Glasgow labourers, Lawrence's colliers, Arnold Bennett's potters, Charles Dickens's Londoners, to George Eliot's rural workers in *Adam Bede* (1859). Dickens, however, tends to use dialect, as do many of Bragg's contemporaries, for comic effect, thereby unwittingly reducing the speaker's status at the same time as relegating their legitimate concerns to the margins of discourse. Bragg avoids this trap and writes in the tradition of Eliot, and of Walter Scott's Lowland Scots English before her, in demonstrating that dialect has a role to play in conveying deep emotion and serious intellectual ideas.

North Staffordshire regional novelist John Toft values dialect as the 'language of our forbears', and draws attention to the curious social phenomenon noted by John Blackwood, Eliot's publisher, 'that the dialect Eliot recorded "arose from hearing her father when with his brothers he reverted to his native dialect. She could not tell how the knowledge and feeling came to her, but when Lisbeth is speaking George Eliot felt it was a real language that she heard" … She did much painstaking research to get the voices right' ('Midland Voices' p.30) because she felt that this particular dialect was a language of its own. The following is an example of dialogue faithfully recorded by Eliot:

> Lisbeth ventured to say as she took it in,
> "Thy supper stans ready for thee, when thee lik'st."

1. Family relative Margaret Armstrong has little doubt that Bragg has called upon memories of his own grandfather, Herbert Bragg, in creating the fictional Tom Paislow: 'Herbert was a fiery man and did jobs around the church and market hall. Boys ran from him when they had been misbehaving in the park. His language was ripe.' (email 30 March 2011)

"Donna thee sit up, mother," said Adam, in a gentle tone. ...whenever he wished to be especially kind to his mother, he fell into his strongest native accent and dialect, with which at other times his speech was less deeply tinged. "I'll see to father when he comes home ... how is it as father's working so late?"

"Its none o' thy feyther as is a-workin' - thee might know that well anoof, if thy head warna full o' chapellin' - it's thy brother as does iverything, for there's niver nobody else i' th' way to do nothin'."

(*Adam Bede*, p.45)

Bragg's stark mixture of dialogue and Standard English stands comparison with that of Eliot -

'Tell us just one thing,' Tom demanded.
'They havent a hoos.'
'I know. Another.'
'Theyll niver hev one.'
... 'Theyre aw muddled up,' he said.
'Naybody knows who belongs who!'
'What do you mean.'
'Well ... theres a fellar theer - a
father 'til his own wife; and a woman
that's a niece 'til her own husband.'
... 'You see,' his grandfather said,
'they'll be folk that niver had
nowt. Theyll niver hev learnt
owt and if anybody's telled them
any-bit-thing that wasn't for their
bellies ' they they'll have forgot it.'

(*WN*, pp.45-46)

- to an extent that were her nineteenth century characters to meet up with Bragg's twentieth century ones, they would 'niver' have any difficulty in recognising their literary kinship.

Bragg shows dialect becoming broader not only in the security of family life, as in the Eliot example, but, perhaps more importantly for its symbolic value, in reaction to class antagonism. When Old Tom clashes with the hunt after shooting the fox it was chasing, his dialect rapidly broadens, becoming an index of class difference and hostility between himself and his daughter Annie's brother-in-law:

> 'Dis thou mean to tell me that thou was among that lot
> that tried to kill me?'
> 'I kept well away from it.'
> 'Ah bet thou did! Ah bet thou did! Thou'd be flaight
> enough te cum alaal bit nearer case sumbody might
> remember we were related. Ah bet thou kept away!'
> .... Tom crept right to the bottom of his mind, curled up,
> and tried to forget everything. His grandfather's
> muttering - in broader and broader dialect as he became
> more and more angry  - spattered against his ears like
> hailstones.
> 'Aw mad! Aw't' family ... Garn up't' Saddle on a horse ...
> crackers ... oor Annie shd niver ha bothet hessel ...
> Crackers! ...' [last four ellipses included]

(WN, pp. 20-21)

As with Eliot's *Adam Bede*, Bragg creates realistic terms for the novel in which he can stress the everyday, even the unseemly use of language, to emphasise the socially orientated nature of actions. Where Bragg differs from Eliot is in stepping back from authorial comment, allowing his characters to define themselves through dialect/dialogue. Even so, it is noticeable that the predominantly middle-class reading public of Eliot's day, 'usually thought of as very class-conscious and conventional, took all the dialect in their stride' (Toft, 'Midland Voices', p.30) in much the same way as today's broader based readership recognises and accepts linguistic codes as an integral part of the regional novel.

It is instructive to pursue further the issue of the exploration of working-class identity, not at the level of plot development but at that of a character's choice of language. Old Tom's use of dialect, and expletives, textually undermines his grandson's assumed mastery of Standard English as a necessary prerequisite for university entrance. His fixed certainty of class consciousness denied his younger namesake becomes apparent when we reflect that his first recorded speech - 'Damn an blast, an hell and bugger it!' (*WN*, p.11) - shapes his last recorded dying words of unbroken class hostility - 'Aah'll git them, the buggers. Aah'll git them!' (*WN*, p.183). Behind his profanities is an implied sophisticated silent recognition of class differences that no amount of argument can bridge - 'Tell them nothing. Tell them not one thing!' (*WN*, p.19) - that is in conflict with the linguistic/grammatical codes that we watch Tom mastering on the journey from village Primary School to the 6th Form of Thornton Grammar School. Yet the paradox is clear: Old Tom is environmentally rooted in his lack whilst the grandson experiences disillusionment and anomie at the novel's end, despite following the trajectory of the classic Bildungsroman success story of the move from the provinces to the metropolis.

This seeming paradox is further extended by Bragg's introduction of another rooted, but minor, character who plays an important part in shaping Tom's future. The local postman, Mr Wiggins, is steeped in the use of dialect and yet becomes the mouthpiece for advancing the cause of education, the adoption of Standard English, and the promise they carry of an escape from the confines of local community. Tom is seen drinking - and he is under-age - in an out-of-town pub in an effort to block out an earlier violent confrontation with a school colleague that threatened to re-open an ever-present 'panic, hysteria and blackout depression' (WN, p. 217). Mr Wiggins keeps an avuncular eye on Tom and finds a suitable moment to advise him against throwing his life away when his educational successes to date have opened up a world of possibilities for him. The following passage is fascinating on several levels:

> [Mr Wiggins's] voice, when he spoke, and even his stance, was shy.
> 'Gaen home, lad?' he asked, eventually
> ' Yes.'
> Tom's voice slipped into broad dialect unconsciously. The very feeling of the words made him feel warmer.
> 'Ay, well!' said Mr Wiggin. 'Let me tell thee summat, lad, eh?'
> 'Ay.'
> Mr Wiggin cleared his throat; skin ran up and down his neck like ripples on a lake.
> 'If Aah was thee - an Aa'ed thy chances, yen way an' another - Aa would keep oot o' spots like this. Ther ne gud for folk like thee. The can du thee nowt but 'arm'.
> 'Aa don't know.'
> 'Well. Tek my tip. Aa *do* know. Thou just keep away fra

that sort o' stuff.'

Tom was too thankful for this interest and advice to do anything but nod, silently.

(WN, pp. 222-223)

In terms of speech patterns alone it becomes difficult to tell Tom and Mr Wiggins apart as their idiolects merge under the influence of shared conventions, coded terminology - 'spots like this' - and stylistic nuances which all serve to assert their shared membership, despite age and educational differences, of a particular closed community. As the brief exchange runs its course the individuality of their voices tends to blur and a kind of echolalia seeps into the text as Mr Wiggins picks up on Tom's words: 'Aa don't know' and 'Aa do know'. What is noticeable here is that without the surrounding text and the guidance of a narrator's voice it becomes difficult to tell which character is speaking. Tom drops into dialect under the older man's influence and this might be read as a form of reductionism celebrating the power of the local environment to undercut notions of a sovereign self. Bragg raises questions about the coherence of character and a belief in the ideology of subjectivity[2] that remain problematic in the novel's closing pages. The passage also suggests a relationship between the Cumbrian environment and character by way of an apt trait-connoting metonym: '... skin ran up and down his neck like ripples on a lake.' Deep waters, unruffled movement, a sense of calm, all predicated upon the central existence of the Lakes and all expressing personality as a sense of local attachment and, importantly in contrast to Tom, presenting an undivided personality where environment and character are as one. We might also reflect on the significance of this decisive chance encounter, in which Bragg uses a minor character to represent the caring kindness of community, marking the final use of Cumbrian dialect in the text.

If Mr Wiggins seems to have evolved from water, leaving his skin 'like loose-hanging crepe' (WN, p.218) and with hands 'which looked as though they had been pushed inside oversized gloves made out of dried-out skin' (WN, p.219), Old Tom is very much a creature of the earth, even working part-time in the grave-yard and to be found close to death 'coated with mud' (WN, p.188). He is autochthonous, having sprung from the soil with '[h]is skin so textured with the stripes of the earth that it

---

2. These concerns are a central issue in other Bragg novels and are explored in considerable detail in *The Maid of Buttermere* (1987).

seemed he would live for as long as the ground he walked on' (*WN*, p. 190).[3] He feels more at home in his hut than in the family cottage, a dwelling which is itself an extension of the land and indicative of his relationship to it: 'so much more a part of the fields than the cottage that the birds and animals treated it with no more nervousness than a tree or a bush' (*WN*, p.31). It also reads as a museum of memory to a miner's and countryman's way of life, even as a cemetery for discarded but treasured objects dislocated from changing times: '[r]abbit-hutches crowded one wall ... Above the door, an old harness flouting old ribbons. On another wall a gallery of implements: a pick-axe, saw, hammer ... Two highly polished miner's lamps swung from the ceiling' (*WN*, p.31). This inventory possesses a distinctly other-worldly character, and though these relics of a way of life may captivate Tom's imagination, they have little connection to his own future. At the time Bragg was writing, Britain still had an economically, culturally and politically important coal industry supporting vibrant local communities. From the perspective of the early twenty-first century, however, the shed embodies the wreckage of a way of life, of pre-Thatcher England with its careless assumption of continuity and tradition. With its miner's lamps, harness and a variety of labouring tools the shed now reads as a fossilised reminder of old working-class certainties and, in its masculine isolation from the domestic cottage, of old gender hierarchies. But for Old Tom the shed and its contents are a manifestation of his autochthonic nature and a material defence of his notion of masculinity. This latter aspect is expressed visually by '[o]ne patch of wall [which] was crowded with photographs of football teams, royalty and soldiers' (*WN*, p.32). Conspicuously absent are any personal family pictures, not one connection to any notion of sentimentality (or softness). He has buried the photographic record of his past beneath a 'dirty layer of bank notes' (*WN*, p.189) in a tin box which he opens on his death-bed. It contains a history of his repressed private life, released like a last breath before a literal return to earth:

> There was one, hardly visible, brown and curly-edged,
> of the old man's parents: innocent and white-haired,

3. I am indebted to Richard Godden's *Fictions of Labour. William Faulkner and the South's Long Revolution* (1997) for the concept of the 'autochthon'. Autochthons appear not only in *Absolom, Absolom!* (1936), the novel featured in Godden's study, but in other Faulkner texts, such as *The Hamlet* (1940), the subject of John Earle's thesis *Faulkner after the War* (2008) dealing at length with autochthony. In my private conversations with Bragg he identified Faulkner as one of several influential American writers he read in his later teenage years.

piercing the fading brown with their steady eyes. There was a photograph of the old man himself when he had been at the mines: squashed in the middle of about forty black-faced and grimy men - all with stern faces, all with their arms around each other's shoulders. There was a photograph of Mr Paislow's wedding: bride and groom standing at attention with never a sympathetic touch or glance or line of movement between them.

(*WN*, p.189)

When Tom visits his grandfather's grave he exhibits a continuity of repressed emotions, having 'guarded himself against feeling and now his feelings defended him from almost all responses' (*WN*, p.270). The evocation of the graveyard gives an impression of the earth as actively malevolent in reclaiming its own and reducing it to nothing: 'He weighed nothing in the earth he had dug and worked' (*WN*, p.230).

One consequence of Old Tom's death is the almost simultaneous disappearance of Tom's vivid day-time fantasies. From the novel's outset Tom has constructed a private and elaborate fantasy world[4] that assumes a species of reality in his imagination and in a very important fictional sense lays the groundwork for Tom's putative fictional/Bragg's actual future literary careers. Bragg merges fantasy and reality in a seamless flow unbroken by any form of punctuation or narrative separation to create a particularly impressive vivid organic form for a first novel. His opening sentence is a fantastic collage of Western movies, jungle adventure, Empire battles and World War II - it is worth recalling that the novel is initially set in 1950 when the War was only five years distant and images of German soldiers and Japanese kamikaze pilots were then the staple fare of children's comics[5]: 'Though a score of Indians, Nazis, pythons, Zulus and midget Japanese aircraft had been shattered by Tom's index and middle finger ...' (*WN*, p.11). Even the everyday geography of

4. One of several possible comparative novel fantasy sequences is Keith Waterhouse's *Billy Liar* (1959) in which the eponymous hero creates a fantasy world to escape the sheer boredom of his job in a funeral parlour. The difference, however, is that, unlike Tom, he deliberately and knowingly invokes his fantasy world of Ambrosia, entering it by choice whereas Tom has no control over the timing or frequency of his fantasies.
5. I can vividly recall that my own reading of comics such as *Eagle* in the early 1950s contained precisely these graphic images of a defeated enemy that fed into and enlarged my imaginative interpretation of an otherwise somewhat culturally deprived immediate post-war world.

the Cumbrian countryside metamorphoses into a site of exoticism and threat conjured up from unknown regions of Tom's imagination:

> To his left the tarn stretched out, flat, grey and empty. His mother could have gone swimming in it one day and suddenly been chased by an alligator. With a long yodel, Tom plunged in and raced across the water, knife between his teeth. Over and over he rolled, the alligator thrashing the water with its tail, all the other creatures of the lake scurrying down to the bottom edges for safety. He stabbed and stabbed again, losing his knife in the scaly belly, forcing apart the great jaws with his bare hands. Blood spurted on to the surface of the water and spread like oil. He was hurled into the air by some last concentration of the reptile's force, but with that effort the alligator died.
>
> And then his mother would admire him and praise him and tell everybody what he had done, and never shout at him again. (WN, pp.11-12)

This fluent contraction of boyhood adventure stories from the pages of Henry Rider Haggard or G.A. Henty can also be read as a symbolic account of the onset of puberty and a compulsively Freudian desire for the mother's love, an underlying theme throughout the novel. There remains a disturbing ambivalence lurking just below the surface narrative of fantasy which hints at masturbatory eroticism, death, sexual arousal and relief: 'The octopus slowly settled its arms around him and sucked him into a jelly blackness; filthy green sewage ink squirted all over him, eating through the part of the skin that it touched. It had started to snow' (WN, p.17). The seamless narrative transition from fantasy filth to actual snow hauls Tom back to reality, and, by the invocation of snow's whiteness, to a state of innocence. The dialectic between innocence and knowledge is mediated throughout Tom's adolescence by Bragg's use of fantasy at moments of personal crisis, particularly those concerning the search for identity. After his grandfather's death Tom comes to accept the double self that is almost a *sine qua non* of the novelist. His last recorded fantasy is a revisionary account of an earlier experience of a body under attack: 'Tom walked along the dour road. He was covered with crawling black lice which bit and sucked at his skin, drawing all blood away from him. His skin trembled with a passion which could not find a reason to explode and so broiled inside him with scaly heat' (*WN*, p.177). Now he finds himself 'sliding towards that double consciousness, double vision, double existence' which will eventually provide him with the imaginative platform to become a legitimate story-teller in his own right/write if the promise of Oxford is to be realised. In part, then, *For Want of a Nail* functions as Tom's/Bragg's Kunstlerroman in which the narrative of Tom's search for self-identity runs parallel with the artistic search for a satisfactory imaginative form to portray the experience.

From the outset of his writing career Bragg routinely calls upon the Lake District landscape not only to validate his own writing practice but also to demonstrate just how thoroughly geographical location can help develop a character's self-identity and influence crucial aspects of their decision-making. Bragg's landscape language moves beyond the establishment of a purely objective visual setting for narrative action to incorporate a subjective self-reflective stance in which, for example. Tom becomes conscious of his psychological engagement with, and physical participation in, its elements:

> Every so often, he would stop and look at the silhouettes
> of the hedges against the sky. Or he would listen to the
> noises which rustled and gathered around him until the
> whole earth seemed to be trembling with muted battles
> of passion. He wanted to grasp the blackness with both
> hands and tear it and nurse it and let it settle into him
> until he, too, died into the night.
>
> He walked beside the ebony river and matched his
> own humming to its endless gurgle of spray; he passed
> over fields of black ice, skating on the dry rustling grass
> which swished against his feet, against his feet so far
> away that they walked a path of their own; he nuzzled
> against the tangy freshness of the quiet, hidden ground.
> He walked in aimless exaltation.          (*WN*. p.104)

The appearance of the pathetic fallacy[6] is qualified by 'seemed to' but not

6.  In the years since *For Want of a Nail* was published, the developing discipline of ecopoetics has come to regard Ruskin's pathetic fallacy as not merely a Romantic indulgence, but an inevitable and positive component of human perception. Neil Evernden's essay 'Beyond Ecology. Self, Place and the Pathetic Fallacy' expresses a belief that the pathetic fallacy and metaphor are central to creating a sense of place:
   For once we engage in the extension of the boundary of the self into the 'environment,'
   then of course we imbue it with life and can quite properly regard it as animate -
CONTINUED P. 28

before admitting the landscape's relational role in Tom's simmering 'battles of passion'. The biblically inflected outburst of 'aimless exaltation' that concludes Tom's reverie is an integral response to his landscape experience that will eventually comment dialectically on his first sensory and intellectual responses to the very difference landscape of Oxford, experienced after sitting his scholarship papers. In Oxford the 'fields were empty  of animals, people and all feelings of fertility' (*WN*, p.257), and an overwhelming sense of oppressiveness arising from a subjectively perceived purposelessness in the landscape so affected Tom that he 'walked heavily' (*WN*, p.257).  Every human attempt to know, describe and define the phenomenal world is of necessity filtered through the value system of the human observer. Tom's first experience of the Oxford fields configures them as exhibiting the 'air of waste land, ready to be churned up, packed with cement and rubble, levelled into yet another route for the incessant driving traffic. They were out of place as fields' (*WN*, p.260). Writing about Henry David Thoreau's *Journal*, Sharon Cameron suggests that 'to write about nature is to write about how the mind sees itself '(*Writing Nature*, p.44). Whereas Tom felt embedded in the landscape of the Lakes, he clearly fears becoming as 'out of place' as the fields themselves in an Oxford environment where it might be argued that his mind faces the prospect of being 'churned up' and 'levelled into yet another route' for the transmission of knowledge/'rubble'. Entrenched in a highly charged moment of being, Tom's thoughts express an apprehension about the commodification of nature - 'yet another route for traffic' - linked to his own doubts about his place in a new world whose values threaten to destabilise his sense of identity.

The Oxford experience relates the negative way in which human emotion may interact with the landscape. Oxford's apparent lack of fixed reference points contrasts with Tom's many acts of naming personally significant places, from mountains to small clearings, in his home environment. There the very act of naming becomes a part of the

6. CONTINUED  - it is animate because we are a part of it. And, following from this, all the metaphorical properties so favoured by poets make perfect sense: the Pathetic Fallacy is a fallacy only to the ego clencher. Metaphoric language is an indicator of 'place' - an indication that the speaker has a place, feels part of a place. Indeed, the motive for metaphor may be as Frye claims, 'a desire to associate, and finally to identify, the human mind with what goes on outside it, because the only genuine joy you can have is in those rare moments when you feel that although we may know in part ... we are also a part of what we know.'('Beyond Ecology', p.101)

process of establishing a sense of place that in turn reinforces a sense of self-identity within the community. Fiona Stafford sees precisely this symbiotic process at work in William Wordsworth's series of 'Poems on the Naming of Places'. Each poem is a 'verbal monument to particular rocks, lakeside or clearings' in which his private naming - Emma's Dell, Joanna's Rock, Point-Rash-Judgment - becomes a 'contribution to the life of the community inseparable from its surroundings' (*Local Attachments*, p.45). Bragg situates Tom within this long tradition of naming local landmarks in response to personal experience:

> There was a tiny wood near the school that had never had a name. Tom would sometimes go there after school with the Turney brothers. They had discovered creepers curled around the trees and, carefully, they had unbound them. They were strong enough to carry the weight of all three of them and the wood had become a playground. Everyone swinging from one hummock to another on the long creepers. Tom had started to call it 'Creeper Wood'. The name had caught on. Now, no one would think of talking about it without mentioning its name.
>
> If there was a rock there, he could call it 'Dagger Point'. He would have to climb up it to see. Or he could just call it 'Death Point'. Then he need not climb it at all. Or 'Horse Leap'. 'Huntsman's End'.
>
> (*WN*, pp.37-38)

Stafford writes of Wordsworth's penchant for naming as contributing to a local history of place: 'As Wordsworth attended to the special character of the Lake District, marked out the different cottages, rocks, or clumps of trees, he recognized the way in which particular places could continue to cradle feelings long after individual events had occurred' (*Local Attachments*, p.47). Likewise for Tom, he expects his naming of 'Creeper Wood' to become part of the local language of place. It is this close identification between person and place and the stability of self-identity that is momentarily ruptured by Tom's Oxford experience.

At the visual and emotional centre of Tom's adolescent development is the very real physical and imaginative presence of the mountain Bragg calls 'The Saddle'.[7] During his childhood in the village before moving to the nearby town of Thornton, ostensibly for the convenience of living nearer to the Grammar School, Tom starts every waking day with a view of the mountain:

> From his window it looked like the soft pencil swell of a hillock, with its central dip no more than an innocent curve. Now, beside it, he saw the open jaw of rock which made that slit look like a trap of sharpened flint, ready sprung; and the side of the fell, so soft when dark, now seen to be covered with slithering, shifting screes, balanced, unsupported rocks, wire bushes with thread-brittle roots.
>
> (*WN*, pp.12-13)

When, at age eleven, Tom first sees the mountain at close range, it discloses a physical harshness and hint of danger that suggests an animate role in the story of Tom's disreputable grand step-father who for a drunken bet rode his horse up 'The Saddle' but had a fatal accident in the pitch darkness. This story, which takes on the form of a contemporary folk ballad, is recounted in a suitably melodramatic fashion by Old Tom: 'They gave him a lantern to carry to see he didn't fiddle it ... They aw' blew their horns and cracked their whips ... And then t'lantern went oot. They could hear t'horse screamin' its heed off' (*WN*, p.33). The mountain then invades Tom's dreams 'The flint jaws snapped together and the horse disappeared' (*WN*, p.35) - and has such a powerful grip on his nocturnal unconsciousness that its images of seeping fluid merge with his own emissions - 'The rock split and a dark liquid came seeping out of it. He woke up. The dank smell comforted him. But he had wet his bed' (*WN*. p.39). The dream/nightmare is an articulation of the narrative's awareness of just how disturbing a presence the mountain and its associated personal tragic history are for Tom. It extends to metaphorically structuring his waking determination to discover the truth about his origins - 'He would smash rocks against mountains if he

---

7. This is Blencathra, a mountain close to Keswick. 'Blencathra (2847 ft) - also known as Saddleback - could keep hikers occupied for a fortnight. Wainwright details twelve possible ascents of its summit, and, though made of the same slate as Skiddaw, 'it's a far more aggressive proposition' (*The Rough Guide To The Lake District*, p.158). The names of its narrow ridges - Sharp Edge, Foule Crag - are indicative of the challenges offered to climbers. The name Blencathra probably derives from 'Blain' and 'Cadeir', from the Celtic 'hill of the chair'.

unleashed himself on this' (*WN*, p.185). As if responding to an Oedipal myth, it will be 'The Saddle' that leads Tom to the truth. Tom's sensing body is caught up in a near deterministic reciprocal interchange with the mountain and its surroundings. The mountain's animate form - 'The flinty jaws snapped together' - makes an active and dynamic contribution to Tom's perceptual experience.

Something of Blencathra's ('The Saddle'/Saddleback) sheer force of magnetic personality imprinting itself upon an ecologically awakening youthful imagination is apparent in Bragg's recollection of his own teenage encounter with the mountain. Recalling the experience in his highly personal history of the Lake District, *Land of the Lakes* (1983), Bragg writes:

> ... the bareness enhances the feeling of great solitude ...
> I remember going up Blencathra one day, from the north, a bright day in the middle of winter, and never meeting a soul from start to finish. By the end of the walk I was willing everyone to keep away. The isolation was marvellous. It had been like scudding across empty water.                                             (pp.23-24)

I choose to linger a while over Blencathra and its immediate environment because it offers a clear example of Bragg's turn to the local at the outset of his writing career in such a way as to link him immediately to the tradition of canonical Lake writers. This is not, at this stage, to make any kind of comparative qualitative judgement, other than to observe its importance as a marker of Bragg's attachment to a sense of place and a clear aesthetic awareness of how the idea of the Lakes in the popular imagination has been shaped as much by poetry and prose as by geography.

Robert Southey liked to take his summer visitors up Blencathra to enjoy the views. John Ruskin favoured Blencathra over the Swiss Matterhorn, writing in his autobiography, *Praeterita*, of 'Skiddaw and far-sweeping Saddleback as the proper type of majestic form' (quoted in Thomson, p.201). Samuel Taylor Coleridge also favoured the use of the more colourful topographical title of Saddleback but when it came to close observation he made detailed scientific notes on his climbs, including one of a waterfall on Blencathra: 'For the first eight or nine feet it falls perpendicular, water-colour, then meets rock and rushes down in a steep slope, all foam, till the last two feet when the rock ceases but the water preserves the same colour and inclination as if it were there' (ibid., pp.174-176). Coleridge's influence, it seems to me, is particularly germane to Bragg's choice of Blencathra as the dominating natural feature of Tom's adolescence. His fictional and factual recall of 'The Saddle'/Saddleback may be traced in part to Coleridge's 'A Thought Suggested by a View of Saddleback'[8] and I quote it in full because not only does it demonstrate the line of ecopoetic inheritance but also because it is one of two Coleridge poems chosen by Bragg for inclusion in his anthology *Cumbria in Verse* (1984):

> On stern Blencathra's perilous height
>     The winds are tyrannous and strong;
> And flashing forth unsteady light
> From stern Blencathra's skiey height,
>     As loud the torrents throng!
> Beneath the moon, in gentle weather
> They blend the earth and sky together.
> But oh! The sky and all its forms how quiet!
> The things that seek the earth, how full of noise and riot!
>
> (*Cumbria Verse*, p.13)

This line of continuity of representation is a vital component in the definition of ecopoetics in what Jonathan Bate calls an experiencing of the earth: 'Reverie, solitude, walking: to turn these experiences into language is to be an ecopoet (*Song*, p.42). In an illuminating discussion of Gaston Bachelard's *The Poetics of Space* he posits the notion, central to my argument for seeing Bragg's Lakeland dwelling and textual representations as heir to the Romantics, that the 'interior order of the human mind is inextricable from the environmental space which we inhabit. Sanity depends upon grounding in place. But it also depends upon grounding in time ... our identities are constituted by a combination of environment and memory' (*Song*, p.173). In his imaginative re-recreation of 'The Saddle' and Tom's emotional response to its being, Bragg pays due textual attention to the active interplay of mind and place

8. The full title is 'A Thought Suggested by a View of Saddleback in Cumberland' and it was first published in *The Amulet* (1833) but never included by Coleridge himself in any collected edition. It was most likely composed in the autumn of 1800 when Coleridge first saw the mountain. According to William Keach in the edited *Penguin Complete Poems* (1997) the first line is adapted from a poem by Isaac Ritson, itself quoted in Hutchinson's *History of Cumberland* (*Complete Poems*, p.559).

over time in a way that helps shape ideas of an environmental aesthetic. Such an aesthetic provides an increasingly important counter-balance to Anthony Gidden's dispiriting, but not uncommon, exegesis that the 'advent of modernity increasingly tears space from place by fostering relations between "absent" others, locationally distant from any given situation of face-to-face interaction' so that 'place becomes increasingly *phantasmagoric*: that is to say, locales are thoroughly penetrated by and shaped in terms of social influences distant from them' (*Consequence*, pp.17-18). The defence of the increasingly beleaguered local as a unique site of experience may appear a heavy responsibility for a first novel to shoulder, but in allowing Tom to know the 'long path around "The Saddle" away from the farm so well that, for rose-hips, raspberries, ash branches, for wild strawberries, dandelions for his grandfather's rabbits, nests, hawthorn blossom and crab-apples, it had become his personal forage-land' (*WN*, p.29) Bragg simultaneously stakes a claim to the Cumbrian landscape as his personal 'forage-land' together with an expressed joy in the minutiae of the natural world that Wordsworth would have recognised.

In his loving and comprehensive illustrated survey of Blencathra's many aspects, *Blencathra. Portrait of a Mountain*, Ronald Turnbull concludes with the confident assertion that '[t]o know the whole world, it is enough to simply see, and be on, Blencathra' (*Blencathra*, p.173). Whilst not making quite such an extravagantly all-embracing claim for Wigton, Bragg undoubtedly writes the town as a synecdoche for the rest of England. The documentary case for the validity of Wigton's fictional metonymic status is made explicit in Bragg's *Speak for England* (1976), a twentieth-century oral history of the town's cultural changes as witnessed and recorded/related by its inhabitants. Bragg likes to quote Blake in support of his belief that all human life is to be found in Wigton: 'To find the world in a grain of sand ... a sound method in science and art since men started looking for answers' (*SE*, p.5). The appeal of/to Wigton as England in microcosm has been a persistent trope in Bragg's work for the past half century it was, for instance, very much to the fore during his 2011 talk at Keswick[9] on 'Back Then - Remembrance of Times Past in Wigton' about his formative years in Wigton, and specifically the

9. 'Words by the Water Festival of Words and Ideas', 4-13 March 2011 at the Theatre by the Lake, Keswick. Bragg is President of the Festival and his constant support of the 'Words by the Water' is yet another example of his commitment to Cumbrian culture. I was able to record his 'Wigton' talk, and will refer to it as valuable source material when discussing his later novels.

Proustian remembrance of dance. During his talk he again quoted Blake in defence of his passionate belief in the value of the known local community as a source of universal meaning. For invaluable background reading to the novels, *Speak for England* is to be highly recommended. It is a substantial volume of over 500 pages, but in essence the modest, unassertive, kindly and good humoured stories told, all serve 'in their serious plainness, and in their persistence' (*SE*, p.8) to represent an elusive but essential quality of Englishness.

The Wigton portrayed in the novels maintains its geographical boundaries whilst steadily expanding its textual ones to quietly argue for a particular view of Englishness seen through a range of diverse local characters in a variety of situations and acts. Bragg's local attachment to Wigton proves the starting point for an English journey that has its literary antecedents in, for example, Arnold Bennett's Burslem/Bursley, one of the fictional Five Towns of Stoke-on-Trent, with which it shares a textual space mid-way along the rural-urban continuum. Whilst Wigton, like Burslem, occupies an actual co-ordinate on ordnance survey maps, Bragg's literary texts bring to it an imaginative coherence that encourages it to become part of the readers consciousness as a navigable space, linking textuality to the very real environment of one small town, 'one grain of sand', in order to comment upon the cultural and political state of England. Writers such as Bennett, and also Thomas Hardy, are seen by the American academic Robert Squillace as setting themselves the task of replacing the lazy caricature of too many guide books, with a fuller, more rounded and life-like picture of place.

> At the same time, they themselves claim a dispro-portionate share in shaping perception of the actual place. As narrators, they at once occupy the privileged position of the native by reason of their intimate knowledge of phenomenon unknown to their putative readers... and they occupy the differently privileged post of the cosmopolitan outsider, able to coordinate the details of native life and understand them in a broad perspective unavailable to the characters who inhabit their provincial landscape.
>
> ('Imagined Town', p.1)

This is a near perfect outline of Bragg's narratological position as both the 'native' who maintains close links with his provincial roots - he has a cottage in High Ireby - and the Hampstead dwelling 'cosmopolitan outsider' calling upon wide cultural frames of reference. The latter position[10] is important for both aesthetic and commercial reasons in allowing the writer greater access to and flexibility to understand and negotiate cultural hierarchies, and to understand the ways in which popular fiction is produced and marketed.

In *For Want of a Nail* Bragg appears ambivalent over relinquishing total authorial control over his depiction of Wigton, choosing at this early stage to disguise its identity as the fictional Thornton. Yet by mapping the action along Wigton's named streets - King Street, Church Street, Duke's Lane - and staging set pieces at locatable sites - Mason's Garage - there clearly exists an unspoken intention to include the town itself as a very real character in its own right. Indeed, intending Wigton flaneurs who prefer physically exploring terraces to texts can still today recognise and visit many of the places and buildings mentioned in Bragg's novels. For the reader wanting a pictorial guide to Bragg's Wigton/Thornton - and particularly some of the fast disappearing sites of the early 1950s - Trevor Grahamslaw's *Wigton Through Time* (2010) will prove an invaluable guide. In his book, for example, Mason's Garage still stands with its wall signage offering 'Cars for Hire' and 'Motor Repairs' in a 1930s sepia photograph where today a bland Associated Tyre Services Shed occupies the site. Bragg's novel cannot avoid becoming by default a guide to time past and a portrait of a particular variety of small-town Englishness now being reconfigured under the pressure of global influences. His description of Thornton's town square in the early 1950s, for example, chimes with my childhood recollection of a similar square in the old town of Hemel Hempstead before the spread of the post-war London overspill building programme destroyed its community-intimacy.

10. Bragg's distinguished broadcasting career and his role in disseminating culture and the history of ideas to a wide general audience is a subject for a book in its own right. He has been writer, editor and presenter of *The South Bank Show*, first on London Weekend (1978-2010) and from 2011 on Sky Arts. He presented BBC Radio 4's *Start the Week* from 1988-1998, only relinquishing his anchor role when he was made a life peer - and in the latter role he regularly speaks on legislation affecting broadcasting and the arts in general. He continues to preside over the long-running BBC Radio 4's *In Our Time*, which he describes as a 'discussion forum which had its origin in one of the oldest and most influential of all intellectual forms - the "Dialogue of Plato"' (*In Our Time,* p.x). Although strictly outside the scope of the present study, I will refer to Bragg's broadcasting (and film) career where it directly influences, sometimes in an autobiographical manner, his literary fiction.

> [The church] stood as the fourth side of a little
> square. Opposite was the 'Lion and Lamb', flanked by
> tall, narrow-doored houses. To the left, a row of shops -
> always more shut than open - a leather shop, an old
> shoemaker, a failing cake-shop, a wool and patterns
> shop. To the right, a wavering rank of low-roofed
> cottages two up, one down - with a hole blasted in the
> middle for the road to go through.
>
> Two children were pressing their noses against
> the shop windows. Three women were clustered
> around one of the cottage doors, smoking, talking.
>
> (*WN*, p.68)

The 'hole blasted in the middle' to make way for a road is a small but significant sign of change to come.

Bragg does not, however, wallow in a utopian vision of a past snug and safe world, framed and distanced without any disturbing details to threaten an otherwise idealised picture. The insanitary living conditions, the near ubiquitous presence of tuberculosis, the almost casual gang violence, sharp class differences, even rape, are all featured in Bragg's Wigton novels, yet somehow without destabilising a cherished way of life. In *For Want of a Nail* change is read largely through the educational and social experiences of one individual, Tom Graham, whereas in later novels a much wider community of characters is involved in the disruption caused by two World Wars. In charting historical change in a sympathetic way arising from a personal understanding of the issues involved, Bragg is able to use the traditional realist form of the regional novel to espouse social and political values - in *For Want of a Nail*, education - that contradict the conventional application of a conservative label to it and similar texts. *For Want of a Nail* is, in effect, the first of a sequence of novels that aspire to a form of rationalist modernity, increasingly common in post-war fiction, in which fictionally translated discourses of a small but universally recognisable community aim to create an evolving reciprocal understanding between text and reader.

This understanding is mediated via Bragg's portrait of a projected self as a young man formed from a dialectic between memory and invention and through which he filters the 1950s small town world of Thornton. Tom's intense inwardness and self-absorption, as he explores perennial existential adolescent dilemmas, co-exists with an impression of the multiple facets of social and cultural life of early 1950s England. Tom's initial awakening of interest in the hidden life of the community meshes with questions of personal identity and is expressed in sociological rather than political terms. Coming across a partially demolished house on the outskirts of Thornton he imagines 'some giant paw ripping away the roof-tops and revealing all Thornton in its hidden third of life' (*WN*, p.143). This seemingly innocuous but deftly inserted visual image might profitably be deconstructed to reveal its own hidden secrets. Bragg was an early devotee of cinema, enjoying greater freedom to view than Tom's weekly Saturday treat when his mother went shopping in Thornton: 'He went in with his mother on Saturday afternoons; she gave him sixpence for the "Matinée": collected him with all her other parcels an hour and a half later and then they walked back home' (*WN*, p.29).[11] Made in America in 1947, Walt Disney's *Mickey and the Beanstalk* (part of a cartoon feature, *Fun and Fancy Free*) includes a disturbing sequence in which a predatory giant lifts the roofs off the townsfolk's homes. On release in British cinemas in the late 1940s/early 1950s, there is every likelihood that Bragg saw the film and was no doubt impressed, however unconsciously, by its graphic imagery.[12] This observation is not to make any extravagant autobiographical claim, beyond drawing attention to Max Saunders's belief that the 'autobiographer does not just recover memory, but elaborates and narrativizes it; loses it, perhaps; certainly turns it into something quite different ...' (*Self Impression*, pp.55-56). The recovery of such memories is the novelist's literary capital and, in this case, a particularly felicitous one - for what metaphor better encapsulates one of the writer's major endeavours than removing barriers to the truth and 'revealing [the] hidden third of life' (*WN*, p.143)? Tom's feeling of pleasure at the sight of a house exposing its inner fabric makes him think that '[e]verything would be revealed' (*WN*, p.143). Easily overlooked when concentrating on discreet images is the emotionally and technically adroit manner in

11. The cinema would have been Cusack's Cinema in Meeting House Lane. Owned by Joe Cusack, it was known locally as 'Joe's'. Admission was tuppence for the front row, sixpence and ninepence for the balcony. All the major films of the time were shown, although they tended to be on a few weeks after general release in the large city cinemas. It can still be located but has now become a café.

12. I was an uncritical admirer of all Disney's films in the early 1950s, using their visual language as an exotic back-drop, where appropriate, to my youthful reading. At the time I would have been unappreciative of Disney's frequent and psychologically disturbing references to the absent/missing father, but am aware now of their inter-media commentary on *For Want of a Nail*'s interest in identifying the father.

which Bragg uses structured moments of suspected revelation to connect seemingly disparate parts of the plot. The exposed house lingers as an agent of exposure on the edge of the consciousness of both Tom and reader, only to reappear at a moment of epiphany, to underscore and emphasise the text's overall thematic unity. Towards the novels climax Tom revisits his first home, now a 'cracked and shoddy little cottage, the garden so overgrown that it looked like a toy jungle, the peeled doors and smashed windows', and by climbing the 'broken low roof of what had been the washhouse' (WN, p.293) he is able to reach a window and look in. The post-coital sight of his mother and Uncle Henry finally reveals the hidden third of life that has haunted Tom throughout the novel.

For Tom, the personal overwhelms the political and whilst at moments of reflection he recognises the need for wider cultural change, his adversarial attitude lacks any coherent vision of what might be required to give it the necessary traction. There is one specifically ideologically important short passage in the novel when Tom, in Oxford, expresses an authentic political consciousness, but in such a psychologically disturbed mental state that its emotional legitimacy, basic social accuracy and moral truth fail to integrate any notion of idea, experience and action:

> Yet there were moments of ideas, which stirred him. When he thought of the injustice of a world which would give one man seventeen houses, five wives, incredible luxuries, power, success and ease - and another so little food or protection that he died of disease and starvation - then he was appalled at his own soft rottenness. When he understood the death and battle which had been fed into the nation which had given him a free rein to educate and exercise himself as he wished - then he was contemptuous of his pampered self-regard. Men had lived who had blasted great valleys through mountains of ignorance; they had discovered the whole world and brought it to the possibilities of understanding; they had discovered worlds within their own world and given themselves the potentialities of destruction. And he swung, tightly bound, in a hammock of self-pity.
>
> (WN, pp.257-258)

Tom's marginalised political consciousness is heavily context-dependent and his sense of helplessness part of a more widespread disaffection from contemporary social forces. The year is 1957 and Tom is 17 years of age. The shadow of apocalyptic nuclear disaster was a constant of the times and CND marches to 'Ban the Bomb' a popular political phenomenon of mass protest. In 1956 the British Conservative Government was forced by American pressure to make an ignominious retreat from Egypt and the Suez Canal, one of the last of a long line of imperial misadventures. John Osborne's *Look Back in Anger* opened at the Royal Court in 1956 with a portrayal of a rebellious and anti-establishment anger by its working class characters that Tom may well have empathised with. Whilst none of this fear and unrest surfaces overtly in the novel's text, it nevertheless clearly provides a disturbing backdrop to Tom's sense of a divided self, caught between the experience of his private life and the wider social/political world. As a potential novelist, Tom needs time and distance from his home town roots if he is to find the necessary objective space to record accurately his experiences. What remains crucial in this process, however, is that the sense of attachment to place - as expressed, for example, in the passages on Blencathra - is the motivating factor behind Tom's potential, and Bragg's actual, life as a writer.

MELVYN BRAGG

The
Second
Inheritance

By the author of 'The Maid of Buttermere'

# TWO
# CODES OF MASCULINITY
## *THE SECOND INHERITANCE*

Bragg's next novel, *The Second Inheritance*, announces its literary ambition in an extended opening chapter that adopts the equivalent of a cinematic aesthetic, presenting a series of discrete visual images to convey a momentary frozen sense of historical time and place, together with a rapid cinematic cutting technique. This propels the introductory narrative through a 'time passes' sequence of more than eighteen years duration. With this telescoped historical time-span Bragg juggles a combination of themes. He juxtaposes the closed domestic interior and the untamed, often bleak, natural world, both of which provide the stage for the drama of two contrasting family histories. He makes an early reference to the Roman Wall as a symbolic marker of a class division that extends its reach to the unconsummated nature and frustrated potential of a submerged homosexual relationship. All these elements combine to show the importance of the natural and social environment, of instinct and heredity and the accidents of history in determining generational outcomes. From the outset, the novel sets these features in a series of timeless tableaux that might have come from the pages of a Thomas Hardy novel and it is not until several years have passed that the reader acquires the information 'It was the summer of 1947' (*SI*, p.24). Bragg's cinematic time shifts (reminiscent of Virginia Woolf's 1922 'Time Passes' section of *To the Lighthouse*), the unannounced changes in narrative perspective, and the placement of symbolic allusions, might be regarded as more representative of the modernist novel than the social realist narrative. Here, however, they are central to his interrogation of the social and geographical terrain he established as his signature motif in *For Want of a Nail*. The seeming dislocation of the opening chapter echoes through the rest of an otherwise comparatively conventionally structured and omnisciently narrated text, finally coming to rest in the concluding chapter, whose sense of stasis is in stark contrast to Chapter 1. The would-be self-determining John Foster, the inheritor of a rural tradition he cannot bring himself to forsake, becomes a figure in the Cumbrian landscape, dwarfed by a plangent romanticism promoting a sense of place unconsciously guiding the fate of the individual.

What looks on the surface to be, in the words of the anonymous *Times Literary Supplement* reviewer of the day, 'a straightforward and traditional family novel, firmly structured and neatly written [and] set in Cumberland' (p.589) is, on a deeper level, an exploration of the novelistic possibilities of using the rural experience to investigate assumptions about human-nature, using a combination of symbolism and naturalism. Bragg's debt to late nineteenth and early twentieth-century naturalist writers in this novel is apparent in his refusal to idealise the rural experience, and by his observation of natural law as a motivating and controlling factor in human behaviour. His literary characters, here, are formed by a mixture of physical and hereditary factors, which include the outside pressure of the city intruding upon the social mores of country dwellers and the economic imperatives of the countryside. At the same time, as Glen Cavaliero warns in *The Rural Tradition in the English Novel 1900-1939*, the 'rural novelist's task also involved something that urban fiction generally omits: a response to a way of life more directly conscious of living form, and of being in touch with non-human forces - what may be called a more elemental way of life, and this aspect in particular called for intelligent treatment if absurdity or pretension was to be avoided' (p.17).

An unpretentious depiction of the hardness of rural character and landscape, and a notion of absurdity attached to the disconnect between social classes, is invoked by Bragg from the very beginning. Farm labourer Nelson Foster courts the daughter of a local farmer more for her expected inheritance than for her self. Her father's own lack of any romantic inclination is symbolised by his imprisoning clothing, from the 'clipped white collar and a stiff black waistcoat' (*SI.* p.8) to his 'stiff cuffs' and whilst he is clearly 'living in imitation of his former force' (*SI*, p.9) Nelson is equally clearly preparing to inherit not only Elizabeth's half-share of the farm, but also her father's now fading work ethic. Unable to impress Mr Webb socially as a prospective son-in-law, Nelson guarantees his inheritance by what is, in effect, a brutal rape of Elizabeth:

> He took her by the shoulders. She did not know whether he was going to throw her away, or embrace her. Fiercely, slowly, he pushed her on to the ground. While she continued to cry, he undid her blouse; then he lifted her skirt and drew off her pants. Still she cried, hopelessly: he had never taken her.
>
> Even when he had finished, she was still sobbing.
>
> (*SI*, p.12)

Nelson's act of sexual aggression, and the resultant birth of his son John, is an early and textually important illustration of the way in which inheritance, in *The Second Inheritance*, becomes subject to the vagaries of the individual will rather than to the operation of the legal wills and entails intended to safeguard the English estate of, say, Jane Austen's *Mansfield Park* (1814). In Austen's novels the physical structure of the estate was indicative of an enduring inherited structure of morality and manners, immune to sudden change. Austen clearly distrusts and disapproves of the Crawfords because they are careless of cultural heritage and are therefore improper agents of social change. In *The Second Inheritance* Arthur Langley is an improper agent of social change, not because he threatens to disrupt traditional relations between house and church - indeed, he finds the Reverend Craddock an amenable colleague on archaeological digs - but because his latent homosexuality represents a physical and culturally-determined end to the line of inheritance. His freely taken decision at the novel's end to leave the house and land and return to London settles the question of who are the appropriate heirs in favour of Nelson and his son John, thereby ensuring the continuing fertility of the farmland/estate but at the expense of the Langley line. In this respect, Bragg's text rejects any intrusion of social nostalgia whilst maintaining the sense of character associated with the land itself. The novel concludes on a far more deterministic note, redolent of post-War social and economic factors than does, for example, the early twentieth-century text of E.M. Forster's *Howards End* (1910) in which the question of an appropriate heir remains undecided although, unlike in the case of the Langleys and the Fosters, there exists an uneasy rapprochement between the Schlegels and the Wilcoxes.[1]

In *The Writing of Fiction* (1925) Edith Wharton observes that 'the bounds of a personality are not reproducible by a sharp black line, but that each of us flows imperceptibly into adjacent people and things' (p.10), reflecting a belief in the interdependence of character and personal identity with the external environment. The Roman Wall in *The Second Inheritance* is both an integral feature of the landscape and a symbolic marker of class membership and individual personality. In the depths of a

1. There are a number of intriguing parallels between *The Second Inheritance* and *Howards End* that might be further explored. These include the disruption of stable and legitimate Edwardian inheritance patterns when Leonard Bast impregnates Helen Schlegel and, as Frank Kermode writes, the 'novel [*Howards End*] makes clear that Forster regrets Bast's education and wishes he could revert to the admirable condition of the simple farm labourer' (*Concerning E M Forster*, p.97).

particular severe winter Nelson and his brother Dickie desperately attempt to build a protective sheep fold to prevent further frozen deaths in their flock by using a pile of large stones from the wall. They are seen by the neighbouring land-owner, Major Langley, who authoritatively bellows 'Those - stones - are - not - your - property!' and who, despite Nelson's reasoned pleas insists that 'Those - stones - have - to - be - left where - they - are' (*SI*, p.21). For the Major, the Wall is a long-standing guarantor of his social authenticity, and any tampering with its structure, or crumbling of its base, threatens not only his sense of ownership but also his sense of superiority. In the early post-War setting of the novel, the middle and upper-classes felt particularly vulnerable to the Labour government's espoused policy of redistribution via nationalisation and fiscal policies encompassing higher estate duties and inheritance taxes. Families such as the Langleys would have been apprehensive of any trespass upon their property rights, however justifiable in terms of natural justice. Nelson's removal of a few seemingly innocuous stones is therefore a highly charged symbolic act, threatening the stability of class relations rather than of the Wall itself. There exists a history, particularly from the early 1700s onwards, of larger landowners in Cumbria using their economic and political muscle to seize and enclose former common grazing land, and the Wall is an obvious historical structure for the Langley family to appropriate as part of a policy referred to as 'intakes'.[2] Class deference, with its concomitant influences upon dialogue, emerges from the symbolic nature of enclosure and separation so that elements of relatively recent material culture link to the history of Roman conquest to form an inextricable whole. So determined is the Major to maintain his class position that, having demanded the restoration of the Wall, he does not trust Nelson to comply without his 'staying to watch the dismemberment of the new wall, the cowed, bitter transfer of the stones to their original rubble-heaps' (*SI*, p.21). Thus the battle lines are drawn in a highly symbolic opening skirmish over who is to control and inherit the land.

Close textual reading reveals unexpected parallels between otherwise unstable distinctions of the human and non-human. The finding of a sheep, 'stretched stiff, ice melting its wool; birds had pecked out its eyes' (*SI*, p.20) re-emerges in another context to question the value

---

2.  The privatising tendency of 'intakes' was offset to a limited extent by a co-operative measure enabling farmers to get their sheep to the open fells using passages called 'rakes' or 'outgangs' in the otherwise encircling walls. Melvyn Bragg's home in High Ireby is called 'Outgang Cottage'.

and definition of the human and human cultural values. This occurs in the next chapter where the scene switches abruptly to a London doss-house and now it is the human animal in a state of decay whose eyes are denied any sense of social vision or comprehension:

> Most of the men were old, many were covered with sores, scabs, flaring cuts, debilities which came from another century. All were filthily dressed and unwashed for weeks ... Goitres, palsied shaking, matted hair - thick, visibly matted with grease like rotted toffee -loose mouth [which] sucked at the dribble spilt down unshaven skins. And eyes - empty, dead, dozed, hidden, frightened, lost, mad. Stunned sockets of eyes.　　　　(*SI*, p.37)

Such a stark convergence of the (dead) animal and (barely alive) human divide raises important assumptions about the nature/culture divide that is central to a reading of the regional rural novel wishing to avoid the problems of literary fragmentation diagnosed by Cavaliero, where the divorce between the urban and rural novel is absolute. Confronted by appalling levels of human degradation in London's worst post-War slums, Arthur Langley despairs of any meaningful political, economic or personal response to a vision of overwhelming horror and is left physically and mentally exhausted with 'eyes ... stare-wide open' (*SI*, p.41). His return to Cumbria is not, however, an admission of moral surrender to economic realities, for he never stops questioning the privileges of a rural inheritance that seem 'to be suffocating his conscience' (*SI*, p, 255).

In sharp contrast, Nelson is determined to see, without necessarily comprehending, everything that happens within his literal fields of vision. He is therefore extremely frustrated to discover that his assumed panoptic surveillance of both his land and family fails to detect a harmless encounter between his wife and a twenty year old Arthur Langley, home on army leave. Lizzie and her three children are enjoying a picnic close to the neighbouring Langley land. John, now aged ten, is engrossed in his mother's reading aloud and wants to see the book's illustrations:

> It was an engraving of a forest of silver birches.
> 'Like ours', said John
> 'Yes. Lovely, like ours.'
> 'But not as big.'

'How can you tell from a picture?'
He screwed up his face at the trees. Then he shook his
head.
  'Not half as big.'
Someone [Arthur] laughed.

(*SI*, p.25)

This brief passage is richly contextual, raising questions of relative value
analogous to the comparative size of the adjacent farms, of literary
pictorial representation and interpretation extending to embedded
symbolism, and, proleptic of John and Arthur's later literary intimacy
and questioning in Arthur's library.

Bragg brings Arthur and John together beneath the book leaves of
fictional silver birch trees. The silver birch has long been regarded as
sacred by indigenous people throughout North America, Europe and
Asia where it has assumed a powerful symbolic image indicative of
collective renewal and survival. It is also entirely appropriate that John
and Arthur meet in the presence of a literary representation and an actual
stand of a tree that, in Scandinavian mythology, carries a promise of
unconditional love. Nelson, however, takes a contrary view, privileging
the social power of ownership over landscape aesthetics. The birch trees
prevent him from seeing the picnic encounter from the farm house and he
is frustrated by this lack of 360 degree vision:

Outside was the garden - shortened to a mat-patch by the
extension of the top field - and on its boundary  the three tall
birch-trees. Nelson looked out and shook his head.
  'Beats me,' he said. 'Upstairs, downstairs, their bedroom,
our bedroom, back, front - every damned window there is in
the place, and I still couldn't see you.' He laughed.
  'It would be from that window,' said Lizzie. 'Or the one
upstairs.'
  'It's them trees,' he replied. 'You can't see that bit for them
three trees.'
Two days later, when he chopped them down, she felt hit by
every strike of the axe. The soft silver bark flaked off gently
where the blade struck.                              (*SI*, p.28)

Such acts of destructive tyranny belong to a narrative that overturns the
English tradition of natural description that expects nature to please.  In
cutting down the birch trees Nelson removes both a temporal and a

spatial landmark, making the text-mark of Lizzie's book all the more important as a memory grounding her son to a local sense of lost place.

Gaston Bachelard, in *The Poetics of Space*, explores the concept of the ontology of the poetic and the way in which, through the construction of images, 'the distant past responds with echoes, and it is hard to know at what depth these echoes will reverberate and die away' (p. xvi). The image of the felled trees has a symbolic ontological textual reverberation when 200 pages later, in an act of symbolic castration, another blade puts an abrupt end to Nelson's dominance of environment and family. '"He was dyking," Shirley began. "He would never wear gloves. And those sickles are as sharp as razor-blades. The way he keeps them"... She spread out her hand and drew a line down the webbing between thumb and forefinger, almost to the wrist. "It was hanging off"' (*SI*, p.236). Bragg has methodically deployed a contested and unfolding reverberatory representation of nature - from dead sheep to silver birch - to dramatise the human predicament whilst avoiding a sentimental representation of rural life. It is in such passages that I read the novel as positioning itself as part of a distinctly Cumbrian contribution to the contemporary ecopoetical debate on modern discourses of nature.[3]

Bragg depicts the fictional town of Aldeby on a Saturday as a psychic semi-urban landscape of a place 'entirely withdrawn; not expectant, deserted [whose] houses were low-roofed and poor-looking' (*SI*, p.85) matching the unforgiving nature of its surrounding countryside. Hearing that a game of Pitch and Toss is underway in a nearby clearing, John and his uncle Dickie abandon the soulless town in search of activity. To reach the clearing they have to pass a patch of allotments whose 'owners, squinting up to look at the loud-footed passers, were as survivors on a rubbish dump' (*SI*, p.85). This conflation of residence, inhabitant, and context extends to the London of Arthur Langley's doss-house and suggests a discourse where only the most self-willed of individuals will escape a form of environmental determinism. The powerful image of 'survivors on a rubbish dump' - an image set in the context of the Cold War

3. Part I, 'Romantic Ecology and its Legacy' in Laurence Coupe's edited *The Green Studies Reader. From Romanticism to Ecocriticism* 9200) provides an introductory set of essays, ranging from William Blake to Raymond Williams, establishing the historical background to the contemporary ecopoetical debate. Particularly interesting as a prototype in establishing the importance of an ecopoetical perspective within any text is the excerpt from Samuel Taylor Coleridge's *Biographia Literaria* (1817) and the philosophical attempt to formulate a theory of the imagination able to accommodate both the interiority of the human mind and the exteriority of the natural world.

of the 1950s and its accompanying apocalyptic fears of nuclear destruction - is an uncomfortable yoking of provincial and metropolitan life.

In the context of a possible impending endgame, the continuing existence of the traditional game of Pitch and Toss is not only a marker of regional identity but also a sign of continuity. Bragg captures the game at its zenith before changing patterns of leisure and consumption saw it rapidly decline, and almost die out, in the early and mid-Sixties. Seamus Heaney reads such descriptive passage of traditional activities as the necessary defensive love of a writer's geographical and emotional territory seen as under an increasing threat from the levelling tendencies of mass commercial culture:

> Their terrain is becoming consciously precious. A desire to [textually] preserve indigenous traditions, to keep open the imagination's supply lines to the past, to receive from the stations of Anglo-Saxon confirmations of ancestry, to perceive in the rituals of show Saturdays and race-meetings and seaside outings, of church-going and marriage at Whitsun ... a continuity of communal ways. (*Preoccupations*, pp.150-151)

These traditional pursuits are recalled and celebrated across Bragg's fictional oeuvre, as well as in his anthropological participant observers documentation of Wigton, *Speak for England* , in which he turns to 'a tradition, a culture and energy, a recognisable face' (p.4) to define contemporary meanings of Englishness. In featuring Pitch and Toss in the novel as the sole example of a purely group leisure pursuit, Bragg directs attention to the dynamics of an all-male close-knit social group, acting in opposition to the law and the 'withdrawn' nature of the town. A look-out is posted to keep a watch for the police[4], the simple rules are rigidly

4. Dave Farrer's essay for the 'Durham Miner Project' sets out the rules of the game as played in the Durham coalfields and makes clear the wisdom of posting a look-out at a time when games of chance not officially licensed were illegal: 'If caught the miscreants were brought before the local magistrates and fined quite heavily, this probably had a greater effect on the player's wife and family than the man himself ... there was a sliding scale of fines employed by the courts ... eventually after 4 or 5 appearances a term in jail usually 28 days was given.' (www.keystothepast.info/miner/projects) As Peter Hennessy summarises the situation: '... there was one illegal activity in which millions indulged every year - gambling ..."in most pubs, in nearly every factory or workshop and on the streets of every working-class community there was a bookmaker with whom he could make that bet. There was one problem: it was illegal." (*Having It So Good. Britain in the Fifties* p.87). I can well remember in the mid-50s having my hair cut by Charlie Wilding who would, mid snip, disappear to the fishmonger's next door to place an illegal horse-racing bet. The Betting and Gaming Act 1960 established a framework for the appearance of legal betting shops whose proliferation ended  illegal back-room bookmaking.

enforced and all the players take the contest seriously. It is as if the very illegality of the game is a necessary contributing factor to group cohesion. John's rash drink-fuelled attempt to re-define the rules of the game for the benefit of a socially inadequate player with 'the face of an old grape, dried to grey slits but still somehow shining from the seeping desertion of its last juice' (*SI*, p.87) provokes a narrowly avoided violent response: 'If you don't like our rules - go back to where you come from' (*SI*, p.90). Taken out of context John's actions appear inexplicable, but positioned within the overall narrative structure they loop back and around in time to recall an earlier episode in a holiday camp in which, enacting an element of the folk tradition, he stood alone against the crowd.

The Pitch and Toss episode, far from being a vaguely interesting but narratively disassociated digression, serves two important purposes. First, it offers a commentary on an activity reflecting shared group values and knowledge which preserve historical elements of local culture necessary to an enduring sense of place. Second, it raises again the centrally vital psychic question for John of what it means to be a man in the company of men.[5] John's puzzling intervention on behalf of a marginalised socially inadequate male player is entirely in character and is reminiscent of similar behaviour described in Chapter 3's holiday camp scene of overt male violence descriptively coded as a moment of displaced sexuality, and which I will discuss in more detail a little further on. Nicola Humble writes that '[t]raditionally, literary criticism has tended to see [the] emergence of queer culture as a feature of the bohemianism of key high-cultural literary groupings ... But is seems to me that this presence is in fact the sign of a much more general visibility of homosexuality, and an increasing cultural interest in it' ('The Queer Pleasure of Reading', p.4). In considering the shadowy but pervasive homosexual/homoerotic presence in *The Second Inheritance* it is necessary to remember the distinct lack of public visibility of homosexuality at the time of the novel's publication in 1966, and, perhaps more importantly, the stigma attached to perceived forms of male sexual deviance in the

5. One of the poems included in my 1973 edition of Iona and Peter Opie's *The Oxford Book of Children's Verse* is Rudyard Kipling's *If* This much quoted guide to acquiring the qualities of masculinity includes a reference to Pitch and Toss as a metaphor for life:

> *If you can make one heap of all your winnings*
> *And risk it on one turn of pitch-and-toss,*
> *And lose, and start again at your beginnings*
> *And never breathe a word about your loss; ...*
> *You'll be a Man, my son!* (p.324)

novel's immediate post-War setting. This was a time when no Member of Parliament could afford to admit to being homosexual and when even the most prominent of London's theatrical knights - Sir John Gielgud - could be arrested and fined for importuning. Read against this background, Bragg's novel assumes critical importance as a realist regional text intent on building upon the portrayal of male relationships in, for example, *Women in Love,* and capable of sympathetically presenting significant but suppressed homosexual characters and encounters.[6] In assessing the importance of Bragg's move beyond standard post-war literary definitions of masculinity based on physical strength and strong heterosexual drive,[7] however well written and welcome as a popular resurgence of the working-class novel, I need to return to the contemporary review which found its undertone of homosexuality and incest and its permutations of partners derivative of Iris Murdoch's formal patterning whilst failing to integrate them into the text and therefore failing to say anything. I want to argue that this is a misreading of both Bragg and Murdoch, and to show that Bragg's realistic representation of repressed male same-sex desire(s) is in direct contrast to what W.S. Hampl, in 'Desires Deferred: Homosexual and Queer Representations in the Novels of Iris Murdoch' calls Murdoch's non- or anti-realistic picture of sexual attraction in which, in a semantic devaluation, 'homosexual ultimately becomes an arbitrary label of little descriptive value' (p.663). This is a critically important area of textual debate for *The Second Inheritance,* intended to reach a wide popular audience, including homosexual readers. If, as Hampl contends, Murdoch's critically unchallenged portrayal of homosexual characters in her novels of the 1950s and 1960s is 'at times alarming, inaccurate, and/or nonsensical' (p.671), then in retrospect, this can be seen to call for a more informed and nuanced reading of Bragg's foray into queer literary territory.

Hollywood's Western films of the post-War period provide a focus for investigating and understanding Bragg's approach to defining

6. It is salutary to remember that many of the literary avant-garde texts published in England and testing the boundaries of homosexual representation in the early 1960s immediately prior to the publication of *The Second Inheritance* - William Burroughs, *Naked Lunch* (1964), Hubert Selby Jr., *Last Exit to Brooklyn* (1964) and itself prosecuted for obscenity, John Rechy, *City of Night* (1964) - were American. As late as 1980 English playwright Howard Brenton's The *Romans in Britain* at the National Theatre was the subject of a private prosecution for alleged public indecency.

7. Alan Sillitoe's *Saturday Night and Sunday Morning* (1958) and David Storey's *This Sporting Life* (1960) are two of the most highly regarded post-War novels defining masculinity - and also the most widely known as a result of the commercially successful film adaptations.

masculinity and desire in *A Second Inheritance*. I have drawn attention to Bragg's early exposure to, and love of cinema, in the previous chapter. It is difficult to underestimate the influence of this art form on Bragg's choice of narrative, use of symbolism and stylistic techniques, often analogous to film editing. Bragg has written in his British Film Institute monograph *The Seventh Seal* of just how deep-seated cinema's influence on him and his generation was:

> I was born in 1939, and like millions of others I grew up with the cinema. It was the one exotic plant in a dour, soberly dressed, religious and some might say rather drab town ... The cinema was a wonder, It brought us people and stories we didn't quite dare to believe were true or in any way part of the real business of life ... The cowboy films with the fake bullets, the fixed fights, the simple morality tale, were as fantastical as [musicals, Tarzan and War films]. All films, the flicks, were Another World. (*SS*, p.14)

Sixty years on, Bragg recalls his formative childhood cinema visits with the same enthusiasm as that boy who 'was happily obsessed with the movies' and who, because he had free admission thanks to his father displaying the cinema's posters in his pub, could for many years go 'two or more often three times a week, thus catching all three films' (*S S*, p.15) in the weekly repertory system.

This saturation of images at an impressionable age plays an important role in providing Bragg with a large canvas to draw upon in his own later creative years as a writer. Cinema in the late 1940s/early 1950s was often the working-class child's passport to a world beyond that of the 'drab town', enlarging his/her visual vocabulary en route. I find a compelling argument for reading Bragg's trajectory of John's development, from a self-centred determined child of eleven to an equally self-contained but now physically mature adolescent of nineteen, in the light of the classic Western's portrayal of the search for the elusive quality of masculinity/manhood as a dialectic between the self's impressionable body and a society with an agenda detrimental to that body's very existence. The literary equivalence extends to a 'simple morality tale' in which John is the lone central character prepared to defend the weak - the equivalent of the lone cowboy in a shoot-out on behalf of a town that refuses to get involved - but in a holiday-camp, not a saloon bar or ranch. One of the more detailed studies of recent years to address the psychology of issues of masculinity in film and literature is Lee Clark Mitchell's *Westerns. Making the Man in Fiction and Film*, and, specifically for my reading, his chapter 'A Man Being Beaten'. Mitchell here draws attention to the manner in which he sees the Western as fetishising the male body as a site for enduring pain and humiliation as a necessary part of a cultural process of 'proving ones male body (or rather proving the body male) - a proof that, ever since [Zane] Grey has required a series of ever more elaborate confirmation' (*Westerns*, p.151).

For John, proving the body male begins at age eleven when his father challenges him to carry an eighteen-stone sack of wheat on his back up the granary steps. The route to masculinity is clearly delineated - 'Your grandfather could do that easily as your age' (*SI*, p.28). John buckles under the sack's weight but, in keeping with the Western tradition, his prone body - Mitchell makes much of the prone body as the precursor to 'miniature convalescence sequences in which the hero is reduced to a prone position so that the camera can display him recovering himself' (*Westerns*, p.151) - not only recovers but is determined to prove itself equal to the task: 'Much later, when work had strengthened him, he could have run up the steps with the weight slung on his back' (*SI*, p.31). The comparison with the confident non-exhibitionist Western hero reluctant to prove his gun-slinging skills is made in Bragg's qualifying clause, '... but he would never do it' (*SI*, p.31).

In his reluctance to demonstrate his acquired physical strength and prowess, John exemplifies a central tenet of Mitchell's view of the Western's masculinity, namely that it 'is always more than physical ... favouring an ideal of restraint well beyond bodily considerations [and revealing] how manhood is as much learned as found' (*Westerns*, p.183). By age nineteen John has acquired a gender identity ready to be displayed and tested in a classic Western scenario, but displaced to a holiday camp setting where John feels very much the outsider. Bragg begins this sequence with a voyeuristically inflected close-up gaze at John's body:

> Planting his feet on the pretty little floor, as if to force his
> legs through it and touch the ground, John stretched his
> whole body into a tight, shuddering tremble; holding the
> thick-shivering judder of his body for as long as he could.

His muscles curled to bunched tightness, and he quickened to their sweet pull against the skin. He lifted his head from the bar-counter and slowly, tensely, watched his fingers extend to their full length. He was nineteen.

(*SI*, p.41)

This is not that far removed from the introductory appearance of the Virginian in Owen Wister's eponymously titled 1902 novel: 'Lounging there at ease against the wall was a slim young giant, more beautiful than pictures ... The weather-beaten bloom of his face shone through it dustily, as the ripe peaches look upon their trees in a dry season. But no dinginess of travel ... could tarnish the splendour that radiated from his youth and strength' (*Virginian*, p.4). In both texts it is the male body that is described in sexually attractive terms, and threatening to slide into homoerotic desire. Such consistency across texts and time suggests a generic need for the Western to incorporate pleasing features as essential to the delineation of masculinity.

John is taunted with a string of sexual insults from a gang of five young men frustrated by his stepping in to defend a fellow chalet occupant, Edward, who Bragg describes in terms sharply contrasting with John's 'pleasing features'. Indeed, so extreme is the contrast - 'spindly, buck-toothed, gormless' (*SI*, p.47) that it calls into question the very notion of a definable stable sexual identity; Edward is the Other that paradoxically acknowledges John's masculinity. This near maternal impulse to protect a vulnerable member of the community - an impulse we see repeated in the Pitch and Toss sequence - presents John as hero, incorporating stereotypically feminine and masculine personality traits, creating an ambiguous instability around the terms of his masculinity, an instability that remains unresolved throughout the novel. In three pages consisting mainly of dialogue, Bragg makes the gang member do all the talking while John remains silent. The dead-lock is broken by an arm-wrestling contest in which John forces Alec's hand on to one of the two strategically placed cigarette ends. Even as John then backs out of the room he remains silent, deigning no more than a nod in reply to Alec's threatening 'See you soon' (*SI*, p.46). This entire sequence is illustrative of Mitchell's contention that in the Western masculinity is about something more than a physical ideal, and that in exercising restraint in the face of physical threats, John shows manhood to be about learned responses:

> Restraint, of course, is essential to our most fundamental ideals of selfhood even as it poses a concept difficult to represent. Therefore, the Western [and its literary models] signals restraint always *through* the body, in its vacillations and hesitations under the threat of danger ... Before restraint can be said to exist dramatically, in other words, it needs to be needled, stretched, otherwise exacerbated by the continuing threat of violence.
>
> (*Westerns*, p.183)

For John, the 'continuing threat of violence' reaches a climax when the gang appears at the chalet John shares with three other boys, including the hapless Edward. He is aware that in any confrontation inside the restricted space of the chalet the gang would attack not only him, but also Edward, who 'would scud across the chalet like a brown paper bag' (*SI* p. 47). John therefore makes a break for the children's playground where, in the logic of the Western's body-society dialectic, the outcome is inevitable:

> His ankle turned, slightly, and they were on him with a tremendous thud.
>
> He lashed out with his feet and fists as long as they were free. Soon he could not feel his blows registering.
>
> 'Don't kill him! Keep him!'
>
> His forehead knocked against the hard cement. Someone had screwed his right arm up his back.
>
> 'Keep him for me! Alec.'
>
> They stopped. He could hardly hear them. Again they were arguing. Donal. He was dragged off. To the middle. Quieter. Virgin.
>
> 'This'll do.'
>
> Then they set on him.
>
> (*SI*, p.51)

The Western's concentration on an almost generic necessity for the beating of the lone hero has been interpreted as providing a 'disguised, displaced, inadvisable homosexual pleasure' (*Westerns*, p.175). Whilst there may be an element of such vicarious pleasure in Bragg's text, it is not deemed suitable for universal viewing 'As long as his mother did not see his [bruised] body' (*SI*, p.52) - and the important cultural trace elements and narrative design borrowed from the Western is seen when John offers himself as a sacrificial surrogate for a weaker male with whom he has no intimate relationship. The hint here, and it is never more than a hint, is of a continuum between homosexuality and homosociality, that will be opened up in a readerly context with the novel's other main male protagonist, Arthur Langley. The Western novel is conspicuously absent from Arthur's well-stocked library, but by then its 'simple morality tale' has already been bent to other purposes.

Arthur Langley's relationship with John connects back to a boyhood moment when he longed to be included in the 'enviable noise and warmth' (*SI*, p.17) of the Foster family's farmhouse when they first moved in. He is totally absorbed by the sight of co-operative bustling women preparing dinner for the men, whilst others unload wardrobes, beds, utensils and everyday objects piled high on the fourteen haycarts loaned for the removal. Bragg employs narrational cross-cutting to follow first John and then to cut to Arthur, now a young man in post-War London. Both he and Oliver, his friend since schooldays, have resigned their army commissions to plunge headlong into charity work for a Dock Welfare Group. Here, in a grotesque parody of the Foster's horse-drawn household removal wagons, they collect items donated to the doss-house: ' ... taking the ancient land-rover with them, which they piled high with junk  old shirts, boots, chairs, crockery, curtains, lamps, stools, carpets, coats, tools, wood, books, tins, bust baskets, ruined sofas ...' (*SI*, pp.37-38). For Arthur this collection of society's waste products is emblematic of the deeply problematic and alienating inner-city environment, confirming human identity to be a fragile construct. This question of (self) identity and cultural community built on stable, not disposable, values is at the heart of what Raymond Williams labels 'knowable communities', where in the city 'experience and community would be essentially opaque [but] in the country ... essentially transparent' (*Country and City*, p.165). Arthur's search for a believable self (identity) is hampered by what he perceives as a lack of a discernable separation between subject and object within an ambiguous cityscape, mapped as a wasteland of discarded animate and inanimate junk.

The city's defining opaqueness and ambiguity extends to encompass Oliver who, despite being portrayed as Arthur's closest friend, remains resistant to any clear definition. He has a shadowy existence as a frame character validating Arthur's existence, whilst himself lacking a surname. In this respect he fares worse than his literary predecessor Oliver Twist, who had Mr Bumble 'with names ready made to the end of the alphabet' (*Oliver Twist*, p.25) to write him into his own story. Concealment of a name may be read as a reflection of the anonymity of early 1950s homosexual encounters in an urban subculture wary of blackmail and legal prosecution. This was relatively unchartered territory for the 1960s English realist novel and it is not altogether surprising that when the narrative returns to Cumbria, the text polices itself with a self-imposed restriction to write the romance of the male mind.

Cross-class and cross-generational contact runs the risk of rupturing middle-class ideals of sexual contact and conduct. When Arthur returns to Cumbria and strikes up an intimate friendship with John, the queer novelty of the situation, as in London with Oliver, is never in any textual danger of physical consummation. The two men investigate and interpret their masculinity via the medium of books in the context of Arthur's library.[8] Paul Hammond's *Love Between Men in English Literature* (1996) defines the library in D.H. Lawrence's *Women in Love* (1922) as the 'homosocial space of the English gentry' (p.94), a space of sanctioned intimacy, where whatever happens in terms of sexual exchange will be literary rather than literal. While Bragg describes the library setting in terms preparatory to an unfolding sexual scenario -

> [Arthur] snapped on two side lights and knocked off the main switch, shuffled some loose papers on his desk into a heap, swung the other armchair around so that it was facing the fire, put on two or three pieces of coal ... The room was a series of arcs from the two lights, each thinning slowly to shade, flowing up the walls and on to the segmented ceiling. As the light from the bulbs went upwards, the area in front of the fire  - between

8. The early 1950s class chasm that John crosses in accepting Arthur's hospitality is not to be underestimated. Bragg describes something of his personal experience of 1960s class-consciousness in an account of entering a house in London's Knightsbridge to film a South Bank programme about Francis Bacon: 'I looked around with all the connoisseurship of a twenty-four-year-old to whom privately owned grandeur had been hitherto a small suburban semi-detached house acquired on a mortgage with much difficulty ... I went several times, oscillating between brash and nervous, wondering when the recent patina of Oxford and the powder of the BBC Arts Department would wear off and reveal the working-class northerner with one good suit and nothing but his often over-forcefully expressed opinions to sustain him' (*South Bank Show*, p.96).

Arthur and John - seemed lit only by the yellow flames
which looped up from the spitting coal.

(SI, p.159)

- it is not inevitable, and interpretation of scene and situation remains
very much a matter for the reader. S/he may register a sense of gendered
ambiguity extending to the fabric of the library itself where, representing
classical Freudian psychosexual difference, decisive masculine action -
'*snapped* on two side lights and *knocked* off the main switch' - results in the
passive feminised '*flowing*' of light (italics added).

Identity is also coded in the library's contents. John draws
Arthur's attention to a copy of Charles Dickens's *Oliver Twist* with the
suggestion that if he could empathise with the fictional Oliver's condition
he might begin to understand 'what it was like to be an orphan in a
workhouse' (*SI*. P.161). There is no indication that Arthur senses the
spectral presence of his friend Oliver or of the doss house/workhouse in
the library at this point. For the reader, however, the triangular
homosocial relationship and the London/Cumbrian continuum is
metaphorically visible when, by way of reply, Arthur gives John a copy
of Henry Mayhew's classic 1851 sociological study *London Labour and the
London Poor*. Arthur's recommending Mayhew's study brings the two
friends' first literary encounter to an end in what might be regarded as a
strategic move towards self-censorship, a refusal to accept the
opportunity to discuss his relationship with the real Oliver outside of a
philanthropic investigation into the plight of the unknown London Poor.
The psychosexual triangle linking Arthur, John and Oliver is insulated
from the social, political and cultural ruptures of 1950s discourse
hovering just beyond the texts margins by the safe backward turn to
Dickens and to Mayhew.

The contrast in reader reception between a fact based sociological
study such as Mayhew's *London Labour and the London Poor* and a novel
such as *Oliver Twist* with an invented structure and characters, albeit
drawn from close observation, are due to both the conventions of their
respective genres and to the ideological frame - which itself changes over
time - within which they are encountered. The aesthetic criteria that
discriminate between Mayhew and Dickens operate in Arthur's library
within a strongly biased masculine discourse in which any ideology of
the feminine is conspicuously absent:

A set of Dickens, bound in green leather with two or three books in each volume. Aldous Huxley - many of his - D.H. Lawrence, Somerset Maugham, John Steinbeck, Ernest Hemingway, Albert Camus, P.G. Wodehouse, Graham Greene.  There was a fat book entitled *Stubb's Sermons*, a book of Francis Bacon's *Essays*, another with the quaint name *Lark Rise to Candleford*, a set of small volumes labelled The British Plutarch. And he passed names he had read in reference but never in fact; Laurence Sterne, Jonathan Swift, Thackeray, Chaucer. There were hundreds of books.                    (*SI*, p.158)

The library's contents make an important interpretive statement on a reading of *A Second Inheritance*, locating the culturally conscious focussed relationship between Arthur and John within a literal reality and a metaphorically gendered paradigm excluding feminine values and relationships. The sole literary intruder into this masculine mind-set is Flora Thompson's *Lark Rise to Candleford* trilogy; there are no eminent Victorian women novelists and no sign of their twentieth-century sisters, such as Virginia Woolf and Rebecca West, who were setting an agenda in conflict with the values represented by the Langley family.

At first glance Thompson's book, an autobiographical recollection of a vanished world of late nineteenth-century village life, agricultural customs, and rural culture, appears to present little radical threat to the shelves of canonical male writers. The unsettling paradox, however, surrounding the trilogy's appearance in Arthur's masculine defined library is that this backward-glancing text is the most chronologically modern volume on his shelves, published in 1945 when he would have been absent from the family home, and therefore highly unlikely to have purchased it for himself or, indeed, to have been aware of its arrival. Evelyn Waugh's *Brideshead Revisited* was also published in 1945. Unlike Thompson, Waugh nostalgically mourns the collapse of the country house and its associated cultural values and orderly patterns of inheritance. Waugh is conspicuously absent from Arthur's library. Thompson, like Arthur's sister Pat, is very much the cuckoo in the library nest, threatening to disrupt it as a site of masculine retreat and to question assumed lines of inheritance. For, despite its dismissively attributed quaint name, there is little fanciful or whimsical about Thompson's depiction of rural life, regarded by Cavaliero as 'probably the best account of late nineteenth-century village life that we have outside the work of George Sturt[9] (*Rural Tradition*, p.28). In his introduction to the book, written in 1944, the anthropologist and nature writer H.J. Massingham interprets it as offering a radical agenda for a post-World War II world - 'Thomson's simple-seeming chronicle of life in hamlet, village, and market town are, when regarded as an index to social change, of great complexity and heavy with revolutionary meaning' ('Introduction', pp.9-10) - ready to re-evaluate the consequences of industrialism and war. In recent years, thanks in part to the popular success of the television adaptation, *Lark Rise to Candleford* has indeed been seen as 'quaint' - the cover of the 1973 Penguin edition shows a detail from Helen Allingham's *Country Scene* painting of an idyllic country garden frozen in time and blossoming with sunflowers and an equally sunny child - but it radically glosses Bragg's text, and John's dismissive glance at its title will prove both ironic and prophetic.

In his *Regions of the Imagination. The Development of British Rural Fiction*, W.J. Keith asserts that a 'common complaint against the regional novel... is that it tries to ignore time and change; initiating what Raymond Williams [in *The Country and the City*, p.253] has called a "sustaining flight to the edges of the island, to Cornwall or to Cumberland", an escapist retreat to the backwaters where the illusion of a stable regional world could still be kept up' (p.9). In a similar vein, K.D.M. Snell notes a continuity of ideological pattern in the regional novel in which '[f]iction from Walpole to Bragg has extolled the yeoman hardiness of Cumbria's independent "statesman farmers" and their workers' (*Regional Novel*, p.38). Thompson would have recognised the essential sameness of Bragg's concluding potato picking scene, which today, 45 years on, reads as an elegy to the hardiness of Cumbria's independent farmers and farmworkers. Far from being a quaint backward-looking text when it arrived in Arthur's library, *Lark Rise to Candleford* anticipates the arrival of a growing number of upwardly mobile individuals such as John who will ensure an immediate post-War stability in patterns of land-owning and agricultural practice whilst acting as agents of underlying social change: 'A little better educated, a little more democratic, a little more prosperous than their parents had been... with just enough malice to give point to their

---

9. George Sturt (1863-1927) wrote two countryside classics, *Change in the Village* and *The Wheelwright's Shop* and is seen as linking the intellectual world of John Ruskin and William Morris with that of D.H. Lawrence. Himself sometimes accused of writing about quaint survivals of rural customs, Sturt was concerned rather to put the experiences of the past at the service of contemporary political and social reform in the interests of community and tradition.

wit and a growing sense of injustice which was making them begin to enquire when their turn would come to enjoy a fair share of the earth they tilled' (*Lark Rise*, pp.535-536).

On the one hand, then, Bragg's novel sits comfortably within the regional rural tradition, whilst on the other its concluding pages split into entwined and tensely antagonistic frames of reference, with implications for future stability, at exactly the same moment as his depiction of the old governing class structure is showing internal signs of instability. Bragg develops Thompson's underlying theme of inevitable change to suggest a transitional moment in both gendered values and in class/economic structures. Having appeared uninvited in her brother's library to disrupt his intimacy with John, Pat is ready to enjoy sex with John, but when he suggests marriage she finds herself unable to cross the self-imposed rigidities of class barriers. Her socially inherited reticence is mirrored by Arthur who is adept at finding excuses for not consummating his personal sexual inheritance with another man, even though this was 'the company of a man whose difference from himself swept him into a brightened knowledge of passions outside his own cocooned and unimpinged bare loneliness' (*SI*, p.262). Ironically, the outcome of this seeming sexual/social stasis and individual refusal to connect is to instigate a far more socially and politically important structural change, with the sale of the Langley farm to the Fosters as Arthur returns to the army and Pat moves to London. I have argued for a reading of *The Second Inheritance* that foregrounds issues of gender, masculinity and homosexuality within the comfort zone of the parameters of the post-War regional novel. There remains, however, a certain irony, and perhaps a conservatively rural textual inevitability, that these controversial themes are allowed to fade from the readers view, and from John's memory - 'It was over' (*SI*, p.270) - in a final concern with rootedness, a sense of belonging to a highly localised personal space in the English landscape which might itself have been inherited from the feminine intruder into the masculine library:

> John loved the empty tractor ride to the town, hedged
> by autumn golds and yellow browns, with all the land
> around him fluttering steadily to sleep and the air
> spanking his face still brown from the summer. He saw
> the tails and flashes of animals amiably scurrying to fit
> themselves out still more for a plump hibernation; the
> birds flocking together even where they were not

gathering for flight; and the great heaved swell of land
which had worked yet another rich year's crop.

(*SI*, pp.263-264)

In the interplay between psyche and landscape it is the latter that
dominates the concluding events. The depiction of the annual potato
picking harvest realises one of Phyllis Bentley's defining qualities of the
regional novel's 'transcendent merit' of verisimilitude. This quality
includes a 'detailed faithfulness to reality, a conscientious presentation of
phenomena as they really happen in ordinary life on a clearly detailed
spot of real earth' with the result that the 'regional novel occupies in
fiction the place of the Dutch school of painters in art[10]' (*Regional Novel*,
p.45). Yet something else important has occurred against this enduring
physical backdrop that is in danger of being forgotten in a conclusion
which sees John remaining a part of the marginalised space he was born
into. Ultimately *The Second Inheritance* tells a story of near-misses and
unfulfilled potential, but in reaching the cusp of a personal and social
breakthrough that never quite materialises Bragg analyses deep sexual
anxieties in a realistic manner. He creates a sense of the intimacy of loving
and mutually semi-articulated pledges of homosocial fidelity, possessing
the same 'transcendent merit of verisimilitude' as does the landscape that
shapes and defines them. In Lawrence's *Women in Love* there comes a
reflective moment after Rupert Birkin and Gerald Crich's asexual naked
wrestling when they try unsuccessfully to explain the experience: '"At
any rate, one feels freer and more open now - and that is what we
want"'(p.308). Whilst *The Second Inheritance* leaves relationships
unfulfilled and class structure undisturbed, it opens up a similar
reflective space for a freer and more open liberating discussion of the
meaning of masculinity within a wider debate about sexuality beginning
to be aired in England in the novels of the 1960s.

10. In her private journal record of all Bragg's novels Margaret Armstrong singles out the
potato harvest scene in *The Second Inheritance* to comment on its 'brilliant picture of "tatie
picking" week as it was just after the war' (document copied to the author). Phyllis
Bentley's reference to the 'Dutch school of painters' and regional fiction might today find
a more apposite painterly comparison nearer to home. Cumberland artist Sheila Fell
(1931-1979) included a number of paintings of potato harvests in her portfolio, several of
which are reproduced in Cate Haste's *Sheila Fell. A Passion for Paint* (2010). Of these *Potato
Field, Aspatria* (Brayton Road) and *Potato Field, Cumberland 1* capture on canvas exactly the
sense of a timeless agricultural tradition central to Bragg's prose. Interestingly for a wider
discussion of influences on Bragg's work, he made his directing debut with a film about
Fell for the BBC flagship art programme *Monitor,* which was shown four years prior to
the novel's publication.

# THREE
# LANDSCAPE FOR THE MIND
## *WITHOUT A CITY WALL*

*Without a City Wall* marks a significant interpretive shift in emphasis from Bragg's first two novels as the narrative viewpoint changes from that of indigenous native to that of metropolitan newcomer. The vivid depiction of a sense of place underlying the previous novels' combination of symbolism and naturalism remains unchanged and central, as does the atmosphere of instability and 1960s political, social and cultural mores. Whereas Tom Graham, in *For Want of a Nail*, and John Foster, in *The Second Inheritance*, are two young men born and raised in Cumbria and able to call upon its landscape in both personal and mythical terms as part of their understanding of self, Richard Godwin, the central protagonist of *Without a City Wall*, enters text and landscape as an outsider.  He is a young man of twenty-four who has self-consciously chosen a form of exile from London in favour of one very specific Lake District village location in an attempt to re-evaluate his life in a setting which he believes will be conducive to renewal. Tellingly, he has moved from the most metropolitan/cosmopolitan of British urban regions to its perceived binary opposite, the hoped for idyllic village of Crossbridge.[1] Initially then, unlike in the earlier novels, landscape and character are not immediately linked but rather must await synthesis in the expectation of a coming sympathy, one to the other.

The arrival of the outsider as narrative catalyst in regional fiction has well established antecedents. Lockwood's outsider function in Emily Brontë's *Wuthering Heights* (1847), for example, is, in part, an attempt to interpret the directness of Yorkshire rural manners and the primary importance of seasonal farming demands over the needs of visitors. In Elizabeth Gaskell's *Cousin Phillis* (1865) Paul Manning is able to approximate the detached view of the general reader in presenting a view of life at Hope Farm from the position of a remote relative. Hardy remains today perhaps the most important and successful regional novelist to

1.  Crossbridge is Bragg's fictional name for the village of Lamplugh, where he frequently stayed as a young boy with his Aunt Mary.  It is also the setting for *The Hired Man* and there is a fuller description of the parish and of Bragg's association with it in the chapter on that novel.

make use of the expository device of introducing an outsider to a localised scene, whose invasion and subsequent disruption of established behavioural patterns serves to point up the clash of local regional and cosmopolitan values. Bragg's outsider, Richard, does however have at least the advantage of recognising his outsider status, and this level of self-knowingness makes him a suitable candidate to usher the reader, him/herself a likely outsider, into the intimate regional connections that exist between the rural inhabitants and their surrounding landscape:

> ... he was a stranger, largely ignorant of rural economy, uninformed when daily life ran in deepest ruts of generations' knowledge; he had been hesitant because he did not know where to go, uncertain because he was perpetually wondering what on earth he was doing there anyway, enclosed distant, submerged ... willing and waiting to be guided on to a course which fitted the obscure instructions which supported it.
>
> (*WCW*, p.134)

His 'course' threatens to remain' submerged' despite his best intentions to fit in, and some eighteen months after his arrival Richard remains unable to recognise and name even the most fundamental markers of localised place:

> ... Richard was still ignorant of plants, flowers, trees, and animals with an ignorance which became depressing as daily it cut him off from that which was the texture of his senses, the everyday landscape for the mind.
>
> So again he had begun to learn the names of the flowers in the garden. Each evening, Wif told him all the names and when he went for a walk he would try to pick them out in the hedge-banks and fields.
>
> (*WCW*, p.259)

The phrase 'landscape for the mind' is of central importance for the belief that character and place in regional fiction are unified wholes. Hardy exemplified this belief in recognising and celebrating the minutiae of everyday local existence when creating his sequence of Wessex novels: 'I am convinced that it is better for a writer to know a little bit of the world remarkably well than to know a great part of the world remarkably little' (*Personal Notebooks*, p.60). Bragg's frequent recourse to Blake's 'world in a grain of sand' - referred to in my chapter on *For Want of a Nail* - as an ontological definition of Cumbria's (and Wigton's in particular), window on to an understanding of a much wider world from the circumscribed margins of regional space, echoes Hardy's insistence in the interpretative values of localised place.

Whilst the text insists on the centrality of localised place, Bragg's epigraph to Part I, 'The Land of Cockaigne', uses the overblown rhetoric of bucolic utopian irony to question the meaningful existence of a rural hinterland as a peaceful, abundant and curative space even before the questing subject has installed himself. Here the epigraph acts as an agent of ambiguity which works by way of a thematically disruptive metaphor inasmuch as the word 'Cockaigne' does not appear anywhere in the main text of the novel, but which symbolically calls attention to the central object of the outsider's search for a Cumbrian Cockaigne. Given my interpretation of its privileged textual position, it is worth quoting the epigraph in full, before considering further its implications for Richard's retreat to the village of Crossbridge, as part of a long tradition of pastoral literature which will reverberate throughout the novel:

> The Land of Cockaigne is the name of an imaginary country, a medieval Utopia where life was a round of luxurious idleness. In Cockaigne the rivers were of wine, the houses were built of cake and barley sugar, the streets were paved with pastry and the shops supplied goods for nothing. Roast geese and fowls wandered about inviting people to eat them, and buttered larks fell from the sky like manna.
>
> (*Encyc. Britt.*)

The utopian fantasy of a land of lost content has a well-documented history in Western culture, stretching back to the Old Testament's Garden of Eden - and it is contextually appropriate that Bragg's epigraph to Part II, 'Every Tree of the Garden', is from the Book of Genesis, threatening expulsion from a place of plenty - and firmly establishing its English fictional credentials in, for example, William Shakespeare's comedy *As You Like It*, where the main players retreat from the corruption of court life to the green spaces beyond its jurisdiction to re-evaluate their values before an inevitable return to reality. More recently, Susan Sontag's metaphorical exploration of the 'rejection of the city' (*Illness*, p.74), in terms of a generalised trope for depicting such major twentieth century diseases as tuberculosis and cancer may be taken as marking a point at which, in literature at least, the city's contagion has totally infected its hinterlands so that hermetically sealed utopian spaces have become unimaginable.[2] In this respect it is salutary to reflect that the Cumbrian writer Sarah Hall's 2007 novel *The Carhullan Army* paints a dystopian vision of a futuristic attempt to establish a feminist commune in the remote Cumbrian fells.

Richard's flight from London in search of physical relief and mental renewal is part, therefore, of a long-held belief in the sanctity of rural retreat as a restorative and curative space. It also enters the debate surrounding the comparative values of aspects of national space in post-war Britain, whose contours are explored in the literature of the 1950s and 1960s, collectively labelled 'Angry', and exemplified by a number of Northern regional texts. Peter J. Kalliney defines this genre of literature of the period as 'a literary form of home anthropology as a means of articulating political dissidence [bearing] all the markers of regional protest - in this case the region being provincial England, in contradis-tinction to the pan-British state and its administrative center - London' (*Cities of Affluence*, p.143). The novel's opening paragraph colludes with the idea that in escaping from London, Richard has indeed stumbled upon the epigraph's land of Cockaigne. 'His legs gobbled up the placid country road' (*WCW*, p.13) in metaphorical anticipation of his later gobbling up the equally placid and compliant '[r]oast geese and fowls [wandering] about inviting people to eat them' (Epigraph, p.11). He has only to 'forage' with his eyes to spot 'loot in the quite ordinary ditches and hedges and fields' and his arms are ready to 'plunder the air' (*WCW*, p.13), Cockaigne's rivers of wine (*WCW*, p.11) seem to have soaked into the very signposts so that the' names on the tipsily slanted signposts' are themselves too metaphorically drunk to help a stranger locate his/her destination, whether Cockaigne or the alliterative Crossbridge.

Taken by his future father-in-law, Wif Beattie, soon after his arrival in Crossbridge, to the agricultural show at Ennerdale, Richard persists in his blinkered view of rural life, seeing only evidence of plenty despite

---

2. 'When travel to a better climate was invented as a treatment for TB in the early 19th century, the most contradictory destinations were proposed. The south, mountains, deserts, islands - their very diversity suggests what they have in common: the rejection of the city.' (*Illness*, p.73)

Wif's insistence on the reality of rural deprivation. Richard's restricted field of vision focuses on the 'spoils of a whole community. Flowers, vegetables, eggs, fruit, every sort of home-baked cake, knitting, sewing, paintings, woodwork, metalwork' (*WCW*, p.58). The text itself is complicit in misdirecting Richard and reader towards Cockaigne with its implied supply of 'goods for nothing' (Epigraph, p.11) by euphemistically removing the notion of monetary exchange and substituting the value-free 'distributed': 'There were scones, rock-buns, chocolate cakes, apple pies, tea-cakes, loaves of bread - now being distributed as the prize-giving was over' (WCW, p.59). This is very much the uninformed metropolitan outsider's view of a rural arcadia of plenty all for the asking, and stands in stark contrast to Wif's more accurate picture of the economic realities of rural life:

> - you know, there are a lot of kids around here who have nothing. I mean they wear shoes and they're fed but that's about it. Have you met Pat Gregory? Well he's got ten - it's why he's been on the dole, to be honest, because the family allowance with his dole is more than he could earn as a working man - there's a lot like that, you know, and they poach and labour a bit on the side.
> (*WCW*, p.56)

Put in a national context, Wif's giving a human face to the statistics of rural deprivation comes at a time when the national media are engaged in propagating a picture of an affluent nation looking towards the antics of swinging London for inspiration. Wif's oppositional and highly localised view from the regional economic margins hints at the beginnings of the urgent national debate on welfare reform that will characterise the 1970s and 1980s as the benefits bill expands with rising unemployment. Any lingering national myth of a land of Cockaigne expires with the 1970s.

Even as Bragg moves from the economics of the showground, and Wif's tentative and limited construction of a politics of place, to Derwentwater and the aesthetics of landscape as a poetics of place, he allows his central character to indulge in one last conflation of Cockaigne with the Lake District. Bragg's closely observed depiction of Derwentwater is representative of his acknowledgement of a nonhuman context which is absent from much contemporary mainstream fiction where the social realm exercises a far more powerful presence than nature. H.J. Massingham, chronicler of rural England, and the author of *The English Countryman* (1942), argues for an essential connection between regionalism and art: '... a specific quality manifests itself in the complete presentation of a region, in precisely the same way as it does in a work of art. A region thus presented is a work of art' (*Remembrance*, p.81). On a pleasure trip to Derwentwater Richard and Wif's daughter Janice become an integral part of a scene described in the language of Cockaigne, matching human desire with the pathetic fallacy of land/dreamscape:

> Coming to the lake once more, quite near their boat, they stood and looked at the tranquil scene before them, suffused with its loveliness as the lake itself was now infused with the reddening sun. All was gentleness. No waves to lash up fears, or unscalable rocks to rip at dreams, no endless water to awe or density of sameness to crush - the perfect proportion of hill and lake, with roads, trees, farms, villages, islands, clouds, boats - all exactly placed, it seemed, painted on the winter day with such docility as made it redolent of an imagined world.
>
> (*WCW*, pp.162-163)

The narrative moment of perfect harmony between human mood and surrounding environment, expressive of the Romantic movement's looking to nature for signs of a divine presence, is sharply broken by Richard's impending note of a post-Cockaigne 'caution ... which did not wish to pluck at what it could not surely eat' (*WCW*, p.163).

Bragg then proceeds to articulate Derwentwater as Romantic space through the unique lens of a J.M.W. Turner painting.[3] Coming to Keswick at the outset of his career at the impressionable age of twenty-one, his subsequent impressionist - not topographically accurate -

3. Arriving in Keswick in the final week of August, it rained for much of his visit. Although unable to see the mountain tops for cloud cover he nevertheless made a number of sketches that he was later able to imaginatively reconstruct in his studio. His 1835 watercolour of Derwentwater, with Lodore Falls and Borrowdale in the background, is worked up from a partly-coloured drawing in his 1797 sketchbook. In his *Land of the Lakes* (1983) Bragg writes that 'Turner did the greatest paintings of the Lakes' able to transmit 'the feeling of a place not only in its particular sense but also in its most general terms'. He concludes 'Turner came and saw the landscape with a terrible directness and painted it as it had never been painted before and never been painted since' (pp.179-180).

representation of the region was in part responsible for helping to create the Lakes' national image evoking the Romantics interest in the regenerative quality of natural landscape. In the passage below Bragg takes narrative time out to develop the aesthetic qualities of landscape mediated by art, enabling him to construct a literature of place that is a multi-layered and multi-accented cultural text, free from a dominant literary metanarrative.

> In many of Turner's paintings the sky is such a scoured, braised red, so burnished with streaks of hard colour and lashed with whites and yellows, such a fury of broiling sunset and yet, at the same time, such a frame of calm, that it is difficult to believe there is anything in nature to approach them. This late afternoon sunset did. From the edge of the lake the hills rose up black, like a waistbelt, cutting off the water from the sky. On the sky itself the sliding sun, blood red, drew great tumulus of clouds around it, clouds which leapt up and away from it like frozen oceanic waves, thick at their base, thinning to feathery-tipped edges - and all were blooded by the sun which seemed to be sucking in through them the fires of a day's blazing. Yet the clouds were few, clustered around the sun like the dust around a desert-marching army, leaving the rest of the sky clear - and that was of such a dense blue, of such a solid mineral sapphire shading to jet, that it was as amazing as the gaudy rubied clouds. And the water of the lake, split pearls the tips of the wavelets, turquoise plateaux the reaches in the distance, the water in the path of the sun a ruby-jewelled treasure chest.
>
> (WCW, p.163)

For a frozen narrative moment the painterly virtues are called upon, in Deborah Bright's formulation, 'as proof of the timeless virtues of a [Lake District] Nature that transcends history but which is not the open field of ideological neutrality' (quoted in Campbell, p.63), in which 'a ruby-jewelled treasure chest' once seen will remain resistant to commodification, whether in the form of mineral extraction, wind turbine or encroaching tourist developments. There is perhaps an implied ideology in regional writing that sees the individuality of place as a fundamental characteristic of central importance in understanding human problems and their resolution. Richard's understanding of his to-date ignored quotidian problems of place is soon to be tested as his Cockaigne inflected certainties unravel in Part II of the novel's post-Genesis grappling with reality as presciently indicated by Bragg's deft insertion of an unsettling qualifying final sentence, as the lovers' 'black boat moved slowly, like the last homecomer in a dying paradise' (*WCW*, p.164).

Within months of this episode David and Janice are married and for a brief time euphorically happy 'wanting only to be naked and wound into each other's body' (*WCW*, p.193), unaware of their impending metaphoric expulsion from a private constructed mythological Edenic space. The catalyst for change is the appearance in Crossbridge of David Hill, a companion from Richard's university and London life. He tries to tempt Richard into abandoning his heroic quest to create a private utopian Cumbrian space, running in parallel to contemporary reality as defined by a metropolitan agenda, to join him in presenting a new series of regional television programmes for North-West TV, with the hope 'of getting one of his programmes nationally networked - for the first time in that region's history' (*WCW*, p.241). This is an understated insertion into the text of what was to become an increasingly important part of a national debate about the cultural power relationship between London and the regions. The full extent of the visual media's penetration of regional cultures was still in its infancy at the time of *Without a City Wall*'s publication and it would have been difficult to envisage just how insidiously destructive of Richard's lococentric self-marginalisation from the capital it was to become. For a while, particularly at the time of the novel's late 1960s setting, independent regional companies such as ATV were actively encouraged, in the interests of retaining their broadcasting licence, to search for and produce regional drama in situ. (This challenge to London's cultural hegemony has now all but disappeared with the merger of previously independent companies into the monolithic giant of ITV and with the increasingly aggressive encroachment of BSkyB with its interest in trans-Atlantic markets.) Now it might be argued that not only London but also New York threatens to erase indigenous regional cultural traditions with a formulaic uniformity. Bragg's work for the BBC in 1960s London, directing and producing programmes such as *Monitor*, would have alerted him to the potency and excitement of the media so rhapsodically glossed by David but not, perhaps, to its longer-term threat to regional autonomy. It is interesting in this context that when David offers Richard the opportunity to 'become the hero of the silver screen in regions as far flung as Dumfries and Barrow in Furness' and to 'dine with the cream of Cumberland society all in the name of communication' (*WCW*, p.243), he does so in terms that remain paradoxically couched entirely within a regional sense of place.

Richard determinedly counters David's tempting offers with an initial commitment to teaching in local schools and involvement in local politics as a necessary and valuable part of matching character to place. Bragg underscores Richard's stand with a textual awareness of similar arguments propagated by Henry David Thoreau, particularly in *Walden* (1854), against the inevitability of modernity as a diminished state of being. In thinking about Edwin Cass, his village rival for the love of Janice, and the unremitting demands upon Edwin's time in attempting to start up his own engineering repair business at the same time as dealing with a parasitically drunken mother, Richard concludes that the 'work and his mother were driving him to transparent desperation' (*WCW*, p.251). Lurking at the back of his mind is a persistent thought which will not let him sleep: 'Who lived their lives according to what?' (*WCW*, p.251). The reader will recognise and make the connection with Thoreau's unsettling notion that '[t]he mass of men lead lives of quiet desperation (*Walden*, p.9) lies behind Richard's characteristic 1960s search for an alternative life-style capable of countering alienation and allowing for personal authenticity. As Bragg's narrative unfolds there is, however, an awareness of the bitter ironically conditioning sub-clause to Thoreau's main statement, to the effect that '[f]rom the desperate city you go into the desperate country' (*Walden*, p.9). Nevertheless, Thoreau is an important influence on those aspects of 1960s sensibilities that surface in Richard's early attempts as an outsider to establish a balance between the individual and nature and in living a useful community life as performance rather than as material end product.

Community as performance comes to the fore in Bragg's atmospheric anthropologically inflected account, in Chapter 6, of the Ennerdale Show. In the twenty-first century, Cumbria's agricultural shows remain popular focal points for the local community to come together and, increasingly, to attract tourists to the area. The Ennerdale and Kinniside Show, held annually in the last week of August, is one of several smaller shows around the County which, whilst diminished in scale, remain a much anticipated and enjoyable part of the rural calendar. Bragg's fictional recreation of this still vibrant, bustling society is an important element in his contribution to the historical continuity of the regional novel, deserving detailed examination.

This echoing sense of continuity is clearly evident when comparing Bragg's description of the Ennerdale Show with that of Constance Holme of the Bluecaster Show in Chapter 13 of her regional novel, *The Lonely Plough*. Holme (1880-1955) wrote a series of novels recording the scenery and traditions of an area bordering on Morecambe Bay, just south of Bragg's Cumbrian region. Like Bragg today, she drew a picture of a region that was both a social and an economic unit, and nowhere more so than in representing the agricultural show as a space where trade and community meet in a state of suspended harmony. Both novelists track their narratives through similar physical features, small towns and recognisable landmarks, so that the overall effect is to suggest a level of local cohesiveness. Bragg further develops the idea of a fictional cohesiveness by means of an intertextual reference to Wif Beattie having once worked for the Langley family featured in *The Second Inheritance* - 'And when aa was hired at Major Langleys - before t'was - right up in t'middle of nowhere he lives, on t' Scotch border (*WCW*, p.55) - which links character to a particular topography of regional space.

Although Holme's novels are seen as capturing the historical moment before Ypres - 'significantly, a moment referenced by Bragg in his locating of Ennerdale on the historical continuum - when her rural world of established attitudes and assumptions, based on an unquestioned hierarchical class structure, was about to pass into history, there remains a remarkably clear line of inheritance between the Bluecaster and the Ennerdale Shows. In both texts it is with the show-jumping scenes that the crowd comes to life and it is here also that we note one crucial difference - unlike Holme's Bluecaster, Ennerdale is no longer a place apart, a hermetically sealed social unit largely immune to outside influences. The threat to the region's rural culture is no longer the physical one of the incursion of railways and roads, but rather from the more insidious one of broadcasting, specifically the medium of television. There is a noticeable marked contrast between the discussion of horses and riders at Bluecaster which is locally restricted in scope to known locals - 'he comes from Saddleback way ... owner is a blacksmith in his spare time' (*Lonely Plough*, p.142), and at Ennerdale where recognition occurs on a national scale through the mediation of television:

> 'See her', said Wif, pointing at a young woman of about thirty leading a grey mare up the slope to its box, 'that's Anne Duvan'. He waited for the reaction.' She jumps on television. I saw her there only a week ago. She'll be up for the Horse of the Year Show again this year. At the White City in London. My God, she can make that thing go...'
>
> Richard watched her for a few moments, saw the respect in which she was held by the way in which younger riders kept passing close to her, looking out for a nod, laughing outrageously when she passed a remark, glowing in the light. (*WCW*, pp.60-61)

Perhaps not surprisingly Anne Duvan 'won everything she entered' (*WCW*, p.63), marking her entry into the competition as symbolic of the wider threat posed to traditional customs by the incursion of a national celebrity culture led by a more spurious inclusiveness of the new media. At the same time, however, as Anne Duvan might represent the outsider whose professional sporting superiority gives her an unfair advantage, her modernity is countered by a nearby 'group of men straining to tumble a beast up a slippery ramp [who] could have tagged along to Canterbury with Chaucer's Miller' (*WCW*, p.62). Alongside the local men, the young girl riders also deny modernity and 'could have waited for a decade in castles or sat patiently in Capability Brown landscapes' (*WCW*, p.63). Here we encounter the regional essentials of romance contributing to the historic continuity and specificity of the spirit of place. Watching and affected by all this, Richard becomes aware that in 'London he had rarely noticed faces' because 'his own haste had blurred the images' (*WCW*, p.63). Now he feels himself to be 'part of all generations; there was no rush, they would all pass, and in that last security he felt that he finally accepted the union between himself and his newly chosen ground' (*WCW*, p.63). Writing in 'Art dévenément' on early cinema's search for temporal meaning, Jean Epstein refers to the 'fragments of many parts come to bury themselves in a single now. The future mixed among memories. This chronology is that of the human brain' (quoted in *Classical Hollywood Cinema*, p.42). Bragg's cinematic cross-cutting between

Chaucer's pilgrims, maidens in castles, Richard's childhood, London, and the Show, within a single consciousness works to fuse perceptions of past and present in an on-going causal regional chain. It is precisely this union of 'chosen ground' and consciousness in the regional novel that will be vulnerable to outside pressures when David visits Crossbridge to offer Richard the same level of national recognition as a television presenter as that enjoyed by Anne Duvan as a show-jumper.

The seemingly unstoppable dialectical transformation of England from a series of culturally vibrant regional particularisms to a hegemonic metropolitan culture is further played out at the Ennerdale Show by the appearance of an eighty-one year old countryman and his two Clydesdale horses, representing a shrinking space in England as a knowable archaic place. Hector Lowell's age emphasises both the continuities of rural life and their fragilities as one generation with a changed agenda replaces another. Hector's Clydesdales, 'fit to plough for twelve hours at a stretch, to haul cannons through mud' (WCW, p.64) hark back to the early years of the twentieth century and are here harnessed as a metaphor for a particular view of English history and community cohesion in which the young men at the Show become part of a long line that 'would have followed the drums from Marston Moor to Ypres' (WCW, p.63). Cumbria's Clydesdales are an integral part of the region's history in much of Bragg's writing. This becomes clear in his 1976 oral documentary study of Wigton's history, tellingly titled *Speak for England*, reflecting his view of the importance of regional identity contributing to a multifaceted national culture. Talking with Joseph Benson, in his early fifties, they begin with a nostalgic reflection on the auctions of the 1940s:

> 'You could have a catalogue entry of anything from a thousand to fifteen-hundred horses. Mostly Clydesdales in those days ... People used to come from, well, you might say Land's End to John O'Groats ... I think if anybody was looking for good Clydesdales in those days they would come to Cumberland to seek them. There would be Clydesdale horses exported out of Cumberland for years and years back [whereas today] if you get about twenty or thirty Clydesdales, all told, you do well.' (*SE*, p.190)

When, later in the novel, the spooked Clydesdales drag Hector to his death in a mocking parody of his Greek namesake's dead body being dragged around the walls of Troy, there is the sense of the passing of an era. The horse as a harbinger of death haunts Bragg's early novels, playing a role clearly unavailable to them in contemporary fiction of metropolitan city centres. In *For Want of a Nail* the young central character's grandstep-father dies on a drunken ride up Saddle[back] mountain with 'th'orse screamin' its heed off' (*WN*, p.33). In *The Second Inheritance* Colonel Langley's horse has to be shot after breaking a leg, setting in motion the old Colonel's decline and death. Television drama might relish depicting the visual immediacy of such life and death events, but their very sensationalism would in effect distort the reality of day-to-day life experienced in the natural world. Even watching Anne Duvan on television encourages a sense of artificially heightened drama through shot selection and editing whilst the viewer sits back passively waiting to be entertained. By way of contrast, attendance at the agricultural show provides an opportunity, readily embraced by Richard, to directly experience a sense of physical and emotional embeddedness in the natural environment of region. The intrusion of David's North-West TV franchise into this world threatens to substitute for the real what James Shanahan calls 'a simulacrum of a real environmental experience' (quoted in Armbruster, p.224). Both Bragg and Holme, however, approach the agricultural show to create a microcosm of social life where the slower pace of rural life acts as prerequisite for understanding a world where, in Karla Armbruster's belief, you 'must be willing to look for the small and the unobtrusive [and] be willing to put up with some degree of physical discomfort, with heat, cold, damp and dirt' ('Creating the world', p.224). Margaret Armstrong recalls how '[t]hrough the years the [Cumbria shows] have remained basically the same' writing that Bragg's depiction of the Ennerdale Show is superb in bringing to life one of the region's social and agricultural highlights. She goes on to relate that the' first year I came up here my husband took me to Dalston Show where the loos were just a pole over a pit behind a screen. Quite a shock for a city girl!' Bragg's sense of the primacy of regional place extends to situating Armstrong's loos within a synthesis of the sacred and the profane: 'the sacred beer tent and its two acolytes, the Ladies' and the Gentlemen's' are a scatological/eschatological integral part of a scene that viewed from the 'top of Grike or Crag Fell ... must have looked like a pageant as formal, perhaps, as those of the Druids' (*WCW*, pp. 58-59). In her 1931 'Preface' to a new edition of *The Lonely Plough* Holme writes of a regions tenacious clinging to its distinctive characteristics: 'Old customs have obstinately re-established themselves, as if war were the mere gesture of a day, and they the things eternal' (*Lonely Plough*, p.vii). Written more than half a century later, Bragg's post World War II novel records a remarkable continuity of a region's community life, focused on the details of 'things eternal' which, whatever the inroads of modernity, the regional text continues to occupy as a defining space of its own.

It has become a literary commonplace to read London as a synecdoche for the condition of England as a whole, and in the process consigning the regional novel to a generic ghetto, vulnerable to any number of derogatory critical misconceptions. This leads, in David James's analysis, to a much reduced critical presence in which its unrealised potential 'polemical scope is thus confined to narrative items of the provincial imagery as bounded, parochial or largely insensible to the dialectic between local and national concerns'. The result is a blinkered labelling of the regional text as an 'inherently conservative genre' (*Contemporary British Fiction*, p.46). The Cumbrian regionalism of *Without a City Wall* counters this perception by avoiding creating a text redolent of sentimentalised pastoral conservatism at the same time as displaying an acute sensibility to the wash of a national historical narrative. This is a quality Bragg's prose strives to share with the regional poetry of Ted Hughes, Geoffrey Hill and Philip Larkin, all three of whom are defined by Seamus Heaney as the 'hoarders and shorers of what they take to be the real England ... aware of their Englishness as deposits in the descending storeys of the literary and historical past' so that '[t]heir very terrain is becoming consciously precious' (*Preoccupations*, pp.150-151). In a similar vein I am prompted to quote David Gervaise's view of Wordsworth as a poet for whom there was 'no hiatus between thinking of his native fells and the thought of his country as a whole' (*Literary England*, p.31) as a defining quality of Bragg's regional positioning. Bragg envisages 'no isolation by simple distancing' (*WCW*, p.130), being all too aware that Wordsworth's 'one impulse from a vernal wood' (ibid.) may be shattered at any moment by the supersonic bang of an aircraft flight. Yet the turn to Wordsworth's advice to the young William Hazlitt ('The Tables Turned') is entirely apposite in the context of Richard's attempt to learn for himself 'the love which nature brings' (*Lyrical Ballads*, p.83),[4] even though he realises that any notion of the isolation of the fells from outside events is no longer valid except as a metaphor. In the tradition of Wordsworth, Bragg represents Richard's consciousness not only as a state of mind, an interior monologue expressing a desire for, and an understanding of, regional belonging, but also as an analysis of the condition of England mediated through a regional immediacy.

Bragg's panoramic sweep of the inter-connectedness of regional and national history as read through environmental aesthetics comes to the fore in an extended four page descriptive passage as Richard climbs Knockmirton Fell. The passage records a progressively felt sense of alienation from nature created by the despoliation associated with the early nineteenth-century industrial revolution and subsequent changes to the national economy. The 'power beneath the surface' (*WCW*, p.40) of an area stretching from the coast 'right back to the fell' (ibid.) has reduced the surface landscape to a series of 'gutted workings [which] lay over the fields like an old skin, crinkling, splitting, worn, wrinkled, useless' (ibid.). The stitching together of land and body in the language of decay draws attention to the precarious nature of each and the metaphoric embeddedness of the human in its habitation. Even though Richard detects signs of an agricultural renaissance - 'Farming was doing well. At Crossbridge Hall a new milking parlour had just been built' (*WCW*, p.41) - the overwhelming impression is one of the transitory nature of human dwelling compared with the deep survival and longevity of the geological landscape. One section in particular deserves a closer look to appreciate the quality of its engagement with the poetics of a specific landscape and the universal feeling of a cultural and physical distance from a space that we occupy for an insignificant moment of time:

> ... here it seemed that the lowland beneath was nothing
> but the shrinking away from the massive hills, the feeble
> train, the necessary but totally unimpressive link which
> was unfortunately needed to connect the whale-backed
> fells to the sea. Here, as he looked around him, the fells

4.  Wordsworth's 'The Table Turned' (1798) is one of nine poems, or extracts from poems, by the poet included in Bragg's *Cumbria. In Verse* (1984) anthology. Bragg's 'Introduction' speaks of Wordsworth's poetry being 'as local as the slate. Lake District places, names, incidents, people, legends and landscapes - feared or loved - permeate his poetry, which rooted itself in rigorous autobiography and reached out for the ungraspable. He made an immense and resounding world out of the few square miles of his native Cumbria'. (p.x)

took the area to themselves. Part of the Caledonian range which stretched at one time from Scandinavia to the Atlantic Ocean, they were supposed to be the oldest mountain range in the world. They were bare. Limestone, slate, granite and Ordovician rock. Scree would scale down a steep side here, there you could see a gash of brown rocks, a legendary wound long cauterised; a tumble of rocks marked some fall years ago, cairns pointed at the sky on the tops, dry walls clung to the hillsides in regular order, bared veins of slate - the whole feeling was of bareness, ageless existence. Celts might have been there, Romans, Norsemen, Saxons, French, English, Scots; traces of none remained save it was a place which insisted that any life would be brushed away, fluff; any change would merely alter for a while, all impulses would shrink to ironic inconsequence.

(*WCW*, pp.41-42)

The view from Knockmirton Fell presents a multi-faceted variety of shifting perspectives: spatial (the immediacy of the lowland farms and the Atlantic Ocean); temporal (from the clinging fell walls of agricultural enclosure to the turbulent passage of England's ethnic tribe across geological time); and ultimately psychological (the minuscule ironic consequence of individual action). There is no doubting the profound emotional impression the scene makes upon Richard, not least the estrangement from social and political practice located within the passages concluding jeremiad.

The politics of despair permeate the text at several points, making it all but impossible to isolate personal and regional autonomy from national and international politics. It is worth recalling that the novel was published in 1968, when anti-American demonstrations against the Vietnam War were at their height and when, for a brief moment, it seemed possible that an alignment of students and workers in Paris might topple De Gaulle's French government. It is against the background of these social and political realities that David delivers a parodic obituary upon the death of the regional novel unless it too can incorporate, and contribute to, the prevailing zeitgeist of alienation and destruction:

> 'Murder in the Mountains'.That any good to you? We
> haven't had a farmer as an ace detective. Detectives are
> out - he must be an agent. Bring a load of gypsy girls in
> and a mad scientist who's hollowed out that fell of
> yours to launch rockets on London and you're away.
> Chapter One: 'It was a normal day in Crossbridge, but
> Huckleberry Armathwaite smelt disaster. At first he
> thought it was pig-shit, but as his fine country nose
> twitched further ...'
>
> (WCW, p.309)

The soundtrack to Richard and David's pub conversation is provided by
a demonstration against Ian Smith's unilateral declaration of
independence for Rhodesia: 'A good case for bombing. The automatic
liberal reflex given spice by the prospect of a bit of justifiable homicide'
(WCW, p.310). The Vietnam War enters Crossbridge through television
newsreel footage of 'such violence unimaginable as burning chemicals on
childrens' arms'[5] (WCW, p.317). These are the very actions and images
that Richard fled from the city to the country to avoid - 'Pugwash
conference ... arms race ... biological warfare build up' (WCW, p.24)  -
along with a prescient vision of global warming - 'carbon monoxide fumes
from the earth lining the atmosphere so that in ten to thirty years, man, the
atmosphere will rise five degrees and there will be floods' (ibid.). When
man-made and natural disasters recognise no artificial state boundaries,
the flight to the regions becomes a futile attempt to circumvent the
dangers inherent in making the existential choice of living when the 'bomb
was near enough to everyone' (WCW, p.97).

For a while Richard's solution to softening his metropolitan
outsider status is to become actively involved in the local Labour Party.
The experiment in engagement is short-lived, ending when Richard
refuses to be nominated for local office as he comes to regard the
organising of an Old Folks' Club as an impotent gesture in the face of the
national Party's reneging on its manifesto commitment to nuclear

5. On 8 June 1972 a South Vietnamese plane dropped a napalm bomb on a group of civilians
mistaken for North Vietnamese combatants. Associated Press photographer Nick Ut was
awarded a Pulitzer Prize for his photograph of a nine year old girl, PhanThi Kim Phùc,
running naked to escape the napalm. She was badly burned but recovered and went on in
1997 to establish a Foundation in the U.S.A., providing medical and psychological aid to
child victims of war.

disarmament. Richard's political consciousness finds it impossible to break out from the aesthetic to become praxis. He remains, until the novel's final page of oral traditional discourse, wedded to a literary view of rural values expressed through an eclectic range of intertextual references: Shelley, Chaucer, Lawrence, Thoreau, Ruskin, Wordsworth, Auden. In considering the obstacles facing the urban/university educated consciousness in accepting the dictates of a rural life-style, it is interesting to consider the way in which the novel's title, redolent of religious connotations, from Mrs Alexander's 1848 hymn 'There is a green hill far away' to 'Proverbs' 'He that hath no rules like his own spirit is like a city that is broken down, and without walls' (25:28), functions thematically by way of metaphor in illustrating Lawrence's summation of the difficulties inherent in translating a city aesthetic to a rural setting:

> Upon the vast, incomprehensible pattern of some primal morality greater than ever the human mind can grasp, is drawn the little pathetic pattern of man's moral life and struggle, pathetic, almost ridiculous. The little fold of law and order, the little walled city within which man has to defend himself from the waste enormity of nature, becomes almost too small, and the pioneers venturing out with the code of the walled city upon them, die in the bonds of that code, free and yet unfree, preaching the walled city and looking to the waste.

> (quoted in *The Rural Tradition*, pp.46-47)

Even Richard's choice of pop-record, 'The House of the Rising Sun', the lament of a young prostitute warning her sister not to follow her example, as a temporary aural escape from worrying about the complexities of meaningful engagement in the local community is not without unintended irony. Brought with him from the city as part of his record collection, Eric Burdon and the Animals' 1964 recording is one of several 1960s recordings reversing the normal cultural flow from city to region. The Animals were based in the North-East of England, an area which, along with Liverpool and Manchester, temporarily dictated the terms of the national debate on popular culture. Burdon, however, would probably have learned the song from Bob Dylan's 1962 Columbia album, and he in turn would have been familiar with it as part of American folk culture.[6] The gramophone needle left 'clicking in the end groove' is the background noise to Richard's 'looking to the waste' that is universal.

Bragg has written of his frustration with the fact that the 'Arts establishment in 1978 had little truck with popular culture which had been much of [his] background and even less inclination to treasure it' (*South Bank*, p.2). His ability and willingness to skip from the music of Monteverdi to the Animals within a single paragraph, without any hint of condescension towards the latter, is one of the qualities of cultural inclusiveness defining Bragg's writing and broadcasting and which marks him out as one of the more generous writers of his generation. In a matter of pages, the misery and despair of a young girl inveigled into a life of prostitution links to the melancholia of Tennyson's *In Memoriam*, as Richard empathises with the poet's 'years of melancholy wandering after the death of his friend, Hallam; between grief and nothingness' (*WCW*, p.297).[7] Whilst his recalling of the line 'Thou shalt not be a fool of loss' represents a firmly grounded personal response to grief, it is also proleptic of the novel's concluding theme of universal loss. Poem and novel also meet on common geological ground, specifically in Section LVI, interpreted in Isobel Armstrong's *Victorian Poetry. Poetry, Poetics and Politics* as envisaging the obliteration of the human species and the end of human history as the logical consequence of the fracture of 'scarped cliff and quarried stone' (*Victorian Poetry*, p.262). Richard, we recall, takes a

6. Bragg's choice of Eric Burdon and the Animals as a soundtrack to Richard's confusion on how best to play a part in the local community is more apt than he may have realised. In 1967 Burdon's geographical trajectory extended from Newcastle to London to San Francisco, U.S.A., as he became part of the Haight-Ashbury community's countercultural dream of establishing an hallucinogenic utopia on a scale beyond Richard's more prosaic expectations in Crossbridge. Burdon's 1967 recording 'San Francisco Nights' urges his British listeners to 'fly Trans-Love Airways to San Francisco, U.S.A.' where they can expect to find a new definition of place, policed only by aesthetics and recognising no political barriers to entry. Burdon's ecstatic rock lyric contributes to what Timothy Gray describes as a search for 'an exit from place' and a 'being together in placelessness' in a space 'of raw aesthetics that anchors a territory but also marks "coefficients of deterritorialization" that point beyond that territory's boundaries, gesturing toward a heretofore unrecognized "interassemblage"' (*Gary Snyder and the Pacific Rim. Creating Counter-Cultural Community*, p.233). Both the San Francisco hippies and Richard are searching for a sympathetic psychic and physical place/space whilst remaining connected to global discourses. Eric Burdon's appearance in *Without a City Wall* contributes to these cross-cultural energies.

7. Tennyson's *In Memoriam, A.H.H.*, was written between 1833 and 1850, in memory of A.H. Hallam, a gifted and intimate friend who died aged twenty-two. One of its best known lines is from section LVI: 'Tho' Nature, red in tooth and claw'. T.S. Eliot's reading of it as a poem of despair, albeit of a religious nature, accords with its intertextual function in the novel. Bragg devoted one of his B.B.C. Radio *In Our Time* broadcasts to a discussion of the poem on 30 June, 2011 (bbc.co.uk/radio 4/inourtime).

similar view from Knockmirton Fell of the permanence, albeit shifting, of geological formations set against the transitory nature of human settlements.

In the novel's last chapter Richard again climbs the fells around Crossbridge and experiences an epiphany as he gazes 'at the vast landscape' devoid of human dwelling except, in an echoing reference to the novel's title, for 'the walls which, however broken or derelict, yet encircled the highest tops' (WCW, p.369). No longer either awed or intimidated by the grandeur of the scene, he feels at one with the landscape and, in a relaxed frame of mind, lies down and dreams. Upon waking he 'could remember only the last flurry of it, an army of men suddenly gulped into slit trenches like those in the Great War' (WCW, p.370). Not only does this imagery of immolation offer a landscape specific gloss on the national poet laureate's vision of humanity 'blown about the desert dust, / Or seal'd within the iron hills' (In Memoriam, Section LV1), but it also prefigures World War I as a social landmark which will become as important as the physical ones in Bragg's next novel. Earlier, Richard viewed his own sense of melancholia through a reading of In Memoriam heavily dependent on images imported from Flanders Fields: 'the silt of retreated love'; 'the blocking silt' (WCW, p.297). Now, awakening from his dream, he has a fading remembrance of men whose 'khaki uniforms made them seem at once soldiers, destroyers of life and, on the brown, slit ground, so close in colour and movement to what sustained them that they disappeared as if they had been called to the earth rather than wiped from it' (WCW, p.370).

The dream on a Cumbrian fell is complex and open to analysis on a number of levels: the picture of a wasted bare landscape contrasting sharply with its depiction in the Lake District poems of the Romantics; the vision of nothingness as the men are 'called to earth'; the gender reversal of Tennyson's grief for the loss of a male friend with Richard's feeling of guilt over his being seen with a prostitute contributing to Agnes's death; the memory of Mrs Cass slipping from the dockside and being smothered in the tidal mud (WCW, p.314). Richard's literary sub-conscious appears unable to free itself from Tennyson's vision of 'A monster then, a dream, / A discord. Dragons of the prime, / That tare each other in their slime' (In Memoriam, Section LV1). His mud/death inflected dream is also reminiscent of images used by Bragg's autobiographical inclusion of Old Tom, a figure based in part on his paternal grandfather,

82

who is found close to death coated in mud (*WCW*, p.188) in his first novel. His grandfather's presence fights to make itself heard in *For Want of a Nail*, broods over *Without a City Wall* through Bragg's paratextual dedication,[8] and will be the inspiration behind *The Hired Man*. In the present novel, his is the figure behind its concluding detailed and committed turn to the tradition of the local.

Having raised the possibility of returning to London - '[b]ut there's no hurry' (*WCW*, p.372) - Richard joins the bereaved Wif in his cottage garden where the older man reflects on the local history of a cottager named Lloyd who lived apart but became part of the fabric of oral folk history. His name makes his national identity problematic for Wif, but he is in no doubt about his acquired identity as a local inhabitant:

> Dis thou know, Richard, he said, eventually, 'there was a fella used to live in yon cottage - beyond yon top road. It's nivver lived in now. An' he was a fella wouldn't mix, thou knows; a terrible man for bein' on his own. You couldn't have dragged that fella intill a company. Couldn't have dragged him in. Lloyd, his name was. But he wasn't Welsh in his talkin', even wid' a name like Lloyd. Well,' Wif pointed to his cigarette, straggly, botched with wet thumb-marks, smokable only with some willpower, 'well he'd got this trick off of bein' able to roll a cigarette one-handed. Nivver met anybody else who could. Nivver one.' (*WCW*, pp. 372-3)

Listening to Wif's voice keeps Richard/reader in touch with the resilient character of quotidian rural life, whilst directing attention to the demands of a given moment. Bragg quietly but insistently attends to the reality of common speech as part of an oral poetic tradition traced back to Wordsworth. Wif here represents a rhetoric of local feeling, inhabitation, and historical community depth which is at risk of erasure by the hyperreal orality of populist television talk shows such as those planned by David's North-West TV station. Wif's voice is part of a contested site in the social and political struggle between region and centre over identity and agency. Whereas, however, at the novel's beginning

8. The paratext refers to all those signs - author's name, book title, preface, footnotes, epigraphs etc. - that surround the main, or type area, text. Philippe Lejeune regards the paratext as 'a fringe of the printed text' (quoted in Gérard Genette, *Paratexts - Thresholds of Interpretation*, p.2).

innocence was Richard's anticipated destination, by the novel's end it has become very much a point of departure, leaving open the choice of Crossbridge (local) or London (metropolitan) as preferred habitation.

The story of the reclusive Lloyd would have been at home in Ronald Blythe's influential oral history of the Suffolk village of Akenfield, published a year after *Without a City Wall*, and forming part of a 1960s trans-Atlantic revival of interest in documenting ordinary lives on tape.[9] The net result is a suturing together of an otherwise diverse private body of significant local voices. Lloyd's story is a fragment in the democratic mosaic that Phyllis Bentley sees as defining the essence of the regional novel: 'It expresses a belief that the ordinary man and the ordinary woman are worth depicting ... In regional novels the characters always appear, for indeed they always do in provincial life, strongly individual, because well known to all in that district; in their own home town or village persons never become anonymous "masses", but remain individual men' (*Regional Novel*, p.45).

Bragg's animating of voices from the margins of regional life extends to one very specific material feature of the book in its dedication to his grandfather, Herbert Irving Bragg. Not only does the dedication appear at the intersection between the books circumreferential paratextual signs, but also between that of fictional and autobiographical fiction. The dedication is an invitation to the reader to look beyond the actual text towards a sign that Bragg wants his family history to emerge into literary visibility as part of the complex cultural history of the Cumbrian region. Herbert Bragg died in 1970, the year that Bragg's next novel, *The Hired Man*, was published. It tells the 'personal story of the sort of man whose life is rarely written about' (Preface to *The Hired Man. The Musical*,pp.vii-viii), rescuing his grandfather's family voice from Bentley's 'anonymous masses' to present a regional history of the English working class in the early twentieth century. Herbert Irving Bragg on the text's opening margins and the fictional Lloyd on its closing page bookend an assumption about the importance of promoting the visibility politics of an otherwise overlooked and culturally dismissed voice. Kelly Oliver's *Witnessing: Beyond Recognition* discusses contemporary theories

---

9. The work of George Ewart Evans in books such as *The Pattern Under the Plough* (1966) has had a significant influence on Bragg's own documentary oral history of Wigton, *Speak for England*, as well as on several of his Cumbrian novels. In America at this time, Studs Terkel deployed the same techniques of oral history in his study of Chicago, *Division Street America* (1966) and of everyday voices in *Hard Times: An Oral History of the Great Depression* (1970).

of society and their culture in terms of power being related to visibility, making the point that

> [v]ision, like all other types of perception and sensation, is just as much affected by social energy as it is by any other form of energy. This is why theorists can talk about the politics of vision or the visibility or invisibility of the oppressed. To see and be seen are not just the results of mechanical and photic energies, but also of social energies.
>
> *(Witnessing*, p.14)

The novel makes an important contribution to those social energies dedicated to establishing the permanency of regional voices. It is to Richard, the putatively disruptive outsider, who shares with Tom Graham, in *For Want of a Nail*, the aesthetically inclined potential to record the history of the region, that the oral history of Lloyd is transmitted and entrusted. In turning from Lloyd to John Tallentire in *The Hired Man*, Bragg engages with the full potential of the regional novel as a form of documentary poetics allied to the oral folk tradition. Inspired by his grandfather's unknown history, Bragg returns to 'the blocking silt' (*WCW*, p.297) in order to construct a politics of visibility for a generation of otherwise unrecorded voices.

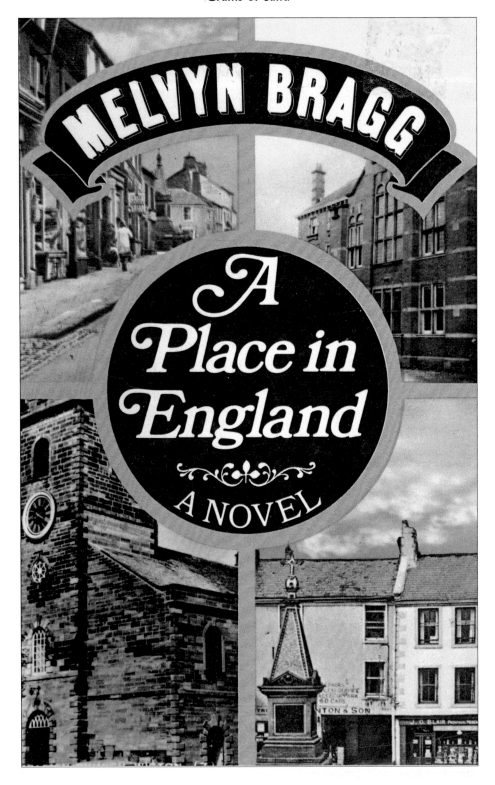

MELVYN BRAGG

A Place in England

A NOVEL

# FOUR

# THE THROSSELL NEST OF ALL ENGLAND
## *THE HIRED MAN*
## *A PLACE IN ENGLAND*
## *KINGDOM COME*

Published in 1969, *The Hired Man* is the first of a trilogy, along with *A Place in England* (1970) and *Kingdom Come* (1980), that traces the changing social and political structure of English society through the fortunes of the Tallentire family from late-Victorian times to the contemporary concerns of the 1970s. The trilogy's social dynamics are firmly rooted in the detailed specifics of the Cumbrian towns and countryside whilst its preoccupations of personal identity, work and leisure pursuits, upward mobility through education, class and family loyalty/betrayal, working-class politics, and the disintegration of knowable communities,[1] are played out against the increasingly intrusive narrative of national history.

Any pastoral tendency the trilogy might have towards an elegiac inflection is challenged by its large cast of imagined and semi-biographical characters whose experiences of brute realities unsettle any notion of an unquestioned nostalgia for time past. Bragg as omniscient narrator is also personally and emotionally implicated in the unfolding drama of generations of working-class artisans to such an extent that his narrative involvement and method self-consciously raises a number of interesting metafictional questions. He writes his family into the epic at an early stage in *The Hired Man*, naming the Braggs as one of ten inter-related labouring family names in the village of Crossbridge. His textual warning that 'care should be taken in talking of someone because you would be certain to be addressing his relation; if you offend one you would be certain to offend all' (*HM*, p.54) might apply with even greater force to the sensitive

---

1.   Raymond Williams devotes a chapter to 'Knowable Communities' in his *The Country and the City* (1973), beginning with the assertion: 'Most novels are in some sense knowable communities. It is part of a traditional method - an underlying stance and approach that the novelist offers to show people and their relationships in essentially knowable and communicable ways' (p.165). In practical terms the idea of a community is related to a notion of maximum self-regulation, so that wherever possible decisions are taken by those most affected. Bragg's treatment of knowable communities challenges the conservative rhetoric of community justifying the preservation of social inequalities whilst avoiding the danger of becoming a value-free assertion of romantic regional localism.

position of the semi-autobiographical writer determined to construct an honest history but also wanting to retain the goodwill necessary to maintain his own cherished place in a loved community.[2] These concerns feature prominently towards the conclusion of *A Place in England*, where the supposedly social realist text questions its mimetic authenticity by the metafictional device of drawing attention to its own fictional status, and in the process surmounting the perceived generic limitations of the regional novel. I will look in greater detail at this aspect of the trilogy and the implications for Bragg's more overt autobiographical fiction in due course.

We have already encountered an early, partial, and unacknowledged representation of Bragg's paternal grandfather in the character of Old Tom in *For Want of a Nail*. Bragg's 'Preface' to the 1984 published script of a musical version of *The Hired Man*[3] unashamedly reveals the autobiographical impulse to record a lasting memory of fleeting glimpses of his grandfather's life as a representative integral part of the largely unrecorded collective history of the Cumbrian rural working class at the turn of the nineteenth-century:

> My paternal grandfather died in 1970. I would guess that he had never read a book in the twentieth century. He left school at the end of the nineteenth century when Queen Victoria sat securely on a vast Empire, rich and varied beyond belief. His part in it - like that of the great majority of people in this country - was humble; he worked. First on the land, where, like many farm labourers his exhausting working life was in some way relieved by his love for the horses he worked with and the landscape he saw every day. Then as a miner where close friendships gave some relief. Like so many others of his generation he was swept up into the First World War; unlike many others including some of his brothers he

2.  Bragg raises the issue briefly, and somewhat guardedly, in his 'Preface' to *The Parish of Lamplugh*, writing: 'I do not remember why I called [the village] Crossbridge instead of Lamplugh. There was a fashion at the time to change the names of real places. There was also a certain sense in it because I wanted to change things and if it had been the real Lamplugh I would, quite rightly, have had protests if I got anything factually wrong. Crossbridge gave me a little more room for manoeuvre' (p.6).

3.  *The Hired Man. A Musical*, with music and lyrics by Howard Goodall was first performed at the Nuffield Theatre, Southampton on 2 February 1984. It reached London on 31 October that year, playing the Astoria Theatre. Since then it has been performed many times at venues across the country.

survived it to come back to a land which promised
nothing but more sweated labour. A few years after that
war, his wife died leaving him with four children: he had
four more by his second wife.            ('Preface', p. vii)

This then is the stimulus for the novel that Bragg was determined to write
when, in the late 1960s, he first realised that his grandfather, with whom
he had become particularly close during his own father's absence on
active service during World War II, was close to death. Many of the novel's
details of his early life, such as his relationship with his first wife, are pure
fiction, but the remaining outline of a hard physical life is an accurate
portrayal of the 'lives of tens, even hundreds of thousands of the people of
this country in the first quarter of the twentieth century' (ibid.).

My reading of the trilogy explores Bragg's ambition to create a
realist fictional account of the social history of a segment of working-class
society over a period of some 70 years, as seen from the perspective of four
generations of a representative family network, deeply embedded in its
Cumbrian community. To an extent Bragg's intention is to realise a fictional
equivalent, on a reduced time-scale, of E.P. Thompson's achievement in
capturing and celebrating the process of self-discovery and of self-
definition of otherwise unexamined lives in his *The Making of the English
Working Class* (1963). *The Hired Man* appears just seven years after
Thompson's study and its creation of a social realist regional community of
agricultural labourers, travellers, miners, tradesmen, factory workers and
publicans, mirrors Thompson's credo of 'seeking to rescue the poor
stockinger, the Luddite cropper, the "obsolete" hand-loom weaver, the
"utopian" artisan ... from the enormous condescension of posterity'
(*Making*, p. 13). Bragg expresses a similar sentiment as: 'It was from the fells
that the Tallentire family had come ... But such families as his were merely
the numbers to the alphabet of history. "Labourers 10": "Estatemen 16":
"Foot-soldiers 17": or more commonly, "and a number of men"' (*HM*, p.14).
In choosing to rescue forgotten lives in the form of a semi-autobiographical
fictional family epic, pitched alternately between the personal and the
public, Bragg asserts his right to know this 'number of men' whilst
maintaining what Philip Davis refers to in *Memory and Writing* as authorial
critical distance through 'the *public* privacy of the novel' (p.224).

When the trilogy opens, in 1898, its central protagonist, John
Tallentire, is 18 years old and about to abandon his apprenticeship as a
blacksmith to seek work as an agricultural labourer so as to support his

new young wife with that proud sense of 'independence he thought essential to a married man' (*HM*, p.14). On his way to the agricultural hiring fair in Cockermouth John stops off to visit his grandparents, Harry and Alice. Whilst John respects his grandfather's knowledge of the land acquired over a life-time of farm labour, he is unwilling to acquiesce automatically in what he sees as a demeaning social deference. Their shared close physical relationship with the land, 'the most demanding of gods' (*HM*, p.12), is described in terms that link labour, marriage and fecundity. Harry has 12 surviving children, scores of grandchildren and half-dozens of great-grandchildren, whilst John's Emily has recently conceived their first child. Luck and care combined are seen to be the requisites for a good land harvest and Bragg's agricultural referencing serves to describe Harry's abundant family structure and John's newly acquired marital status: '"husbandry" it was called, a word accurately descriptive of the necessary bond of intimacy [for] a good harvest' (*HM*, p.12). Bragg further links grandfather and grandson in their shared preference for an early morning taste of dried bread. Before setting out, John 'put some dry bread in his mouth. Bread a few days old, you could not beat it in a morning, he thought' (*HM* p.14), whilst almost simultaneously a few miles distant, 'downstairs there was a piece of dry bread waiting' (*HM*, p.17) for his grandfather. The dry bread is important as a small-scale version of the spaced mapping of a whole community at the heart of the trilogy, and specifically telling in its depiction of the simplicity of rural life, establishing shared morals as much as a culinary distance from a leisure class still likely to arrive at a late breakfast evincing 'an unusual attachment to silence and soda-water' in consequence of a Pickwickian 'unwonted dissipation of the previous night' (*Pickwick Papers*, p.96). But this same staple diet of dry bread also becomes a measure of the crumbling of inter-generational patterns of social deference.

With the claim that John's walk to his grandfather's cottage 'was paved by no treasured remembrance of things past' (*HM*, p.14), Marcel Proust's *A la Recherche du Temps Perdu* is alluded to in such a way as to equate the humble piece of dry bread with the famous madeleine as triggers for the authorial recovery of memory in both texts. Harry takes his 'bread out into the garden to share it with the blackbird he was taming' (*HM*, p.17). In naming the bird 'Dizzy'[4] Harry symbolically aligns

4. 'Dizzy' became a term of popular affection for Benjamin Disraeli (1804-81). It was common for crowds to chant 'Dizzy, Dizzy' at the sight of him in his carriage in the streets of central London. Hesketh Pearson's classic biography is titled *Dizzy: A Life of Benjamin Disraeli* (revised for Penguin Classics, 2001).

himself with the considerable number of the working class who in 1898 looked to the late Prime Minister and leader of the Conservative Party, Benjamin Disraeli, and his successors, as the natural elite rulers of Britain and perennial promisers of material benefits and social improvements.[5] Harry espouses a deferential attitude to social and political authority that makes him a suitable candidate for Dizzy's ideological taming: 'In the inarticulate mass of the English populace, [Disraeli] discerned the Conservative working man as the sculptor perceives the angel prisoned in a block of marble' (*The Times*, 18 April 1883, on the second anniversary of Disraeli's death, quoted in McKenzie and Silver, *Angels in Marble*, p.ii). Harry extends his identification with the upper classes to matters of dress, in which he 'was as careful and conservative as those "above" him and always wore a hard hat' (*HM*, p.18). The hard black 'Dizzy' hat's message of deference is the one aspect of his grandfather's life that confuses John, who sees in it 'his grandfather submissive to the place given him by others' and, to complete the symbolic breaking of dry bread, 'and to notions which were the crumbs scattered by his masters and manners aped' (*HM*, p.24). Despite his deep love for his grandfather, John 'could have knocked off that hard hat' (ibid).

In the event, Bragg signals John's determination to break free of paternalistically structured class attitudes by his refusal to adopt another of his grandfather's customs of class identification. Harry adheres to the region's traditional signifying practice associating straw with both the land and with those who work it: '"Thou'll have to have this", he said, handing [John] a piece of straw he had brought. "In my time they twisted it under their hats so it popped out of the ears. They suck it now"' (*HM*, p.23). John, however, spits out the proffered straw in disgust, asserting his personal sense of a coherent inner self wishing to distance itself from an all-too-visible marker of a dependent status: '"I can be hired without that," he replied, over-curtly' (ibid.). Here Bragg touches on the notion that in accounts of changing times it is crucial to historicise the boundaries that exist between thing and person. Commenting on Bill Brown's relatively new development of Thing Theory, John Plotz

5. The period 1898-1914 may be seen as one of limited improvement in the standard of living of the Cumbrian working class at the same time as many small independent farmers struggled to maintain their status as the more successful landowning class became increasingly absorbed into the upper echelons of social class. The Gosforth *Parish Magazine*, begun in 1887, inadvertently documents the region's social stratification with long and detailed obituaries of the deceased gentry, while the great majority of the population are fortunate to merit a single line.

suggests that 'what counts as human attention to [an] object is not a metaphysical project but a genealogical one, and the shifting boundaries turn out to reveal shifting ideas about the location of selfhood and subjectivity' ('Can the Sofa Speak?' p.114). A sense of shame attached to the visibility of the object as an ideological statement poised at the boundary between a present self and a traditional world view extends from straw to Emily Tallentire's attitude towards the still-ubiquitous form of domestic/industrial footwear: 'What caused Emily most shame was her clogs' (*HM*, p.59). She is self-consciously aware that their visibility signifies a 'rigid liaison between money of a certain quantity and goods of a specific type' (ibid.), and in consequence 'she hated them and would take any opportunity to tuck her feet away under her dresses or lean on one foot so that she could draw the other back' (ibid.).[6]

By the 1940s and 1950s of *A Place in England* the categories of class signifiers may have changed but their power to fix class and status remains intact. Married to John's son, Joseph, Betty Tallentire adamantly refuses to have a telephone installed in their tenanted pub, even though she recognises that it would assist in its efficient management. Betty foresees its appearance as a status symbol likely to place a barrier between landlord and regular, suggesting a claim to an unwarranted social superiority: 'a telephone, like a car, would, she thought, be a clear and justified object of scorn and envy' (*PE*, p.159). This association of messages contained in objects, involving established ideological opinions about where human labour or human thought might be read as residing, is apparent in Arnold Bennett's 1910 essay 'The Hanbridge Empire' in *The Nation* (reprinted *Paris Nights*), where the appearance of clogs as a form of popular music-hall entertainment leads him to reflect upon their historical message: 'And when I think of clogs I think of the knocker-up, and hurried fire-lighting and tea and thick bread, and the icy draught from the opened front door and the factory gates and the

6. Published in 1956, and based on fieldwork conducted in 1950-52, W. M. Williams's study of the Cumbrian parish of Gosforth, on the western fringe of the Lakeland fells, records that whilst the wearing of clogs is fast disappearing their signifying power remains: '... clogs are very rapidly disappearing and are now to be found mainly on farms where they still general for everyday use. In the village, clogs are rare and are certainly a sign of low class position. One housewife ... said defensively of her children, "They wear clogs to school, but they takes them off the minute they get (home) and anyway it don't matter what they has on their feet. Anybody can look at what they wear above (their clothes) any time." Clogs are "old fashioned", boots less so, and shoes are a token of modernity, and for this reason shoes are preferred by those who are anxious to "better themselves"'. (*The Sociology of an English Village. Gosforth*, pp.113-4).

terrible time-keeper therein, and his clock; all the military harshness of industrialism grimly accepted' (*Paris Nights*, p.282).[7] Bennett recognises what John and Emily intuit, namely that objects, such as a piece of straw and a pair of clogs, may be interpreted hermeneutically in the sense in which the inert physical thing becomes the semiotic marker for some wider social truth and political reality. Knowing this, Bennett writes that '[a]n artist who is truly original cannot comment on boot-laces without illustrating his philosophy and consolidating his position' (*Books and Persons*, p.284). Bragg, too, understands that there is no unmediated seeing and in the Cumbrian Trilogy marries realist narrative to theoretical self-consciousness in the same accessible way as distinguishes Bennett's craft.

Ordinary and everyday things are important components of Bragg's text, depicting the material world of early twentieth-century rural social structures operating as a system of signs indicating a character's present aspirations and offering clues to his or her social background. They convey a very real sense of the way human relationships were often conducted as a corollary of human-object ones, where one class treated the members of a socially inferior one as readily disposable and replaceable. The opening sequence of *A Hired Man* rejects any notion of a golden Edwardian age, of a 'land of lost content', but rather one where the ageing labourer faces uncertainty, impoverishment and the prospect of a hastened physical decline. Bragg does not lecture the reader on the heritage industry's partial and misleading nostalgic mythical reading of rural times past, preferring to let his characters - who share a common but unanalysed psychology - speak for themselves in their own regional dialect, which takes on a peculiar dignity in the face of adversity. Harry perceptively likens his enforced retirement to the very treatment of the things he has spent his life getting rid of: '"They used me up and cast me off. Like the chaff, John, sent away from the barns to be burnt"' (*HM*, p.105). Harry's life has been fairly and

7. The reference to Arnold Bennett in the context of a discussion of Bragg's regional fiction is no accidental choice. Early twentieth-century novelists like Bennett deliberately set out to create rounded life-like portraits of place, viewed from a position of privileged insiders. As narrators they are subsequently able to claim a disproportionate share in shaping the outside world's perception of the actual place. This remains true today of Bennett's fictionalised portrait of Bursley (Burslem in Stoke-on-Trent) and is also applicable to Bragg's introduction to Crossbridge (Lamplugh) and, more importantly, Thurston (Wigton). As will be argued later, there is a marked historical continuity between Bennett's presentation of Burslem and Bragg's of Wigton.

unsentimentally portrayed as one of hard manual work, not far removed in time or nature from that depicted in Wordsworth's 'Michael', where work was a community's chief means of finding a cultural identity for itself. Harry's lament is a warning not to dismiss his contribution to rural culture by parodying him as an entertaining rustic character whose concerns therefore do not warrant being taken seriously:

> 'Aa can still work. They know that. But it's - "No, Mr Tallentire, thou must retire." "Yes, Mr Tallentire, we want thou to have a peaceful old age." They didn't kick me out, John - Aa could a' kicked back then - they Mothered me off the job! Whativver Aa said against it - they laughed - mekkin' out Aa was a comical old character - as couldn't think of what to do widdout his work and wasn't that so very comical! But it isn't a question of fillin' time, lad. Nivver was. Not my way. Aa can't be interested in piddlin' aboot like a soft-bladdered old nag. Aa'm nothing widdout work. Nothing! No man is.'
>
> (ibid.)

His conclusion is that 'it might be better nivver to be born' (ibid.).

In assessing the documentary accuracy of Bragg's fictional portrait of a farm labourer it is instructive to note its marked resemblance to that of a real-life contemporary, Frederick Bettesworth, whose final years are affectionately recorded in George Bourne's[8] *Memoirs of a Surrey Labourer*. Bourne tells how, in 1903, he realised that the elderly villager Bettesworth, whose age he estimated to be the late 60s, was increasingly unable to find work: 'He would never get another employment; to cut him off from this would be like saying the world had no more use for him and he might as well die out of the way. But I had no courage to condemn him to death because my lawn was ill cut' (*Memoirs*, p.82). Bettesworth is as reluctant as Harry to 'do without his work' but, 'with aching limbs - his ankle where he had once broken it pained him cruelly at times - went slaving on for his own satisfaction, when [Bourne] would have suggested to him to take things easily' (ibid.). Bettesworth's companions also provide the

---

8. George Bourne is the pen name of George Sturt (1863-1927), born in Farnham, Surrey. He wrote an account of changing traditional local craftsmanship and relationships in *The Wheelwright's Shop* (1923), under his own name and based on the long-established family business. The most comprehensive recent study of his work is to be found in David Gervais's *Literary Englands. Versions of 'Englishness' in modern writing* (1993).

documentary evidence for Harry's anxiety: 'There was Carver Cook, for instance. He was seventy-seven year old and fretting because he was out of work: "I en't earnt a crown, not in these last three weeks"' (*Memoirs*, p.176). Bourne was only just in time to chronicle the disappearance of a long-held rural way of life and the organic community, seeing his role as that of artless recorder with his only claim to art being in his faithful reproduction of Bettesworth's dialect without the artifice of authorial arrangement. Bragg's use of dialect is similarly objective, letting it speak for itself at the same time as his sober prose reproduction of the texture and substance of its delivery - 'the clatter of cheap forks on thick china' (*HM*, 105), provides as eloquent and accurate comment on a way of life that is passing.

The trilogy shows culture in the process of development such that there is, therefore, no static point outside this process in which to call an arbitrary halt to sum it up. The complex and developing interaction of character and social forces gives the three novels the positive quality that Raymond Williams thought lacking in his comparison of twentieth-century fiction with their nineteenth-century forebears, regretting an absence of history in the former, where a character's experiences seem to exist and develop independent of, and undetermined by any larger forces. 'In the same way when a place is introduced [such as Crossbridge or Thurston], it is not just the site of an event as is typical of contemporary fiction, but the materialization of a history which is often quite extensively retraced' (*Politics and Letters*, p.275). In Williams's view 'the [novel] series is the only technical solution which is open to a contemporary novelist who is interested in a broad band of social experience' (ibid, p.274). Bragg's expansive 819 page narrative over the course of the trilogy accords with Williams's formulation, successfully negotiating what Dominic Head describes as the economic pressure of the publishing industry 'creating an ideological squeeze on the novel, demanding the omission of social history, and the exclusion of the kind of political embedding that would be necessary in a fully realized working-class fiction' (*Modern British Fiction*, p.63).

*The Hired Man* makes clear its ambition as a political novel at the outset through the character of Seth Tallentire, one of John's brothers, who is a passionate advocate of workers' rights and their realisation through the collective action of unions and the newly formed Independent Labour Party. We first meet him at the Cockermouth Hiring

Fair where he is bitterly complaining to John and to Isaac, the third Tallentire brother, about the lack of industrial compensation for an activist uncle, Ephraim, involved in Co-operative and union organisation, whose recent mining accident means he will never be physically fit enough to find future employment. I quote in full the paragraph that stands as an introduction to Seth's ideological position because in its compassing of political theorists, political history and a personal hatred of inequality it announces itself as a textual manifesto whose concerns will echo throughout the trilogy:

> 'All wrong' was how Seth saw the world. The ideas of Ruskin, Morris, Owen, Engels and even Marx wraithed themselves around the columns of the British status quo as smoke from an ignored fire. But Seth had caught a whiff of them through their popularizers in the threepenny pamphlets his uncle Ephraim bought, and from some of the speakers who came to West Cumberland on their way to building up the Independent Labour Party - and this scent he had followed. For it seemed to him All Wrong that men should slave while others lorded it, All Wrong that the sick should suffer while the rich wore pearls, All Wrong that a man should be ripped from school to work at an age when many of those who would never work were just beginning their schooling, All Wrong that there should be hovels for some and palaces for others, All Wrong that a man should be shut out from learning at the very time he might see the sense in books. All: Wrong.
>
> (*HM*, p.30)

The litanised 'All Wrong' carries the weight of a political slogan demanding active redress, and the passage ends with something of the preacher's pulpit oration, with the capitalised and spatially separated 'All: Wrong' exhibiting the powerful secular certainty of a prayer's 'Amen'.

It is worth recalling that the passage quoted above appeared in print at a time when the French student-led rebellion of 1968 had failed and when the revisionists in the Labour Party were embarking on an attack - successfully realised some 25 years later - on the Party's Clause Four commitment to 'secure for the worker by hand or by brain the full fruits of their industry and the most equitable distribution thereof ... upon the basis of the common ownership of the means of production, distribution and exchange, and the best obtainable system of popular administration and control of each industry or service.' Bragg's novel now reads as an emotional and brave, if somewhat forlorn, defence of traditional socialist values, written against the grain of the emergent postmodern playfulness of the period - John Fowles's *The French Lieutenant's Woman* and B.S. Johnson's *The Unfortunates*, for example, both appeared in 1969. But *The Hired Man*'s enduring value lies precisely in its almost unique qualities as an avowedly political text.

Seth Tallentire is a complex character, representing as he does a transitional phase between localised and sporadic workers' collective action and a fully organised national trade union movement. He can be heard making the case for co-ordinated action 'Every man that isn't in the Union is for the masters' (*HM*, p.148) - arguing for the exclusion of blacklegs from the workplace, before there exists a general willingness to sink individual interests in favour of the collective. John, however, proves an adept protégé, travelling a path of developing political consciousness from his earliest working days as a hired agricultural labourer to joining his brother Seth in the mines of Cumbria. As an eighteen-year old there were no statutory regulations to stop him working 'all the hours God sent. There was nothing to hinder exploitation' (*HM*, p.71). Joseph Arch's 1872 agricultural union 'fizzled out in the damp of the long agricultural depression and Arch saw his work undone' (ibid.).At the age of twenty-six - the year is 1906 - John has joined the miners' union and is fighting for the Eight-Hour Day. Whilst intellectually convinced of the truth and value of Seth's political analysis, John nevertheless remains disturbed by the tenor of his brother's fanaticism.

Chapter 14 of *The Hired Man* is a succinct and accurate exposition of the political and social forces at work in 1906 England, a time when industrial unrest and political battles over welfare provision, along with growing female militancy demanding the vote, were unsettling notions of a stable democracy. Bragg captures something of this turbulent atmosphere in an account of a union meeting at which Seth cannot prevent himself from running ahead of the objective reality of a still emerging union movement, to press for a syndicalist State: '... we can take all over - education we can tek, governing and workin'. I would do away with all companies - parliament - everything - only the Union that is democratically elected by the men on the spot would run things' (*HM*, pp.148-9). At the heart of Seth's impassioned plea for action now, Bragg inverts a knowing proleptic reference to William Beveridge's 1942 social welfare report, *Social Insurance and Allied Services*, promising care from 'the cradle to the grave', with Seth's belief that syndicalism could deliver welfare 'from the cot to the cemetery' (*HM*, p.149). At such points *The Hired Man* assumes an overtly political fictional form, articulating the interaction of individual interests, family and community relationships, and national movements, in such a way as to demonstrate the inclusiveness and continuity of working-class history.[9] The trilogy is a profoundly historical/political construction sharing many of its characteristics with Raymond Williams's 1960 *Border Country* in which, as Tony Pinkney argues, a panoramic medley of 'voices, styles, forms, all these histories, jostle for predominance in a novel whose own grand historical project, the recovery of a past both personal and social, will grant each their appointed place and local validity in its own overarching temporal framework' (*Raymond Williams*, p.37). Seth Tallentire shares many of the virtues and defects of Williams's *Border Country* rail-worker union organiser in the 1926 General Strike, Morgan Rosser; both men are ultimately defeated in their time by the pressure of external factors on their local communities as well as by their own ideological fanaticism. Seth's over-determined promotion of values which will come to be seen as conventional wisdom 30 years on, leave him a partially isolated and ineffectual figure. He is, however, a pivotal figure, illustrating complicated emotions and relationships in a state of tension between past and present working-class consciousness, regional and national events, and the potential synthesis between the two.

There is a sustained historical narrative between *The Hired Man* and *A Place in England*, both in the presentation of the individual self and in the continuing social identification of a collective project. The main

---

9. Tony Benn's essay 'The Inheritance of the Labour Movement' reiterates the importance of individuals such as Seth on the development of the more important trains of thought and action from which the origins of the British Labour Movement can be traced: 'The real history of any popular movement is made by those, almost always anonymous, who throughout history have fought for what they believe in, organised others to join them, and have done so against immense odds and with nothing to gain for themselves, learning from that experience and leaving it to others to distil that experience and to use it again to advance the cause'. (Tony Benn *Arguments for Socialism*, p.44)

protagonist of *A Place in England* is John Tallentire's son, Joseph, and both men enter their respective textual domains at the age of eighteen and, significantly, given the political novel's need for the formation of a vision for the future, both awake on their respective novels first pages from dream to reality. The year now is 1931 and Joseph is searching for work in Cumbria in the midst of the decade's deepening economic crisis. Seth's arguments for collective action are now all too apparent as the working-class is made to bear the brunt of the Government's austerity programme whilst the middle-class is able to marginally benefit from deflation's downward pressure on consumer goods' prices and on house prices.

Cumbria is seen as representative of the country at large, with 'workless men moving ceaselessly; largely ignorant of the system which had brought them to that state, largely ignored by those who ran the system' (*PE*, p.38). Two years on and the events surrounding the Jarrow March have politicised Joseph's young wife, Betty, to the extent that she believes the ruling elite 'should be shot for letting this happen' (*PE*, p.70) and cannot wait to be old enough to vote, to give Labour 'a weapon for them to use' (ibid.). Betty's synonymic use of 'vote' for 'weapon' is indicative of her deep sense of injustice and shame in the face of a system where 'towns were as in mourning' - for her, the Jarrow March marks a political awakening. The trilogy commands credibility as a political text, in part, because Bragg immerses it in touches of authenticity involving place, for example Jarrow, in the context of social and economic relations that are timeless in their portrayal of the unequal distribution of power and resources. There is an insistent pattern of prefiguration in the novels, linking the psychological make-up of the Tallentire men to their social situation that finds expression in the formative experiences of living through such historical events as World Wars I and II, the Great Depression, the 1945-50 Labour Government's creation of the Welfare State, the Cold War, the counter-cultural movement of the 1960s, the industrial unrest of the 1970s - all within a carefully contextualised narrative of which Jarrow as a trope for inequality is an example. It is also an example of the need for working-class texts to present a history told from below in contradistinction to official history's often distorted version of the past judged by the standards of elite culture. Kenneth Burke expresses the need as: 'If a small class ... happens to have expressed itself in literature, and a large class through being illiterate happens to have expressed itself in dancing, when our savants examine this era [the 1920s] they will find nothing but the literature remaining, hence must offer it as the "essence" of the times' (quoted in Charles Scruggs, 'Jean Toomer and Kenneth Burke and the Persistence of the Past', p.55). Dance as a feature of community life is invoked in several of Bragg's Cumbrian novels, but here we are invited to read the Jarrow March, along with similar nationwide displays, as a politically choreographed dance whose movements display bonds of class solidarity under stress from economic despair and demanding a response from Government. Literature such as *A Place in England* matters because it merges aesthetics and politics in a way that assumes a dynamic relationship between a text and its audience, informing about past truths in the hope of influencing future thought and policy.

The relationship between text and writer, and the latter's right to interpret family and community history of which he or she believes themselves to be a part by virtue of genealogy and a personal sense of place, also receives extended scrutiny in the final sections of *A Place in England*. For the moment I am interested in Bragg's semi-autobio-graphical character Douglas Tallentire, preparing himself for university, and asking the pertinent question 'Who from the working-class - really from it, no school-teacher-mother-literary-uncle in the background, has spoken accurately and lastingly?'(*PE*,pp.186-7). Douglas is John's grandson - the same relationship that was the catalyst for Bragg writing *The Hired Man* - and through him Bragg raises the uncomfortable issue of the reluctant upwardly mobile distancing of the educated child from a close-linked community class structure as a class/status linked education system operates to separate generations. (The 1944 Butler Education Act is often seen as having this unintentional social-engineering effect.) Douglas's ambition to capture Thurston in fiction is in part a solution to the dilemma, as the text itself works towards a definition of literature as work, a sedentary but satisfying variant of his ancestors' physical labour in its depiction of the visibility of his literary output: 'He put down the typescript and drank some more coffee. The draft of the novel was scattered all over his table ... he groaned to think how many times it might have to be re-written' (*PE*, 226). The result of such laborious re-writes is the successful capturing in prose of memories of his father's pub and translating the work routines of everyday life into a balletic performance of aestheticised labour:

The cellars opened outside the pub, in front of it, a large trapdoor, and he would stand at the bottom, as of a pit, and see the wagon towering with barrels and crates, one of the men stalking over it like a warrior among plunder. The way they swing down the crates was beautiful to watch. Each crate held two dozen bottles. One man on the wagon would pass them down to the other, two at a time. He would stack them around the edges of the trapdoor. Lift one, pause, lift another, swing around, the man below took the first, the second, turned and stacked them, turned back, two more waiting, a slight jostling thud each time a crate was placed. The way a stack of crates was reduced was like seeing someone scything down a field of hay. Then the man who had been on the wagon jumped down into the cellar and the crates were slid down the long ramps, two at a time, and again the co-ordination. Harry - who was mad on Rugby League and went to see these two play whenever he got the chance - was sure he observed in their actions the same rhythm and balance which entranced him when he saw fast open play.

(*PE*, pp.147-8)

The continuity with agricultural labouring history is apparent in the 'scything down a field of hay' metaphor, whilst the threatened class gap is narrowed by Bragg/Douglas's likening of the delivery men's technique to the play of Rugby League. In short, the passage stands as an example of memory turning a lived life into art in a lovingly observed reconstruction of the minutiae of working-class lives and the culture of the ordinary.

The beer delivery passage sits comfortably within a perspective on masculinity defined by physical strength and manual dexterity, and endorsed by the trilogy's history of agricultural-rural labour. Throughout the novels, gender and sex are taken as biological and social givens within an ideological paradigm which Kaja Silverman, in *Male Subjectivity at the Margins*, refers to as 'the dominant fiction' (p.12). It is, therefore, all the more unexpected to find a sensitively written interlude featuring cross-dressing at the Thurston carnival, where its potential to disrupt conventional views on gender and sexual differentiation might have been expected to cause confusion, distress and even open hostility amongst the local community. Bragg's detailed description of the carnival preparations does nothing to alert the reader to what is to come.

'There was a man called Kathleen[10] who was to lead it this year' (*PE*, p.106).This unadorned statement of fact introduces cross-dressing and transvestism as a sign of what Marjorie Garber, in *Vested Interests: Cross-Dressing and Cultural Anxiety*, calls a 'category crisis' (p.16), foregrounding the performative character of identity. Kathleen's mother so desperately wanted a girl that when she gives birth to a baby boy she insists on dressing him in the 'little dresses with "Katie" embroidered on them ... and even on the panties' (*PE*, p.106). By the time Kathleen's father finally insists his son wears trousers for school it is too late to undo the psychologically gendered sexual identity that he/she accepts as a state of unremarkable queerness. During adolescence Kathleen ignores the rude chants and remarks of others, remaining calm and polite, and growing into a strong youth who '[a]lways did labouring jobs and always did them well' (*PE*, p.107), thus conforming to the stereotype of masculine performance, but wearing the label of femininity. In due course Kathleen drinks in the local pub, goes to hound trials, attends local football matches, using his/her new-found toughness to come out and protest and preserve the qualities that labelled him/her feminised in the first place.

Kathleen's finest moment as a cross-gendered performatively presented self comes when s/he parades in the first of Thurston's post-War carnivals 'dressed up as Mae West ... Immaculate. A long cigarette holder and high heels, silk stockings, the lot' (*PE*, p.108). Far from becoming an object of fun or hostility Kathleen is awarded 'first prize for Gentleman Individuals' and, in an ironic piece of gender reversal, 'shared the Certificate of Originality with the woman who came dressed as King

---

10. This reads as a direct echo of Johnny Cash's version of the Shel Silverstein song, *A Boy Named Sue*, which he performed and recorded live at San Quentin State Penitentiary, U.S.A. on 24 February 1969. Julie Wyman's 2001 documentary, *A Boy Named Sue*, tells the story of Theo, a transsexual, in this case raised female but becoming male, and featuring Cash's song on the soundtrack. Kristine McCusker and Diane Pecknold's 2005 collection of cultural essays, *A Boy Named Sue: Gender and Country Music*, Mississippi University Press, explores the role of gender in American country music. More recently, the first of Jimmy McGovern's television series, *Accused*, broadcast on 11 August 2012, featured Sean Bean as a transvestite. The look of his powerful physique, clad in miniskirt, high heels and a blond wig, suggests something of the visual shock that Kathleen's appearance must have caused.

Kong' (ibid.). The following year Kathleen is invited to lead the procession, dressed as Two-Ton Tessie O'Shea. Several aspects of Kathleen's textual cameo appearance strike me as deserving further comment. Provincial towns in the late 1940s were not renowned for their tolerance of any type of queer behaviour, and yet in this instance Bragg celebrates an all-inclusive community strong enough in its own sense of identity to incorporate, or license, the existence of a marginal personality. It is worth recalling that this episode of acceptance of the radical otherness of queer identity occurs shortly after the defeat of a Nazi regime that persecuted, sent to concentration camps, and murdered transvestites and others it labelled sexual deviants. It is instructive in this context to read this small Cumbrian town as a model for post-War conciliation and social inclusiveness.

Kathleen also embodies the natural excess of carnival: 'carnival day in Thurston did disjoint the town: people set out most purposefully to get drunk; those who dressed as conservatively as all England did at that time put on wanton plumage; others, like Kathleen ... played out a personal vision or desire at once harmlessly and at the same time challengingly' (*PE*, p.109). The procession 'was like a dream made tangible and quite unexpectedly laid over a normal waking life' (*PE*, p.111) inspired by Hollywood's Dream Factory. Carnivalesque excess was also a feature of many of the British films of the late 1940s and early 1950s, and whilst none proposed the level of radical change that would overthrow or seriously reform the prevailing economic orthodoxies, the casting of, for example, Alistair Sim as the headmistress in *The Belles of St. Trinians* (1955) might be seen as a contribution to the carnivalesque and the puncturing of officialdom's pomposity. Bragg, however, makes a more serious observation in linking Thurston's carnivalesque, as seen through Betty's eyes, to the governing Labour Party's programme:

> There was nothing 'laid on' about it, neither from hands of the mighty dead nor from the hands of the rich living. In that way, Betty thought, it was like the Labour Party which proclaimed that people were now equal with regard to their health and their basic livelihood, and more equal than before in regard to education and the systems. She would respond emotionally for the Labour Party on any subject - but especially now, at this time, when they were in power with Clement Attlee as Prime

Minister and 'making a really good job of it considering the mess there is to clear up after a war'. Somehow, the carnival was directly related to the Labour Party's term of government - but more importantly, it was related to people peacefully enjoying themselves. She loved to be in crowds but feared it terribly when the slightest ripple of nattiness stirred. Here was a time when there was none. (*PE*, pp.115-6)

Suddenly politics and the personal find a generational link. New to village life in Crossbridge, Emily Tallentire enjoys most 'those occasions when *everyone was part of the crowd* - the day of the Club Fair (called a Walk) when the band played all day in the field behind The Cross' (*HM*, p.100, italics added).[11] The continuity of community celebrations and their long-established association with politically motivated movements is given a human dimension by the expression of both women's desire to be part of a friendly crowd. All of which takes me some distance from the initial introduction of the surprise transvestite guest at the party, yet I am aware that the critical study of cultural phenomena needs to be attentive to such unexpected presences as Kathleen - the woman who is not there and the feminine presence which is - and to all that s/he makes possible. Kathleen's decision to publicly announce his transvestite self in the most conspicuous of community settings is the culmination of several years of hesitation and deliberation. His/her display can be read as both a means of self-discovery and of social transformation enabling him/her to recognise who s/he really is. Kathleen is able to inhabit a place in Thurston/England that is sufficiently liberal to tolerate, and even celebrate, difference. A similar pattern of hesitancy, self-discovery and

11. Betty Marshall, a life-long resident of the fictional Crossbridge's actual village of Lamplugh, tells me that 'Lamplugh Friendly Society was known throughout the County as Lamplugh Club. It was the second oldest Friendly Society in the County and had many traditions.' The day of the Walk was 'an important day in the Lamplugh Calendar'. She goes on to say that the 'Club was stopped when WW II was declared as many members were in the forces etc. I do not remember an actual Club Walk but my Grandfather was the last secretary and treasurer and I can remember "old men with long white whiskers" coming to the house to pay the Club Money on the day it was due. This stopped of course when the Welfare State was introduced' (private correspondence, 16 February 2012). Betty Marshall's summary factually bridges the gap between Club Day 1898 in *The Hired Man* and the carnival/Welfare State in the late 1940s of *A Place in England*. I am indebted to Betty for sending me a copy of *The Parish of Lamplugh* (1993) which contains, among many invaluable details, an account of the Friendly Society and the Club Walk (Ch.13 'Clubs and Societies).

transformation, this time of an intellectual as opposed to a physical/psychological journey, is soon to be apparent in the construction of the text itself.

Towards the end of *A Place in England* Douglas is preparing for university and is shown making tentative attempts to write poetry, inspired, not by the Lake Romantics, but, significantly for the novel's final metafictional twist, by a trio of modernists - e e cummings, Ezra Pound and T.S. Eliot. The aesthetic shift from Romanticism to Modernism is symbolic of Douglas's determination to escape from the shadow of his ancestors as hired men, but is also textually significant as a stumbling stage in his mirroring of Kathleen's hesitancy in announcing his new self: 'He was aware of a necessity for secrecy. Everybody he knew in the town would think such urgency directed to such an end as writing as proof of conceit or senselessness' (*PE*, p.185). Abandoning his poetry, Douglas picks up a notebook in which he has been making preliminary sketches for a novel. Bragg's description of Douglas's intentions reads as a manifesto for the trilogy's ideological stance:

> It was to span three generations and concern a family much like his own. The more he read, the more he thought that his sort of people appeared in books as clowns, criminals or 'characters' and it offended him. Everywhere, it seemed to him then, on the wireless, on television, in films and magazines, ordinary people were credited with no range of feeling, no delicacy of manner, no niceties of judgment: and women like his mother laughed at as 'chars', their opinions and attitudes thought to be trite because their expression was, often, commonplace. One reason for writing the book would be to set that right.
>
> (*PE*, p.186)

The scale of Douglas's literary ambition is announced in its distinctive class-oriented self-fashioning to be measured and judged against an impressive canonical ancestry: 'A family history which concerns a family who do not consider themselves a family (unlike The Buddenbrooks or the The Brangwens) and have always been strangers to history, even their own' (*PE*, p.186). Both families are well chosen -

Lawrence's *The Rainbow* (1915)[12] and *Women in Love* (1921) suggest the continuity of the regional novel, whereas Thomas Mann's *Buddenbrooks* (1901), on the theme of family disintegration, written with a decidedly autobiographical slant, offers a key to Douglas's own planned epic. But Douglas is confused about the sort of novel he ought to aspire to, sometimes attracted to a modernist stream of consciousness story 'told inside the head of a man who was dying' and then reverting to traditional realist models and writing 'out such as he considered "the facts"' (*PE*, p.187). The perceived binary of modernism/realism is an important one both for Douglas's fictional fiction and for Bragg's actual fiction. Douglas's attitude to realist texts is ambiguous, sometimes thinking 'that the writer of such fiction was a dinosaur' and then reconsidering such an attitude as a scholastically learned 'pose, adopted from the intellectual essays in which most things he wanted to do were described as decaying, or disintegrating or dead' (*PE*, pp.187-8). Something of an advanced warning about the Trilogy's formal status is signposted here, alerting the reader against a too complacent acceptance of the realist text. Whilst *A Place in England* is opposed to what John Carey labels, in *The Intellectuals and the Masses*, as the class-bound elitist modernism of, say, Virginia Woolf or Wyndham Lewis, Bragg nevertheless has a modernist/postmodernist surprise in store, every bit as revelatory as Kathleen's transformation.

In Part Four of *A Place in England*, called 'Arriving', Douglas has arrived professionally as a successful novelist, with two books published

12. Douglas's reference to the Brangwens sets off a multi-faceted intertextual link. In *The Hired Man*'s opening pages the schoolmaster, Mr Stephens, reads aloud Wordsworth's poem *Yew Trees* (1804) to Douglas's newly married grandparents. Not only is 'Yew Tree Cottage' the name of the farm to which the Brangwens move in *The Rainbow*, but it is also quoted at length in *A Hired Man* and is one of nine Wordsworth poems chosen by Bragg for inclusion in his *Cumbria In Verse* (1984) anthology. Particularly pertinent to my reading of the trilogy is Tim Fulford's *Landscape, Liberty and Authority* (1996) which offers a radical and convincing analysis of *Yew Trees* as a patriotic and nationalistically inflected narrative, making the 'Lorton yew an object so steady, permanent and single, yet so old and rooted in a named English landscape that it embodies English history', suggesting 'a sturdy independence resulting from a rooted attachment to a local place [that] is a defining characteristic of Englishmen' (p.198). I would also draw attention to Fulford's argument that *Yew Trees* is symbolically divided, providing the raw material for weapons of national glory - '... those that crossed the sea/And drew their sounding bows at Azincour/Perhaps at earlier Crecy, or Poictiers' - but also arming a rebellious local pride against the monarch - 'Not loth to furnish weapons for the hands/Of Umfraville or Percy ere they marched/To Scotland's heaths ...' (*Lyrical Ballads*, p.194). This sense of ambiguity towards the authority of the national family not only glosses the family disunited theme of Thomas Mann's *Buddenbrooks* but also anticipates the difficult relationships between fathers and sons that recur throughout the trilogy.

and a third in draft. Bragg's insertion of six pages from the planned new novel creates a playful metafictional[13] metamorphosis of Douglas's tentatively titled *The Throstle's Nest* into the materially real book we have in our hands, complete with its 'The Throstle's Nest' as Part Three. It should be said at the outset that whatever the level of textual sophistication at work here, Part Four of *A Place in England* remains a model of metafictional accessibility making no unreasonable demands upon the reader to be familiar with metafiction or its history to enjoy the book. Bragg's framing device only becomes apparent on page 221, with Douglas awaiting a visit from his father and checking 'through what he had just written of the town he had called Thurston. Deliberately using real names, deliberately allowing his own sentimental feeling about the place to find expression, it was, he thought, a message to his parents' (*AE*, p.221). And at this point everything changes and we are forced to reconsider not only the nature of the text but also the extent to which Bragg's seemingly realist novel is engaging with modernism, extending his technical reach, and providing textual cover for a still somewhat reluctant readiness to admit the sheer extent of his recapturing of personal and community memory in semi-autobiographical form. This latter question will not be fully addressed for nearly another 30 years, until the publication of *A Soldier's Return* in 1999.

To date there has not been any serious exegesis of *A Place in England*, with reviewers generally restricting themselves to noting the accuracy and liveliness of the dialogue, or, more interestingly, in the case of *The Times Literary Supplement*, drawing attention to the 'conflict between dialogue and narration which expresses a tension between two styles of language and living [which] Raymond Williams would call ... "educated" and "customary"' (13.11.70 *TLS* bound vol. p.1317). In looking for a suitable theoretical context to widen the discussion of the novel I became engrossed in reading Kerry Higgins Wendt's 2011 PhD dissertation, *The Epigraphic Character: Fiction and Metafiction in the Twentieth-Century Novel*.[14] Wendt defines the epigraphic character as one

13. The critical term 'metafiction' is generally used when describing fiction about fiction. By including Douglas's text within a text *A Place in England* openly comments on its own fictional status.

14. Wendt's study looks in detail at James Joyce's *A Portrait of the Artist as a Young Man*, Flann O'Brien's *At Swim-Two-Birds*, and Graham Greene's *The End of the Affair*. It makes interesting observations about the fictional presentations of writers' writing which alerted me to its usefulness as an analytical tool in discussing *A Place in England*. I am indebted to Kerry for sending me a copy of her dissertation and allowing me to quote from it.

who 'overtly voices ideas about fiction, writing or literature' in novels that 'lie somewhere between conventional fiction and metafiction'. Such novels, of which I read *A Place in England* to be an example, use 'metafictional means to talk about how stories work ... and the epigraphic character [such as, for example, Douglas] is a metafictional element that exists as a central part of conventional fiction' (Abstract, p.1). The joy of Wendt's approach lies in its exuberant catholicism permitting a reading of *A Place in England* alongside the very same Modernists that Douglas/Bragg is exercised over:

> Joyce and Woolf use the epigraphic character differently, of course. What's exciting about the epigraphic character is that, although we can define it, isolate it, identify it, and even trace its origins, the ways authors can and do use it are virtually unlimited. And, although it grows out of modernist concerns with art, modernist compositional structures, and modernist subjects, it is not bound to those concerns. The epigraphic character is modernist in origin, but structural in nature, and thus can appear in any novel about any subject.
>
> (*Epigraphic*, p.10)

We can read Douglas as critiquing fiction from within *The Throstle's Nest* in parallel to Bragg's narrative technique, bringing 'metafiction and conventional fiction together in a paradoxical counterintuitive way - a way which suggests that [their] aims are not mutually exclusive' (*Epigraphic*, p.11). Wendt argues convincingly that a novel - such as *A Place in England* - 'can reflect on itself without employing a special character to do so' but that they can, like Douglas, be 'elevated to that level for brief moments, and then disappear into the story as otherwise "normal" characters. Their main function is as participants in the story' (*Epigraphic*, p.12). The essential requirement for such a character is that he or she be fully committed to the practical/theoretical pursuit of the creative arts, and Douglas clearly fits this profile. Bragg uses him, not only to voice his own ideas about the purpose of the novel - in this instance to resurrect voiceless histories - but also as a character deeply embedded in text and able to provide a structural dynamic.

Wendt concludes that the 'epigraphic novel speaks to the mystery of writerly creation, to fiction as opposed to ideas about fiction, to fiction as it embodies reality' (*Epigraphic*, p.228), and in this context we might reflect upon Bragg concluding his novel with Douglas's father telling him that his fiction falls short of reality:

> 'You've been very careful, Douglas. A bit like a detective, I thought you've covered up where it mattered most. That's what I mean by "appreciate". You haven't got me, though.'
>
> 'No. I had to invent you. I don't know you well enough to describe you.'
>
> 'Now what does that mean?'
>
> 'It means I don't really know what you feel about anything: say about what you've read. A little, a lot; mild, or murderous; flattered, or furious; a bit proud or a bit disgusted - I do not know.'
>
> 'No, Douglas. And you'll never get to know, either! And I'll tell you another thing - you haven't said the half of it about yourself, either. Not the half!'
>
> (*PE*, pp.242-3)

Here, in a brief dialogic exchange, Bragg foregrounds the question of how fiction and metafiction work together in the semi-autobiographical realist novel. *A Place in England* is not a modernist novel but it displays a hitherto critically unrecognised modernist concern with authorial consciousness, narrative perspective, and an exposure, late in the text, of its own fictive status. It has 'come out' and future critical commentary needs to recognise and explore its metafictional turn whilst assessing its contribution to the realist-documentary history of neglected voices asserting their right to a place in England.

The trilogy's concluding novel, *Kingdom Come* (1980), appears after a ten year hiatus and, unlike its predecessors, shifts its centre of gravity to become essentially a London, even a trans-Atlantic, novel. It merits attention in the context of this study as an extended footnote commenting on a Cumbrian culture caught in the textual act of becoming minor. The earlier novels' sense of individual and group progress no longer exists and Douglas's work and marriage difficulties are symptomatic of a larger social malaise. The 1970s setting of the novel was a decade of divisive and damaging industrial disputes fought out against a background of rapidly rising inflation which saw many staple foodstuffs quadruple in price. The miners' strike in 1972 forced Edward Heath's Conservative Government to ration electricity supplies and impose a three-day working week, postal strikes left mail untouched for two months, whilst the public service strikes that occurred during James Callaghan's Labour administration of 1978-9 gave the impression, however unjustified, of a trade-union movement out of control. *Kingdom Come* appears soon after Margaret Thatcher's 1979 Conservative election victory, promising to curb union power and heralding an extended period in which local community voices would be disregarded in favour of a free-market approach to economic management at the same time as central government imposed its diktat on Local Authorities.

*Kingdom Come* sees Douglas returning from a business trip to America and viewing Cumbria from the air at a distance from which 'it seemed, full of strength, ancient and enduring' (*KC*, p.5). The disconnect between appearance and reality is, however, apparent in the shrinkage of a Cumbrian world becoming minor as seen from Douglas's 'god's-eye view, it was all like a charming model in a natural history museum' (ibid.). Cumbria has become a location to be traversed whilst experienced from the liminal enclosed space of an aircraft that encourages an anaesthetised language no longer warmed by memory and place: 'He himself, he thought, would probably die in a motorway car accident, an aeroplane crash or of a heart attack in a side street of a foreign city. With luck' (*KC*, pp.5-6).

'Death', and its unlikely textual companion 'luck' circulates through the novel as a shadow narrative configuring a residue of references that, whilst tangential to its dominant narrative, demonstrates the stresses inherent within it. Part One ends with the death of old John Tallentire, and with his passing goes the source of Douglas's early inspirational semi-autobiographical writing. Attending the funeral, John is 'sickeningly self-absorbed'. "The spiral", he said to himself, "has come a full circle"' (*KC*, p.151). At this low point in his life Douglas is tormented by the mysterious death of an old school-friend, to the extent that he 'had come to identify completely with the man who had sought death and blundered to it in those thin, wet Northern woods' (ibid.). In terms of a shadow narrative it is an admitted 'uncanny identification' (ibid.), that becomes the basis for Douglas's next book, bringing with it the possibility of a lucrative Hollywood contract. The shadow narrative's unanswered question of 'why had Alan gone into the woods and perished; allowed himself to die' (*KC*, p.50) contributes not only an alternative trajectory to that pursued by Douglas, but also one offering an oppositional discourse to the commercially successful story of another loner, the rock musician Raven, whose life Douglas documents on film. Alan and Raven represent opposite dimensions of the dominant culture's values that Douglas confronts in a search to find a language - filmic and textual, documentary and confessional - that simultaneously reinforces and questions those values.

Alan's unexplained suicide in the wooded Fells becomes, in Douglas's story 'Death of a Friend', a shadow narrative in which Bragg suggests the personal and creative tensions inherent in Douglas's own life and in which he attempts to answer existential questions. Did he die 'in order to find some order, some satisfaction in life, some connection with his beginnings, and release the pain and drag of the past'; was he, as Douglas's story will suggest 'within some sight of an illumination' (*KC*, p.99). What excites me about Alan's story is its oppositional discourse, an easy to overlook critical space on the margins of mainstream cultural values which nevertheless has real-life counterparts linking the Fells to the wilds of North America. Jon Krakauer's *Into The Wild* (1996) is the true account, later successfully filmed, of a young man, Chris McCandless, who in 1992 gives away all his savings to charity and abandons all his possessions, and walks alone into the wilds of Alaska: 'When the boy headed off into the Alaska bush, he entertained no illusions that he was trekking into a land of milk and honey; peril, adversity, and Tolstoyan renunciation were precisely what he was seeking' (*Intro*, p. x). He also found death. Even more closely related to Alan's pre-meditated death is that of Beat poet Lew Welch who, in 1971, at the age of 44, disappears into the foothills of the Sierras and is never seen again. He leaves only a note: 'I can't make anything out of it - never could. I had great visions but never could bring them together with reality. I used it all up. It's all gone ... Goodbye' (*I Remain*, Vol.2, p.187). Linking the deaths of Alan, Chris and Lew provides a scaffold for a considered retrospective interpretation of *Kingdom Come*, drawing attention to the semiotics of aesthetics and money, death and luck. As Alfie, the film producer, tells Douglas, 'I read your story [of

Alan] by accident to tell you the truth' (*KC*, p.334) - a lucky accident that carries the ironic promise of realising a radical destabilising oppositional Lakeland voice within Hollywood's culturally conservative hegemonic practice.

A specifically Cumbrian oppositional discourse that addresses national concerns is centred on a strike at Thurston's major factory, its largest employer, and on the internal and inter-union disputes that threaten any sense of workers' solidarity. Thurston is in the textual eye of the storm that disturbed industrial relationships in the 1970s, and Bragg presents the dispute as representative of larger national ills: 'The media were in an orgy of verbal overkill on the desperate social, economic and moral short-term straits Britain was in. The lash of blame provoked shouts and whispers up and down the island' (*KC*, p.294). The novel is cautious in its assessment of localised struggle, led by union steward Harry Tallentire, with a nagging suspicion that appeals to community class solidarity are ultimately futile when capital shapes the national economic framework. The slow draining away of local economic influence is encapsulated in a paragraph that presents Thurston as typical of 1970s communities in turmoil as they become increasingly subservient to national transformations of economic space:

> Like much of the rest of the country, the workers at Thurston's principal factory - which directly supported well over half the work force in the town and indirectly propped up much of the rest - were in a deadlocked dispute. It seemed endemic at the beginning of that autumn. Disputes about pay differentials, about manning, about bonus payments, new machinery, comparability rates and studies, about production targets; management-union disputes, union-union disputes, internal union disputes - all of them lumped together by much of the media and variously dubbed as "madness", "suicide" and "the end of Britain". The reaction was uniformly extreme: the solution, too, was uniform: strikes and picket lines. Instant industrial heroes and victims and martyrs were pulped into prominence.
>
> (*KC*, p.295)

Bragg's coverage of a dispute centred on an industrial grievance and on the self-same issue of the closed-shop versus individual conscience - the chapter is titled 'A Matter of Conscience' - that exercised Harry's great-step-uncles in *A Hired Man*, recovers something of the wounding experience of the ordinary, providing a counterbalance to caricatured and 'pulped into prominence' media accounts of industrial unrest. Bragg's response is far more problematic, far more guarded, aware that strikes can foster individualism as well as group solidarity. I am minded to recall here the sequence in Williams's *Border Country* in which Jack Meredith, a railway signalman, previously only one among many, refuses to join the 1926 General Strike and remains unmoved by local union organiser Morgan Rosser's arguments, countering them with his own tersely argued strong principles. In *Kingdom Come* this dialectic of individual versus group interest is played out between Harry and an older man, Joseph Fletcher, who, having fought and been decorated in the Korean War, has developed a marked aversion to all forms of authority: 'They - i.e. *all* big institutions, bosses, unions, politicians, newspapers - They - were all to be looked at thoroughly sceptically and avoided if at all possible' (*KC*, p.297). Whereas Williams contrives a suitably comradely and peaceful solution to his dispute, Bragg is perhaps more honest in showing the intimidation simmering close to the surface in the unrest of the 1970s. When Fletcher crosses the picket line, Harry is 'ashamed of the bullying taunts and threats which met the man at the gate. And impressed by Fletcher's apparent disdain' (ibid.). Harry is forced to reflect on his deeply held beliefs in trade unionism, and the merits of the closed-shop, when some of the strike committee raid 'Fletcher's pigeon loft [wringing] the necks of all his prize racing pigeons, as well as trampling over all his vegetables' (ibid.). Bragg's unflinching depiction of such events in Thurston is representative of much that was happening elsewhere in the country, not least in London, and is, to my mind, unique in the publishing speed of its response to unsettling contemporary events ignored at the time by other serious literary novelists.[15]

15. At the time of *Kingdom Come*'s publication Bragg was intimately involved in the professional world of metropolitan broadcasting, having worked for the BBC on such series as *Monitor*, and becoming editor of ITV's *The South Bank Show* in 1978. He would, therefore, have been very much aware, for example, of the manning disputes in Fleet Street and at the National Theatre that provide the national factual background to Thurston's fictional strike. Peter Hall's diary entry for 19 March 1979 makes interesting reading as presenting the stark

Continued next page ☞

Novels analysing collective industrial action, and prepared to acknowledge the individual injustices sometimes involved, remain thin on the ground with, perhaps, only Jonathan Coe's *The Rotters' Club*, published two decades later, fully exploring industrial unrest and the eruption of violence within a closely defined community setting, in this instance through the experience of a British Leyland shop steward in Birmingham in the 1970s when the future of the British car industry was in the balance.

It is a notable achievement that Bragg's novel appears almost contemporaneously with the events recorded and competes, therefore, with the immediacy of broadcast and newspaper commentary. It is also sobering to reflect upon the novel's exposure of the vulnerability of working-class communities such as Thurston/Wigton, in the face of national movements and the suggestion, implicit in the novel's closing chapter - 'London Lives' - that the Cumbrian Trilogy is witnessing history passing elsewhere. Bragg knows that there is no going back even while he hesitates to make the final break: 'It would be easy to say that the time had passed when a writer could successfully isolate himself within a rural community - but Douglas knew that ... there would be someone in some remote place contradicting him by turning out fine work' but for him 'the necessities which drove him now were urban. Even in the country he had no escape from the global city' (*KC*, p.309). Yet even now there remains a reluctance to accept the logic of a community in decline and Thurston is privileged with the last word of an inherited sense of place as a young John Tallentire, in an echo of his great grandfather quietly leaving the house in the opening pages of *A Hired Man*, gets up quickly 'so as not to disturb his mother' (*KC*, p.351), to stake out 'his territory' for a day's fishing: 'Then he made his first cast

15 continued....
reality behind the act of vandalism towards Joseph Fletcher:
> Very nasty intimidation going on all day. When the milk float crossed the picket line our peaceful pickets took out their screwdrivers and punctured scores of the little cardboard containers. The butcher had his burglar alarm set off and the back door of his van forced open. Yolande Bird, who'd unwisely left her car in the theatre car park with an NT sticker on it, found that it had been completely smashed up, all windows broken, and her belongings taken. Michael Redgrave's taxi was stopped when he came to rehearse *Close of Play* and he, despite having Parkinson's disease and being hardly able to walk, had to hobble the length of the building to the stage door. Peggy Ashcroft's taxi was finally let through, but she can't walk at all at the moment because of her invalid knee. (Edt. John Goodwin. *Peter Hall's Diaries. The Story of a Dramatic Battle* pp.422-3)

of the day. It was perfect' (ibid.). With these final sentences Bragg deftly avoids narrative closure, allowing the text to reimmerse itself in a persistent sense of place whilst casting its narrative line in such a way as to involve the reader in the contemporaneity of social and political issues articulated and given a historic perspective in a specific Cumbrian place in England.

# FIVE

## 'THIS UNCOMPLAINING ACQUIESCENCE'
### *JOSH LAWTON*

It is tempting to read Bragg's London novel, *The Nerve*, published a year after *A Place in England*, as the novel Douglas Tallentire might have written once he had completed his semi-autobiographical Thurston Bildungsroman. *The Nerve* is also very much the anomic text that Tom Graham, the aspiring novelist of Bragg's first published novel, might have been contemplating after his move from Cumbria to London. Indeed, Ted Johnson, the first-person narrator of *The Nerve*, begins his story with an enveloping sense of anomie brought on by the sound of a dustcart like a 'chained animal' (p. 7) that recalls Tom Graham's awakening in London at the conclusion of *For Want of a Nail* to the sight of a crane that reminds him of a 'great scaffolded tree' (*WN*, 318), both images of the natural world left behind in Cumbria. Given these lingering ties to a Cumbrian textual hinterland it is perhaps unsurprising that in the event *The Nerve* represents no more than a short literary break in London. It is a sharply observed account of mental anguish and urban neurosis that deserves attention on its own merits, but which is notable in the context of this study for its narrator's inability to free himself from thoughts of home. His early morning musings on cosmopolitan attitudes towards the perceived otherness of rural communities provides an illuminating, albeit unconscious, preface to Bragg's next, and very different, Cumbrian novel, *Josh Lawton*:

> My flat is in north London in Hampstead, near the Heath. It's strange and rather amusing that I should be in a district which attracts as many clichés as the one in which I'd been brought up. People in the Lake District - where I was born - were constantly being caricatured as 'Dalesmen', 'Slow-thinking but hard-headed', 'Shrewd countrymen' and so on; so many tourists *wanted* the people to be as unchanging and as easy to identify as the Lakes themselves that there was even more of sloppy social anthropologizing than usual.

Everyone who has lived in a rural area must know how useless it is to attempt to counteract the weight of this patronizing opinion: in the Lake District, a rural area which was also a beauty spot, the weight was sometimes oppressive. And at university - I went to Bristol - there was the cliché of the Northerner to be bored by: where he'd once been thought of as Blunt and Thrifty and Common he was now expected to be Bright and Abrasive and Original.      (*N*, pp.12-13)

Whilst Bragg's originality lies in writing about the lives and tragedies of working-class characters with serious respect, he does so in *Josh Lawton* in a tightly disciplined manner without being 'sloppy' or resorting to cliché. His achievement is to articulate the desires and grief of a markedly inarticulate pair of lovers. The story eulogises the inevitably doomed eponymous handsome, even beautiful, hero who, whilst the object of almost universal desire within a tightly delineated area of the Northern Fells, has few desires of his own and no self-knowledge of his own attractiveness, coupled with little recognition of its effect upon others in the community. Maureen Telford, a girl from a rough amoral working-class family in Thurston falls in love with an image of Josh as a figure of masculinity and erotic energy that she discovers too late he cannot live up to. Her rival for Josh's affection is Cedric Tyson, an ex-soldier displaying a veneer of toughness masking a weak personality, but who is able, nevertheless, along with the local vicar, to express his love in suitably articulate terms that transcend the romantic banalities of cliché and provide the commentary that justifies the *Times Literary Supplement*'s reference to the novel as 'a village *Romeo and Juliet*' (14 July, 1972). In a closing scene of raw brutality that denies any sense of reductive sentimentality or rural whimsy the deaths of both Josh and Cedric are required by their inability to be incorporated into the closed society they inhabit. This is not the socially cohesive Thurston of the Cumbrian trilogy but rather a godless world of loneliness, unpleasantness, brawling, fury and despair that totally subverts any comfortable and distant conventional metropolitan notions of the bucolic contented peasantry of pastoral idylls.

Somewhat teasingly misleading at the novel's outset there is a hint of the traditional and surviving rural England of cultural myth still present in the person of Josh. 'There was something marvellous about him, something bottomless in his willingness to be of service ... the transparency of his good nature brought out instances of goodness and godliness and neighbourliness' (*JL.* p.6). Bragg presents him as the personification of childlike innocence, suggesting a lingering but fragile link to prelapsarian visions of a Golden Age such that '[o]lder people would bring forward comparisons from their youth, those they had known, those they had heard of' (ibid.). Josh, the orphaned farm-labourer is noble, uncorrupted, innocent and as beautifully handsome as Billy Budd and is, therefore, intertextually groomed to meet his doom. The comparison with Herman Melville's story 'Billy Budd' is instructive because in both texts the narrative unfolds within inherently knowable and undividable social and political worlds - ship and village offer classic images of uniform totalities in which spatial damage and spatial recovery are tightly policed. More significantly, both texts are a re-telling of the parable of the Fall. Robert Milder's interpretation of the internal logic of Melville's story might also be profitably read as a commentary on Josh's 'fall'. 'Billy "falls" from innocence to experience, simplicity to complexity, childhood to adulthood; historically, from primitivism to modern civilization; and sexually from androgyny - a happy balance of masculine strength and feminine sweetness and beauty - to a more severe maleness consonant with the repressions of patriarchal society' (Intro.*Billy Budd, Sailor and Selected Tales*, pp. xxxiii-iv).

Josh also inherits a number of intertextual genes from his literary predecessors and I would like to outline these, if only to demonstrate the critical importance of reading Bragg's regional texts in wider historical and international contexts than they are sometimes afforded. To conclude that the regional novel assumes only a practical dimension set firmly within the English rural tradition is to fall victim to the very generalisation that the narrator of *The Nerve* recognises and descries: '-this addiction to labelling is so pervasive that even English class snobbery cannot fully account for it. Probably it is something to do with tribalism - a wish to keep groups both small and quickly identifiable for easier co-habitation or more rapid extermination' (*Nerve*, p.13). In claiming a degree of trans-Atlantic connectedness with 'Billy Budd', I would wish to draw attention in *Josh Lawton* to precisely those problematic and haunting meanings which Melville sets into circulation in specific ways. Both Billy and Josh are, for instance, orphans - Billy is told 'that I was found in a pretty silk-lined basket hanging one morning from the knocker of a good man's door in Bristol' (*Billy Budd*, p.287) whilst Josh is raised by an equally good man, the vicar in charge of the 'Fellways Boys' Home' (*JL*,p.4). (There is, however, a hint of 'the vicar being "funny" and interfering with the boy' (*JL*, p.5) which, although adamantly dismissed by the housekeeper as malicious gossip, nevertheless casts the same shadow over Ullaby as falls over the deck of the *Bellipotent*.) In both boys/men there lurks a yearned-for attachment to a parental figure - Captain Vere/the friar Laurence-like vicar - who will ultimately fail them; the vicar is even refused his request to preside over Josh's funeral.

In both narratives the young heroes are slow to anger and anxious to placate rather than fight and yet both establish their masculine credentials, under interpretative misreadings from their feminised good looks, at an early stage in their respective stories by a sudden and unexpected turn to physical force. Deliberately provoked by a fellow sailor who suspects Billy's feminised good looks to characterise physical weakness, Billy 'forebore with him and reasoned with him in a pleasant way' (*Billy Budd*, p.283) until a final insult leads him to give 'the burly fool a terrible drubbing' (ibid.). Similarly, when a visiting football spectator from a neighbouring village verbally abuses Ullaby residents before singling out the vicar as an 'embarrassment' who is only saved from the madhouse by his dog-collar, Josh warns the mocker to stop, and when he persists he flies at him like a 'whirlwind', flooring the three friends who go to his aid (*JL*, p.8). Both men's retaliatory violence is an explicit instance of directly expressed and then soon forgotten anger. This is in stark in contrast to Josh's friend Cedric's resentment over an insult that slowly festers before surfacing in a cowardly attempt at revenge taken upon the tormentor's dog. Josh and Billy share a disposition towards an 'uncomplaining acquiescence all but cheerful' (*Billy Budd*, p.281), 'something bottomless in his [Josh's] willingness to be of service' (*JL*, p.6). Billy has 'a nature that, as Claggart magnetically felt, had in its simplicity never willed malice or experienced the reactionary bite of that serpent' (*Billy Budd*, p.311), or, as Josh's fellow farm-worker Norman succinctly puts it, 'There's no bad in that man' (*JL*,p.37). Above all, both texts open with the common shared theme of the handsome, even beautiful, orphan boy, an unselfconsciously charismatic figure who is presented as a cynosure for all to admire. Billy has a 'smooth face all but feminine in purity of natural complexion' (*Billy Budd*, p.286) whilst

Josh has a 'sweet, clear face which in feature and complexion was lovelier than any in the village' and which 'stayed unblemished' to an extent that 'girls came up and asked him what he used for his skin' (*JL*, p.5). And all this persistence of outward perfection despite both men living a working life exposed to all weathers.

Melville and Bragg are exercised not so much by the prevalence of evil in a fallen world but, rather, by how such a world responds to the unexpected presence of pure innocence, which, in these two instances, is personified in the nature of two simpletons. Whilst *Josh Lawton* differs radically from 'Billy Budd' with the introduction of a complicating female love-interest, the intertextual echoes deserve more than a passing parenthetical glance in terms of an equivalence of embryonic coding directing us to read Bragg's text as a dense reflection of the nature, function and allure of young male beauty, whether within the closeted space of a British man-of-war or within the still ostensibly sacred configurations of the rural family.

Cedric Tyson may also be read in the shadow of Melville's Master-at-arms, John Claggart, with whom he shares a closeted past whose unknowability makes both men subjects of suspicion. In Claggart's case '[n]othing was known of his former life' (*Billy Budd*, p.299) and because he 'never made allusion to his previous life ashore; these were circumstances which in the dearth of exact knowledge as to his true antecedents opened to the invidious a vague field for unfavourable surmise' (*Billy Budd*, p.300). Something of a reverse history of privacy prevails in Cedric's case, a character who is initially well-known as born and raised in Ullaby but whose twenty-five years of overseas army service in the Far East remain a subject for conjecture, unknown beyond the occasional sexual boast that Cedric slips into bar-room conversation to ingratiate himself with 'the lads' (*JL*, p.9), and whose lack of promotion from the ranks, given his professional boasting, remains problematic. Added to which, his willingness at age forty to exist solely on his army pension and to live with a mother for whom he shows callous disregard, combined with his ostentatious display of a body image dressed in 'black leather jacket, black boots and black gauntlets' (*JL*, p.3) whilst overseeing Josh's fell-running from his big motor-bike, only adds to an air of person-place dissonance. There is indeed 'something about him that the more respectable people in the village instinctively shrank from' (*JL*, p.9). Although not explicitly stated in the text, Cedric's time in the Far East coincides almost exactly with the final years of British rule and a concomitant conclusive period of prolonged systematic violence. Cedric represents part of the jetsam of Empire that, in his case, washes up in a closed and isolated regional community where English parochialism and insularity have screened out the messier realities of colonial occupation. His sudden reappearance threatens to reveal aspects of rural community life that otherwise remain repressed or occluded.

There is no specific unambiguous reference in *Josh Lawton* outing Cedric as a homosexual character, although the text directs (some of) its readers to reach this conclusion by knowing hints that remain short of irrefutable textual evidence. In this respect the reader is very much in the same judgemental position of those long-term Ullaby village residents who may, or may not, be aware of the clues on offer and are able to decode any camp epistemology. A good example, from early in the novel, is of Cedric's presumed yearning gazes and subtle glances of homoerotic sexuality that find expression in his obsessive need to be with Josh, encoded in his multiple viewings of the film version of Norman Mailer's World War II novel *The Naked and the Dead* (1948) as well as reading the book itself. Cedric has fantasies of himself in the role of a Royal Canadian Mounted Policeman, or as the sort of tough-guy character portrayed in films by Robert Mitchum or, significantly, as 'that soldier in *The Naked and the Dead* he'd seen the film four times and read the book' (*JL* p.21).[1] Mailer's novel is noticeable for a distinct lack of any descriptions of lasting happy family life or, indeed, of any long-term successful male-female relationships. Susan Gubar, in her essay 'This Is My Rifle, This Is My Gun; World War II and the Blitz on Women' summarises the novel's misogynist drift: 'Whether they are dead, disloyal, or frigid wives, randy girlfriends, or raunchy whores, the female characters in *The Naked and the Dead* play no part in the action except as "gauges" located in the "Time Machine" section that returns us to civilian life before the war' (p.253).

Any doubts about the level of homoerotic frustration in Cedric's

---

1. The film version of *The Naked and the Dead* was released in 1958. Reviewing it in the U.S. on 31 December 1957 the magazine *Variety* found it bore little more than a surface resemblance to the novel, with the emphasis entirely on action scenes. Contemporary posters for the film depict three gun-toting marines, with a much smaller image of a female dressed in a negligée relegated to the visual margin. Cedric would most likely have read the novel in the 1961 U.K. Panther paperback edition.

gaze are overtly removed when, faced with Josh's marriage to a 'bloody effing tart' (*JL*, p.72), he transfers his near-pathological detestation of women onto his vulnerable mother. The text makes clear that 'his preoccupation was Josh' (*JL*, p.71) when Cedric sadistically delights in telling his mother about the time when his army 'mate used [Cedric's knife] to skin those Malays they caught in the jungle. He learnt to skin them alive from the Ghurkas. Every inch of skin off the man and him still not dead' (ibid.). He warns his mother that the same will happen to her if she breathes a word of this in the village. But the reader has been given what James Creech refers to as the wink that 'emerges out of taboo and secrecy' (*Closet Writing*, p.93). If this knowing reader extends their textual cruising to the novel's cruising, they may well reflect on this same knife's role within the novel's hermeneutic code as it becomes the object that kills its tormenting owner, but in the hands of Blister, Cedric's chief male tormentor.

Cedric's personality and sexual orientation are sharply contrasted with those of Josh in Bragg's description of their respective domestic spaces. Cedric's bedroom has a sinister aspect of secrets closely guarded and of repressed onanistic desires kept literally under lock and key. There exists a feeling of chill loneliness in the description of a retreat that is tellingly referred to as 'Cedric's Empire', a marginalised space in retreat from the real thing and in which the subaltern exile cannot accommodate himself:

> In his bedroom - the door he secured with a double lock he'd fitted on himself - was Cedric's Empire. The walls were a mind-swirling montage of heroes and heroines, faces and bodies carefully cut out of shiny magazines and glued on to the uneven surfaces - athletes, body-builders, models, champions of motor-bike and racing-car, film stars, footballers, famous personalities - faces and limbs everywhere, sometimes three or four layers deep where he'd found new idols and been forced to cover the old. Sometimes he'd just lie on the bed and look around for hours, try to pretend he was going out with some of these people, what they'd say, what he'd do, where they'd go. He could have a good laugh sometimes when he'd think of things that could go wrong. Or he'd read, in this room,

one of his war books perhaps and not feel exposed as
he'd often felt in the barracks nor yet lonely because of
all the familiar faces that would do as he wanted.

(JL,p.12)

The image here is of a dead space, enclosed by photographic images, a multi-layered palimpsest of erotic longing from a distant unattainable world. Cedric's room might be compared with my earlier description of Old Tom's shed in *For Want of a Nail*, where the photographs and objects, whilst removed from any family links, had at least the merit of being intimately connected to the working history of Tom's community life, whereas Cedric's images and books are impersonal and culled from a world far removed from the local community.[2]

In *The Poetics of Space*, Gaston Bachelard proposes a study of images of intimacy residing in the poetics of the house as 'a provisional refuge or an occasional shelter' (p.xxxvi) providing the 'ground for taking the house as *a tool for analysis* of the human soul' (p.xxxviii). If Cedric's bedroom as a space of enclosed immobility and secrecy provides a psychological insight into his disturbed state of mind, then Josh's move into the marital home reveals him as an aspiring 'poet of furniture' (*Poetics*, p.78) whose enthusiasm and diligence in cleaning, painting and preparing the rooms for his bride Maureen's arrival suggest a holy space, reflecting her impression of her husband as 'the brightly painted saint he reminded her of' (*JL*, p.59). Josh attempts to create a pure space 'all re-done by himself, papered, painted, mended, plastered, fixed, wired' (*JL*, pp.88-9) in which '[e]verything fitted in' (ibid.) and is safe-guarded by a 'picture of the blessed Virgin Mary and Child' (ibid) hanging on the kitchen wall. Where Cedric's room threatens to hollow out his soul so that '[s]ometimes in his mind he would machine-gun the entire village' (*JL*, p.12), Josh's kitchen is a living space and his 'love for the house' cannot be contained and is expressed in a rare outburst of song:

---

2. Cedric's perceived strangeness and isolation from intimate village life means that even when he tries to ingratiate himself at the local pub his stories are usually taken, and encouraged, as the boasts of a fantasist, with the result that when he argues on the basis of verifiable fact he is still disbelieved. His contention, for example, that the athlete Herb Elliot trained under Percy Cerutty who revolutionised training by making all his athletes run up and down sand dunes on the Australian coast is greeted with derision (JL,pp.21-2). Yet '..I was galloping over sand-hills ... and splashing through the surf ...' (Herb Elliot, *The Golden Mile*, Cassell, 1961 (p.70).

'My cup's full
And running over.'
He began to sing it - loudly and tunelessly
'So the Lord save me
I'm as happy as can be
My cup's full
And running o, O, O, O, O, Over!' [3]

(*JL*, p.89)

In a novel where Josh finds it painfully difficult to express his feelings, it is significant that it is within the space of his very own personalised dwelling that his voice is no longer anaesthetised. It sings a holy song for an innocent man.

The house as structural metaphor also helps define the vicar's identity. The description of his den carries a sanitised echo of Cedric's photograph-covered bedroom walls, but with the essential difference that the portraits of the young boys/men with whom he is cocooned are personally known to him: 'He looked around his cluttered, crowded room, stuffed with school photographs, college photographs, photographs of relatives and youthful friends and everywhere snaps of the Boys he had fathered' (*JL*, p.183). His room takes on the quality of a shrine to the male - and we note the capitalisation of 'Boys' as a secular equivalent to 'God' - with little space in its claustrophobic surroundings for more than the merest hint of a feminine presence ('photographs of relatives'). The overwhelmingly masculine display indicates the compromised autonomy of the vicar as a voice representing a mixed rural community, relegating him to a classic Victorian ideology of separate spheres of identity. The very choice, or inheritance, of furniture operates as a drug designed to keep the present at bay, whilst providing nostalgic and comforting images of a time when the role of vicar was respected irrespective of the incumbent's personality: 'The furniture was comfortable, Victorian, substantial, too big and too grand for the cottage' (ibid.).

Where Cedric turns to Mailer for his model of post-War masculinity, the vicar keeps faith with the implied solidity of his Victorian furniture, significantly ignoring the Bible in favour of a classic

3  The song is based on a line - 'my cup runneth over' - from Psalm 23, verse 5, and remains popular today. A lively version can be accessed, for instance, sung by *The One Man Quartet* on youtube.com.

Victorian text of male adventure: 'On his lap was *King Solomon's Mine*s, one of his favourites that he read again and again' (ibid.). It is as if the vicar is seeking a vicarious experience of the certainties of Empire that Cedric finds slipping from his grasp in the reality of post-World War II de-colonisation. Henry Rider Haggard's *King Solomon's Mines* (1885) is an African adventure in which male identity is forged at the expense of, and, as in *The Naked and the Dead*, to the exclusion of women.[4] Sex has been exiled from the heart of the narrative so as to make textual space for the construction of the perceived Victorian ideal of masculinity in the figure of the gentleman. The vicar's nervousness around Josh, and reluctance to be seen to influence him in ways which would be his by right as a real rather than a surrogate father, is in keeping with the ethos of innumerable Victorian novels defining gentlemanliness as incorporating the suppression of unsuitable desires, and in particular the repression of any hint of sexual appetite. The ideal of the gentleman and the ideal of Platonic male relationships are both, in this context, problematic. The vicar expresses this conflicted state of being in a secular prayer that is the counterpoint, albeit in the event ineffectual, to Josh's holy song:

> 'Help me to be strong in my dealings with Josh. I taught him Your ways and he believed. I see his soul in his eyes and it is in danger. *I pester him too much*, I know, and I confuse him with my talk which is always serious. *I cannot be at ease with him*, O Lord. His virtue as a boy struck me with awe and even now, when he is sadly mistaken, I run to him to see the working of Your grace. Let me not press him further. Let me leave him

---

4. Gail Ching-Liang Low's *White Skins Black Masks. Representation and Colonialism* looks in detail at *King Solomon's Mines*, interrogating the 'association of women with nature in the Haggardian adventure' in which the 'adventure story's displacement of woman returns in the form of the geography of the land [but with] male identity [being] forged at the expense of - and to the exclusion of - women. In *King Solomon's Mines*, adventurers are obliged to cross Sheba's breast to Kukuanaland to seek the treasure that remains buried in the caverns of this eroticised and feminised bodyscape' (p.49). From the textual evidence available, it seems likely that the vicar has kept his innocence intact through multiple readings of the novel since his own translation of a feminised landscape lacks all physical anatomical detail, and calls upon Greek authority: 'Turning over in his sleep like the huge goddess she is, and across her limbs scurry the night creatures and on her brow is the dew. The Greeks were right about all that' (*JL*,p.41). The metaphoric construction of a woman-landscape identity is an important element of *A Time to Dance*, which I deal with in Chapter 9.

to Your safe-keeping who guards us all, through Jesus
Christ, Thy only beloved Son, who for our sake came
down from Heaven, and was made flesh. Amen.

(JL, p.183, italics added)

The vicar, as an intelligent and remarkably assiduous reader of Rider
Haggard, would understand the novelist's philosophy as, in Gerald
Monsman's summation, a form of 'neo-Platonic romantic *thanatos*, in
which life has corrupted the universal One into many flawed particulars;
but Death, releasing the buried divinity within, permits man to merge
again with the ideal world beyond temporality' ('H. Rider Haggard's
*Nada the Lily*: a Triumph of Translation', p.391). The vicar's tragedy lies
in his being divided from Josh in life and remaining so in death, when,
at his funeral, he 'walked last' (*JL*, p.192). It is Josh and Cedric, purity
and corruption, whom death joins together 'beyond temporality.'

When Maureen Telford, the novel's main female character and
Josh's nemesis, makes a delayed appearance on the scene in Chapter
Four, she brings with her the gender and genre politics of Rider
Haggard's African colonial texts. The vicar, for instance, might well have
sought comfort in Alan Quatermain's (the narrator of *King Solomon's
Mines*) suggestion that one of the attractions of his tale was the virtual
absence of women: '...I can safely say that there is not a petticoat in the
whole history' (p.24). In the novel's sequel, *Alan Quatermain* (1887),
women cannot be entirely excluded, with the consequence that the
eponymous hero and narrator becomes disturbed by his colleagues' first
encounter with the Zulu sister queens and the fatal agency of women's
beauty: '...the beauty of a woman is like the beauty of the lightning, a
destructive thing and a cause of desolation' (p.168). Similarly, Cedric is
apprehensive that the outcome of Josh's infatuation with Maureen will
be desolation - 'You've WASTED yourself!' (*JL*, p.51) but fails to avert
tragedy, in part because he has no personal knowledge or understanding
of the power and energy of determined female sexuality. Herself
possessing the destructive beauty of a Zulu queen, Maureen also inherits
a literary gene from another, domestic, sexually arousing Victorian
woman, namely the handsome barmaid Arabella Donn of Thomas
Hardy's *Jude the Obscure* (1896). Maureen seduces Josh in the same
calculated manner as Arabella seduces Jude Fawley, where
conventionally the male anti-hero would seduce the innocent virgin.

And Josh's innocence is what initially attracts Maureen, unused in her previous relationships or among her troublesome family, to 'such tenderness, nor reticence, nor lack of malice and viciousness' (*JL*, p.59). In her defence, there is little doubt that Maureen has no choice but to take 'command' (ibid.) if there is to be any future in the relationship, but her 'command' is entirely sexual: 'It was when they made love that she saw her power and knew that she could use it' (*JL*, p.63). Their marriage is the union of an ill-assorted couple and based on a sexual premise that is short-lived and all but ended by the birth of a child. As in *Jude the Obscure*, '...their lives were ... ruined by the fundamental error of their matrimonial union, that of having based a permanent contract on a temporary feeling which had no necessary connection with affinities that alone render a life-long comradeship tolerable' (*Jude*, p.76).

The birth of a daughter effectively ends their intimate relationship because, whilst Maureen decides against having any more children, Josh refuses to use contraceptives.[5] Encouraged by her sister Beth, Maureen takes up with the local bully, Blister, and thus initiates a tragic downward spiral. Interestingly, for a novel published in 1972, Bragg inverts the still strong social code that it is the woman's/wife's responsibility to mind the home and bring up the children - Josh

---

5. This is not, however, an entirely logical explanation, because Maureen would have the option of choosing an oral contraceptive, although as a lapsed Catholic this might have caused her a lingering ethico-religious dilemma. Josh's reluctance to use condoms is at one with his textual depiction as one of Nature's simple souls, unable to separate or interfere with the natural progression of cause and effect. An added consideration is that in a tightly-knit village community such as Ullaby there would be a general unexamined historical consensus towards viewing marriage as linked to reproduction. Certainly this appears to be the case in Williams's study of the Cumbrian village of Gosforth in the 1950s in *The Sociology of an English Village* (1956), Chapter III 'Some Aspects of the Life Cycle', where even the 'unborn child is referred to as 't' babby' very much as "living" children are (p.59). On the wider literary front, Sandra M. Gilbert and Susan Gubar's *No Mans Land. The Place of the Woman Writer in the Twentieth Century. Volume 3* (1994) notes that 'improved birth control, legal abortion, women's growing economic independence, and the beginning of the gay liberation movement made it possible for women to uncouple sex from reproduction and to insist on their own capacity for (and right to) pleasure' (p.321). Discussing the new discourse about female eroticism and sexual rights Gilbert and Gubar list such titles as Helen Gurley Brown's *Sex and the Single Girl* (New York: Random House, 1962), Anne Koedt's 'The Myth of the Vaginal Orgasm' (in *Notes from the Second Year: Women, Liberation, Major Writings of the Radical Feminists*. New York: Radical Feminism, 1970), and Nancy Friday's *My Secret Garden* (New York: Pocket, 1974), to which list might be added Germaine Greer's *The Female Eunuch* (London: MacGibbon & Kee, 1970). This is but a very small sample of the feminist texts emerging in the 1960s-1970s, none of which, however, appears a likely best-seller in Thurston and, whilst relevant to Maureen's sexual identity, are written at an ideological level beyond her educational competence.

becomes in effect a single parent in all but accurate nomenclature, leaving Maureen free to indulge in extra-marital sexual adventures, becoming in the process the subject of vicious village gossip. In many respects Maureen can be read as the female equivalent of such 1950s/60s sexually predatory male characters as Arthur Seaton of Alan Sillitoe's *Saturday Night and Sunday Morning* (1958) and his closely modelled successor, Alfie Elkins in Bill Naughton's *Alfie* (1966). Like them, Maureen is aggressive and unrestrainedly hedonistic in the pursuit of pleasure and sexual satisfaction. As the sexual aggressor, Maureen negates still prevalent social notions of the feminine subordination of the silent, acquiescent wife and lover, undermining any lingering 1950s' Freudian view of female sexual incapacity - and making this point at the moment in the early 1970s when the women's liberation movement began to take shape as a potent social and political force. It is perhaps Maureen's unfortunate timing to be enmeshed in an isolated time-warped Cumbrian village, where the increasingly invasive cosmopolitan levelling of tropes of gender difference have yet to take a hold, so that the social roles Ullaby women were expected to fulfil remain fettered to those of Victorian home and family. In her study of femmes fatales in Victorian literature, Nina Auerbach's *Women and Demons: The Life of a Victorian Myth* (1982) sees characters such as Ayesha from Rider Haggard's *She* (1887) and Lady Arabella from Bram Stoker's *The Lair of the Giant Worm* (1911) as symbolically embodying a radical realignment of women's roles as they attempt to free themselves from nineteenth-century domesticity. Bragg's anti-heroine may unconsciously aspire to be part of this tradition but she crucially lacks sufficient self-knowledge, independent economic power and a supportive sisterhood to change her Hardyesque tragic role in the novel's inevitable deathly outcome.

*Josh Lawton* is essentially an unhappy book whose few redeeming moments of joy are finally swamped in its concluding pages by disturbing images of dead and dying hunted animals, prefiguring the loss of human life. The vicar's last desperate attempt to persuade Josh to take Maureen away from the isolation of village life takes place in the woods with the rabbit Josh has killed between them 'smudged with blood at the neck, the fur stiffening' (*JL*, p.113). In the seconds before Josh's manslaughter the hounds are 'barking savagely; they had seen their prey and needed no scent' (*JL*, p.197) as they move in to kill an already injured vixen. The linking of animals and men in death is again indicative of Bragg's debt to Lawrence's animalistic vision in understanding what Tianying Zang, in *D. H. Lawrence's Philosophy of Nature*, labels a 'deep correspondence between natural man and natural world [in which the] myriad things of the universe mirror men and correspond to man's understanding of himself' (p.41). In this, as elsewhere, there is a disciplined aesthetic at play, controlling what Bragg, in his 'Foreword' to Sid Chaplin's regional novel of the North East, *The Watchers and the Watched* (2004), calls 'a territory of life long neglected through ignorance of its nature or fear of ridicule from the Metropolis' (p.5) and in the process transforming a chronicle of the 'English Lower Depths - as they could have been called' (ibid.) into an art form.[6]

The very art of the novel's intertextual construction means that the reader reaches its final pages with a rather depressing prospect of meaninglessness on a social, cultural and personal level in a world of existential fragmented isolation. The darkness and despair that frame the novel are only marginally counterbalanced by a hint of community remorse as the 'women felt the clutch in their throats and yielded' and the 'men, too, had to fight their emotions' (*JL*, p.193) as the coffins were lowered into their graves. In his writing of the universal theme of love and death in the village of Ullaby, Bragg exemplifies the quality that he praises in Lawrence - '...that exchange of sexual needs so often suffocated in repressive conformities and inarticulacy' ('Intro. *The Prussian Officer*, p.ix). As for love's companion, the vicar is one of the village's few inhabitants able to articulate the truth of the novel's denouement: 'It is sad how easily men can be brought together for death' (*JL*, p.175).

---

6 Bragg has remained a consistent defender of his belief in the aesthetic of the ordinary in its regional setting. Nearly 40 years prior to espousing these values in his 'Foreword' to Chaplin's novel, Bragg had set out his credo in the conclusion to *Speak for England*: 'The only propaganda that this book aims at is to demonstrate my conviction that everyone repays attention, that the most surprising lives come out of the most unexpected places and that the generalisations of most affluent intellectuals, at each end of the political spectrum, about "the masses" or "the workers" or even "the people" that such herd-like descriptions are worthless' (p.478).

# Grains of Sand

'A strong and solid novel, with a totally convincing figure,
at once fallible and admirable, at its centre'
*Sunday Telegraph*

# MELVYN BRAGG

## *The Silken Net*

# SIX

# INTO THE LABYRINTH
## *THE SILKEN NET*

Spanning the first half of the twentieth-century *The Silken Net* (1974) is an ambitious novel following the life of a female protagonist from infancy to middle-age as she searches for spiritual and aesthetic certitude in defiance of the epigraph's threat of imprisonment in a 'gilded cage', taken from William Blake's 'The Prince of Love'. Rosemary Lewis was born in France in 1908 of a French mother and an English father, both of whom have unfulfilled artistic dreams, and neither of whom she ever sees again after the outbreak of World War I, when she is sent to live with her father's unmarried relatives in Thurston. Her father is killed in action and her mother enters a downward spiral of bohemian existence, finally dying in a 'small, cheap hotel in Marseille' (*SN*, p.7) in 1923, when Rosemary is just fifteen years old. The mother's ashes are buried in that same Thurston cemetery that saw the interment of Josh and Cedric in the closing pages of *Josh Lawton*.

The *Silken Net*, however, is ultimately a far more life-enhancing novel than Josh Lawton, which, despite travelling to the outermost limits of despair to reach the truth about human relationships, ends on a note of survival. Bragg invokes the Greek myth of the Minotaur and the Labyrinth to illuminate Rosemary's quest. It is one of many intertextual references Bragg uses to negate any threat of regionalism restricting a literary fiction's artistic horizons within a self-contained locale - in this case the locale being Thurston/Wigton. By mapping her own route through local and mythically inflected labyrinths, Rosemary's story incorporates regional aesthetics into wider, more universal contexts, demonstrating that social and economic change, particularly that initiated by World War II, is capable of transmuting place-based identification into the 'world in a grain of sand'. As I will demonstrate in what follows, the novel's many references to other literary texts, often eliding the separation between ancient myths and present realities, together with its broad time-sweep, move the text beyond any limiting protocols of a community's spatial and formal restraints with the result that the emotions unearthed, far from being diminutive, become universal by the very virtue of being deep-rooted. In its study of conflicting temperaments between otherwise well-intentioned individuals, and of the misunderstandings that arise out of their quests for emotional honesty, *The Silken Net* privileges that search for the truths of the human heart that Nathanial Hawthorne's 'Preface' to *The House of the Seven Gables* places as central to the aim of romance:

> The [Romance] - while, as a work of art, it must rigidly subject itself to laws, and while it sins unpardonably, so far as it may swerve aside from the truth of the human heart - has fairly a right to present that truth under circumstances, to a great extent, of the writer's own choosing or creation. If he thinks fit, also, he may so manage his atmospherical medium as to bring out or mellow the lights and deepen and enrich the shadows of the picture. (p.1)

These 'lights' and 'shadows' appear in the, by now, familiar setting of Bragg's Thurston, which, along with the wider Lake District environs, plays a major part in the shaping of lives caught between the dialectic of community tradition and custom and increasingly intrusive cosmopolitan/global innovation.

It is difficult to over-emphasise the importance of Bragg's developing fictional portrait of Wigton, thinly disguised as Thurston, in providing a personalised authorial anchor from which to explore universal themes of human behaviour, albeit increasingly informed by his own experiences as a media professional in a cosmopolitan world. A sense of place implies a sense of belonging, which in turn allows for a developing sense of understanding of, and empathy with, the lives of those placed under a fictional microscope for the enjoyment of readers and, increasingly, the encouragement of tourists, while carrying with it a level of personal responsibility. Bragg's life-long commitment to Cumbria and his home-town of Wigton provides him with ready access to a personal privileged site of geographical feeling opening up the potential for representing the familiar as authentic experience in contrast to merely imaged fictional spaces. Accuracy of local depiction, both emotional and structural, becomes of ever-more paramount importance if, as David Harvey claims, global readings must of necessity extrapolate from local experiences simply because 'for most people the terrain of sensuous experience and affective social relations (which forms the material grounding for consciousness formation and political action) is locally circumscribed' (*Spaces of Hope*, p.85).

All this is by way of a prologue to an extended look at the accuracy and sensitivity of Bragg's recording of Wigton's topography to create Thurston as an on-going and important recognisable fictional/factual location over a period that now covers more than 45 years of publishing history. The pivotal importance of Thurston/Wigton will appear again in later novels, but I feel that with *The Silken Net* I have reached the point at which to reflect on Bragg's sense of place-based identification, coupled with his intimate knowledge of his home town in weaving a literary web whose threads encompass, among other things, personal intimacy, emotional depth, moral commitment, social bonding, the march of time, and a focussed nostalgia. Alan Sillitoe makes a trenchant observation in *Mountains and Caverns* that applies to Bragg's regional fiction: '... a sense of place for a writer also involves a sense of distance. He has to look at things from under a magnifying glass, and from the sky as well' (p.71). Discussing Sillitoe's panoramic vision of landscape and Nottingham's physiognomy within it, David James argues for a scrutiny of place with precision, along with an awareness of vulnerability to national trends, in terms that I wish to bear in mind when venturing into Thurston's textual alley-ways:

> The town centre's 'maze of streets' locates his survey as he moves beyond Nottingham's horizon; local specificity thus extends [the writer's] broader critique, lending focus to that prospect-view he climatically assumes ... Oscillating between ambient atmospherics and frank dialogue, aerial depictions and street-level conversations, [he] shapes a multivocal method for addressing the lived experience of urban planning and imminent change.
> (*Contemporary British Fiction and the Artistry of Space*, p.51-2)

Thurston's sense of local identity within the national economic framework is established early in Chapter Two, where it is described as 'a typical northern market town with a couple of small factories which joined it to Industrial England' (*SN*, p.8). Helping it to lay claim to an Everytown status are its 'four thousand inhabitants [who] were a fair microcosm of English life' (ibid.).

Arriving in Thurston as a young girl at the outset of World War I in the care of her father's brother and sister, Lawrence and Sarah Armstrong, Rosemary is enrolled first at 'the Church of England primary school behind Market Hill, then up to the National School and on to Thomlinson, a girls' school' (*SN*, p.8). Such 'street level conversations' are important aspects of Bragg's documentary precision in which the accuracy of historical place intersects with the lives of fictional characters to ensure that narrative plot remains fully integrated with setting. Readers curious about the past, and present, of the schools that Rosemary attends are able to find their history recorded in, for example, T.W. Carrick's 1949 classic *The History of Wigton* (see specifically Chapter XIV, 'The National School' and Chapter XV, 'The Thomlinson School') and, more recently, in Trevor Grahamslaw's *Wigton Through Time* (2010).[1] The latter book, referred to several times in the course of my study, is particularly useful in making the link between nostalgia and progress with, for example, photographs of both the National School (p.26) and the Thomlinson School (p.30) as they were around the time of Rosemary's attendance, and in their adaptation for continued use today. Past and present also coalesce in Rosemary's adolescent dreaming of Thurston's history and making it the focus of a future nostalgia in terms remarkably similar to Stanley Baldwin's contemporary eulogising on England's countryside: 'She could draw a picture which would seem ageless: the vicar and the choirboy, the spinster teachers and the cheerful shopkeepers; the "characters" and the old families of modest means and pretensions; the fields which came into the town, inlets of farming with the taste of real country ... Peace at night without traffic or rowdy behaviour' (*SN*, p.17). By 1939, however, the 'inlets of farming' are in retreat, making problematic the permanence of fixed-place identity and suggesting that community space may be as dialectical as time. As Rosemary's local lover, and soon-to-be husband,

---

1. Grahamslaw's brief history of Thomlinson Girls' School divulges interesting, if easily overlooked, details placing Wigton in an unexpected national and international context. He writes that the school opened in 1899, was named after John and Robert Thomlinson, and has today been converted into Wigton Junior School. It was originally 'built on the site of Flosh House by John Westmorland a wealthy merchant *who made his fortune managing Jamaican plantations*' and that it was later 'owned by Isaac Pattinson - *the textile manufacturer*' (*Wigton Through Time*, 30, italics added). Wigton stands revealed as an integral constituent of England's textile manufacturing base and, perhaps more importantly, as implicated in the slave trade upon which West Indies plantations depended for their wealth creation. Events on the imperial periphery of eighteenth and early nineteenth-century Britain are thus seen to infiltrate such unlikely distant regional locations as Wigton, making it a part of a wider historical narrative and part of the labyrinth of Empire.

perceptively remarks when he contemplates buying fields for residential development: 'The town's starting to creep away from itself' (*SN*, p.107). Despite such intimations of change, Rosemary clings tenaciously to her romantic nostalgic view of Thurston, 'snuggled in its nest, the church tower solid in the centre of it all, dark sandstone and slate holding their ground, a sturdy compact place' (*SN*, p,142), whilst becoming increasingly aware that in many respects she has outgrown the confines of such an all all-enveloping environment. Having 'outgrown her old cocoon' she would either 'devote herself to spinning another [Blakeian net] or she would attempt to fly as she had bid herself to do' (ibid.). Both Edgar and Rosemary are articulating a map of personal and community potential in which, in James's formulation, 'visual perceptions give way to intimations of progressing, revealing the way such writers [as Bragg] bring the exactitude of literary naturalism to the task of envisioning environmental renewal' (*Contemporary British Fiction*, p.52).

Early years spent freely roaming and exploring Wigton's central maze of streets and alleyways empowers Bragg to bring an authoritative ethnographic insight to his portrayal of Wigton/Thurston's places and characters. Bragg's topographical references to specific locations and buildings throughout the novel are too many to itemise and quote in full here, but by way of a representative sample they include the following locales, all of which can be found in *Wigton Through Time* (*WTT*): 'New Street and past the old jam-works' (*SN*, p.20; *WTT*, p.79); 'up Longthwaite Road, a seventeenth-century alms cottage' (*SN*, p.52; *WTT*, p.12); 'Union Street' (*SN*, p.54; *WTT*, p.93); 'Church Street' (*SN*, p.79; *WTT*, p.56); 'the Rayophane mill was employing almost a hundred men, Redmayne's took in about two hundred women.' (*SN*, p.94; *WTT*, p.66); 'a pub came up to let, The Mitre' (*SN*, p.174; *WTT*, p.33); 'They soon came on [a cottage] up at Highmoor, near the old mansion' (*SN*, p.223; *WTT*, p.7 and p.8). This last example, which refers to the married Rosemary and Edgar Crowther's move from their tenanted pub to a pleasantly situated detached cottage, is typical of Bragg's historical accuracy in presenting the town of Thurston/Wigton as a document in its own write/right, displaying the public face of its history, allowing it to be read as a palimpsest and marrying structural change to bodily health:

> ... there had once been a lime tree on the mile-long avenue leading to the big house [Highmoor] ... Now the zoo was gone, the pond was neglected, the golf course

was farmland, the mansion was eleven flats, the avenue of limes was an avenue of two- and three-bedroomed houses on one side and neat garden allotments on the other. Yet the place remained; the lovely Georgian house and on top of it, the imitation Venetian tower, planted there by a nineteenth-century owner who had loved Venice; now a landmark. Once there had been a bell in the tower whose strike could be heard for ten miles around; but it had been too heavy or badly slung and threatened to destroy the entire building. It had been removed. Rosemary saw a parable in that, the tongue being taken out for fear it would destroy the body. She amused herself drawing simple parallels between her own situation and this odd structure, this extravagant foreign stalactite on the calm and reasoned Georgian proportions. [2]

(SN, p.223)

Rosemary's musings on the bell-tower's mortality add a metonymic dimension to the textual microgeography, establishing a contiguous relationship between tongue/female body and bell/bell-tower, in an association technique that highlights Rosemary's often uncomfortable position within the local community and her struggle for self-definition.

Edgar's identity, by way of contrast, is a function of his natural habitat of the streets as a natural extension of his body. Their names are ever-ready to trip off his tongue and they act in collusion with his

---

2. Grahamslaw reproduces an early 1900s photograph of the avenue along with the text: 'Through the gate was an elegant tree lined avenue stretching for a quarter of a mile to Highmoor mansion. When Highmoor estate was auctioned in 1909 the avenue was sold separately, being developed in the 1930s when the trees were felled and houses built on the avenue's southern side. The avenue road remained separating the houses from their gardens on the northern side. Today the Lodge is a private residence with the gateway pillars and perimeter wall surviving' (WTT, p.6). He also sketches a brief history of Highmoor: 'Highmoor mansion built in 1810 by Joseph Hodgson a textile manufacturer. Later owned by William Banks and then his sons Henry and Edwin, who enlarged the estate and added an Italian style tower. Equipped with chiming clock, large bell and a carillon of bells which played tunes during the week and hymns on Sunday, the tower dominated Wigton visually and audibly. In 1909 the then owner Edwin Banks was declared bankrupt and the house sold. In 1934 Highmoor mansion was converted into flats whilst private housing has subsequently encircled the house' (WTT, 7). There are further pictures, and text, of Highmoor Pond and the view from the Lodge on pp. 8-9. Grahamslaw's sepia reproductions are testament to the camera-like lucidity of Bragg's historically inflected eye.

personality and desires:

> ... he whipped through the warren of back-alleys, through Reed's Lane and the Warren and Water Street, up to the top of Church Street to meet her at the church square as casually as if he had just strolled down from the auction. It was then that the network of alleyways and yards which made up the centre of Thurston struck him as being so friendly. They kept his secret. They sped his passage. They nurtured his desire.
>
> (*SN*, pp.78-9)

Immediately prior to this passage, Rosemary has likened Edgar to the Minotaur of Greek mythology. Here, whatever the implied threat to one particular young virgin, he is spectacularly free to roam Thurston's labyrinth of terraces, back-streets and alleys at will and with deliberate speed without fear of ambush. Person and place read as one as Edgar negotiates Thurston's myriad entrances and exits, an intricate network where he is a Prince of Love. He does so with an intensity and an excitement, a responsiveness to life and physical sensation that helps explain his attractiveness to (some) others. Approaching the sawmill where Edgar works, Rosemary sees only a 'small area bleak with walled industry', and is unable to summon up any of Edgar's contrasting 'worth of ... vision of the place' (*SN*, p.110). It is Edgar, at home in his native environment, who is able to transform a lumber yard into a performative space and in the process assume a locational identity with definite associations and concrete meanings. Edgar's busy energy and multi-tasking at speed strike me as remarkably similar in style to the equally frantic and spontaneous performances that Jack Kerouac's real-life friend, Neal Cassidy - Dean Morriarty in *On the Road*[3] (1957) - turns in as a parking-lot attendant. Here is Dean in action:

> ... he can back a car forty miles an hour into a tight squeeze and stop at the wall, jump out, race among the fenders, leap into another car, circle it fifty miles an hour

---

3. In Bragg's *Crossing the Lines* (2003) the main semi-autobiographical protagonist, Joe Richardson, is thrilled by the spontaneous prose style of Jack Kerouac's *On the Road*: 'And his head pulsed excitedly with its transatlantic, free, druggie, rolling life, free-flowing prose. What a sound!' (*CL*, p. 283). Bragg/Richardson's interest in the Beats spills over into *Remember Me...* (2008), the fourth novel in the sequence, where he uses Kerouac's exclamatory enigmatic 'It' to describe a jazz performance: 'This is IT!' (*RM*, p.160).

in a narrow space, back swiftly into tight spot, hump, snap the car with the emergency so that you see it bounce as he flies out; then clear to the ticket shack, sprinting like a track star, hand a ticket, leap into a newly arrived car before the owner's half out, leap literally under him as he steps out, start the car with the door flapping, and roar off to the next available spot, arc, pop in, brake, out, run;

(*On the Road*, p.9)

And here is Edgar, his English counterpart:

The whine of the machine soared into the darkening sky as he walked between the yellow planks, heaving large branches of stripped timber onto the plate, pushing them towards the sawing wheel and back again as the log was executed. The process hypnotized Rosemary. Edgar was so capable. He could attend to so many things at once - kicking the belt of the saw, stopping to pick up the log with one hand while sliding the branch back with the other, stacking the log as he turned ... she, who hated noise, found it enjoyable, even a little exciting.

(*SN*, p.110)

In both instances a small working-class stage becomes the arena for a display of a particularly virile type of universal kinetic physical masculine pride that transcends the merely local. W.J. Keith believes that '[o]ne possible way of distinguishing a regional novelist from his merely local or provincial counterpart is to note how the former writes of a specific locality but for as wide an audience as possible ... while the latter may be seen as writing primarily for the inhabitants of the area itself' (*Regions*, p. 89). The respective paeans of praise to Dean's and to Edgar's Anglo-American balletic athleticism both capture the essence of a philosophy of living in the present that narratively elides the local in demonstrating a moment of effusiveness that offers a key to both men's restless character.

Where Edgar's extrovert character can be illuminated by comparison with a classic 1950s masculine-orientated American text, in a similar vein Rosemary's more introverted nature may be seen as sharing the concerns of an equally iconic 1890 feminist American text, Charlotte Perkins Gilman's 'The Yellow Wall-Paper'. Confined to her attic room on account of a suspected nervous breakdown, Gilman's heroine becomes obsessed by patterns in the wall-paper, visualising a woman trapped behind bars - 'by moonlight, it became bars! The outside pattern I mean, and the woman behind it as plain as can be' (p.13) - and denied the right to live her own life. Without access to pen or brush she expresses herself through the wall-paper, transferring her own need for communication and recognition into a form of feminist interpretation:

> The front pattern *does* move - and no wonder! The woman behind shakes it!
>
> Sometimes I think there are a great many women behind, and sometimes only one, and she crawls around fast, and her crawling shakes it all over.
>
> Then in the very bright spots she keeps still, and in the very shady spots she just takes hold of the bars and shakes them hard.
>
> And she is all the time trying to climb through. But nobody could climb through that pattern - it strangles so; I think that is why it has so many heads.
>
> They get through, and then the pattern strangles them off and turns them upside down, and makes their eyes white! (p.15)

Clearly the figure behind bars is both the narrator and the narrator's double, whose plea for visibility is also apparent in Rosemary whose 'violence and changeability of her passion' (*SN*, p.11) as a school-girl finds an outlet in her drawings: '... there was some evidence that their morbidity had caused offence and the headmistress herself judged them "far too worrying". Both the drawings showed a girl, sketched boldly, an angular, distressed girl, trapped behind bars while out of walls came malevolent heads of demons and in the walls themselves were outlines of skulls. The colours were dark, the subject matter powerful.' On the eve of her marriage to Edgar, Lawrence destroys 'two unhappy paintings' (*SN*, p.163) he had been keeping since her adolescence, believing her at last ready to live her own life. But he cannot destroy painful memories of her original love for her cousin Wilfred, captured in her drawings, and the presumed flight to freedom paradoxically ends when, with no time for painting as a liberating exercise, she finds herself returned to a version of Gilman's world, where, living in a pub which she hates, she grows ever-increasingly 'wearied in this *prison*, as she saw it' (*SN*, p.183, italics added), and begging Edgar to free her. Later, she will again express herself through art, but in the immediacy of post-War Britain she finds herself literally serving time behind bars, echoing Gilman's 'I wish John would take me away from here' (*Yellow Wall-Paper*, p.11). What is striking is both the connection between texts separated by time and geography in dealing with a feminist perspective on confinement in texts/pictures and homes, and the continuing viability of feminist tropes of textual/architectural confinement over a period of some 60 years.

Growing up as an unofficially adopted child in a household where she is materially well cared for but left craving emotional warmth from her surrogate mother, Rosemary is aware from an early age of a painful sense of displacement and of not quite belonging. Leaving school to work in a library in Carlisle, Rosemary continues to express artistically her predicament in being caught between two worlds, executing pictures of emotional stasis in which, although free from childhood bars, she remains poised between sky and earth, 'between the edge of the page and the centre' (*SN*, p.80) in a fierce debate arguing for 'her to leave her fortress and come into the world' (ibid.). When she does so it is only to find herself caught between a sexual attraction to the physically appealing Minotaur-like Edgar and an intellectual bonding to her older academic London cousin Wilfred, a contest that will cause much pain and distress throughout the novel. But Wilfred is himself severely emotionally damaged as a result of what he sees as his guilt in the death of his wife, from whom he had separated after quarrelling. Walking and climbing with Rosemary on Skiddaw, lecturing her on Wordsworth and Coleridge, it is not to the expected Lake writers that Bragg calls upon to underpin his psychological depiction of Wilfred's emotional distress, but to the far darker iconic Northern face of Edvard Munch's 1895 painting *The Scream*, with its open mouth expressing an inner anguish matched by nature's turbulent waters and inflamed sky. Camille Paglia sees Munch's work as addressing 'Late Romantic themes of sexual menace' with his Scream '[f]rozen on the bridge of history over the abyss of nature' (*Sexual Personae*, p.505), a depiction which describes Wilfred's immersion of personal pain into a landscape suddenly transformed from Wordsworthian sublime to a harbinger of death: 'Why did he not scream his pain onto this landscape which had seen so much unjust blood and loss?' (*SN*, p.118). Wilfred is framed as Munch's deranged scream, singing out 'with sick rage the guilt and pain in the skull', wanting to 'let howl and tear [his] hair' (ibid.). Two aspects of this scene arrest my attention, one strictly, but fascinatingly, textual, the other more painful, relating to the author's personal demons in the early 1970s. The former is perhaps the more easily objectively, even ludically, dealt with, but both are relevant when discussing the expansive boundaries of Bragg's regional texts.

It may be that Bragg sometimes makes unconscious cultural connections that have beguiled me into claiming unwarranted deterministic associations, but given his wide knowledge of literature and the arts in general I feel justified in maintaining that nearly every allusion is intentional. Plot allusions to Gilman's story 'The Yellow Wall-Paper' are, in my earlier exegesis, structural to function, and are in turn intensified by the thematically coded allusion to Munch's *The Scream*. The text's accompanying allusions to Wordsworth's abandoning his French lover, Annette Vallon, leaving her to bear his child in the turmoil of the French Revolution, and to John Stuart Mills's breakdown (SN, p.119) complete the four corners of the intertextual structural and thematic allusions that invite consideration for a clearer understanding of the novel's serious intent.

'Why did he not scream his pain onto this landscape which had seen so much unjust blood and loss? Munch like the sheep went the jaw of the lecturer. Sang with sick rage the guilt and pain in the skull' (SN p,118). For D.F. McKenzie, in his essay 'Typography and Meaning: The Case of William Congreve', 'it is impossible to divorce the substance of the text on the one hand from the physical form of its presentation on the other ... To the eye the pages offer an aggregation of meanings both verbal and typographic for translation to the ear' (p.200). Wilfred's repressed scream of pain is given enhanced meaning by the grammatical interplay of typography that makes the scream and the 'pain in the skull' centrally contiguous to the M/munch of his jaw bone. Meaning drifts between printed text and spoken word 'Munch', opening up the space between ear and eye. Added to which we have the evidence of the homonym (a word that changes its meaning when the initial letter is capitalised) - munch/Munch - positioned on the page to create parallelism and connection with the related words in the type area bookending it. To me then, it is clear that Bragg's novel has meanings and rewards that are only fully disclosed when a straightforward reading of the plot is disrupted by searching for and interpreting the signs that are free-floating from the type area text.

I have already drawn attention to marked semi-autobiographical aspects of Bragg's fiction and, although not itself a biographically inflected text, The *Silken Net* harbours a painful and remarkably recent part of the writer's history. For most of the novel Bragg successfully creates the narrative illusion of events represented as part of a cultural stance rather than as a personalised identifiable individual one. Discreet sections of Chapter Seventeen and Chapter Twenty, however, introduce unsettling and difficult questions concerning the presentation of character, memory, and moral responsibility in the light of the authorial perspective's rendering of those characters, together with the recall of specific events surrounding them. Wilfred is objectively free to contemplate resuming a relationship with Rosemary after his wife has died of cancer, but even with Rosemary on Skiddaw (Chapter Twenty) 'again and again he thought of the death of his wife' (*SN*, p.118) with the accompanying 'guilt and pain in the skull' (ibid.) because their separation meant he was absent when most needed. The Munchian reference to skulls echoes Wilfred's earlier admission that he 'felt no relief inside the skull' (*SN*, p.102) even when sharing the tragedy with Rosemary as a sympathetic listener. It is almost as if the personal is leaking into the public text through the chance of plot, surreptitiously releasing Bragg's own demons.

For there are demons. Bragg's first wife, Marie-Elisabeth Roche, committed suicide in 1971 and it is a matter of public record that he felt/feels guilty that because of their separation he was not on hand at a crucial time. These events are dealt with honestly, movingly and cathartically in Bragg's 2008 novel *Remember Me ...* , a searing semi-autobiographical narrative which tells the story of Joe Richardson, Bragg's fictional *Doppelgänger* and central protagonist of *The Soldier's Return* sequence, and his relationship with a disturbed French poet, Natasha, who closely resembles his late wife. The novel, which falls outside the main parameters of this study, is an outstanding example of contemporary semi-autobiographical and confessional fiction, deserving of a full critical analysis in its own right. My interest here is to flag-up those brief flare-ups of authorial guilt in *The Silken Net* that subsequently remained hidden from the public gaze for the next 34 years, before Bragg finally feels able to share them in a brave act of self-analysis. As he himself wrote in the *Sunday Times* at the time of paperback publication in

2009, 'Fiction can reach into a mind, even a spirit. It has a possibility to divine and articulate what is often otherwise hidden and silent. In *Remember Me* ... I wanted to get to the heart of what had been and still is a time of my own darkness.'

The *Silken Net* is Rosemary's story, a feminist Bildungsroman shaped by the Cumbrian Fells, and Wilfred is not Bragg, with whom he shares little in common except in the breadth of his early literary reading. If anything, Wilfred plays the part of mediational being whose distressed utterances represent an early, but unsuccessful, attempt by the author to write himself free of those memories and situations that have so damaged him. There may be an element of doubt here about the extent to which Bragg controls Wilfred as a fictional creation in his fictional world in which his fictional outbursts read as both self-implicating and self-analysing. Two excerpts, both taken from the confessional Chapter Seventeen, provide the evidence:

> 'Everybody feels guilt at the death of someone close to them,' he said, 'it must be part of the sense of loss. But what makes it difficult in my case is that we had quarrelled, we had separated and Stephen had become a rope in a tug of war. It's not as if her death can be set apart from what happened between us; the illness she had was quick and sudden, it ate her up like grief or despair. The point is that I was not there, and not only that, I was in the process of following through a terrible argument, a vendetta it would be better to call it. We had disappointed each other so much that revenge was the only consolation.' (*SN*, p.101)

> 'And I did not realize how weak she had become,' he said. 'What I did not understand was how much she loved me. Not me as a man - though that, too, sometimes - but me as a husband and as a father, as a provider, as a companion, as all those people she needed in order to live. There are letters she wrote but did not post. I read them. And those she did post, if I had only read them with understanding. There is no doubt in my mind that I killed her: by default.'

> (*SN*, pp.104-5)

If we can bear to read these fictional passages in the full knowledge of the biographical truth that powers them, it becomes clear that Bragg is attempting a kind of truth-telling in laying bare his fictionalised self in all his personal errors and omissions so as to try to understand, and possibly heal, himself. This latter must await the publication of *Remember Me ...*, but meantime the narrator of *The Silken Net* has made a first tentative foray into incorporating an exploration of both the conscious and unconscious structure of the writer's mind.

There are further links between the two novels in that both Rosemary and Natasha are painters, one amateur the other professional, whose work is the subject of symbolic textual interpretation. Both women are drawn to view contemporary relationships through a prism of mythical allusions drawn from ancient Greek lore, in particular, the story of Icarus. Natasha paints the young university student Joe Richardson as 'Icarus ... the closed eyes, the fall of the head (so clearly Joe), the resignation of the boy who flew so close to the sun that his waxen wings melted' (*RM ...*, p.82). Early in their relationship Rosemary fantasises that Wilfred could attain god-like status, carried on a stream of air bubbles 'to lift you up and throw you into the sky. You would be like Icarus' (*SN*, p.31). Both women's dreams of a mortal Icarus fail to take flight. In Rosemary's case, she is rejected by the professionally high-flying, but ultimately cynical and frustrated, Wilfred, turning to the earth-bound Edgar, who dramatically enters her life in the guise of a Minotaur driving a herd of young bulls directly into her path.

Bragg's mythical allusions to the Minotaur and the Labyrinth are complex, dealing with ideas of female submissiveness and self-expression, hidden female sexual passion, sacrificial demands, feelings of being buried alive,[4] endurance, all within the labyrinth that is at Thurston's heart and all against the reader's background knowledge that it is Ariadne who has the clue that will thread a way through the Labyrinth only to be deserted. Such a conclusion may be read as inherently conservative, although it is in tune with the social mores of the

---

4. The labyrinth and the Minotaur are fairly common tropes in fiction. Will Ladislaw's expressed disgust at Dorothea's marriage to the elderly pedantic scholar Casaubon, in George Eliot's *Middlemarch* (1871-2), for example, is equally expressive of Rosemary's choice of Thurston for domicile when her head yearns for the intellectual freedom of London and her heart for the warmth of Provence: 'You have been brought up in some of those horrible notions that choose the sweetest women to devour like Minotaurs. And now you will go and be shut up in that stone prison of Lowick [Thurston/The Mitre]: you will be buried alive' (*Middlemarch*, p.153).

early 1950s, but more constructively it sets up a model of feminist altruism and alterity that equates to Ariadne's gift of the thread.

Rosemary's realisation of the personality difference between Wilfred and Edgar, and of the nature of the choice she must make, is triggered by a moment of clarity entirely engendered by the immediacy of the landscape. Climbing to Surprise View to look at the 'spectacular vista of Borrowdale, Catbells and the valley floor, waterfall and sheer rock face', Edgar balances precariously close to the sheer drop. Instinctively "It makes you want to fly," she said and then remembered Wilfred and Icarus who would always be her guide. But Edgar was not to do with that. He was the Minotaur' (*SN*, p. 90). And she decides to marry Edgar/Minotaur but not to become a victim trapped in his labyrinthine home territory. Indeed, once relocated to the outskirts of town from the tenanted pub, she resists all entreaties to re-enter his maze: 'Edgar begged her to move out and go into the middle of the town, to Church Street in a place near his warehouse, the street which snaked through the heart of Thurston and poked its alleyways into several covert archway exits: but she would not budge' (*SW*, p.264). Consequently their estrangement deepens at the same time as Rosemary is increasingly drawn to examine her predicament in the context of myth. Visiting Edgar's mother, Rosemary walks 'the twisting lanes to the Crowther farm [thinking] of herself as Ariadne,' unable to comprehend why Theseus could abandon her after defeating the Minotaur.

*The Silken Net* consistently and insistently gestures towards the Minotaur and the Labyrinth in contemporary, aesthetic terms that remember and incorporate the mythic narrative of the past in order to illustrate the events of the present. Nowhere in the novel is the fusion of past and present, myth and history, more apparent than in Rosemary's choosing to name her and Edgar's daughter Eleanor. Born soon after the outbreak of World War II, her name is a reminder to her mother of Eleanor of Aquitaine and Eleanor of Provence (with whom her own mother is for ever associated), both of whom contracted alliances with England, an alliance now being challenged by the German invasion of France. Named also after Helen, daughter of Jupiter and Leda, Rosemary has consciously registered her child's name as part of a modern mythical epic being played out 'at the northern edge of a beleaguered England which settled down grimly to find in itself the strength to endure the terrible assault from the Nordic will to power through fire' (*SN*, p.164).

This private but ambitious gesture, offering the child from Thurston as a symbol of Englishness and cultural survival, transcends the regional at a moment of national crisis.

Invalided out of the army, Edgar, however, reverses the trajectory of myth back from national to personal and it is a part of the reader's hermeneutic pleasure of textual detection to be able to unravel such patterns. It then becomes prophetically clear that Edgar's role/fate as a modern Minotaur is early coded in his distaste and avoidance of Thurston's industrial scene of the bull's death. 'A friend of his father's took him on in the butchering business but the steaming entrails overpowered the thought of eventual triumph as a merchant prince' (*SN*, p.56). Nor can he be persuaded into a partnership raising pigs when he stops to recall 'his nauseating experience in the slaughterhouse' (*SN*, p.59). The pathology of sacrifice is prefigured, bound up with a secrecy that locates the slaughterhouse, the site of nemesis, almost hidden in Thurston's inner maze. It is here in an extended and deliberate graphic sequence that Edgar's fate is to be read in the entrails of the beast, when, lost in the maze, his lover Jessie witnesses the death of the beast:

> She turned into the arched way which was the entrance to Church Street and was chilled by the gloom of the place. No sun fed that twisty narrow street, and in it she felt less sure of herself. Afraid that someone might slip out of one of the many odd-shaped houses which opened directly onto the straitened way and confront her. She hurried and looked around rather wildly for the warehouse which Mr Ismay had so laboriously described.
>
> But he had given her the wrong references ... to the left she went and found herself in the slaughterhouse. The beast had been shot and hauled upon the pulley. She came just as the big belly was slit open and the innards tumbled out with a gleaming stink. Though country born and bred, she had never been able to overcome her squeamishness and the sight of the guts and intestines of the beast heaping up on the concrete floor while the sallow man in rubber boots and apron and gloves leaned in to scoop out more and more of the freshly dead animal's entrails startled and sickened her.
>
> (*SN*, p.307)

Such vivid imagery presents an unwilling Jessie consulting the Oracle and being given an authoritative pronouncement of her future that dovetails with her later contemplating a sleeping Edgar with 'the head awkwardly flopped to one side as if the neck were broken' (*SN*, p.362), herself morally confused as 'the simple truth disappeared into a labyrinth' (ibid.). We last see Edgar, remorse 'now set in him, as fixed as the alcohol in his blood' (*SN*, p.385), warning a liberated and surviving Rosemary to steer clear of a frisky bull on the hillside after a cathartic visit to his new home. The slaughterhouse is an important site of ekphrasis, in which Bragg consciously invites the reader to contemplate an image of death which is part of the novel's thematics of sacrifice surrounding debatable protocols of sexual love and marriage.

These protocols come under further scrutiny when Rosemary is told by Wilfred that he is engaged and therefore no longer free, her response is to turn away from the physically present Edgar, with whom she has already made love, and attempt a telepathic literary connection with the man she insists on seeing as her destiny. She measures and records her distress against historical poetic versions of unhappy or unrequited love, repeatedly copying out in long-hand a passage from Book IV of John Dryden's translation of *The Aeneid of Virgil*: 'What pangs the tender breast of Dido/When, from the tower, she saw the covered shore' (*SN*, p.153) in an hysterical push towards a poetics of presence, wanting to become one with the person who is her ideal. Her room becomes an anthological labyrinth of 'sheets of paper, stuffed in drawers, in pockets, under pillow, heaped on the window-seat, everywhere' (*SN*, p.152) a thought process given materiality in the search for escape from an emotional impasse. 'Poems should echo and re-echo against each other', in the Californian poet Jack Spicer's words: 'They should create resonances. They cannot live alone any more than we can' (*Collected Books*, p.61). Rosemary's quoted Aeneid is a trajectory of wish fulfilment, resonating with Wilfred's handwritten verse from Wordsworth's *A Slumber Did My Spirit Seal*:

> No motion has she now, no force
> She neither hears nor sees,
> Rolled round in earth's diurnal source
> With rocks and stones and trees.
>
> (*SN*, 153; *Lyrical Ballads*, p.131)

Finding these fragments, Sarah is aware of 'a bond she could not understand', but clearly moved she textually unites the poets - 'She pinned the two pieces together' (ibid.) - in her material act of emotional wish fulfilment that runs strangely counter to the two poetic extracts' different take on social relationships.

References to Wordsworth in Bragg's novels are not the mere caprice of chance, but rather a calculated positioned gloss on narrative events. The Lucy poems, of which *A Slumber Did My Spirit Seal* is part of the sequence, all tend to follow a similar arc in which Lucy's fixed dying into the landscape enables the male (writer's) gaze to retain its autonomy and move on. In Wilfred's choice of poem Lucy/Rosemary becomes pure disembodied object - 'Rolled round in earth's diurnal course/With rocks and stones and trees' - and destined in *Lucy Gray* to become pure spirit. It might strike a more deconstructive reader than Sarah that it is very convenient for Wilfred to place Rosemary by metaphoric poetic association in a Lakes landscape setting where, whatever the strivings of lovers, the cosmos remains sublimely indifferent to the fate of any particular human dwelling within it. By contrast, Rosemary's quoting from Dryden's *Virgil* gives precedence to Love as all powerful, determined to only connect until the moment of death. Wilfred's choice of verse appears to privilege the autonomy of the male self, whereas Rosemary's quoted extract foregrounds her sense of identity within the realm of committed human relationships. Bragg's focussing on poetry as a socially critical medium involving layers of meaning on numerous 'twisted pages' (*SN*, p.153) exposes two very different, gendered, and insightful versions of self. The irony inherent in this duality of outlook in Romantic imagining is that by the novel's closing pages Rosemary has survived violently contradictory emotions to seemingly make good her escape from Blake's epigraphic net only to self-inscribe Wordsworth's mourning verse 'as an epitaph in her mind' (*SN*, p.382). There is an unsettling ambivalence in an ending that sees its central female subject gazing on the Lakes landscape 'as she held on tightly to the glory of the moment, full of life' (*SN*, p.386), whilst sometimes experiencing 'the dizzy sensation that she did not exist; that she had passed through one band of reality and entered a zone of spirits' (*SN*, p.382). She has metaphorically died into the life of the exemplary poetic Wordsworth heroine.

Chapter Twenty-Four ends with Sarah storing these poetic, and other, fragments of Rosemary's recent past, and burning her sexually explicit drawings, removing them from sight in an attempt to forestall the occurrence of painful memories. Chapter Twenty-Five, however, immediately opens a dialogue with its predecessor over the efficacy of texts as healing documents in circumstances where their retrieval is sensitively handled. Laurence, and his like-minded antiquarian friend Harold Sowerby, set about restoring Rosemary's fragile mental balance by prompting a re-engagement with the present via a judicious choice of philosophical and cultural textual fragments. Harold initiates the healing process by making a daily delivery of 'immaculate copper-plate and black ink' (*SN*, p.155) handwritten extracts from *Reflections for Every day in the Year on the Works of God in Nature and Providence from the German of Christopher Sturm* (Sturm, 1740-86). At first glance the subject matter appears arbitrarily chosen and not readily appropriate to Rosemary's circumstances - February samples range from 'A Temperature Always the same would not be good for the earth' (February 3) to 'On the use of mountains' (February 23) - and yet Harold appears to have chosen wisely for '[t]hey brought [Rosemary] great pleasure' (*SN*, p.156). Perhaps Bragg harbours hopes that the curious reader will be motivated to share the pleasure of Rosemary's reading experience by seeking out the less than readily available volume with its less than seductive title. Were s/he to do so it becomes apparent that at least some of the sociocultural values ascribed to by Sturm are also those which, from what we know of her history, Rosemary might be expected to bring to his text, evidencing a number of common experiential and ideological parameters. For example, one of the passages Harold copies out contains sentiments which match Rosemary's insistence on the constancy of truth and virtue in a changing world whilst, at the same time, inevitably stirring memories of Wilfred/Icarus in the context of ill-judged ambition. Here is the complete 'Reflection':

> 'The Sun', February 8
> Such is, likewise, the instability of all human transactions; we can never promise to ourselves durable pleasures, and uninterrupted felicity. This consideration should render us careful and circumspect in the hour of prosperity, and moderate our desire for earthly joys, since every thing is subject to change and inconstancy. Virtue alone is immutable; virtue alone makes us support with unbending firmness, the vicissitudes and the

contingencies of life, unmoved by the frowns or the smiles of fortune; and enable us to sustain the mocks and the scorn of the world, whilst we pity and compassionate the weak children of delusion, who show their gilded wings in the sunshine of to-day and to-morrow are heard of no more. (pp.54-5)

There are complex runic and elliptical connotations between Sturm's populist philosophical 'Reflections' and notions of human frailty exposed in the Dryden and Wordsworth verses, the latter now hidden from Rosemary's view. In turning to an eighteenth-century text as a healing prescription, Harold has used his antiquarian knowledge to good effect, sharing in Milton's belief that 'books are not absolutely dead things, but do contain a potency of life in them to be as active as that soul whose progeny they are; nay they do preserve as in a vial the purest efficacy and extraction of that living intellect that bred them' ('Areopagitica', p.720).

Not to be outdone, Lawrence counters Germanic lore with indigenous Cumbrian dialect and folk-tales. He sets himself the ambitious task of interesting Rosemary in the philosophy of the Cumbrian dialect with the help of William Dickinson's *A Glossary of Words and Phrases Pertaining to the Dialect of Cumbria* (1859). Bragg clearly relishes the opportunity to let loose across the page a fizzing sample from the more than 7,000 words, and their definitions, collected by Dickinson: 'the small upstairs bedroom sounded with the cracking of that strong old language. "Brig" - bridge, "Bummel" - blunder, "Cadger"- retailer of small wares. "Carl" - a coarse fellow, "Cat-wittin" - conceited, "Chunter"- to reply angrily, "Cockly"- unsteady, "Cofe"- calf - and on through the alphabet...' *(SN,* p.156). Bragg makes the related point in *The Adventure of English* that people from Wilfred's, Harold's and his background 'were encouraged to wipe that dialect off our lips' (p.27). Today they would be part of 'the efforts being made by dialect societies and local publishers to keep the tongue alive' *(AE,* p.29)[5] In 1938 Lawrence's decision to contextualise the dialect definitions and bring out something of their poetry by reading to Rosemary from John Richardson's (1817-86) *Cummerlan' Talk* was an inspired advanced educational technique. Although Bragg does not

5. At the 23 May 1998 Annual General Meeting of the Lakeland District Society, Bragg was made an Honorary Member. The post-business talk included a number of quotations from Dickinson's *Glossary.* The *Glossary* was first published in 1859 with a revised and enlarged edition following in 1879. This latter collection is currently available in a 2006 edition, edited and published by Richard Byers.

detail Richardson's chapters, it is worth searching out the originals to find just how closely some of their titles, and even content, run parallel to Rosemary's experiences and moods: 'What t' Wind Sed', 'This Love's a Curious Thing',[6] 'T' Woefu' Partin'', 'Git Ower me 'at can'. The healing credentials of Wilfred's performative didacticism is evidenced in Rosemary's taking the phonetic properties of Richardson's dialect and articulating them in a simile expressive not only of the language's sonic qualities but also of their atavistic Cumbrian origins: 'Like the slapping of butter it sounded, she thought' (*SN*, p.156).

However fincly attuned Rosemary becomes to the sound and meaning of local voices there remains a persistent echo from a foreign shore reminding her that she can never renounce her French inheritance. One of her mother's infrequently posted gifts from abroad is a Georges Sand novel which Rosemary reads avidly, in the original French, and comes to know almost by heart by her teenage years. The otherness of France assumes a mythical colouring equivalent to the world of Greek mythology,

6. The 1871 edition of John Richardson's *'Cumberland Talk'; Being Short Tales and Rhymes in the Dialect of that County,* together with *A Few Miscellaneous Pieces in Verse,* published in London by John Russell Smith and locally, in Carlisle by Geo. Coward, is accessible in an on-line digitised format (archive.org). To give a flavour of the richness of the dialect that Rosemary would have enjoyed I include here a full transcript of 'This Love's a Curious Thing':

> Ya bonny summer neet it was,
> When dayswarlang, leàtt on I' June,'
> At efter I'd me derrick de˘n,
> I had an earen'd into t' toon.

> 'Twas gitten dusk when I com back,
> For t' sun had sunk doon into t' sea;
> An' burds the'r merry sangs teun't up,
> Ameàst fra ivvery bush an' tree.

> When just a bit fra t' toon I gat,
> I met a young an' gradely pair;
> I saw 'at they war gentry fwok,
> For beàth leuk't smush, weel dress't, a' fair.

> He had his arm around her waist,
> An' she leuk't smirken in his feàce:
> Thinks I, be aw the powers abeòn,
> That's just anudder cwortin' keàse.

> They seem't as happy as two burds,
> 'At flit frae tree to tree I' spring;
> For sceàrse ten yerds I'd gitten by,
> When beath began to lilt an' sing.

> Thinks I, this love's a curious thing:
> Them two gaan wi' the'r barfet feet,
> Seem just as happy as yon two;
> Their kiss, nadoot, 'ill be as sweet.

Bragg also includes Richardson's poem 'It's Nobbut Me' in his *Cumbria In Verse* anthology.

encouraging Rosemary to embrace the past, 'fondling long in memory what she had often scarcely even caressed in life, making in those catacombs of thought secret contacts, meanings, patterns for survival' (*SN*, p.195). Such textual survival techniques surface in, for example, Rosemary's finding and re-reading of an old letter from her mother shortly before she meets Wilfred's son, Stephen. Writing to her then teenage daughter, the mother wistfully muses that if only they were closer in age, 'Then what fun we could have on this wicked ancient sea' (*SN*, p.194). Shortly afterwards Rosemary becomes intoxicated with Stephen's youthful, lively company as they exchange views on favourite writers, culminating at the moment of Edgar's arrival with Stephen reading aloud some French verse. Bragg gives us six lines of the original French without either ascription or translation.[7] The effect is to trigger a moment of reader empathy with Edgar, both being, at least momentarily, excluded from 'thought secret contacts'. Uncovering the poem's identity as Paul Valéry's great work *The Graveyard by the Sea* allows us to make an obvious connection between poem and letter. The title suggests a collusion between the poetic and the personal, reminding us that Rosemary's mother died in France, by the sea, whilst the narrative itself alludes to Rosemary's psychic investment in Greek myth, with its final lines on the Greeks' excited cry in Xenophon's *Anabasis*, *'Thalassa, thalassa!'* on reaching salt water during the Persian wars.

Stephen, too, is excited by the poetic complexities of Valéry's mind, and Bragg, much later, returns to the French connection in setting his youthful enthusiasm against the world-weariness and lack of intellectual engagement seen in his father when Rosemary visits him in London for one last time, only to find a man now steeped in convention - the formerly ambitious soaring Icarus firmly grounded under Heathrow's flight path. When asked what he is currently working on, Wilfred reduces the excitement of poetic discovery to the everyday mundane: 'Oh nothing important. Boring really. Attempting to make sense of a man called Claudel ... You won't know about him. Nobody does except those of us who are paid to. Still, somebody's got to read the poor bastard.'(*SN*, p.374). Reluctant at first to help Rosemary make the geographical connection between the poet who worked in Provence and the mother whose ashes came to Thurston cemetery in a Provencal urn, Wilfred eventually relents, allowing memories

7. Paul Valéry, (1871-1945), *Le Cimetière marin*: 'The high shrieks of tickled girls, the eyes, the teeth, the damp eye-lids, the charming breast playing with fire, the blood shining in lips surrendering, the final gifts, the fingers that defend them everything goes underground and returns back into play!' (*The Penguin Book of French Verse. 4*, p.69. Edited by Anthony Hartley.)

to flood back. What Wilfred, unlike his son, singularly fails to do is to direct Rosemary to any of Claudel's output. Had he done so, Rosemary might well have rejected his contemptuous assessment of Claudel's worth, finding verse that spoke directly to her, as in, for example, these lines on withered roses and distance and time destroying memory in *Strasbourg*:

> Qui n'asenti quelquesfois, dans les tristes après-midi d'été,
> Quelque chose vers nous languir comme une rose desséchée?
> Ah! De ceux ou de celles-là que nous étions faits pour comprendre et pour aimer,
> Ce n'est pas la distance seulement, c'est le temps qui nous tient séparés,
> L'irréparable temps, la distance qui efface le nom et le visage:
> Un regard seul pour nous seuls survit et traverse tous les âges![8]

'Boring' does not describe a poet who knew Genet and whose ballet *La Femme et son ombre* was performed in harness with Genet's only ballet, *Adame Miroir*, in 1948, this latter being set in a hall of mirrors imprisoning the dancers searching for an exit from the labyrinth.

One of the rewarding aspects of a close reading of *The Silken Net* is in negotiating the reflectivity of the dense inter-textual allusions used in constructing a textual labyrinth, the aesthetic equivalent of Thurston's geographical maze. In addition to those already mentioned, they include Eliot's *The Waste Land*, Shakespeare's *King Lear* and *Henry IV Part I*, Lawrence's *Story of a Man Who Has Come Through*, Shelley's *Ozymandias and Adonias. An Elegy on the Death of John Keats*, and the eighteenth-century French lullaby *Au Clair de la Lune*, together with passing references to books that mark Rosemary's growth to maturity, from 'the Oresteian Trilogy by Aeschylus' (SN, p.21) to Carl Jung's psychology and James Frazer's *The Golden Bough* (SN, p.348), all seamlessly stitched into the text's net.[9]

8. Paul Claudel (1868-1955), *Strasbourg:* 'Who has not sometimes felt on a sad summer's afternoon something languish towards us like a withered rose? Of the men or women we were made to understand and love, it is not distance only, it is time that keeps us separated, irreparable time, distance blotting out name and face: a single glance lives for us alone and crosses all the ages!' (*The Penguin Book of French Verse 4*, pp 32-3. Edited by Anthony Hartley.)

9. Bragg's choice of Walter Scott's *Redgauntlet* (1824) as Rosemary's reading on her daily bus commute to Carlisle (SN, p.95) would have provided her with some interesting reflections on the risks of transgression to person and social identity. She might also have been attracted by Scott's attempt to build a mythical past for Scotland, linked to a rhetoric of mourning and loss, mirroring her own life history. Another interesting inter-textual feature is the inset of 'Wandering Willie's Tale', a story told in dialect within the main narrative, very much resembling the ideological intent of the dialect inserts of Sturm, Dickinson and Richardson in *The Silken Net*.

It would be a little misleading to conclude this chapter on a deafening note of sophisticated textual referencing, however apposite it may appear, when there are other more straightforward pleasures also deserving a mention. Glen Cavaliero, an astute and esteemed literary critic of the poetics of landscape and place, reviewing the novel for the *Eastern Daily Press*, praises the intensity and concentration of vision that recalls Lawrence in its 'shrewd and interesting study of conflicting temperaments'.[10] He is especially impressed by the clarity and tone of the dialogue that brings out the way the 'underlying quest for emotional honesty can be misunderstood'. He is thinking in particular of an extended passage of dialogue when Rosemary visits Edgar's mother in an attempt to discover whether her husband's amoral behaviour has its roots in his childhood experiences. The exchanges are finely nuanced to portray irreconcilable differences, so that however much Rosemary defers to her mother-in-law - 'You are so much wiser than I am' (*SN*, p.321) - her amateur attempts at Freudian psychology are met with incomprehension and mounting sarcasm - 'don't follow you Rosemary. You must remember I am not an educated woman' (*SN*, p.323) - in a refusal to emotionally connect. Rosemary's asking 'Did he love his father?' proves a probing too far, cutting off further exchanges. Cavaliero reads the exactly caught dialogue as the clue to why and 'how slowly modern attitudes take place in a country setting.' Mrs Crowther is condemned by her words to remain wandering in the labyrinth, as lost as any of the tale's main participants.

I began by describing *The Silken Net* as a comparatively optimistic novel, and so it is, but only to the extent that the ending is held in a cinematic freeze frame of narrative uncertainty as Rosemary is last seen alone in the landscape, as motionless as Wordsworth's Lucy, but holding on 'tightly to the glory, full of life' (*SN*, p. 386) in a moment of being. The reader is presented with a frame split between the montage of fields, cattle and dry stone walls of the Lakes, and the interior narration of Rosemary's mind-set, presaging the hope, but not the certainty, of rebirth. 'Language', writes John Fowles, 'is like shot silk; so much depends on the angle at which it is held' (*The French Lieutenant's Woman*, p. 437). As Rosemary discovers.

---

10. Glen Cavaliero shared with me his thoughts on Bragg's qualities as a regional novelist at the Powys Society Conference in Llangollen in 2011. I am particularly grateful for his later taking the trouble to find and post me his original typed draft review of *The Silken Net*.

# Grains of Sand

# SEVEN

# SLOUCHING TOWARDS BETHLEHEM
## *AUTUMN MANOEUVRES*

*Autumn Manoeuvres* (1978) is an overtly political 'condition of England' novel, set in the late 1970s, as viewed from a Parliamentary constituency in West Cumbria. It is structured around the incumbent Labour MP Jimmie Johnston's campaign for re-election in an imagined 1978 General Election. Despite his track record as a committed socialist and a loyal Labour Party member, Jimmie enters the short sharp three-week campaign enmeshed in 'an endless and melancholy labyrinth of doubt'. He is aware of the many kinds of compromised languages circulating in manifesto texts and hustings promises that are dependent on 'the angle at which [they] are held' for ideological meaning and enactment. The then Labour Prime Minister, James Callaghan, is seen in retrospect to have made a major miscalculation in not calling an election until 1979. Bragg's novel provides part of the background as to how and why no amount of Autumn manoeuvring was able to prevent a Winter of discontent, heralding a Conservative electoral victory under Margaret Thatcher.

The Cumbrian constituency serves as a synecdoche for a troubled nation as Bragg sets local problems and disputes within the wider political context. In negotiating any presumed and illusory differences between the practice of politics and their representation in literature Bragg's novel unites matters political and poetical to achieve the considerable distinction, in D.J. Taylor's estimation, of being 'one of the few substantial political novels of a period when it had already come to seem doubtful whether poetical novels could continue to be written' (*After the War*, pp.213-14). Given the tenor of the Cumbrian Trilogy's realistic portrayal of Labour Party history, espousal of socialist values, and aesthetic appreciation of working-class culture, Taylor's verdict should not occasion any great surprise. Indeed, thirty-two years on Bragg finds himself guest editing a politically inflected issue of the same *New Statesman*[1] magazine

1. In his editorial Bragg reminisces about first reading the *New Statesman* at his grammar School in Wigton in the 1950s, where it 'sat mint and fresh every week on the library table' (p.5). Thus begins a life-time of reading it. An inescapable feature of Bragg's edited issue is the continuity and intensification of the same social and political problems - particularly as featured in Peter Lazenby's article 'The harrowing of the north' - that are identified in *Autumn Manoeuvres* (*New Statesman*, 11 October 2010).

that profiles Jimmie as a centre-right politician held back from preferment by fading good looks and a lack of working-class credentials. Bragg's major achievement as a political novelist alert to the ephemera of much political news media is the ability to combine political interpretation and literary aesthetics whilst providing a unique recording voice of the day-to-day minutiae of constituency campaigning and its wear-and-tear upon its participants. None of the other major politically orientated novels of the period, some of which I look at below, deal with the mundane and the quotidian of political life in quite such unforgiving local detail and at such a provincially depressed distance from London.

Not that every literary critic shares Taylor's and my appreciation of Bragg's left-leaning political-literary credentials. Writing about the literary representation of the political climate in the 1970s, Christopher Harvie, in *The Centre of Things. Political Fiction in Britain from Disraeli to the Present* (1991), in an otherwise valuable historical study on the role of fiction in British politics, contemptuously dismisses Bragg and Margaret Drabble as 'liberal herbivores' whose 'unreassuring tone owed as much to their unsure political footing as to gloomy plots' (p.223). Harvie argues that these two writers, and others of their contemporaries, are ineffectually 'trapped between predatory capitalism and revolutionary youth, trying to present a moral politics, while the economic machinery that preserved the BBC and the Arts Council was seizing up and far below political society something very atavistic was going on'(ibid.). This is to demand that the political novel must, as a necessity of definition, name an enemy and thereby risk a simplistic division of good and evil as part of a monologic purpose. In Harvie's analysis the destabilising changes in political allegiances, that his quoted writers are too liberally inclined to warn of, or prevent, result in the foundation of the Social Democratic Party (SDP) in 1981 which 'smashed the two-party system to pieces'(ibid.). In making his call to radical political-literary arms Harvie has either misread, or not understood, the nature of both Drabble's and Bragg's frustration with the political status quo in the 1970s and the importance of their wide-ranging survey of a contemporary malaise of a lack of involvement in organised politics, that remains as valid today as when they were writing. Perhaps it is not surprising therefore that Harvie's obituary of the two-party system is as foolish as it is premature.

Of the many political novels of the period,[2] Drabble's *The Ice Age*, published in 1977, provides a valuable and comprehensive introduction to the economic condition of 1970s England confronted by the protagonists of *Autumn Manoeuvres*. While both novels are notable for their awareness of the property speculation and related scandals of the day, resulting in the nemesis of several prominent architects and politicians, it is Drabble's graphic portrayal of a national society in a state of paralysis that sets the scene for the localised electoral struggle at the centre of *Autumn Manoeuvres*:

> All over the country, people blamed other people for all the things that were going wrong - the trades unions, the present government, the miners, the car workers, the seamen, the Arabs. The Irish, their own husbands, their own wives, their own idle good-for-nothing offspring, comprehensive education .... The old headline phrases of freeze and squeeze had for the first time become for everyone - not merely for the old and unemployed - a living image, a reality ... A huge icy fist, with large cold fingers, was chilling the people of Britain ... (*Ice Age*, p.65)

But, as Glenda Leeming argues: 'This is not the view of a character, it is an example of the authoritarian narrator, sketching in a depressing picture of Britain, but qualified with an ironic distance' (*Margaret Drabble*. p.59). By way of contrast, *Autumn Manoeuvres* directs the 'large cold finger' of a discomforting political reality directly towards West Cumbria, and at a relatively small cast of almost entirely local characters who play out a closely argued dialectic between the personal and the political in which the latter appears to win a Pyrrhic victory at the cost of

2. Among the more interesting examples I have read are Raymond Williams's *The Fight for Manod* (1979), John Harvey's *The Plate Shop* (1978), Max Egremont's The *Ladies' Man* (1983), Piers Paul Read's *A Married Man* (1979), and Julian Fane's *Revolution Island* (1979). This is far from a comprehensive list but the titles selected give a flavour of the generally angst-ridden depiction of 1970s Britain, although none explore in any detail the mechanics of grass-roots political change. *A Married Man* is notable for its portrayal of the middle-class's increasingly paranoid fear of the putative power of the unions and of government attempt to curb strikes, both official and unofficial ones. *The Plate Shop* approaches the problem from the other side, explaining just how difficult ordinary union members found it to influence even their own union officials. At the most extreme end of the political spectrum *Revolution Island* slides into an unreliable narration of dystopic despair but Fane does succeed in conveying the increasing atmosphere in the 1970s of public disillusion with Labour politicians as opposed to socialist policies.

a future which the reader might deduce as being the narrator's preferred socialist outcome, but which his characters ultimately deny him.

The novel opens with images of autumnal decay and personal illness that all but pre-determine a tragic ending irrespective of its broader engagement with practical and philosophical political issues refracted through Jimmie's belief in the need for the Parliamentary enactment of his branch of Christian Socialist values. Having slept badly during a stormy night, Jimmie's wife Elaine has risen early and is walking in the garden, beneath the family's ancient copper beech, and 'conscious, as she trod, that she was pressing [its newly fallen leaves] to decay'(*AM*, p.3). The interiority of decay is matched by surrounding images that make Elaine dislike the autumn: 'the flowers die, the trees stripped by wind, the hedges become skeletons of themselves' (ibid.) and, significantly, the copper beech oppresses her as being 'too heavy, too dark'(ibid.). Jimmie hears his wife go outdoors and is afraid that she is heading 'into another of her bad times'(p. 5) only to be got through with pills, patience and rest. The dark secret of the source of Elaine's illness is only revealed late in the novel, when its disclosure traumatises her son Gareth - already estranged from his step-father Jimmie and determined to disrupt his election campaign - and leading to the accidental death of Gareth's son that invites a parallel reading of the novel as the demise of Socialism. The novel ends as it begins with a storm, a storm that makes itself felt 'especially in the copper beech' (p.239) that dominates the vicarage and punctuates the text throughout.

The ancient tree stands rooted as a powerful symbol of patriarchal power's resistance to change, both within the family and in a wider political context. In Ford Madox Ford's *The Last Post*, the final novel in the sequence *Parades End*, Sylvia Tietjen engineers the cutting down of the Groby Great Tree which symbolically represented the old order - 'The tree ... the great tree ... It darkens the windows ...'(p.793, the author's ellipses) - and so clearing a metaphorical space for the continued existence of the Tietjen family's genealogical tree. By way of contrast, the Johnston family tree becomes a nodal point for Elaine's youthfully-induced psychoanalytically troubled relationship with the exercise of masculine power. Repeatedly thrusting itself into Elaine's awareness, the tree oppresses her in its association with a constraining male authority that echoes Sylvia Tietjen's experience:

She looked at the copper beech - so enormous and

> domineering and old. It blocked the view. But who
> would ever dare knock it down? As the sun came up it
> cast a cold shadow into the living-room. Yet not only
> this household but to some extent the whole
> neighbourhood was proud of its immense dark copper
> strength and age. (*AM* p.75)

For Jimmie, the tree creates an aura of familiarisation and continuity that
fuses with a beneficial sense of heightened political consciousness:

> ... he looked directly into the copper beech. As a boy he
> had swung on it, hidden in it, dared himself to climb
> higher and higher - testing himself - attempted to
> construct a tree house, made a swing, watched it daily
> exist, just be, there, outside his bedroom window. He
> could not think of life without it now. When he looked
> at it, Jimmie felt that he understood the strange
> religious notion of Wordsworth that there were indeed
> virtues in Nature, moral laws, which the receptive mind
> and heart could perceive. For although it was
> embarrassing to admit, it was true that, on some
> occasions, simply looking at that copper beech tree
> made him feel a better man and determine to act so.
>
> (*AM* p. 164)

The tree elicits a moment of political exaltation in which Jimmie invokes
Wordsworth's belief in the intrinsic power of the poetic word to return
human nature to the sources of simplicity and happiness resident in
nature, nursing his own hope that political activity can help construct an
equally authentic and harmonious social world. But Wordsworth's
troubling *The World is Too Much with Us* also implies that it is the presence
of the human that has depleted nature, creating an emptiness out of
plenty that no amount of political manoeuvring can redress:

> The world is too much with us; late and soon,
> Getting and spending, we lay waste our powers:
> Little we see in Nature that is ours;
> We have given our hearts away, a sordid boon!
>
> (*Lyrical Ballads*, p. 184)

In this reading, Wordsworth's consciousness of loss of human spontaneity in nature mirrors much of the twentieth-century's political entropy.

Where for Jimmie identification with the beech signifies a perceived benevolence of patriarchal power, from a feminine standpoint it represents only loss and lack of influence. Marianne - the single mother of Gareth's son Alan, both of whom also live at the vicarage - reads the tree in the same dark tones as does Elaine, seeing it as an agent of separation from, rather than inclusion in, life. She berates Gareth's half-hearted attempt to make his son a swing in the tree in language that is symbolically prescient: 'You were too lazy to climb the tree to find a good branch - but you just about did it - and there it dangles yet - more like a *hangman's noose* that a boy's swing' (*AM* p. 237, italics added). Earlier in the novel we notice that Elaine underscores the imbalance of male-female power relationships that underwrite the political process, by limiting her involvement with the beech tree to its fallen/cut twigs, which she associates with death:

> Elaine saw the white-ended twigs as wounded. It was a crazy exaggeration - she was aware of that - but her nature was such that she felt the ripped-off wood to be bleeding to death: the water in the vase was simply a stay of extinction. (*AM* p.35)

and

> Elaine took the copper beech twigs from the vase. The leaves were crinkled. She looked, as they walked back, for somewhere to dump them but nowhere seemed appropriate. Hedges newly trimmed, narrow roads free of litter. In the end they were carried all the way back home to the rubbish heap on which the others had been laid. (*AM* p.151)

The prominence of the symbolism of the beech tree is not an evasion of politics via a diversionary tactic into nature, but rather a demonstration of the centrality of nature to a political-aesthetic discourse specifically located in a Lake District context. It serves to highlight the critical ambivalence always likely to be present when trying to endorse a text as both an aesthetic creation and a call to political action. In *Autumn Manoeuvres* the presence of the beech tree bookending the novel invites a discussion as to whether it suggests an exit from politics or whether it redirects the reader to the bedrock of familial politics that underlies the most important political questions of authority and its legitimacy.

In a similar interpretative vein, Elaine's mother, Mrs Burns, who lives at the vicarage, might be wryly amused and somewhat sceptical to find her private domestic occupation of patchwork quilting annexed by the 1970s feminist aesthetic-political agenda. Nevertheless, her commitment to a form of quilting that spills out from the privacy of her room to the vicarage at large represents an essentially feminist activity that has increasingly come to be interpreted, in such texts as Elaine Showalter's influential 1991 study *Sister's Choice, Tradition and Change in American Women's Writing*, as a metaphor for 'a Feminist Aesthetic, for sisterhood, and for a politics of feminist survival' (p.146). Mrs Burns's retreat to a room of her own is viewed as a positive move 'out of which came an endless line of well-sewn patchwork quilts which she did - one of her few boasts - with "her own eyesight"' (*AM* p.32). In Showalter's thematics, Mrs Burns's quilting is part of a generalised intertextual tradition linking women's rites to women's rights via a feminine impulse to nurturance and thrift that characterises Mrs Burns's life-style and on-going care for her damaged daughter. At the same time, by restricting her aesthetic activity to quilting she is also maintaining an ideological definition of feminism as marginal to the political mainstream in its characteristic reproduction of a separate sphere of domestic femininity. As Showalter expresses it: 'Quilts, like those who write about them, are thought to be trifling; they have been seen as occupying a female sphere outside of high culture' (*AM* p.147), so that it is little wonder that throughout *Autumn Manoeuvres* quilting remains marginal in a text which has nothing to say about Mrs Burns's political ideals and aspirations, but which concentrate on her hard work in the kitchen or laundry room. It is the advance of the women's movement in the decade of the novel's publication, linked to the subsequent widening scope of feminist research and scholarship in the field of literary textual analysis that has prompted a radical reappraisal of the art/craft of quilting as documenting an important aspect of women's lives.

Mrs Burns and her contemporaries might find it difficult to identify her interests with any of the plethora of poster images plastered on the walls of the squatter's house where Weston, the Workers Revolutionary Party (WRP) activist, has established his entirely negative electoral campaign base: 'The walls were plastered all over with posters - Che, Mao, Buster Keaton, Angela Davis, Soledad Brothers, Shrewsbury Three, Meetings, Declarations, Demands, Threats and Promises'[3] (*AM* p.155). Their immediately most striking feature is of an entirely unfocussed political montage of multiple and even contradictory messages defying a coherent response from the viewer/reader. The most charitable critique would be to submit that a state of contradiction holds few epistemological fears for Weston and his supporters, since no single cause, position or reified image holds sufficient cultural or logical superiority over another to demand priority. Read/viewed thus they become representative of a capitalist system that can equally accommodate film stars and revolutionaries as evidence of its own internal contradictions which the Far Left exploits for subversion from within. E.L. Doctorow puts a poster collage to similar use in his 1971 novel *The Book of Daniel*, an impassioned account of the controversial trial of Julius and Ethel Rosenberg in early 1950s America, in which the paranoia of Edgar Hoover's FBI is represented by the display of clashing images - 'Shirley Temple in her dancing shoes' appears alongside 'a chain gang working on the road' and Mickey Mouse cavorts beside 'a black man hanging from a tree' (p.140) - all aimed at the hegemonic premise calling for revolutionary change that 'EVERYTHING THAT CAME BEFORE IS ALL THE SAME!' (p.141). There is, however, one striking difference between Doctorow's and Bragg's choice of radical iconic images - every one of Doctorow's twenty-six images is indigenous to American culture, whereas Bragg's posters range internationally - U.S.A., South America,

3. The semiotics of the poster art referenced here could claim a chapter of its own, dealing as it does with the autonomy of an art form which in itself might encourage political apathy, in a paradoxical relationship with the encouragement of active political engagement. Weston's wall display limits its statement to a visual expletive in a context lacking any authentic or political evaluative criteria. It would, for example, be useful to know of the direct connection between the Soledad Brothers and Angela Davis posters. The Soledad Brothers were three Afro-American inmates of Soledad Prison, charged with the murder of a prison guard. One, George Jackson, was killed during an escape attempt in 1971, whilst his two remaining 'Brothers' were acquitted of the original charge one year later. A detailed account of these events is in *History is a Weapon. Soledad Brothers: The Prison Letters of George Jackson* (www.historyisaweapon.com). The Soledad Brothers Defence Committee was led by none other than the feminist black activist Angela Davis, whose 1971 essay 'Reflections on the Black Woman's Role in the community of Slaves', whilst a powerful analysis of American slavery's effect on women is difficult to translate to the British historical experience in the 1970s. The intrusion of a Buster Keaton poster I find particularly intriguing, appearing at first sight as being as incongruous in such surroundings as is Mickey Mouse in Doctorow's political collage in *The Book of Daniel*. It might be justified by Keaton's screen persona's pricking of pomposity from the position of 'the weakling lost in a world of gigantic he-men' (*The Rise of American Film*, 414).

Cuba, China - displaying only one British candidate, that of the 'Shrewsbury Three'.[4] This lack of a local identity is seen by Jimmie as a fatal weakness, exposing the WRP's lack of coherent and relevant programme; yet Jimmie is acutely aware that in a marginal constituency such as his, the loss of disaffected Labour to the Far Left risks handing the seat to the Conservatives.

Jimmie caricatures Weston's WRP followers as a 'clutch of hare-brained thespians, disaffected television producers and sadly gullible apprentices'(*AM* p.58). Here Bragg touches on a little explored in fiction, but culturally important, part of the British scene in which the media, and the BBC in particular, are seen in some quarters as having undue influence on public political opinion. Vanessa and Corin Redgrave were both active in the WRP - a party of no more than 3,000 members at its height - lending credence to Dominic Sandbrook's assertion in *Seasons in the Sun. The Battle for Britain, 1974-1979* (2012) that '[f]or some strange reason, the WRP had a particular appeal to the acting profession' (p.303), and 'was particularly marked among the writers, directors and producers who worked on the BBC's *Play for Today* strand'(ibid.). Given Bragg's first-hand experience of working at the BBC in the 1970s it would be fascinating to know whether he shares Jimmie's fictional hostility to the WRP (and the Socialist Workers' Party). Certainly Bragg appears to have modelled Weston on the real-life leader of the WRP, Gerry Healey, regarded by many commentators as a bully attempting to mould a small band of fanatics into the sort of citizens' army ridiculed in the BBC television sitcom *Citizen Smith* (1977-80), where the prominence of the Che Guevara poster was a substitute for any serious ideological positioning. In *Autumn Manoeuvres* Weston is finally exposed as a serial seducer who deserts his wife and family, leaving them without any financial support, and who is guilty of assault and the manipulation of committee votes to achieve his ends. Here again it is difficult to avoid the suspicion that Bragg has Healey in mind, a leader who solicited funds from the Libyans, helped himself to party funds, sexually abused female comrades and assaulted male colleagues who disagreed with him. If it dealt only with a picture of the radical Left, *Autumn Manoeuvres* would be a valuable addition to the political fiction of the 1970s, but it does much more than this in addressing a question that is always to the forefront of

---

4. Accounts of the trial of these building-worker pickets, from two opposing viewpoints, may be found in Roy Jenkins's 1991 autobiography *A Life at the Centre* (391-3) and in Ritchie Hunter's *Justice for the Shrewsbury Pickets* (www.catalystmedia.org.uk) .

Bragg's credo "'If Weston wants to address himself to big questions, I'll give him one. Where are we, English, British now? Or, much harder ... *who are we?* What is that identity without which nations are as lost as individuals?" (*AM* p.59, author's italics) and which goes to the heart of mainstream electoral politics.

Gareth is obsessed with discovering the truth about his own identity and, on the eve of the election campaign, has resigned from his populist broadcasting job to travel to Cumbria in search of answers. His final recorded interview goes on air whilst he is with the family in the vicarage, subliminally raising confusing notions of identity by the accompaniment of an otherwise seemingly innocuous set of musical cues. Gareth's voice is first heard as an American heavy rock number is faded out: "'Flapjack Mack and *Million Dollar Baby* - another funky black sound out to make a fortune'" (*AM*, p.73). His editorial comment on the ubiquity of capitalist commodified entertainment values is an expression of his political ideology but the irony of the claim 'they are just like us, we are just like them'(ibid.) is at this stage lost on both Gareth and the reader, and must await the novel's concluding revelation about the identity of his biological father. The faux-American phraseology involving listeners 'coast to coast'(ibid.) is followed by an abrupt change of musical identity as 'a full Hammond Organ chord bulged out of the radio and then turned into the first few bars of "Greensleeves" played in a minor key' (ibid.). This quintessential English love ballad, dating back to 1584, is the ironic prelude to hearing a distraught mother publically sharing her intimate story of how her crying baby was killed by her drunken partner.

This snapshot of a dysfunctional Britain, transmitted in the context of an unfocussed trans-Atlantic soundtrack, elicits significantly contrasting responses from different generations of listeners. Jimmie represents a dying tradition of inclusive Christian Socialist values and cannot understand the growing influence of the mass media's 'vague populism'(*AM*, p.75) feeding off 'a tawdry and misguided exploitation of human frailty' (*AM*, p.73). Contrastingly, Helen Wilks, a young PhD research student helping Jimmie's campaign while gathering material, respects Gareth's ability to present and make visible social problems in a way in which ordinary listeners can empathise with, even though she personally finds the underlying truth of their message unbearable. The broadcast exposes differing responses to the location of meaning as dependent on variable social and historical constructs, even though all those listening at the vicarage are conscious, each in their own way, of the absolute value of a past sense of Englishness that is being lost. The values that Jimmie's generation attribute to Englishness linger on in the political process but the contingency of its beliefs and commitments is demonstrated as much by the unethical business practices of colleagues, such as the property speculator Harold Ruthwaite, as by the performative staging of political anger by Weston's WRP followers. The latter, although few in number, signify a major shift towards political campaigning as a contested category away from the traditional English belief in fair play as the default setting for measuring political behaviour. Jimmie's commitment to argumentative persuasion, the compromises necessary for ideologues of Left and Right, the slow tortuous but democratic process of candidate selection, the cumbersome legislative process itself, are all challenged by the disruptive intervention of such groups as the WRP who have learnt to subvert the ethical legitimacy of the majority by using the more extreme tactics of some American civil rights and anti-Vietnam war demonstrators, allied to the mob mentality of Fascist thugs. Gareth encapsulates this flight from Englishness when his first response to Jimmie's attempt at opening a reasoned dialogue is to stand 'to attention, Gestapo heel-clicking style, and [giving] the Black Power salute' (*AM*, p.140). Later, WRP attempts to disrupt the visiting Prime Minister's speech with choreographed shouts of 'Sieg Heil!' (*AM*, p.197) are countered by a display of fair play by that most traditional of Northern English community institutions, the local professional rugby league team, whose members carry the protestors from the hall.

A particular merit of *Autumn Manoeuvres* as a political novel is its ability to accurately summarise Labour Party history and identify its leading members in such a way as to provide the necessary political background without either glamorising its participants or threatening to deliver a didactic tract. Bragg outlines Jimmie's Party involvement in four succinct pages (*AM*, pp.6-9), showing Jimmie to be a complicated character whose alignment with the Christian Socialist moderate right-wing of the Party, and a belief in Clement Attlee's government's 1945 welfare reform programme, does not prevent him from being emotionally susceptible to Aneurin Bevan's passionately adversarial left-wing pronouncements - '"Bevan brought poetry into Labour politics"(*AM*, p.7). In a neat psychologically revealing touch, Bragg traces Jimmie's belief in pragmatic Socialism, practised within the boundaries of the capitalist system as exemplified by Hugh Gaitskill, back to his boyhood reading of Arnold

Bennett's best-selling 1908 self-help manual *How To Live On 24 Hours A Day*. Bennett himself was a Socialist, a one-time Fabian Society member, who argued the need for a fair and open meritocratic society, without challenging the basic tenets of capitalism. His book is a call to work, not to arms, and the fact that Henry Ford purchased 500 copies to distribute to his staff is perhaps evidence enough that in citing it 'as the foundation on which he could build his life' (*AM*, p.5) Jimmie is early predisposed towards the safe middle-ground of Democratic Socialism in the interests of welfare capitalism. But, as a non-literary man, he fails to learn Bennett's dictum on the benefit of close reading. In his enthusiasm for providing affordable housing for his constituents he readily accepts the word of his friend Harold Ruthwaite on the legality of various business contracts and is then unprepared for the disclosure of contractual irregularities that find their way on to the pages of *Private Eye*.

In naming the satirical magazine *Private Eye*, Bragg is able to chronicle recent public events to contextualize effectively the related events of his fictional narrative. The references to *Private Eye*'s pursuit of Reginald Maudling, Jeremy Thorpe[5] and James Callaghan is an effective condensed economy of presentation indicting the entire political spectrum and suggesting in its inclusivity the levelling cross-currents at work in contemporary political culture that so exercise Gareth and his like-minded friends. Bragg skilfully shapes the naming of actual personalities so as to reveal that the extent of political corruption extends beyond the involvement of any one individual or political party. Jimmie's earlier recall of the hounding from office of Maudling, for example, reverberates with Ruthwaite's fear that *Private Eye*'s investigation of his business dealings will lead, not only to his own term of imprisonment, but also will in the process taint his friend Jimmie and harm the Labour Party locally: '"They got Poulson. Locked him up. They got Dan Smith. Locked him up. Cunningham[6]

5. Jeremy Thorpe's homosexual entanglements while leader of the Liberal Party, and his alleged payment for what turned into a wildly surrealistic attempt by a hired hit man to kill his blackmailer, Norman Scott, but who only succeeded in shooting Scott's dog, found its way into the pages of *Private Eye*. Auberon Waugh, a satirist who wrote the magazine's regular Diary entry picked up the story in his local paper, *West Somerset Free Press*, under the headline 'Mystery of the dog in the fog'. Read in full, including the subsequent trial and Thorpe's fall from grace, the story has elements beyond the imaginings of all but the most inventive of fiction writers.

6. Andrew Cunningham was jailed in 1974 for his participation in the corrupt practice of both Poulson and T. Dan Smith. In return for financially beneficial favours from Poulson he steered lucrative building contracts toward Poulson from the many public-bodies he chaired and the Labour councils he could influence. At one time he was a regional secretary of the General & Municipal Workers' Union and a member of Labour's National Executive Committee.

- as Labour a man as you, my friend - locked him up. They nosed out Slater.[7] That was serious'" (*AM*, p.98). Bragg is highlighting the issue of property speculation and petty corruption that stained the reputation of several prominent public figures in the 1970s. The crooked West Yorkshire architect John Poulson's contacts included an influential network of politicians and council officials, prominent amongst whom was Reginald Maudling, a former Conservative Home Secretary, revealed to have taken bribes from Poulson, and Newcastle's flamboyant Labour leader T. Dan Smith. Both Poulson and Smith were eventually jailed on corruption charges. Maudling's demise would have been at the forefront of Jimmie's mind in contemplating his own guilt by association with Ruthwaite's property development scam, even though he entered into it for the best of motives and made no personal financial gain. It is worth remembering that at the time of *Autumn Manoeuvres* publication, these events would still have resonated in many readers' minds, contributing to the late 1970s general sense of disillusionment with the Labour Party as a vehicle for representing the interests of its core working-class supporters. The albeit limited electoral appeal of Weston's WRP antics becomes more understandable if thus contextualised, and in giving them narrative space Bragg is drawing attention to the early stirrings of what will become a near terminally destructive battle for the ideological soul of the Labour Party in the 1980s.

The novel's political climatic set-piece is the Prime Minister's visit to the constituency and his speech in the local ballroom in the presence of television cameras. Reviewing *Autumn Manoeuvres* in the *Times Literary Supplement* (2 June 1978), Paul Johnson singles out this episode to write that the 'visit of the Prime Minister is brilliantly done - I dare say Jim [Callaghan] could use a few phrases from the speech'. Reading it today it appears remarkably similar to twenty-first century electioneering speeches aimed simultaneously at physically present local audiences and a wider television one. Bragg equips his fictional Prime Minister with the full range of rhetorical devices, many of which leave Jimmie with the uncomfortable feeling that he is using 'the national feeling; using the overspill of emotion, manipulating, seizing the opportunity,

---

7. Edward Heath's financial assets had been managed - at a fire-wall distance - by Slater Walker, who invested them in special situations not available to the general public. The result was a 60 per cent return on £30,000 in two years. Although no direct impropriety attached to Heath, his reputation suffered damage from the *Sunday Times*'s investigation of Slater's methods.

wheeler-dealing' (*AM*, p.175). The Prime Minister accuses London newspaper editors and the foreign press of circulating biased gloomy reports of the state of Britain; he flatters his local audience as being the 'people who really speak for this country' (*AM*, p.173); he catalogues the social improvements made under Labour that will be at risk with a change of administration; he blames present economic problems on the Tory inheritance; and he conscripts John Bunyan as part of Labour's heritage: '- we've pulled the country out of the Slough of Despond ... let's march on together to the Promised Land' (*AM*, p.175).

The other notable feature of major campaign speeches that has become firmly factored into electoral broadcasting since the late 1960s, and which Bragg mimetically reproduces, is the importance of being able to deliver a speech crafted for delivery to two separate audiences.[8] Bragg's Prime Minister has learnt to switch abruptly from partisan harangues to the wholly different content, style and tone of delivery for, say, a three minute live insert at the top of a national television news bulletin:

> The Prime Minister waved down the applause and seemed to forget all about the cameras as he leaned forward, jutted out his chin, pushed aside his notes, thought of the eleven to twelve million watching this bulletin, knew in his heart of hearts that elections *could* be tilted in a day, knew there was everything to play for and reached out for votes. "What do you ask of us?" he cried out - and the tone was harsher and more fierce than he had used hitherto.
>
> (ibid.)

There is an undeniable element of cynicism in a practice in which the speaker sees 'the signal from the floor - Back to London in fifteen seconds' and winds up his oration to the accompaniment of maximum applause with split second timing as 'the cameras lingered an extra twelve seconds' (*AM*, p.177) to create an impression of passionate unity but which is ultimately aimed at promoting the Party as the equivalent of any other branded commodity.

Two elements of Bragg's depiction of the big set-piece political speech, and its organisational preparation, strike me as deserving further

---

8. There is a useful chapter on the history and future potential development of television and radio electoral broadcasting - Martin Harrison, 'Television and Radio' - in D. E. Butler and Anthony King, *The British General Election* (1966).

comment. First, as someone actively involved in the 1979 General Election as a Labour Branch Secretary in a similar northern constituency, I am impressed by the documentary realism of Bragg's prose. Looking again at the press cuttings included in my 1978/9 diaries I am struck by an uncanny match between the Prime Minister's fictional speech and that given by the then Cabinet member Roy Hattersley, Secretary of State for Prices and Consumer Protection, when he accepted my invitation to speak locally. The examples quoted below come from the 8 May 1978 issue of the daily regional newspaper, the *Sentinel*, with a readership across North Staffordshire and South Cheshire:

> '"We inherited from the Tories a mess bigger than anything since the war"' (*AM*, p.176) 'Since the war Labour Governments have been repeatedly returned by the electorate to "mop up an economic catastrophe" left by the Conservatives' (*Sentinel*).

> '"Who else could have called on the Unions to help curb the evil of inflation?"' (*AM*, p.176) 'Labour were the only party who could work with the unions' (*Sentinel*).

> '"Look at what they did last time - set off a galloping sickness of inflation and stagnation and unemployment that took us three years to cure"' (*AM*, p.176) '... it would be a disaster for Britain if the pattern of the last thirty years was repeated, and Labour lost power after bringing the country back from economic crisis' (*Sentinel*).

And neither Bragg's Prime Minister nor Hattersley fail to include an ingratiating reference to their immediate audience, with the former praising it as 'people inside a compassionate Labour Party' (*AM*, p.174) and the latter being 'touched by the friendliness and hospitality of the local Labour Party' (*Sentinel*). From a literary critical perspective 35 years on I can recognise that Bragg's deployment of political language/diction and aesthetic language are not mutually exclusive antagonistic categories. Any number of novels with an element of social resonance lend themselves to a political reading, but *Autumn Manoeuvres* is concerned with actual political struggle and affiliation, inviting readers to take sides in a generalised Left-Right political debate. I would suggest, then, that we critique *Autumn Manoeuvres* both for Bragg's connection of the personal and the political within a multi-themed text and for its openness and willingness to itself become part of the existing cultural power structure in a realistic and pragmatic way.

Closely related to the above discussion is the second noteworthy element of Bragg's coverage of the election. Whilst Bragg is openly associated with Labour Party politics - and now sits on the Labour benches in the House of Lords as Lord Bragg of Wigton/Thurston - he carefully structures *Autumn Manoeuvres* so as to avoid any simplistic division between Labour and Conservative as one between good and evil. We remain aware of his ideological preferences, both in this novel and from several of his other works, including the non-fictional *Speak for England*, whilst simultaneously being presented with a critique of Labour values from within the text, both by access to Jimmie's conscience and by listening to Ruthwaite's vitriolic attack on the hypocrisy of Labour values. Jimmie's private doubts surface in the midst of the Prime Minister's big speech, punctuating its positive message with precisely the troubling issues likely to be at the forefront of concerned readers' minds in the late 1970s:

> Yes, his conscience was split over the closed-shop issue and his loyalties torn by the parochial attitudes of the big unions towards their smaller "brothers"; by the hypocrisy of the rich Labour men who used the private schools and hospitals and by the hypocrisy of the Labour left which was so selective over what it saw in Eastern Europe. (*AM*, p.175)

Ruthwaite mounts his more telling attack on Labour in general and on Jimmie in particular from the position of a working-class boy who becomes a successful business man who feels alienated from the party to which he naturally belongs by birth-right.

> I'm a crude feller, I'm vulgar, successful and pushy. I'm a bit like all the Englishmen of the past you never actually get round to talking about, Jimmie - the sweatshop merchants and industrial swine who made us rich - the cruel bastards who scared the hell out of Foreigners from Shanghai to Amsterdam - all those unpleasant sods who fail to appear in your Peter Pan History of England. I like your speeches, Jimmie, truly I do. You can bring a lump to my throat. But to go out and get the lucre that makes the world go round you

need a lump somewhere else. All you state-subsidised socialists pretending to be the voice of the working class - what you've done is grab the microphone! None of you has ever *made* work, *made* jobs, *made* money, come up with 'the goods' - interesting word that, eh? No, you can shake your head until it rolls off, old son, but you can't ignore what I say. You'd like to ignore it. Just like your father, the great Canon, ignored all those poor little Asiatic bastards actually working in the rubber plantations where he deposited his famous inheritance and where it vanished - an Act of God, that, if ever there was one. There's a lot you like to ignore. You ignore Elaine when she talks - except maybe when she talks about her father - oh how *interesting* that the chap made brass horseshoes in his spare time. And *what* a pity he was killed by cheap pit-props. Made on an English rubber plantation, no doubt, by somebody who went on to add lustre to the land. You were probably at school with his son.

(AM, p.100, author's italics)

I have quoted the passage at length in part because it is illustrative of the sort of attack upon Labour made by characters in several novels of the period, but, as in for example, *A Married Man*, usually by members of the comfortable but disaffected middle-class. More tantalisingly, the passage raises the sort of hidden questions about Imperialism and Englishness - and then, admittedly, subsequently ignored in the rest of the text - first deconstructed in the light of a critical analysis of the English novel in Edward Said's 1993 *Culture and Imperialism*. But, by at least giving space to Ruthwaite's oppositional voice, Bragg maintains the possibility of a multiplicity of interpretations within the politics of a literary text.

I am equally interested in exploring the way in which Ruthwaite's disclosure of hidden, forgotten or wilfully displaced texts plays out in the parallel context of the novel's own dark domestic secret. Ruthwaite's accusation that Jimmie, along with his socially like-minded friends, conveniently ignores any versions of the truth that might disrupt his preferred version of reality, finds its fullest expression in the representation of the novel's long-deferred, central primal scene, the war-time rape of Elaine. Lured from a local dance at an American base to the beach she is gang-raped by three American G.I.s who escape punishment and are quietly sent home to avoid scandal. Elaine refuses an abortion, marries the sympathetic Jimmie, and gives birth to her son Gareth. The rape has been kept secret from Gareth until now, and its sudden revelation threatens to destabilise any remaining remnants of a self-identity. The knowledge leads indirectly to his symbolic enactment of the abortion his mother refused when he becomes responsible for the death of his own son.

But there is already something of a festering secret in Gareth's own life which helps to explain his urge for self-destruction. His brutal battering of Peter Fraser, 'a fashionably coiffured, edgily arrogant boy-man' (*AM*, p.117) whom he lures to his London basement flat in a desperate attempt to silence what appears to be the threat of homosexual drug-related blackmail, has elements in common with the behaviour of the American rapists. Leaving the scene of the attack Gareth admits the full extent of his sensual arousal: 'it had exhilarated him, the violence, it had made him wholly alive' (*AM*, p.118). At this point Bragg re-ignites a question that rumbles along beneath the surface of the electoral plot, that is the extent of any link between individual psychological make-up and political ideology. Gareth makes explicit the recognition that personal violence has a direct correlation with certain types of extreme political behaviour: ' ... he saw himself having nowhere else to go but to the extreme political position which at least gave him something to grasp' (ibid.). In other words, Gareth exhibits a clinical internalised character synthesis of his political and psychological commitments,[9] leading to an immersion 'in the sense of evil which spread throughout his tense exhausted brain like a poisonous root' (*AM*, p.120). Disturbingly invasive, this sense of evil extends to Gareth imagining himself capable of the same violent behaviour towards a woman he sees out walking as exhibited by the serviceman who raped his mother: 'What if he tried to rape the woman? What if he did the vilest things he could imagine? What was there to stop him?' (ibid.). Neither Gareth nor the reader is in a position at this stage of the narrative to relate Gareth's violent imaginings, together with his rejection of societal conventional behavioural restraints, to the rape of his mother. Gareth's propensity to

9. The idea that ideology has a psychological personaity base, also linked to childhood experience, was first explored in detail in the early/mid twentieth-century by Wilhelm Reich, whose analysis of the fascistic personality carapace remains valid, even though his attempts at constructing machinery - the orgone box - to help patients have been largely ridiculed. The most accessible introduction to his work remains Paul A. Robinson's *The Sexual Radicals. Reich Roheim Marcuse* (1972).

violence, together with a suggested ambivalent sexual identity, is apparent when, in the next moment, Peter's face is replaced by an image of the 'haughty yobbishly-chic Dorian Gray face ... he had wanted to beat to insensibility' (ibid.). The image of Gareth's potential towards uncontrollable violence is stored in Bragg's text, in much the same way as Wilde's storing of Dorian's portrait, until its meaning emerges later as part of the Johnston's family history. In the light of Gareth's defection to embrace Weston's fascistic views we might further interpret the Macbeth-like appearance of Dorian Gray's face as an intertextual comment on Gareth's ventriloquizing of Weston's extreme political views as an echo of Dorian's parroting of Lord Henry's views - both are empty echoes, without a mind of their own. It is entirely psychologically and ideologically appropriate to read Gareth as the slave of another's beliefs, having his behaviour and thinking chosen for him, and then in turn manipulating the actions and thoughts of the three women in his life. When he is finally traumatised into an act of self-realisation and attempted family reconnection, the result brings the novel to a destructive conclusion in which personal tragedy obliterates any sense of the value of community politics. The final act of violence makes clear that however carefully private secrets are located within domestic everyday spaces, screened off from a more active and potentially threatening public sphere, the frail veneer of separation is always susceptible to sudden and unexpected rupture.

Gareth, however, is the one character in the novel who actually raises, rather than assumes, substantial questions about the practice of politics and the poetics of their argumentation from within a perspective of deep Englishness linked to the compaction of Cumbrian regional culture. Much of Chapter Twelve, in which Gareth and Helen climb the fells, is devoted to a discussion of ways of representing regional and community time/space to construct regional history and, significantly in the context and continuity of Bragg's other Cumbrian novels, how to approach Cumbria as a regional story in an on-going argument about national identity. The novel's deferred revelation as to Gareth's duality of Anglo-American birth-right helps explain internal contradictions that can wax lyrical in patriotic English expressions of love for his region and its traditions - ' ... remember, just down in Carlisle yonder was Arthur's finest and first court and Merlin's best and last hour'(*AM*, p.112) - at the same time as sceptically exposing the thin veneer of a commodified tourist-orientated commercial present, under the ultimate protection of a physically intrusive N.A.T.O. alliance.

The myth of Icarus remains a potent symbol of self-destruction twenty years on from its appearance in the immediate post-World War II years of *The Silken Net*, only now more immediate and threatening. Gareth alerts Helen's attention to four Phantom jets on a low-level training exercise,

> 'technologically trained to correct all the frailties of Icarus, Super-Icarians in tiny jets practising low-level flying for the day when we shall bomb the world to extinction, streaking low level across England, waking children, disturbing schools, driving cows and sheep to panic, over the heavy shires, over the fallow fields of the old industrial valleys, across the bone of rock and emerald greensword.' (ibid.)

Bragg's tone here is radically different from, say, that of Philip Larkin's 1969 poem 'Homage to a Government' (*Collected Poems*, p.171) written in protest at the Wilson government's demilitarisation of British bases in South-East Asia. Bragg is making Gareth the textual spokesman for precisely those international arguments about the right to maintain a military presence in sovereign countries linked to that surrounding the control over English regional territory threatened by the stationing of American cruise missiles that erupted during the Thatcher-Reagan years. Gareth's lament is both rhythmically poetic and politically prescient. He makes it against a background of perceptual unity between observer and landscape, pursuing an imaginative possessiveness that emphasises his bodily dematerialisation in the experience of a projected deep ecology analogous to the Aboriginal Australian 'Songlines' or 'Dreaming-tracks' celebrated in Bruce Chatwin's 1987 book *The Songlines*:[10]

> ... 'Imagine a giant compass. A Sci-Fi post-Wellsian monstrous Cape Canaveral compass with its bodkin pronged in here,' he pointed down to the top of the cairn, plumb below his body. 'Deep in here, deep in the rock which

10. Bruce Chatwin's book is an imaginative, anthropological and poetic study of the European designated Aboriginal 'Songlines', a labyrinth of invisible psychic pathways that criss-cross Australia. To the Aboriginals they are the 'Footprints of the Ancestors' tracing territorial rights of passage and bestowing personal identity. The Aboriginal notion of a sacred landscape under threat from global commercial and military pressures resonates with Gareth's own 'Dreaming' passage . The English equivalent of songlines is ley lines

might be the rock that stretches out to what might have been Atlantis. And that is so. So. In your imagination, draw, with this compass, a mighty circle, draw, with this stupendous compass, that miraculous never-ending straight line, that symbol of symbols, the circle, and .... Reaching out to the nethermost and uttermost parts of the realm, to the honking gulls of Orkney, to the black cruel rocks of Cornwall, to the friendly silt of Old Father Thames at Tilbury and up to the Wash - draw then this mighty circle and you will find upon this very spot, on this ancient pile .... That you, here, are in the very middle of these islands, the centre, the very plexus of Britain.'                                                  (*AM*, pp.111-12)

All this in the context of a lovingly detailed panoramic view of the Lakes 'in a magical enfolding of valleys' (*AM*, p.110) encompassing Borrowdale, Gable, Scafell, Helvellyn, Bassenthwaite, Blencathra and Skiddaw. Helen sees it as 'a place to gaze on and a spot to live in' (*AM*, p.110), whereas the more cynical Gareth sees it being reduced to a series of commodified images for the postcard industry in which the thinness of the cultural veneer is traced back to the late eighteenth-century tourist influx and 'a little Claude glass' (*AM*, p.111) in which the viewer symbolically turns their back on the actual landscape in order to frame a decontextualized part in a convex mirror, at about the size of a postcard. Gareth's point must surely be to signify the separation between viewer and landscape, the isolation of the viewer from the surrounding environment that is the equivalent of the cockpit view-finder that allows a Phantom jet pilot to release missiles in an act of abstraction from the physical world beneath. Destruction is thus wrought from a disinterested aesthetic distance.

Gareth's tragedy is that, given his ethical insights, he might have pursued a political trajectory in line with Jimmie's appeal to common decency. He does, after all, pause on the mountain to quote George Orwell, a writer who makes England the centre of his world and who is often cited as the epitome of English decency and common sense. David Gervaise, in *Literary Englands*, writes that Orwell's 'England was as if refracted through his anthropologist's curiosity, a commitment that did not preclude neutrality when necessary. This was part of his strength since it enabled him to avoid the more facile and sentimental kinds of identification with the working class that many of his contemporaries went in for'(p.170). Such an identification is a constant refrain in Gareth's attacks upon Jimmie's Socialism, and yet how psychologically telling that in quoting Orwell's poem included in his 1947 essay 'Why I Write' - "'A happy vicar I might have been,'he chanted, 'a hundred years ago, to preach upon eternal gloom, and watch my walnuts grow'" (*AM*, p.110) - Gareth seems to turn from the neutrality of his broadcasting career towards a desire for familial attachment expressed at one remove from Jimmie's canonical family background.[11] Gareth is aware of the divisions opening up between Cumbria's isolated but mythically central past and its globalised present, but he confronts the change in a context where his proneness to nostalgia finds an outlet in the regressive certainties of fascistic ideology, fought out amongst the landscape he loves and which ultimately gives authority to politics of whatever persuasion. In his chameleon-like switches of personality, politics and identity, the tragic figure of Gareth is the contemporary troubling avatar of the anti-hero of Bragg's 1987 deeply-embedded Cumbrian novel, *The Maid of Buttermere*, in which issues of identity politics from the wider world search out even the most historically isolated Cumbrian spaces.

11. Orwell's paternal grandfather was vicar of Milborne St. Andrew in Dorset. In quoting Orwell, Gareth fails to note the writer's openly expressed distaste for homosexuals, 'castigating in private "the pansy left", the "fashionable pansies", Auden and Spender being singled out for especial contempt. Yet he insisted, as usual unpredictable and unfailingly contradictory, that he had "always been very pro-Wilde."' (David Goodway, *Anarchist Seeds Beneath the Snow*, p. 136). Gareth appears ambiguously adrift between Orwellian and Wildean representations of self.

Grains of Sand

'- a frozen cascade of broken rock face lying on the more solid rock waiting only for an impulse to charge it into dangerous motion.' *The Maid of Buttermere,* p.88.

*Honister Crag* reproduced by kind permission of Julian Cooper.

# EIGHT

# THE MAN WHO NEVER WAS
## *THE MAID OF BUTTERMERE*

There is a marked behavioural and psychological fictional compatibility between the identity-searching Gareth of *Autumn Manoeuvres* and the shape changing chameleon John Hatfield at the centre of Bragg's first historical novel, *The Maid of Buttermere* (1987). Both indulge in unrestrained sexual adventures, share a propensity towards self-delusion, behave amorally, are ever ready to blame personal failings and inadequacies on the social and political system, and both have a death on their conscience. The respective novels in which they enact the drama of unrestrained egos are, however, radically different in genre and, importantly, in textual construction. Realistically, the Cumbria of *Autumn Manoeuvres* is depicted as a region suffering pockets of industrial decline and economic deprivation, unlikely to attract the attention of the tourist industry, whereas in *The Maid of Buttermere*, Keswick, Borrowdale, and Buttermere are shown emerging from geographical obscurity and cultural marginality to become putative beacons of Arcadian social stability at a time of revolutionary unrest, set in a timeless landscape of grandeur and harmony.

Driven by the search for a personal hidden paradise, the characters in *The Maid of Buttermere*, both factual and fictional, are motivated by the Romantic vision of solitude and the sublime, in which there is a powerful moral principle involved in the decision to put down roots in a specific place. The poets Wordsworth and Coleridge are at one with the anti-hero John Hatfield in sharing a subjective response to Buttermere and its surrounds that conveys their states of mind and emotional feelings in a concrete way, but whereas the poets can express their response in verse, Hatfield struggles to formulate his response other than in a private cry of wild exaltation addressed directly to Nature. Edith Wharton's *The Writing of Fiction* (1925) makes the related point that the 'impression produced by a landscape, a street or a house should always, to the novelist, be an event in the history of a soul' (p.85), and this is very much the response not only of the Romantic Lake poets but also of Bragg himself who represents Buttermere as a microcosm of the Romantic aesthetic and its programme of constructing a harmonious psychological landscape. The novel opens with a two line epigraph from Wordsworth's 1805 version of *The Prelude*, an epigraph that marks one of the founding moments in the cultural history of the Romantic movement that circulates through the heart of Bragg's novel

> 'Now I am free, enfranchised and at large,
> May fix my habitation where I will'
>
> (*The Prelude*, p.36)

which is both a ringing declaration of freedom and an enquiry as to what uses he will put it. Joe Pace's interpretation of these lines in his article 'Emotion and Cognition in *The Prelude*' extends to Bragg's fictional portrayal of Hatfield's search for a stable identity in a fixed location: 'What will I do with my life? Where is my place in this society? What kind of soul do I have and where will it find its kindred spirit?' (*Romanticism on the Net*). In shaping a response to these questions Bragg has ventured for the first time into the literary genre of the historical romance, stitching together historical and fictitious figures and events in a pattern that appropriates Nathanial Hawthorne's definition of the genre as a 'neutral territory, somewhere between the real world and fairy-land, where the Actual and the Imaginary may meet, and each imbue itself with the nature of the other' (*The Custom House*, p.28). The novel's final, paratextual, page lists 'those characters based on real people and historical figures who also appear in the novel' (*MB*, p.415), suggesting that in the Romance the terms fact and fiction are themselves illusory. This authorial nod towards a text in which mainly historical characters rub shoulders with fictional creations accords with *The Oxford Companion to English Literature*'s definition of Romanticism as representing 'the triumph of the values of imaginative spontaneity, visionary originality, wonder, and emotional self-expression [... arising] from a period of wider turbulence, euphoria, and uncertainty' (p.872).

The viewing of historical characters in their specific time/space setting through a literary lens brings its own difficulties of interpreting the dialectic between reality and imagination and, indeed, the very notion of the extent to which it is possible to recapture and present that time-past directly to a contemporary audience. Much of what follows will include an exploration of Bragg's narratological response to this question, in line with Hayden White's claim that history is as much the product of poetic language as fiction: 'For we should recognize that *what constitutes the facts themselves* is the problem that the historian, like the artist, has tried to solve in the choice of metaphor by which he orders his world, past, present, and future' (*Tropics of Discourse*, p.47). As a graduate of Modern History at Oxford, Bragg brings the academic rigour of historical documentary research to the writing of Romantic fiction.

Set in the early nineteenth century, *The Maid of Buttermere* recounts the true story of Mary Robinson, daughter of the inn-keeper of the Fish Inn in the isolated Cumbrian village of Buttermere, who was thrust unasked into the public limelight after she was featured as a beauty to rival nature's attractions in a best-selling travelogue of the period. Mary became a tourist attraction in her own right at a time when the Lake District was becoming the haunt of choice for poets, artists, and tourists in general, denied the freedom of European travel by the conflict with France. Mary's tragedy was to marry the bigamist fraudster, John Hatfield, then passing as an aristocrat, but who was destined for the hangman's noose when his various crimes came to light. Bragg knew the story well and must have been contemplating its potential as a novel for several years, having, for example, included Wilson Armistead's fairly accurate and comprehensive nineteenth-century account, 'The Beauty of Buttermere, or Tragedy in Real Life' in his 1981 anthology *My Favourite Stories of Lakeland* (pp.18-36). In a preface to the story Bragg opines that 'The writer [Armistead], despite himself, was obviously fascinated by her seducer'. And so is Bragg, bringing all his novelist's imaginative skill to bear in creating a fictional psychological profile to account for the known facts of Hatfield's life. He deploys a large cast of factual/fictional characters against what Amanda Thursfield describes as:

> the brooding landscape of the Cumbria that Bragg knows and loves so well ... his intimate descriptions of the towns and villages, of the paths up and down the fields, the detailed mappings of the meteorological changes in the area and the physical characteristics of the people who inhabit it are almost an act of devotion that one feels Turner or Coleridge themselves might have admired.
>
> (*Melvyn Bragg*, p.3)

There is also an encyclopaedic range of references covering proliferating tales, characters, plots and sub-plots, a familiarity with various arcane forms of local knowledge and ritual, from ballads to rural wedding customs, and an intellectual and political grasp of the wider contemporary scene at the start of the nineteenth century.

This sense of proliferating textual possibilities is apparent in the framing of the novel between an opening chapter of pseudo-real fictional/factual textuality and an authorial factual epilogue of historical record, coupled with an extract from an academic literary journal article linking Mary Robinson's story to twentieth-century sensational celebrity events such as the assassination of John Lennon.[1] Between these polarities *The Maid of Buttermere* emerges as a factual fiction, its double stance emphasised by Bragg's morphing of fiction into journalism's world of observation and commentary via Coleridge's reportal activity. I will return to consider in detail Bragg's use of genuine ideological, reportal, and commentative matter, but for the present I wish to linger over the opening chapter, which is both inventive as well as cognitive and referential in its fictional pursuit of a real past in a way that lends textual authority to its title of 'Rehearsal in the Sands'. Set on the dangerous shifting muddy wasteland margins of Morecambe Sands, the anti-hero Hatfield makes his first appearance in a liminal space between land and sea. The seashore of the Sands is, significantly, a scene of potential new beginnings as well as possible sudden exits, sucking down individuals unacquainted with its notorious tidal patterns.

On to this stage comes a character in search of an identity, referred to throughout the chapter only as 'He/he'. The man to be revealed as John Hatfield is in need of both a name and a persona to fit his next assumed role as a Lake tourist. Bragg imagines Hatfield thinking himself into the skin of John Philip Kemble, one of the most admired actors of his generation, whom Hatfield saw at the Drury Lane Theatre in London, sometime after his appointment there as actor-manager in 1788. Kemble is an inspired choice of role-model for Hatfield, for he not only acted in his own version of Shakespeare's *Coriolanus* at Drury Lane, but was also

1. Donald Reiman, 'the Beauty of Buttermere as fact and Romantic Symbol', *Criticism, Vol.26, No. 2*, pp.139-70, Wayne State U.P., 1984. The essay has attracted critical attention for its extensive survey of the literature which looks at events in Buttermere, both before and after 1802 - see Jerome Christensen, *Romanticism at the End of History*, p.221, John Hopkins U.P., 2000. At the same time it has come under scrutiny for displaying 'a confusion that has become generic to discussion of Robinson when it ascribes to Wordsworth the De Quincey version of the story' and consequently demoting her status in favour of reading her as a key to Wordsworth as poet. (Susan Lamb, *Bringing Travel Home to England: tourism, gender and imaginative literature in the Eighteenth Century*, p.217, Associated U.P., 2009.

perceived to have unconsciously allowed its influence to colour his off-stage private gestures and modes of speech in precisely the sort of presentation of self, founded on the psychological study and inhabiting of a fictional character's personality that Hatfield consciously aspires to. Hatfield declaims 'for the benefit of the sky, the sands, the waters' that he is to become 'Alexander Hope, Colonel, Member of Parliament for Linlithgowshire and brother to the Earl of Hopetoun' (*MB*, p.11). Schooled in prison by an unnamed, but subsequently fictionally important character who claims to have worked with Kemble, Hatfield recites his back-story by heart and ventriloquises the voice of a minor aristocrat, speaking aloud until 'the new voice ceased to surprise [him], then [he] could forget about it: the lines would come easily' (*MB*, p.12). In the process, Hatfield comes to prefigure the emerging Romantic myth of a primal, pre-abstract level of language tuned to a pristine order of meaning encompassing spiritual communion; he becomes 'utterly abandoned in his flow to that moment, those words, the vision, the air and flesh and thing he was: free, unthinking, self-ravished ... finally released in that empty ocean floor' (*MB*, p.13). In reading Bragg's extended account of Hatfield becoming Hope I am struck by its similarities with Peter Brook's description of Paul Schofield's rehearsal practice in which:

> The act of speaking a word sent through him vibrations that echoed back meanings more complex than his rational thinking would find: he would pronounce a word like 'night' and then he would be compelled to pause: listening with all his being to the amazing impulses stirring in some mysterious inner chamber, he would experience the wonder of discovery at the moment when it happened.
>
> (*The Empty Space*, p.124)

The thematics of performance and the construction of identity are central preoccupations in the novel, in which Hatfield will find himself 'compelled to pause' at critical moments of belief in the validity of his own performance. From the novel's outset, Bragg has not only mimetically reproduced the structure of stage-character rehearsal, but he has also prepared the ground for a literary analysis of the structure of social encounters from the perspective of dramatic performance as described in Erving Goffman's sociological depiction of promissory character activity:

> He may wish [people] to think highly of him, or to think that he thinks highly of them, or to perceive how in fact he feels toward them, or to obtain no clear-cut impression; he may wish to ensure sufficient harmony so that the interaction can be sustained, or to defraud, get rid of, confuse, mislead, antagonize, or insult them. Regardless of the particular objective which the individual has in mind and of his motive for having this objective, it will be in his interests to control the conduct of others, especially in their responsive treatment of him. This control is achieved largely by influencing the definition of the situation which others come to formulate, and he can influence this definition by expressing himself in such a way as to give them the kind of impression that will lead them to act voluntarily in accordance with his own plan.
>
> (The Presentation of Self, p.3)

Hatfield/Hope's role-playing meets all Goffman's criteria and he might well have continued his initial success of deception by performance had not his intended restricted regional audience been augmented by a national interest, stirred up in a large measure by Coleridge's series of newspaper articles, all of which feature in Bragg's use of the historical record. The novel's constant interrelation between regionalism, history and romance is notably conspicuous from the outset, with its setting of Morecambe Sands, Kemble's London acting, and Hatfield's self-induced visionary moment. Similar wider textual interrelationships than might at first be apparent arise from the presence of the, unknown to Hatfield, only two members of the audience present at his dress-rehearsal.

Anne Tyson, who makes her living by shrimping along the shoreline, is intrigued by Hatfield's dramatic performance and presence in such a potentially dangerous location, and so she keeps a watchful eye on him. When seen by Hatfield she tells of her daughter's drowning and her concern for a stranger's safety. Viewed from a distance, Anne appears as a care-worn asexual creature, but upon close inspection Hatfield finds her to be a relatively attractive middle-aged lady: *'You can't be older than I am. You play at being the old crone, don't you?'* (*MB*, p.15, italics added). Anne assumes the role of an 'old crone' to protect her sexual vulnerability by deliberately appearing unattractive, undesirable and unavailable. In a performance that successfully evades the predatory male gaze, she achieves the anonymity denied Mary Robinson. In this respect she is equally, if not more, deserving of Wordsworth's valuing of Mary's '... just opinions, delicate reserve/Her patience, and humility of mind/Unspoiled by commendation and the excess/Of public notice ...' (*Prelude*, p.269), leaving her 'Without contamination' (ibid.). Where Wordsworth's *Prelude* displaces the sexual threat to an outcast prostitute, Bragg does something similar with the other member of Hatfield's audience, the servant girl Sally. It is, though, Anne Tyson who travels to Carlisle, unremarked and unobserved, to stand 'apart and alone' (*MB*, p.411) to witness Hatfield's execution in the novel's concluding sentence. She shares both her name, in all but an 'e', and her protective matronly demeanour, with the factual Ann Tyson who, with her grocer and draper husband Hugh, kept a cottage first in Hawkshead, and later in nearby Colthouse, where for eight years she provided the young Wordsworth with a stable and caring lodging while he attended Hawkshead Grammar School from 1779 to 1787. Hatfied vows 'I'll never forget my guardian on the Bay of Morecambe' (*MB*, p.16) in a fictional echo of Wordsworth's tribute to Ann Tyson: 'While my heart/Can beat I never will forget thy name' (*Prelude*, p.142).

The young farm girl, Sally, guards Hatfield's horse while he ventures on to the Sands. Later Hatfield seduces Sally and then utters his seemingly uncontrollable Pavlovian response to any experience/promise of sexual satisfaction: 'We ought to get married, you know' (*MB*, p.19). He imagines a future life by the Bay with her in the same terms as he will later use to fantasise about an idyllic pastoral existence with Mary: 'He could see himself master of a little farm along the Sands, here, living a simple life, some fishing - one of his passions - at ease and lordly in the small community, served and adored by Sally ... He would make his home comfortable, bring in a few books, stroll along the shore on an evening such as this ...' (ibid.). His dalliance with Sally is presented by way of a physical and textual rehearsal of his relationship with Mary, an intertextuality that extends to the (mis)naming of the latter in a textual gesture to the fictional Sally. Captain Joseph Budworth's ground-breaking account of his visit to the Lake District, *A Fortnight's Ramble to the Lakes in Westmoreland, Lancashire and Cumberland*, first published in 1792, rhapsodises over his encounter with Mary Robinson at Buttermere's Fish Inn, comparing her looks, as does Hatfield with Anne Tyson, to those of an angel. For some unknown reason, in the first two editions of his travelogue, Budworth misnames Mary as 'Sally of Buttermere', perhaps out of gallantry to protect her identity, perhaps out of a wish to maintain a sense of private ownership. In any event, both Ann(e) and Sally are names that whisper secrets about performance and textual identity that reverberate throughout the novel.

Performance, disguise and identity are to the fore in a passage that reads as a purely fictional rehearsal of Hatfield's actual elopement with Mary. Bragg imagines a scene in which his two central historical characters cavort with their fictional doppelgängers, who in turn give a referential narratological credence to the novel's historical and regional accuracy. Hatfield, with Mary's help, comes to the rescue of two young lovers, George Shelborne and Catherine Hodge, fleeing to Gretna Green before Catherine's guardian forces her to marry his son. Invited into the Fish Inn, and under Hatfield's direction, the pursuing guardian is deceived by an adroit mixture of costume, make-up and stage setting. Shelborne later explains that his initial appearance under the guise of an old man was achieved with clothes 'got from a pawnshop in Kendal; [whilst] the rouge came from an acquaintance of Mrs. Charlotte Deans (*MB*, p.111). Charlotte Deans (1768-1859) was a talented actress who was well known in Cumbria for her performances as a travelling player, and whose memoirs place her in Keswick around the time of Hatfield's presence there: 'From Cockermouth we proceeded to Keswick for the Regatta, which generally drew together a great concourse of genteel company' (Wordsworth Trust website). The historical/regional link is further strengthened by the fact that Charlotte's father, Henry Lowes, was born in Cockbridge, and practised as an Attorney at Law in Bragg's hometown of Wigton. It was in Wigton, also, that Charlotte's memoirs, *A Travelling Actress in the North and Scotland*, were published in 1837. The increasing textual density of the seemingly casual reference to Charlotte Deans becomes even more apparent when knowledge of her personal history further collapses narrative distance and establishes a regional and historical referent. Mirroring the Shelborne and Hodge elopement story, Charlotte, at age 17, fell in love with an actor, was imprisoned in her room by her horrified parents, escaped and fled to Gretna Green. Hatfield and Mary marry in semi-secret, without eloping, but in a faint fading echo of earlier events they reach Carlisle on their honeymoon at the same time as 'a group of actors advertised a play that evening, to be given by the local celebrity Mrs. Charlotte Deans' (*MB*, p.234). Such a small but significant referential textual pin-prick of historical/regional verisimilitude subtly conveys a theatrical image that, upon readerly reflection, may be seen to inflect the entire novel.

Where Bragg departs from the historical record is with the creation of the entirely fictional Newton,[2] a character who casts a Gothic shadow over Hatfield's every move and who is instrumental in bringing about his capture, trial and execution. Newton is the figure fuelling Hatfield's psychological torment, bursts of guilt, divided self, and a fatal paranoid delusion - all features which *The Oxford Companion to English Literature* (2006) defines as central to the Gothic tradition (p.422). Prison scenes are also prominent features of the Gothic novel, and it is in prison that an unbreakable Svengali-like bond is forged between Newton and Hatfield. Newton's total psychological domination of Hatfield comes close to embodying the Christian notion of absolute evil, leading in the extreme to murder, and it is surely significant that he lacks a Christian name. The fictional Newton is an enigma; he lacks a body, with only 'his white face' (*MB*, p.20) as the sole textual reference to his physical appearance, and, as he tells Hatfield, he moves through the world having 'no scent' and'[n]o marks' (*MB*, p.22) as evidence of his existence. But his presence in Hatfield's life triggers classic Gothic effects of apprehension, fear and claustrophobia.

Margaret Russett's revealing study *Fictions and Fakes. Forging Romantic Authenticity, 1760-1845* (2006) includes a chapter devoted to Hatfield, 'The delusions of hope', in which she draws attention to a similar fictional presence as Newton in an 1841 novelistic retelling of Hatfield's story, *James Hatfield and the Beauty of Buttermere*. In it, the 'worst excesses of the Hatfield character are displayed onto an evil preacher named Quandish, probably based on Robert Wringham, the "Justified Sinner" of Hogg's 1824 novel' (p.102). This observation suggests a case

---

2. Contemporary reviews either ignored Newton completely or mentioned him only in passing, preferring to emphasise Bragg's inclusion of the real-life Lake poets. Andrew Sinclair, for example, in his generally positive *Sunday Times* review writes: 'It is apt that Hatfield's evil companion should be called Newton', without further explanation. Anna Vaux's similarly largely favourable review in the *Times Literary Supplement* simply refers to Hatfield's 'dealings with a man called Newton'. (It is unfortunate that Vaux's review begins by mistakenly referring to Buttermere as 'a small Cumbrian town' as a time when it struggled to meet the criteria of a hamlet.)

for reading Newton as a Gothic character in a direct line of descent from Hogg's malign stranger, who functions as the evil alter ego of the novel's central character, Colwan, who he directs to commit a series of horrifying crimes, including murder. Russett herself draws such an implicit suggestion when she goes on to remark that 'in one of [Bragg's] few departures from the historical record, [he] invents a Svengali figure who drives Hatfield to his most desperate deeds' (p.102).

*The Maid of Buttermere* is in the tradition of Romantic romances, but where it differs from most of its nineteenth-century predecessors is, as Russett recognises, in its scrupulous regard for documentary historical accuracy underpinning any flights of Gothic fancy. Newton commits murder without conscience, leaving Hatfield as the appalled witness to '[t]hroats slashed wide open' (*MB*, p.162), but seemingly powerless to intervene. Bragg comes close to presenting Newton as the Devil's representative on earth, whose 'demonic digging out of [Hatfield's] will and of any trace of sympathy, second thoughts, decency, compunction, was made crystal glorious in the proof it gave him of his power: to take this sensual, strange and curious creature and work him, work him to a purpose ....' (*MB*, p.196). Newton cements his dominant influence over Hatfield during their shared years in prison - Hatfield had actually spent time in the King's Bench prison for debt during his London years, as well as in Dublin and in Scarborough, this last incarceration providing the fictional entrance of Newton - when, 'alone, abandoned, terrified and all the time touching him, knowing as he did, how dependent the man was on touch, on the felt and experiencing pressure of flesh for the desperate reassurance of his vitality' (ibid.). This expression of physical closeness adds a conjectural layer of repressed, and therefore unhealthy, homosexual desire to Newton's leech-like attachment to Hatfield. In searching for possible models for Newton I was intrigued by the occasional parallels between Newton/Robert Southey and Hatfield/Coleridge, thrown up in Richard Holmes's *Coleridge. Early Visions* (1990). Holmes paints Coleridge as 'hypnotically drawn by a man [Southey] of less humour and imagination than himself but with far greater force of character and willpower' (p.64). 'There was also a sexual component to the friendship' with Southey/Newton for his part 'dazzled and enchanted by Coleridge's[/Hatfield's] warmth and generosity of feeling, his spectacular talk, his responsiveness, and superb imaginative flights' (ibid.). My Southey/Newton conflation might but be interpreted as an artistic imitation that has escaped its referent, but certainly it is undeniable that the Lake poets helped create Hatfield's identity in the public mind, none more so than Coleridge whose newspaper exposés were to prove so damning.

Bragg is very space/time specific in linking Coleridge to Hatfield and placing both within the Romantic tradition in a move that gives documentary credence to the novel. He has Hatfield arriving at the Queen's Head in Keswick at the same time as 'a few hundred yards away, [Coleridge] was writing a letter' (*MB*, p.106). Further, Coleridge's letter and Hatfield's journal entry of the previous evening provides evidence of the two men sharing similar language to express a state of personal well-being when acting under pressure:

> Hatfield:  'He would try in his journals that night to express his extreme contentment.'
> Coleridge: 'I have always found a stretched and anxious frame of mind favourable to depths of pleasurable expression.'                              (*MB*, p.106)

I read these two sentences as an example of textual morphing of authorial identity in the service of Romantic identity. The same passage from which they come also historicises textual authority by the use of the Coleridgean association of 'persons and characters supernatural, or at least romantic' (*Biographia Literaria*, quoted in Russett, p.6). By including Thomas De Quincey as a party to the creation of authentic literary and personal identity - 'According to De Quincey, Coleridge had "the largest and most spacious intellect, the subtlest and most comprehensive that has existed among men"' (*MB*, p.106) - Bragg further tightens the bonds of authentic literary and personal identity in the Romantic text. There is nothing of the arbitrary in Bragg's reference to De Quincey since it is in his *Confessions of an English Opium Eater* (1821, revised 1856) that recites the narrative of the thematics of nightmares and degradation that makes for common ground between Coleridge and Hatfield. Holmes writes of the 'black stirred up sediment of the unconscious mind emptying in the hours before dawn' (*Coleridge*, p.355), quoting an extract from Coleridge's *Notebooks*: 'A most frightful Dream of a Woman whose features were blended with darkness catching hold of my right eye and attempting to pull it out' (ibid., p.293). Coleridge and Hatfield both cry out in the night from the torment of their dreams, both hoping for comfort from, respectively, William and Dorothy

Wordsworth, and Mary Robinson. This nightmare bond between the two men extends beyond the demonstrable resemblance of the violence, obsessive sexuality, and horror of their dreams, to a significant intertextual continuity provided by the background figure of De Quincey. On the most obvious level, Hatfield, Coleridge, and De Quincey share a dreamscape of masochistic psychopathology in which demon women and reptilian life-forms threaten to engulf and destroy them; Coleridge's 'most frightful Dream of a Woman' and De Quincey's 'cursed crocodile [which] became to [him] the object of more horror than the rest' (*Confessions*, p.192) have their equivalent in Hatfield's nights of horror:

> ... creatures from under large old moss-green rocks crawled up his legs, leeching on the white skin, wetly sucking the blood, and above him, ropes, rigging nets, a gigantic sagging cobweb of strong and re-strung hemp lines, swayed down to trap him (children crying), and wherever he looked the wide mouths of women, no other feature but the mouth, tongues thick and purple as damsons, teeth white as the flecks on fall water and hands, nails curled and black, clawing at him, at his clothes, his chest, at his face (children wailing), ripping it away, tearing the skin from the skull ...
>
> (*MB*, p.128)

I have quoted the dream sequence in full so as to leave no doubt as to Bragg's deft textual manoeuvring designed to assign a strictly historical Romantic dimension to Hatfield's nightmares, linking them to an entire tradition that begins with Coleridge and De Quincey, and extends through the Romantic/Gothic Edgar Allan Poe to the 'nightmare flatness' of William Burroughs's 1953 novel, *Junky*[3] (p.139).

The novel's Romantic generic connection to Coleridge and De Quincey is emphasised when the images above of ropes, rigging, net, and sagging cobwebs swaying down to trap Hatfield re-appear in the second narrated dream: 'bottomless black-walled glassy-surfaced prison cells and above him the loops of chain and ropes rat-mangled and he a white face struck wide-mouthed in horror as the vast machine turned to crush and break and slowly rip him sinew from bone, inescapable agony' (*MB*,

---

3. The manuscript evidence for a connection between the aesthetic and political programme of Romanticism and Burroughs's invocation of Wordsworth's childhood dream-world is explored in Oliver Harris's *William Burroughs and the Secret of Fascination* (2003, p.77).

p.172). And suddenly I am reminded that De Quincey included an account in his *Confessions of an Opium-Easter* of 'Many years ago, when I was looking at Piranesi's[4] *Antiquities of Rome*, Coleridge then standing by, described to me a set of plates from that artist, called his *Dreams* and which record the scenery of his own visions during the delirium of a fever' (p.188). De Quincey proceeds to recount from memory Coleridge's depiction of 'vast Gothic halls' and 'mighty engines ... cables, catapults', and all indicative of the hopelessness of any unfortunate trapped individual. Hatfield's nightmare has its origins in his own experience of incarceration, but with an intertextual nod towards Coleridge's remembrance of Piranesi's stage prisons. J. Scott's *Piranesi* (1975) further strengthens the argument for a connection: 'Piranesi's etchings of imaginary prisons held a hypnotic fascination for later Romantic writers such as Coleridge and Edgar Allan Poe. The immensity of the architecture seems to embody the workings of a great supernatural power. Below, diminutive figures appear doomed to climb endless staircases without hope of release. The sinister machinery of cables, pulleys, and levers suggest awful horrors' (p.1). What I read is an historical alertness and natural genetic continuity between Bragg's account of Hatfield's nightmares, and Coleridge's memories of Piranesi's etchings, which, as stage sets, provide the ideal performative dream space for a con artist.

Out on the textual and historical margins of Mary's story is the little remembered real-life Newton, who played his own small walk-on part in kick-starting the Lake District as a dynamic imaginary on which to project Romantic fantasies of Arcadian community, romance, myth, the sublime, and possibility, including the radical social possibility of a humble village inn-keeper's daughter marrying into the (supposed) aristocracy. Bragg's first mention of Mary Robinson is the historically accurate one of how, when she was barely fourteen, a 'Captain Budworth, on a walking tour of the fashionable Lakes, met her and planted her firmly in his best-selling book *A Fortnight's Ramble in the Lakes*' (*MB*, p.32). Budworth began his tour in Grasmere in 1792 and his subsequent enthusiastic response to the region might well owe something to the sense of preparatory well-being induced by the breakfast he was served

4.  Giovanni Battista Piranesi (1720-1778) was an Italian artist renowned for his series of etchings, begun in 1745, of Rome and of fictitious and atmospheric prisons (*Carceri d'Invenzione*). The prison etchings are a series of 16 prints showing enormous subterranean vaults. The immensity of the structures is emphasised by the low viewpoint and the small, dream-like size of the figures, and are based on stage prisons rather than real ones.

by a certain Robert Newton. This included 'a stuffed roast pike, a boiled fowl, veal cutlets and ham, parsley and butter; cheese, wheat bread and oat cakes, followed by three cups of preserved gooseberries and a bowl of rich cream' (Thompson, p.136). Robert Newton is no murderer but he nevertheless inadvertently literally fuels the beginnings of a process that will turn both the Lakeland scenery and Mary Robinson into tourist commodities, thereby destroying their original unspoilt beauty that made them so initially attractive. Newton's breakfast menu is evidence of Stephen P. Hanna and Vincent J. Del Casino's premise that 'tourism is not simply an economy or set of sites/sights, but is in itself a set of cultural practices' (*Mapping Tourism*, p.xx) dependent on leisure time, discretionary income and positive local sanctions. Newton's meal demands both consumption time and disposable income, and Budworth's elevation of Mary to tourist attraction is sanctioned by a local economy ready to profit by a commodity in relatively short supply, namely a virginal unspoilt human beauty, seemingly just out of reach of suitors.

It is a necessary condition of Budworth's prefatory contribution to the Romantic view of the Lakes as a wild space promising escape from materialism that inhabitants such as Mary remain in situ - Budworth writes that 'Mary had never been out of the village (and I hope she will have no ambition to wish it)' (*Fortnight's Ramble*, p.251) - as an observational positionality promising a fantasy of unspoilt Rousseauesque nature. The seemingly inevitable corruption of the values of indigenous populations exposed to, and landscapes invaded by, cosmopolitan tourists is outside the scope of Bragg's novel, except insofar as his factual references to Coleridge and Wordsworth mark the start of a writerly process of attraction, still in progress today, and to which his novel makes its own very real contribution.[5] Even within the short space of the ten years separating Budworth's viewing of Mary and Hatfield's fictional response to her beauty, the former's guarded classical allusions to her beauty and tentative reference to her body - 'she had a manner about her which seemed better qualified to set off a dress, than dress *her*' (ibid., italics in original) - has given way to a more penetratingly invasive

5. Wordsworth was initially drawn to the Lakes by their isolated beauty which represented the very opposite of metropolitan noise and bustle. As he grew older he also grew increasingly intolerant of others, often of a perceived lower class, wishing to visit the region and able to take advantage of the newly built railways. The obvious irony is that, as Lynn Withey's *Grand Tours and Cook's Tours* (1997) remarks: 'His own poetry helped promote the popularity of the region, to the point that he himself [in a bizarre literary re-creation of the Mary Robinson phenomenon] became one of the region's top tourist attractions by the 1830s' (p.51).

male gaze: 'he sensed the voluptuous body modestly concealed in a gown which puckered under the breasts and flowed down to her ankles but concealed nothing of her sensuality' (*MB*, p.53). Whilst Hatfield's response suggests a stereotypically sexist attitude that is part of the clue to his character, Bragg also plays with a rhetorical strategy that sharply differentiates Hatfield from the philosophy and purpose of the Romantic literary aesthetic of creating an Arcadian imaginary.

Bragg positions his version of Hatfield, the artisan in aristocratic clothing, so as to partially deconstruct and interrogate the Romantic mythology of the Lakes. Hatfield's use of the gendered rhetoric typical of the early nineteenth century does not obscure the more fundamental political divide between his class and social position and that of the members of the upper echelons of society he seeks to imitate and infiltrate for personal gain. At a time when the escalating violence and social instability of the Paris Terror persuaded many previous sympathisers and fellow-travellers, such as Wordsworth and Coleridge, to renounce their support and adopt a more conservative stance towards political reform in England, Bragg's Hatfield remains a dangerously undisciplined, but ideologically immature, opponent of concentrated wealth and privilege. As Bragg summarises the volte face, the Lakes become a politically neutral uncontentious site for a private individual Thoreauvian experiment in life-style, the 'Arcadia where balked political revolution and faded religion turn to nature for a new radical impulse' (*MB*, 38). The move is perhaps best illustrated by the example of Wordsworth's description of the region in *A Guide Through The District of the Lakes* (1810) as a site of near Republican perfectibility in which 'person and possession, exhibited a perfect equality, a community of shepherds and agriculturists' (p.94) in which Nature provides the agency 'for the production of the few works of art and accommodations of life which, in so simple a state of society, could be necessary' (p.95). Such a view depends on suppressing precisely those aspects of the region's social and economic history, together with any appreciation of an indigenous cultural agency and ambition, that Bragg was anxious to reclaim in *The Hired Man*. Wordsworth's description of Lake cottages in the 'Second Section' of his *Guide* is as one of the picturesque products of Nature seemingly independent of human agency:

> Cluster'd like stars some few, but single most,
> And lurking dimly in their shy retreats,

Or glancing on each other cheerful looks,
Like separated stars with clouds between.
(*Guide*, p.96)

By way of sharp contrast to Wordsworth's 'cheerful' ambience, Hatfield's initial tourist picturesque view of the village of Borrowdale concludes by frankly acknowledging the human want and misery elided by Wordsworth's concentration on the dwelling, not the dweller:

> ... he was tempted to go into the village for some refreshment: it looked charmingly picturesque, even under the dull skin of grey; smoke from chimneys curling, thatch, goats, cheese, the homely clutter of rustic glamour: but as [Hatfield] knew only too well the new picturesque was the comfortable conscience for the old poverty. To [Hatfield] such a scene signalled want, bitter winters, spare victuals, goitres, rheumatism, at best the forgivable disgrace of pauperism.
>
> (*MB*, p.83)

Bragg's bleak but historically accurate picture of early nineteenth-century isolated village Cumbrian life exposes the Romantics' propensity to idealise the local inhabitants' identification with nature, a form of literary forgery attractive to their privileged middle-class readership in a way in which the more disruptive political/social forgery of Hatfield was not. Bragg's inhabitants are not always the strongly rooted and contented independent yeomen of Romantic myth but, rather, casual workers caught up in the capitalist, often profiteering, transformation of the land - 'gangs of men building the giant reaches of drystone walls enclosing even the highest fell-land,[6] the better to take advantage of grain prices in the war' (*MB*, p.88), or:

> ... working the woods, as charcoal-burners, swill-makers, coppice-workers, plain woodsmen; and, as here, men in the high mines   men spread all over the landscape, bondmen of industry, all living out near their workplace, turf huts and teepees, scattered abroad, excluded from society throughout the week of their work and let into its

6. The enclosure of the fell-land and the highly charged symbolic nature of drystone walls as a continuing marker of class division in post-World War II Cumbria is a central trope in *The Second Inheritance*. I draw attention to its importance in Chapter 2.

comforts and pleasures only for a brief Saturday night
escape.[7]                                                    (ibid.)

For Hatfield this is the real as opposed to the picturesque chimerical
Cumbria, and it is in the frank recognition of such reality that fuels his
determination to join the appropriators. At the same time, Hatfield's self-
conscious positioning remains that of the Romantic individual, seeing
'himself as the only point of free will in the landscape before him' (ibid.) in
which 'vagrants, beggars, a sixth of the total population, the abandoned and
the despairing' (ibid.) define the region as the antithesis of pure Nature. It is
as if Bragg is at pains to refute a conceptual division between the two very
different natural and social landscapes, that of the 'prescribed "stations" for
the Claude glass' (ibid.) and the working landscape that affronts Hatfield's
gaze. Part of the critical interest in *The Maid of Buttermere* is in noting the
extent to which Bragg, as a privileged insider, feels able to attempt to
reconcile the aesthetic and contemplative values of Wordsworth, and his
fellow Romantics, with an aesthetically politically attuned appreciation of
an often oppressive human culture, industry and basic subsistence.

Proof that Hatfield's perceptive thoughts on the injustices of
society are indeed genuine, and not merely another aspect of a multi-
faceted forged consciousness, becomes apparent in the novel's closing
scenes. Appalled by conditions in Chester jail where he is put in a 'large
open pen where crones and overnight drunks, harlots, madmen, thieving
children and some of the most vicious of both sexes are deposited with
less ceremony than hogs in a sty' (*MB*, p.367), Hatfield channels his
disgust into an experiment in democracy. This involves a Parliament
elected on an equal franchise between men and women, a school and a
programme of religious study, and equal access to whatever food is
provided. The experiment comes to grief because of the male prisoners'
refusal to sanction a female franchise, triggering a female backlash, which
in turn provokes a prison riot 'which saw several injured, many with
minor contusions, the cell wrecked and finally a number of soldiers
rushed in to enforce order' (*MB*, p.370). Irrespective of the experiment's
failure, mirroring the high hopes of French Revolutionary equality
descending into the Paris Terror and the subsequent authoritarian
dictatorship of Napoleon Bonaparte, by attributing its genesis to Hatfield,

7. These are the otherwise unexamined, unrecorded lives that, in the tradition of E.P.
Thompson's *The Making of the English Working Class* (1963), Bragg brings to the fore in *The
Hired Man*. This project is looked at in Chapter 4, 'The Throstle Nest of All England'.

Bragg raises the universal, and contemporary, question of whether good governance can be delivered by flawed individuals. At the same time, Bragg has redirected the reader's attention to an, at times, uncanny connection between Hatfield and his textual tormentor, Coleridge, and their shared interest in constructing Utopian societies based on sexual equality and a common Christian love for humanity.

Hatfield sets out his political philosophy in his prison journal whilst in jail in Oxford:

> I will propose a system of political order (with a Bill of Rights: and all men enfranchised) and a system of domestic economy (with the poor given land and a minimum wage and the rich dispossessed of vast tracts of their generally illegally gotten gains). I will examine religion and education and make recommendations in each area ... And I shall lay down rules of behaviour both for adults and children ...
>
> I will begin, as all men in solitude must, with love.
>
> (*MB*, p.363)

Hatfield's notion of citizenship at this stage does not include the possibility for women's political participation. This rings true as very few male radicals of the time considered female citizenship a realistic goal. For example, a contributor to the radical Norwich periodical *The Cabinet* (1795) 'argued unequivocally for adult female suffrage ... yet even he recognized that most men would laugh his arguments out of court' (Anne Clarke, *The Struggle for Breeches. Gender and the Making of the British Working Class*, p.146). When the increasingly radicalised Hatfield pragmatically as much as philosophically agrees to extend the suffrage to women - 'As there were almost as many women as men in the place' (*MB*, p.368) - his attempt is brutally rejected. Whilst I accept that in part Bragg has linked Hatfield's political philosophy to that of the seventeenth-century Levellers and Diggers, it is also fascinating to note the extent to which his micro-political system of democratic government within a prison shares common principles with Coleridge's near-contemporary attempt to found a Utopian colony in America on the banks of the Susquehanna river, and organised on the principle of the equal rule of all and the communal ownership of property, a system referred to as 'Pantisocracy'. Holmes defines the scheme as 'a heady cocktail of all the progressive idealism of the Romantic Age' (*Coleridge*, p.63).[8] I read it as significant that Bragg takes advantage of fictional novel history to present the later Hatfield, like Coleridge, a flawed proponent of genuine democratic government. With Hatfield's proposed extension of the franchise to women the similarity between the two men's views becomes marked, uniting them in a minority position. Coleridge writes of the need for women to be freed from domestic drudgery: 'Let the married Women do only what is absolutely convenient and customary for pregnant Women or nurses - Let the Husbands do all the Rest - and what will that be -? Washing with a Machine and cleaning the House. One Hour's addition to our daily Labor' (quoted in Holmes, p.78). For a brief Foucaultian heterotopian[9] moment the historically recorded Coleridge and the political fictional Hatfield are at one, although the latter reached his conclusion after a life-time of abusing women and denying any meaningful equality, whilst the former will gradually recoil from Enlightenment values to embrace a reaffirmation of the traditional sanctions of order, authority, and duty, withdrawing, in E.P. Thompson's resonant phrase 'behind [his] own ramparts of disenchantment' (*History*, p.915). But at the turn of the century the two men's reflections on Christian love make for remarkably similar reading:

Coleridge: 'Jesus knew our nature - and that expands like the circles of a Lake - the Love of our Friends, parents and neighbours lead[s] us to Love of our Country to the Love of all Mankind' (*Lecture*, 1795, quoted in Kitson, 'Political Thinkers', p. 161)

Hatfield/Bragg: 'The sacrificial nature of human love finds its example and the greatest justification in the noblest act performed on earth - the sacrifice of Jesus Christ ... Once the sacrifice of love has been offered, it cannot be reclaimed ...Therefore we have love just as Christ had one sacrifice.'  (*MB*, p.364)

---

8. Chapter Four, 'Pantisocrat' pp. 59-88 of Richard Holmes' *Coleridge. Early Visions* gives a detailed account of Coleridge's Utopian experiment.

9. See the essay 'Different Spaces' (pp.175-185) in *Michael Foucault, Aesthetics, Method, and Epistemology* (Allen Lane, 1998) for a definition of heterotopias as spaces of contestation, both mythical and real. In particular, the essay's concluding comments on ships as floating heterotopias may be read as comparable with the similar enclosed and closely regulated space of a prison.

Reading Hatfield's final expressions of love, sacrifice, and behavioural regret make for an entirely apposite, and critically engaging, inclusion by Bragg of an epigraphic opening section of Donald H. Reiman's journal article *The Beauty of Buttermere as Fact and Romantic Symbol* in which Reiman links the continuing interest in Mary Robinson's story 'to the assassination in 1980 of John Lennon' (quoted in *MB*, p.414). Both men appealed for feminine understanding, Hatfield in his prison cell letter to Mary - 'a letter of hope that you will believe in me' (*MB*, p.346) - and Lennon, with his lyric of contrition addressed to Yoko Ono in 'Woman',[10] and both died violent deaths before the promise of a reformed nature could be fully confirmed.

Apologists for both Lennon and Hatfield might justifiably cite childhood experience as a persuasive explanation, or excuse, for wayward adolescent and adult behaviour. Bragg's shaping of Hatfield's final prison letter to Mary shows a physical and psychologically damaged man groping toward self-knowledge through a biographical narrative of early abuse, malice and instability. Apprenticed as a young boy of seven to a psychopathic draper, Hatfield writes of being treated like a slave: 'There were four of us boys, none of whom had a life better than that of a nigger[11] on a plantation. We worked sixteen hours a day ... two of the boys - older than I, with some spirit left - were chained to their benches and slept in chains' (*MB*, p.314). Whilst Hatfield's analogous use of the phrase 'nigger on a plantation' is justified in terms of youthful forced, and chained, labour it also harks back textually to a psychological explanation of his revengeful exploitative relation with Crump, the businessman and lawyer, who 'had been talking much about the slave trade on which much of his father's great founding fortune had been based' (*MB*, p.131). But the seven year old knows nothing of this wider mercantile context, only that his master is free to sexually molest girls as

10. John Lennon 'Woman', track 10 on the compact disc John Lennon and Yoko Ono, *Double Fantasy* (Capitol Records, 2000) opens with the lines 'Woman I can hardly express/My mixed emotions at my thoughtlessness/After all I'm forever in your debt' and concludes 'Woman please let me explain/I never meant to cause you sorrow or pain/So let me tell you again and again/(I love you now and for ever)'. In addition to making the reformed misogynist link between Hatfield and Lennon, Bragg's concluding epigraphic turn to contemporary popular music is a further example of the ability to recognise and cultivate those same cross-cultural energies discussed in connection with Eric Burdon in Note 6, Chapter 3 *Landscapes for the Mind. Without a City Wall*.

11 John Lennon also uses the word 'nigger' in an equally pejorative sense in the lyric 'Woman is the Nigger of the World' on his 1972 album recorded with Yoko Ono and the Plastic Ono Band (Capitol Records).

young as ten and to arrange forced bare-knuckle fights among apprentices for entertainment. Bragg describes how Whitfield's master 'would occasionally unshackle one of us and haul us off to a cockfighting ring where we would be made to set to with other apprentices - all naked, bare fists and feet flying - while the gentry tossed us coppers and laid side bets' (*MB*, p.315). What I find uncanny about this passage is the way in which, by linking it to the prefixed 'nigger on a plantation' derogation, Bragg's poor indentured whites' fight becomes a trans-Atlantic metaphor for exploitation in its mirroring of the equally young, equally brutalised, young blacks' battle royal in Ralph Ellison's[12] novel *Invisible Man* (1952), exposing black oppression in pre-Civil Rights America. In Ellison's account the blacks are forced to fight blindfold by the local leading white citizens: 'Everyone fought hysterically. It was complete anarchy ... Blows landed below the belt and in the kidney ... [The narrator] bled from both nose and mouth, the blood spattering upon [his] chest. The man kept yelling, "Slug him, black boy! Knock his guts out!" "Uppercut him! Kill him! Kill that big boy!"' (pp.23-24). In his 'Introduction' to the 30th Anniversary Edition of the novel (1982) Ellison writes that 'what is commonly assumed to be past history is actually as much a part of the living present ... Furtive, implacable and tricky, it imprints both the observer and the scene observed, artefacts, manners and atmosphere and it speaks when no one wills to listen' (p.xiii). As Hatfield later realises, his adult behaviour has its origins in precisely such a mentally suppressed historical scene: 'I believe that what happens to us in those tender years of childhood sets up a reel that unspools through the rest of our lives' (*MB*, p.316). The literary point at issue here is that some key words or phrases in a text 'nigger on a plantation' can easily drop below the radar of literary exegesis, when, upon closer inspection, they are shown to enclose and encode disparate peoples/races in historical time and place in which similar social and industrial practices assume a symbolic hold uniting, say, the English regional novel and the black American protest novel.

In Chapter 6, 'Into the Labyrinth. *The Silken Net*', I note that Wigton's history is caught up in the West Indian slave trade. In that novel, however, it remains on the fringes of the text, whereas in *The Maid of Buttermere* it actively disturbs any notion of the Lake District as a

---

12. Bragg puts Ralph Ellison alongside Richard Wright and James Baldwin as one of the small group of influential black American fiction writers of the early/mid twentieth century (*The South Bank Show*, p.70)

domestic idyll, in the person and practices of 'Mr. John Gregory Crump of Liverpool [who] was a very wealthy man indeed' (*MB*, p.124). His wealth is accumulated from trading 'in the form of Ceylon tea, Indian Jute, Irish coal' (ibid.) and an 'encyclopaedia of imports' (*MB*, p.125) with the help of 'partners in the East, in the Indian Ocean, over the Atlantic, around the African coast' (ibid.). Crump's business activities provide as index to an archive of global aspects of production, distribution and exchange that he and his wife hope to convert into a marker of domicile and acceptance into the upper reaches of the English class system by buying land and building a fine residence in Grasmere. But he is blind to the 'deceits and bad faith of exploitation, cruelty, oppression, barbarism, murder and vicious wrongdoing'(ibid.) that underpin the flow of global capital into his chosen sanctum of Grasmere. This catalogue of inhumanity underwrites Hatfield's childhood and informs his egging on of Crump to enthuse on 'the benefits which flowed - especially to the Negroes themselves - from the slave trade even though, alas, it was now becoming uneconomical' (*MB*, p.132). Bragg underwrites the irony of Crump's free trade encomium by picturing him, through Hatfield's consciousness, making a Freudian word association between slavery and personal freedom in his 'throwing over the chains of trade' (ibid.) to escape to the Lakes. Mrs Crump adds to the disassociation between person and place by seeing the inhabitants of the region as symbolic rather than real, a form of branded material for the envisaged good life to be found amongst 'the people ... so natural', 'so simple', 'innocents' (*MB*, p.124). They no more threaten to disrupt her idea of uncomplicated pastoral relations than do the happy slaves of tobacco advertising iconography threaten global trading patterns.

Hatfield, however, can tell a different version of Lakeland economic realities. Whilst the Crumps patronise and caricature the local inhabitants as care-free peasants, Hatfield is prompted to recall a recent graphic account of local deprivation that underlines the doubleness of regional discourse according to subjective positioning. Bragg's tale of a young family with five children falling into poverty and reduced to eating grass before the almost inevitable death of both parents has echoes of Wordsworth's *Lyrical Ballads* poems 'The Female Vagrant' (*Lyrical Ballads*, p.13) and 'We Are Seven' (ibid, p.48) For Hatfield, hearing the father described as 'like a living skeletal' (*MB*, p.130) would have threatened a return to the Gothic and the prison nightmares. What is also evident is that at this stage of events Hatfield and Wordsworth share a common antipathy to putative acquisitive landlords such as Crump who would increase their wealth by buying land and turning independent farmers into tenants:

> Then rose a mansion proud our woods among,
> And cottage after cottage owned its sway,
> No joy to see a neighbouring house, or stray
> Through pasture not his own, the master took:
> But when he had refused the proffered gold,
> To cruel injustices he became a prey.
> His troubles grew upon him day by day,
> Till all his substance fell into decay.
>
> ('The Female Vagrant', p.30)

Without naming Wordsworth 'He writes about butterflies and flowers and birds and in praise of the common people' (*MB*, p.133) Crump recognises the poet as an adversary determined to 'have [him] scoffed and hounded out of the county rather than see [his] house completed' (ibid.), but is unable to decode the language of rural Lakeland as an attempt to articulate an aesthetic challenging class dispossession. Yet by the novel's end Crump and Wordsworth are united in their contempt for Hatfield: 'Of Hatfield, Wordsworth wrote in *The Prelude*:

> Unfaithful to a virtuous wife,
> Deserted and deceived, the spoiler came ...
> And wooed the artless daughter of the hills
> And wedded her in cruel mockery.'
>
> (*MB*, p.404)

The irony is that, whilst Hatfield continues to believe in the revolutionary transformative power of rhetoric until the end, even in prison where forgery and fakery can no longer serve a personal project of upward mobility, Wordsworth's poetic authority from 1800 onwards drifts towards a paternalistic discourse that supports and enhances the values of arriviste landowners such as Crump. Read thus, *The Maid of Buttermere* maps an illuminating route through the regional novel, integrating aesthetic and economic aspects of landscape with the individual psychological and social experiences of those most affected by the increasing pace of change from outside sources.

It is to Wordsworth, and to a lesser extent Coleridge, that Bragg also turns in a brief but seminal passage invoking the former's notion of 'spots of time': 'There are in our existence spots of time,/That with distinct pre-eminence retain/A renovating virtue ...' (*Prelude*, p.479). Such discrete images of experience are seen as presenting life-changing, life-enhancing, moments of 'profoundest knowledge' whose visionary insight reveals '[t]he invisible world' (*Prelude*, p.235) and are understood as valued 'gleams/ Of soul-illumination' (ibid., p.241). The essential features of Wordsworth's first revelatory view of an Alpine village - 'Well might a stranger look with bounding heart/Down on a green recess, the first I saw/Of those deep haunts, an aboriginal vale' (ibid, p.235) - are translated by Bragg into Hatfield's epiphanic moment on Hause Point:

> As he turned Hause Point and caught a clear sight of Mary's Buttermere, the lonely valley, he experienced what seemed a physical soaring of his spirits, a giddy uplift of the heart. He was overcome. It was a true revelation. He held his breath. It was such an unanticipated shock that he froze, to cling onto this unique moment. He could not remember when he had felt as purely happy. (MB, p.94)

In describing Hatfield's vision Bragg uses the language of Romantic epistemology, privileging the imagination's cognitive faculty, Coleridge's 'prime agent for all human perception' (*Biographia*, p.167). Hatfield's instantaneously acquired realisation of an alternative pastoral life-style is in keeping with the Romantics' belief in the illuminatory potential of 'spots of time' to fashion salvational self-knowledge. Such sublime literary moments are often experienced within a quasi-mythical landscape, such as that once walked by Merlin: 'Merlin had been in these parts ... Perhaps he [Hatfield] was Merlin come again, invisible in his magic cloak, looking for the woman who would trap and hold him forever' (*MB*, p.95). *The Prelude* explores the visionary sublime as a gateway to psychic wholeness, a wholeness that momentarily appears to be within Hatfield's grasp. '[H]ow shamelessly it had floated away, that *spot of his time*' (ibid., italics added) as Hatfield's private vision is interrupted by the appearance of the quarryman, Harrison, whose guarded Republican conversation re-ignites Hatfield's own political sympathies. Crucially, Bragg has Harrison compare working in the local quarries to slavery, using the textually plangent simile 'Negroes on plantations do better' (*MB*, p.97). Wordsworth's subjectivity- isolating 'spots of time' on Hause Point suffer a perceptual collapse as Hatfield, and text, are forced back to the political and economic realities that explain, if not excuse, Hatfield's forged identity.[13]

*The Maid of Buttermere* oscillates between realism and romance, between the Gothic and the Folk, between historical documentary evidence and imaginative drama, taking full advantage of the increasingly porous boundary between fiction and non-fiction. If I have concentrated on the novel's fictional aspects, it is largely because Bragg's use of the historical/literary record of the time is both accurate and readily verified. What remains of interest is the extent to which Bragg's referencing of documentary evidence sutures the contradictory elements inherent in matching fictional persons and episodes to a faithful historical account. Scott, widely acknowledged as the progenitor of the historical romance novel, claims in the 'Dedicatory Epistle' to *Ivanhoe* (1819) 'that of the materials which an author has to use in a romance, of fictitious composition, such as I have ventured to attempt, he will find that a great proportion, both in language and in manners, is as proper to the present time as to those in which he has laid out his time of action' (p.49). Responding to such assertions of a basic diachronic stability of language and manners, John Wilson Croker, writing in the *Quarterly Review* raises 'a great objection ... to historical romance, in which real and fictitious personages and actual and fabulous events are mixed together to the utter confusion of the reader and the unsettling of all accurate recollections of past transactions' (quoted in Keith, *Regions of the Imagination*, p.31). This is the essence of a continuing debate that concerns *The Maid of Buttermere* as well as the increasing number of neo-Victorian novels. According to Keith it is an argument that is 'persistent in treatments of regional writing [in which] a novel illustrating the mode of living at a particular moment in time is sometimes inferior to more imaginative "creative" fiction' (ibid.).

It is also a formalist notion of literature that by self-definition

---

13. The question arises as to what extent Hatfield's later prison letter describing his apprentice years as no 'better than that of a nigger on a plantation' (*MB*, p.314) is itself a plagiaristic textual forgery prompted by a recollection of Harrison's simile. In this respect, Hatfield might be seen to keep company with Coleridge's plagiarisms from Schelling (see Margaret Russett *Fictions and Fakes. Forging Romantic Authenticity*, 1760-1845, p.11.)

excludes, as part of an aesthetic rear-guard action, what it regards as deviant forms and the incorporation of stylistic alternatives. A border-crossing genre such as *The Maid of Buttermere* activates its readers to discover and enjoy the tension between representations of fact and fiction. Bragg's use of biography, letters, folk ballads, posters, newspaper headlines and reports, and canonical poetry alongside a fictional narrative and the use of third-person indirect discourse highlights the referential nature of all discourse, in what I see as a successful integration of otherwise discrete categories of fact and fiction. These documentary inserts are part of an ideological as much as an aesthetic tendency, displaying Bragg's former historical training in gesturing to a wider environment in which Hatfield's history becomes an active, if minor, part of the process of a more general social transformation. For all its manifest interest in fakery and forgery, the powerful latent theme of *The Maid of Buttermere* is one of inequality and the unjust distribution of land and property, not only in one region of England but also of Empire. The dissection of regional political and social life as both place-specific and indicative of national trends is by this stage an established feature of all Bragg's Cumbrian novels.

Bragg's narrative insertion of an anonymous Notice offering a fifty pound reward for Hatfield's capture (*MB*, p.304) is the most obvious example of the use of a public document to locate the novel in the reality of a time-specific historical period divorced from authorial subjective expression. The broadsheet's survival and inclusion is important because it, arguably more so than, say, Coleridge's sensational investigative reporting for the *Morning Post*, summarises Hatfield's career in a procedural way that authenticates Bragg's fictional text and, crucially, provides a level of detailed information about the suspect that could only be known to a close acquaintance such as, say, the entirely fictitious Newton. The unanswered question as to the identity of the Notice's well-informed author(s) invites the reader to become a co-adjudicator of the documentary evidence and therefore creator of the text along with the narrator. Such involvement explains in part the pleasure and sense of participation felt in reading pseudo-journalist accounts of real events. The true story rather than the invented one 'enjoys an advantage so obvious, so built-in, one almost forgets what power it has: the simple fact that the reader knows *all this actually happened*. The disclaimers have been erased. The screen is gone. The writer is one step closer to the absolute involvement of the reader that James Joyce dreamed of and never achieved' (Tom Wolfe, p.34). Making due allowance for Wolfe's characteristic hyperbole, he nevertheless draws attention to an important literary tradition to which *The Maid of Buttermere* is heir. The fictional exploitation of newsworthy historical events and the mixing of factually reported events and invented materials goes back at least as far as Daniel Defoe's 1721 *Journal of the Plague Year*. Two of its more prominent and well publicised (and American) post-World War II examples are Truman Capote's *In Cold Blood* (1965) and Norman Mailer's *The Executioner's Song* (1979). Although dealing with very different historical time periods and cultural mores, Bragg's novel shares many features with the Americans' contemporary texts. Their central male characters are involved in violent crime, face prison and trial, and are executed; Perry Smith (*In Cold Blood*) and Gary Gilmore (*Executioner's Song*) are talented artists, whilst Hatfield is the consummate performance artist. All three texts make extensive use of documents; are set in small rural communities; and make use of conventional non-fictional forms such as biography, history and journalism. Perhaps the most interesting feature connecting all three novels is the American concentration on the individual ego as a key indicator of their contemporary socio-economic and political cultures in much the same way as the promotion of the self is to the establishment of the nineteenth-century Romantic myth.

I am arguing here for a considered reading of *The Maid of Buttermere* in the context of a wider contemporary trans-Atlantic ideology of form, referencing documentary realism, encompassing elements of the Romantic and the Gothic. Buttermere (Cumbria) then takes its place in the company of Holcombe (Kansas) and Provo (Utah) as the source and locale for crimes in search of a literary genre and methodology, but able to illuminate them.[14]

I began this chapter with a reference to Hawthorne's American Renaissance inflected definition of the historical romance as a contested

14. For further discussion of the possible benefits of such a comparative exercise see Brian Hardings 'Comparative Metafictions of History: E. L. Doctorow and John Fowles' in *Forked Tongues. Comparing Twentieth-Century British and American Literature*, edited by Ann Mason and Alistair Stead (Longman, 1994). The argument advanced for a more intensive cross-cultural study of Anglo-American regional literature also applies to the quantitatively more demanding task of a globally comparative study to throw light on questions of national identity and cultural difference viewed from the relatively stable but heterogeneous literary position of the regional.

space 'somewhere between the real world and fairy-land'. Whilst *The Maid of Buttermere* carries echoes of Hawthorne's fairy-land pastoral escapism - 'this deeply protected world's end valley, the home as might be of the hidden enchantments of fairy tales' (*MB*, p.74) - I have concentrated on those elements of the Romantic, the historical, the social environment, the Gothic and the documentary, that I see Bragg structurally binding in a unified organic form. Exposing any lingering rural 'enchantments of fairy tales', Bragg has continued the project begun with *The Hired Man* of giving a voice to history's excluded, from the fictional Anne Tyson to the factual Michelle Nation, channelling them alongside the official stories certified by the historical archives. Simultaneously he shows the relationship between a culture's national dynamic elements, such as the growing influence of the investigative Press and the movement of metropolitan trade capital into the rural hinterlands, and the persistence of patterns of daily life and static social relations[15] in a seemingly stagnant and isolated regional backwater: 'Buttermere was nine miles from Keswick by the horse road, fourteen by the carriage road - both steep and difficult passes' (*MB*, p.72). What makes the difficult journey worthwhile for the Romantic sensibility is precisely the promise of an Arcadian landscape that defies change: 'If you rolled a god-like pebble across the valley floor, it would come to rest on the site of the Fish [Inn], for the location commanded every aspect and enjoyed every advantage - surrounded by lush flood meadows, watered by nearby falls and tumultuously clear becks, sweet in its grasslands and serene in its views' (*MB*, p.72). One of the pleasures of reading Bragg's Cumbrian fiction is to encounter such strong and vibrant impressions of a socially grounded landscape, often at odds with the increasingly homogenous imposition of a national cultural and

---

15 An example of a traditional pattern of social relationships is the bidden-wedding, still being held in isolated communities such as Buttermere, but on the cusp of dying out in the early 1800s. Bragg's description - The bridegroom and his friends rode around the village inviting everyone who wanted to come to the day (*MB*, p.55) - is an accurate contribution to the novels sense of regional identity. The following is an example of the sort of notice Mr. Fenton (ibid.) would have read: 'Suspend for one Day all your cares and your labour, And come to this Wedding, kind friends and good Neighbours, NOTICE is HEREBY GIVEN, That the marriage of Isaac Pearson with Frances Atkinson, will be solemnized in due form in the Parish Church of Lamplugh, on Monday next, the 30th of May, instant immediately after which the Bride and Bridegroom, with their attendants, will proceed to Lonefoot, in the said Parish, where the Nuptials will be celebrated by a variety of Rural entertainments. Lamplugh 20 May, 1786.' (Cumberland and Westmoreland Wrestlers Association web site.)

political grid. The camera-eye of a 'god-like pebble' making a decision free of human agency, selects Buttermere as a model panorama of a moral and philosophical system, a vernacular landscape cohering around the popular culture of the inn.

Left in Bragg's hands, this highly selective pebble has a strong homing instinct to roll into his home-town of Wigton and to seek out his adopted hamlet of High Ireby, rattling against the nearby village of Ireby. Passing through the Lakes, Mr. Judge Hardinge breaks his journey at 'The Crown in Wigton for an excellent game pie and a credible local beer' (MB, p.259), although he denigrates the local men as idlers given to spitting. Neatly juxtaposed with Hardinge's superior qualified praise and patronising observations, Bragg invites the reader to turn the page and read the local from a very different class and geographical perspective. On their way to Carlisle for a putative honeymoon, Hatfield and Mary's coach boy wants to stop at Wigton, 'which he had heard of as a mighty place, famous over the globe for its game pie and beer' (MB, p.261). What interests me here is the unexpected contrast between the coach boy's global reading of domestic space from a critically limited social perspective compared with the judge's blinkered local reading from his privileged national, if not global, perspective. Such a minor dialectical play between competing national and local values is indicative of the novel's wider concerns with identity and difference.

Passing through Ireby, Hardinge writes it off as a 'once wealthy village now being set in decline by the new industries' (MB, p.259). Since Ireby remained a busy market town at the time of Hardinge's visit, his condemnation seems both peremptory and premature. And this is the same Ireby that Keats visits in 1818 and hymns for its life-affirming local dance-tradition, an event that Bragg re-visits in his next novel, A Time to Dance. Hardinge and Keats demonstrate the polarities of reading the regional, the one passing through as a consumer, uninterested in making any meaningful personal connections, the other making an overnight stop and becoming, however briefly, part of village life. Hardinge dismisses Wigton and Ireby as having little to contribute to the national imagery, whereas Keats becomes a willing participant-observer at the local dance and in consequence eulogises its youth as exemplars of a beneficent national culture. Rather than distance the reader from any perceived radical alterity of time past, Bragg's novel calls upon the stability of the regional and its continuing visibility on the tourist map to encourage readers to bring their own experience of local history to bear upon Cumbria's relationship to identity politics and national ideologies. His sense of history extends beyond structural persistence to include the essential historical sameness of human history as exemplified in a short semi-autobiographical passage in *A Son of War*, which we can read as Hatfield reflected in Bragg's mirror:

> ... he stared at the heavy, handsome head, looked at it until it became a strange thing to him, a feeling of stone, a sight he saw from another part of the room, this unbodied head reflected more truly in the mirror than in the live skull itself ... (*MB*, p.70)
> ... and stood in front of the mirror over the wash-basin. His plan just to stand there.
>
> It happened soon. The life went out of him. There was this head. In the mirror. A head of someone. It did not belong to him. What was him was not in the mirror. The head was strange to him. Like stone ... You were looking at not you.
>
> (*SW*, P.377)

This semi-autobiographical ghosting of the historical Hatfield might be subconsciously, intuitively grasped, but, whether latent or manifest, it stresses a continuity of identity politics over difference, and does so from a geographical space in Wigton that links the drama of Bragg's youthful conflict in *A Son of War* to that of a figure from the national stage. There is the sense in which national identities are refracted through local knowledge in the hands of the self-analytical regional writer. In this context it is surely appropriate for this particular regional writer to include an 'Epilogue' in search of a strong historical local connection between author and subject as he points the interested reader in the direction of Mary Robinson's 'grave ... a few miles over the common land where this novel was written' (*MB*, p.413), in his Lakeland home of High Ireby. At the same time it cannot escape our notice that Bragg introduces one last mix of historical fact and fiction designed to re-route the regional tale back to one very specific and important authorial setting. He invents a young apprentice coffin-maker, Ike Wilkinson, to put the final nails into Hatfield's coffin whilst 'trying desperately to remember every detail of his visit so than he could turn it over to his parents in Ireby when next he went home' (*MB*, p.407).

*The Maid of Buttermere* encompasses a wide range of diverse expression, from coffin-maker to Coleridge, casting its interpretative net widely over a range of documents, from the aesthetic to the functional. The result is a novel that re-invigorates an enigma of revolutionary times from the perspective of one very small rural space in Cumbria that now claims a special status in fact and fiction as the stage where performance, fakery and forgery almost gulled the establishment. In telling this extraordinary story Bragg interleaves his narrative with a variety of discourses inviting an inter-disciplinary critical response, which includes the crossing of national borders, to the assessment of the regional novel's ability to expand the scope and potential of the genre. Bragg's next Cumbrian novel takes up the challenge to further expand the regional genre by re-visiting and re-writing William Hazlitt's *Liber Amoris* for the late twentieth century.

# NINE

# HAZLITT REDUX
## *A TIME TO DANCE*

*A Time to Dance* (1990), whilst very much a story of modern times, is haunted and shaped by a text from the Romantic period. The novel's relationship to Romanticism, and a canonical link to William Hazlitt's *Liber Amoris* (1823), is established in a central moment of revelation at the 1989 Wordsworth Summer Conference. Once *A Time to Dance*'s metafictional identity has been revealed, the reader is tacitly invited to look at its predecessor to fully appreciate the extent to which its structure closely shadows and reinterprets Hazlitt's confessional Romantic text in a twentieth-century context. Bragg's descriptions of physical passion across class and age boundaries, together with his musings on the appropriate use of language to convey the joy of sexual intercourse, establish an epistemological connection with the Lawrence of *Lady Chatterley's Lover* back to Hazlitt's ground-breaking literary memoir. It is here, with the structure and contents of *Liber Amoris* that a critical appreciation of Bragg's novel needs to begin.

Hazlitt's autobiographical narrative *Liber Amoris, or the New Pygmalion* shocked its contemporary readers and remains today one of literature's most compellingly uncensored self-revelatory explorations of obsessional love and desire. In daring to write prose comprising a heady mixture of high romance and what Tom Paulin calls 'emotional pornography' (*Day-Star,* p.45) to justify his pursuit of Sarah Walker, his landlady's daughter, Hazlitt damaged his personal and literary reputation for years to come. This was due in part to a reaction against the text's sexual frankness but perhaps more importantly to what was perceived as his reckless exposure of an uninhibited crossing of class boundaries by a middle-aged man besotted by a woman half his age. Such alliances were hardly unknown in nineteenth-century England but there existed a generally observed convention of censorship that severely curtailed any acknowledgement of the full range of sexual relationships. In this climate Hazlitt's book appeared as a dangerously explicit act of cultural subversion, anticipating by over a century radical changes to expressions of sexual longing and behaviour only now becoming assimilated into mainstream thinking and writing.

Hazlitt aroused the full force of a male conservative establishment anxious to protect not only its gendered sexual privileges but also a narrowly drawn political authority unwilling to contemplate any fissure in the class structure that might question the legitimacy of its definition of the right to govern. Hazlitt had long attacked what he regarded as an authoritarian despotic State, urging his readers not to abandon the democratic principles that he saw as the lasting legacy of the French Revolution. A.C. Grayling writes: 'There is no question of the depth and sincerity of Hazlitt's outlook in these respects. He was not a party man, but he was a passionate believer in liberty, secular republicanism, and the rights of man, and it goaded him into a rage to think how monarchs and the privileged batter on to the majority of mankind' (*Quarrel of the Age*, p.217). It was a short step to link such radical political opinions to Hazlitt's sexual libertinism. Jon Cook records that in 1819 the '*British Review* claimed that he was one of a "class of writers, whose main aim is to destroy the very foundations of modesty and decorum" and whose style was an abuse of proper English, their politics an abuse of the English constitution, and their fascination with erotic imaginings ... an abuse of respectable morality' (*Hazlitt in Love*, p.29).

Bragg has constructed *A Time to Dance* out of the aesthetic form of *Liber Amoris* whilst foregrounding contemporary issues of class division, education, age, loss and grief, marriage, money and, primarily, sexual obsession, played out against the detailed landscape of the Lake District. Writing in what is for him the unfamiliar voice of first-person narrator, Bragg confronts head-on the challenge to social mores raised by a sexual relationship played out across a thirty-six year age difference. The threatening nature of the predatory male gaze - and its universality - is fully explored and the, admittedly consensual, sexual acts are described in physical detail. Such explicitly transgressive relationships remain the more usual province of lurid popular newspaper headlines but Bragg's sensitive handling of potentially explosive material is what in part distinguishes his novel both from the commercial sensationalism of sexual deviancy and also from Hazlitt's misogynistically inclined confession. Nevertheless, the novel remains recognisably a palimpsest of Hazlitt's text for which the term intertextual applies in the sense that Bragg recalls the events and emotions of Hazlitt's text and times in a way that speaks both to the present moment as well as to its radical historical model.

The novel was published at a time when Hazlitt's work was beginning to attract renewed interest. Stanley Jones's widely praised *William Hazlitt: A Life - From Winterslow to Frith Street* appeared in 1989, followed by a number of important books and studies repositioning Hazlitt as a major polemical writer and, in the process, bringing *Liber Amoris* into the mainstream of canonical autobiographical texts.[1] Of the most recent books, Cook's 2007 study takes a particularly useful look at *Liber Amoris* and the cultural context in which it appeared, with the aim of 'not to attack or defend, but to understand what happened' (*Hazlitt*, p.10). Gregory Dart's 2008 edition of *Liber Amoris* helpfully places the text in the context of Hazlitt's other writings that were influenced by his infatuation with Sarah Walker. Both Cook and Dart draw attention to two contemporary fictional versions of *Liber Amoris*, namely Jonathan Bates's *The Cure for Love* (1998) and Anne Haverty's *The Far Side of a Kiss* (2001). Bates's novel is a psychological examination of romantic love and obsession played out between a male patient and female psychologist, that is steeped in references to Hazlitt's books, essays and life, demanding a considerable amount of background knowledge about the writer if the reader is to decode the mystery involved. *The Far Side of a Kiss* tells the story in the voice of Sarah Walker and its feminisation of Hazlitt's text is an impressive addition to feminist rewriting of classic texts.[2] Neither Cook nor Dart, however, appears to be aware of Bragg's earlier entry into the field. This critical lacuna is unfortunate because not only is Bragg's novel an important and original fictional commentary upon Hazlitt's transgressive text, fully deserving recognition as a precursor to the later novels, but it is also the most directly related to the original in its use of the epistolary format, its non-linear sequencing and its anonymous male first-person narrator. Where Bragg differs

1. Most notably Daniel Robinson 'Taking "Other Liberties" with Hazlitt's Liber Amoris' (1997); Tom Paulin *The Day-Star of Liberty. William Hazlitt's Radical Style* (1998) and his edited *The Fight and Other Writings* (2000); A.C. Grayling *The Quarrel of the Age. The Life and Times of William Hazlitt* (2000); Mark McCutcheon 'Liber Amoris and the Lineaments of Hazlitt's Desire' (2004); Jon Cook *Hazlitt in Love, a fatal attachment* (2007); Duncan Wu *William Hazlitt. The First Modern Man* (2008); Gregory Dart *William Hazlitt. Liber Amoris and related writings* (2008). The Hazlitt Society itself was established in 2005, with Michael Foot as President and an inaugural lecture by A.C. Grayling. This followed the unveiling earlier in the year of the restored memorial stone over Hazlitt's grave in St. Anne's churchyard in Soho, London.

2. This practice is now a literary sub-genre in its own right, notable examples of which include Jean Rhys's *Wide Sargasso Sea* (1966) and Jane Smiley's *A Thousand Acres* (1992).

significantly from Hazlitt is in setting the story in the Lake District and making location an important factor in plot development.

The novel's opening chapter in the form of a letter written, but not sent, to Bernadette Kennedy by the middle-aged anonymous narrator in thrall to her, establishes the link to Hazlitt, a link which Bragg continues to demonstrate throughout his text. It also introduces a reflection upon the classic (male-orientated) literary debate trying to unravel the female angel/whore binary. Hazlitt's unstable appraisal of Sarah Walker switches in the space of two sentences from the elevated language of Milton's *Il Penseroso* to a more earthy appreciation of her character: 'I once thought you were half-inclined to be a prude, and I admired you as a "pensive nun, devout and pure". I now think you are more than half a coquet, and I like you for your roguery' (*Liber*, p.45). Hazlitt constantly struggles, as will Bragg's narrator, to find a fixed definition of Sarah's femininity in the light of what is perceived as her inconstant actions. One moment he begs her to 'bend as if an angel stooped, and kiss me' (*Liber*, p.46) and the next he is writing a fictional letter to the dramatist James Sheridan Knowles, castigating her for having 'no more feeling than a common courtesan shows, who bilks [cheats] a customer' (*Liber*, p.105). Similar violent oscillations are typical of Bragg's narrator who seems unable to categorise Bernadette's femininity. His opening letter - a letter out of narrative sequence, as in *Liber Amoris* - expresses the Madonna/Magdalene binary in unambiguous terms: 'Bernadette, black hair swaying across your eyes and mine, as you knelt above me, looked down, your slim oval face with the solemnity of a Madonna,[3] and locked into me tightly, the wanton Magdalene, leaning your breasts into me ...' (*TD*, p.10). The almost obsessional need to marry the sacred and the profane - when Bragg's narrator closes his eyes in the act of sex he is in a 'darkness which art heaven' (*TD*, p.10) - is a constant throughout both texts. Bragg's narrator recalls how one moment Bernadette 'bucked and wrenched back' in violent sexual activity and the next '[lay] flat and straight as a nun as I plunged into you'. She was 'Now wanton, now virginal, Magdalene Madonna' (*TD*, p.128).

Bragg's indebtedness to the structural details of *Liber Amoris* is readily acknowledged but he himself has also called attention to another

---

3. Hazlitt's vignette from the title page of the 1823 edition of *Liber Amoris* is a reproduction of his copy of an old master, which he thought resembled Sarah Walker. It shows a young girl/lady looking upwards in what could be interpreted as either a pensive gaze of worship or a questioning gaze of anticipated submission to the secular male gaze.

important source of inspiration, from the world of cinema. In his 'Introduction' to his own screenplay for the BBC television adaptation of the novel, Bragg has the narrator, now named Andrew, tell his solicitor friend Christopher 'about seeing the film *The Blue Angel* (which was one of the many starting points for the book)' (*Screenplay*, p.15). This is a particularly interesting reference on several levels. In Josef von Sternberg's *The Blue Angel* (1930) there is a clear line of influence both in the metaphoric use of light (angel) and darkness (whore) in shooting and in the sequence in the Blue Angel nightclub where Lola-Lola (Marlene Dietrich) mesmerises Professor Immanual Rath (Emil Jannings), as she commands the stage and directs the camera's and the spectators' gaze to a display of stockings and bare thighs. Sternberg adopts Expressionist cinema's technique of using light and shade to monitor the stages of his character's loss of self-respect and fall into degradation/darkness. Bragg inserts a cinematic rapid-cut panoramic mis-en-scène into his narrative to suggest not only the sordidness of a determinate location but also the phenomenon of degradation at work in the narrator's mind. He has driven Bernadette to a lonely spot, isolated in the darkness and the drizzle, to rehearse an earlier misunderstanding, when he suddenly breaks off to give the reader a bleak vision of passion's entropic force: 'A couple in a car in an unfrequented place - a feature of lonely suburban road, overgrown lane, remote track, dark alley, underused car park, unlit sidestreet, bare hillside - infidelity and its aftermath in remote stationary cars the length of the land, limbs wrenching against the steering wheel, bucket seats unyielding' (*TD*, p.60). However understated, Bragg has effectively updated Hazlitt's undercurrent of sexual depravity to the twentieth century via German Expressionist film of the 1920s and American film-noir of the 1940s.

Bragg recreates the sexually charged atmosphere of the Blue Angel nightclub in his setting of a fair at Carlisle, which his narrator visits against his better judgement at Bernadette's invitation. Once there he realises how far he has climbed the social ladder and just how far off are the days when he could anticipate with pleasure a visit to a fair: 'A career away ... several generations of class away, respectability away' (*TD*, p.42). Now he finds the fair conjuring up images of historical bacchanalian misrule: '... the bearpit, the cock-fighting ring, yobbo rampage .... the Goose fair of loutish behaviour however Falstaffian ...' (*TD*, p.42). This seemingly casual reference to Shakespeare's Falstaff will find an echo later in the novel.

Read through the narrator's version of events - and there is always the same possibility of unreliability in his narrative as there is with Hazlitt's artistic shaping of events to fit his confessional agenda - the fair-ground becomes a public erogenous zone in which he fears the collapse of moral inhibitions and a related challenge to his notions of masculinity as Bernadette becomes a visual symbol of eroticism threatening to unleash a level of male violence beyond his control. Here, as elsewhere in the novel, the private and the public are in a constant dialectic as performative spaces for the realisation of the narrator's erotic projections.

Hazlitt rhapsodises on the sight of Sarah's arms, imbuing their nakedness with the power to kill. Paradoxically, Sarah expresses distaste for the very garment she has freely chosen to wear, presumably to please her admirer(s):

> H. How beautiful your arms look in those short sleeves!
> S. I do not like to wear them.
> H. Then that is because you are merciful, and would spare frail mortals who might die with gazing.
> S. I have no power to kill.
> H. You have, you have  Your charms are irresistible ...
>
> (*Liber*, p.45)

Bernadette extrovertly re-enacts Sarah's display in the public arena in what the narrator interprets as an open invitation to the public gaze in opposition to his privileged private gaze:

> The first thing I noticed and the thing I noticed most all afternoon was about two hand-spans long. A black elasticated sort of woollen mini-skirt which stretched across your buttocks and your thighs like the peel of a tight apple ... And, short as it wickedly was, it still rode up once or twice ... - you made only the most perfunctory of tugs to conceal the skimpy white lace - G-STRING! underneath. Everywhere we moved I sensed a rabble of lusting eyes swarming up your thighs. The lusts of a hundred young men gobbling up that firm tanned flesh
>
> (*TD*, pp.44-45)

Bernadette is identified as dramatic spectacle very much in terms of the visual grammar of audience-cinema relations, reproducing the culturally conditioned male-female gaze. The reader may even sense an undercurrent of textual masturbatory eroticism as the narrator recalls the excitement of events now very much in his past. He, like Hazlitt, 'would have no one else see you so. I am jealous of all eyes but my own' (*Liber*, p.45) and yet he too is making her display public and permanent through the medium of print.

Two years prior to *A Time to Dance* Bragg published *Rich. The Life of Richard Burton* (1998). Aspects of this biography seem to have lingered in Bragg's memory and subsequently inflected passages in the novel. He writes at length of Burton's infatuation with Elizabeth Taylor and of her ability to sexually arouse him. Bragg includes a passage from Burton's diary that not only provides an accurate template for Bernadette's display but which also reflects upon the effect of such a display upon the male onlookers:

> Elizabeth was looking infinitely sexy. She wore mesh white leotards and the shortest mini-skirt I've ever seen. It barely, and when she moved didn't, cover her crotch. The beach boys around, who all appeared to be stoned, were beside themselves. And as we left they shouted various invitations to her and offered to kiss her in various parts of her anatomy - the mini-dress was also very low cut - including sundry offers of fornication. They were careful that I was on the boat and moving rapidly away before these generous offers were made.
>
> (*Rich*, p.245)

Bragg comments that, from the safety of the departing boat, '[it] is almost sweet that he calls up his street macho. The sexual intoxication and possession jealousy is heavily in evidence and clearly Burton is in thrall to her at this time' (*Rich*, p.245). Bragg's narrator, a much less 'street macho' character than Burton, has no similar ready means of retreat from such a sexually charged scene, and his refusal to run suggests an interesting parallel with the Western movie heroes of Bragg's youthful cinema-going days. Bragg interrogates the identity of the familiar (Western) action hero, questioning assumptions about masculinity which were an inherent part of the nineteenth century's vituperation of the so-called Cockney writers to whom Hazlitt belonged. Revealingly Bragg writes that Bernadette 'whooped around the fair like a *cowboy* in a rodeo' (italics added, *TD*, p.45), suggesting that Bragg sees her as subverting the Western genre in order to appropriate the male gaze in an unconscious attempt to reverse the cultural power dynamic in her relationship with the narrator.

By way of contrast to Bernadette's Western film image, Bragg depicts his narrator as a chivalric English Knight intent on defending his maiden's honour against '[y]oung men with tattooed arms gathered to stare ... the ragged army of the new English mob' (*TD*, p.45). Bernadette rewards his bravery by having sex with him soon after, and Bragg again turns to the cinema, and inter-media textuality and Shakespeare's *Henry V*, when searching for an image to describe his feelings. His narrator suffers 'worries flying into my head like those arrows at Olivier's Agincourt' (*TD*, p.48). Later we read how Bernadette's smile 'darted like an arrow to its target' (*TD*, p.59). Coincidentally, Bragg published a study of Laurence Olivier in 1984, featuring a full-colour poster for Olivier's 1945 film of *Henry V*, in which a flight of arrows crosses the skyline (*Olivier*, between p.48 and p.49), and in which the text notes 'Olivier's control and Olivier's ambition *thudded into the bull's-eye*' (italics added, *Olivier*, p. 73).

Arrows may suggest a phallocentric approach to sexual metaphor, but Bragg is concerned in *A Time to Dance* to open up a rather more wider-ranging gendered debate on sex and language in literature. In *The Adventure of English* (2003) he looks briefly at the nineteenth century's censorship of the more sexually frank novels of Smollett, Fielding and Richardson:

> Johnson had omitted "shit" from his dictionary. By the nineteenth century, in polite print in England, this delicacy of feeling or squeamishness had grown stronger and English was being whipped into line. Chaucer, who had an immense number and range of swear words would I think have been puzzled at what had happened to that vigorously rude English element in his repertoire. Morality censored language.
>
> The result was that coarse language withdrew from public view. It went underground or into the work of

outraged and outrageous writers, from Rochester to Lawrence.

(*AE*, pp.232-234)

Rochester probably wrote more frankly and publicly about sex than any English writer before Lawrence. In referencing Lawrence, and to a lesser extent Henry Miller, in *A Time to Dance* Bragg is setting the terms of the aesthetic challenge he is renewing. Critically the odds appear stacked against him. D.J. Taylor, for example, is damning of the modern novel's attempts to replicate the physicality of intercourse on the page, citing its 'portentousness and the excitable language of wildly exploring tongues ... the sense of incongruity which invariably emerges whenever a novelist tries to write in a romantic context about essentially unromantic physical detail' (*After the War*, p.235). In Taylor's view, the 'most effective modern writing about sex ... tends to avoid this gloating over physical detail and approaches the sensation of the sexual act from a more oblique angle' (*After*, pp.235-236). Taylor's choice of terms is fairly representative of the loaded response awaiting Bragg's attempt to combine sensitivity with the use of frank Anglo-Saxon wordplay. Bragg makes clear his wish not to hide behind an 'oblique' indirect approach to the sex act, whilst simultaneously taking pains to write in such a way as to avoid accusations of arousing the reader to gloat - 'feast eyes or mind lustfully' (*Concise Oxford Dictionary*, p.521).

The question of how sex/sexuality can be rescued from secrecy and brought into the realm of language was central to the Lawrence of *Lady Chatterley's Lover* (1928) and is likewise a major preoccupation of Bragg: 'In [*A Time to Dance*] the writing about sex is an attempt to be open and graphic, to be emotionally involving and erotic without being pornographic, overheated or crass. It was difficult to do but the discovery of his eroticism was fundamental to [the narrator's] life, just as a more refined discovery proved essential to Bernadette' (*Screenplay*, p.16). We catch here an echo from Lawrence's 1929 essay *A Propos of 'Lady Chatterley's Lover'*: 'And this is the real point of [*Lady Chatterley's Lover*]. I want men and women to be able to *think* sex, fully, completely, honestly, and clearly' (*A Propos*, p.308). Sixty years after the publication of Lawrence's novel, and despite the sexual revolution of the 1960s which cleared the moral ground for the publication of formerly banned works by Lawrence, Miller, Genet, Selby, de Sade and many others, there remains a coyness about the liberation of explicitly vernacular sexual language on the printed page.[4]

Lawrence and Miller provide a framing device allowing Bragg to approach the use of sexually explicit language indirectly by ventriloquising the narrative voice of others in ultimately justifying his own practice. Here, however, Bragg's autobiographical voice appears to replace that of the narrator inasmuch as the reference to 1960s publications imply a critically aware reader able to contextualise their profane, scatological or sexually deviant language within a wider literary and aesthetic debate, encompassing the Hemingwayesque 'second time when the earth did move' alongside 'all the Romantic cliches of Romantic love' (*TD*, p.49). Nor would I underestimate the sheer practical difficulties of the narrator acquiring copies of Miller's *Tropics* in a small Cumbrian town. His success in doing so implies a sophisticated banker/reader who shares a significant part of his intellectual hinterland with that of his creator. The notion of identity between author and narrator, where the lived experience of the former translates into the fictionality of the latter, is susceptible to particular scrutiny in the case of a first-person narrator. Here, given Bragg's frequent turn to autobiography in his novels, the reader might reasonably judge the narrator's aesthetic development to run remarkably parallel to Bragg's own literary sensibilities.

The referencing of Lawrence and Miller to preface the narrator's search for an acceptable form of words to capture the physicality as well as the spirituality of sex is central to the book's argument. The narrator is anxious to move beyond describing 'just sex' but he stumbles from the outset:

> (Perhaps people find this hard to write about because of
> the words: 'love' is a portfolio of a word, a jingle, a
> throwaway, a rubber stamp, a lie, a sell, a compromise,
> a defeat, a defence, a trick, a trash word, a worn word,
> a pulped and victimised word, a raped, mutilated,

---

4. In *Liber Amoris* - and his other writings - Hazlitt was restrained from writing openly about sex, and the result is a disturbingly masturbatory prose of male excitation that appears to revel in the possibilities of sex whilst condemning female physical display for provoking such arousal: 'If I were a law-giver ... no woman should expose her shape publicly unless she were a prostitute ... the thin muslin vest drawn tight round the slender waist, following with nice exactness the undulations of the shape downwards, disclosing each full swell, each coy recess, obtruding on the eye each opening charm, the play of the muscles, the working of the thighs, and by the help of a walk ... displaying all those graceful motions, of which the female form is susceptible these moving pictures of lust and nakedness, against which the greasy imaginations of grooms and porters may rub themselves ...' (*The Complete Works of William Hazlitt*, edt. P.P. Howe, vol.I, p.289; qtd. Grayling, p.87).

bayoneted word, soggy, infirm, a code word, a war word, a dog of a word, don't trust him, unreliable, unbelievable, shot: and 'sex' is worse.) Yet it *was* sex, and it was *love*.

(*TD*, p.49)

Neither Miller nor Lawrence offers him an alternative language beyond 'allusions in hints and metaphors' (*TD*, p.50) with which to describe his moment of sexual epiphany with Bernadette. Miller eventually became an enthusiastic evangelist for Lawrence, writing with a sexual frankness allied to a social and ideological radicalism foreign to the mainstream of the mid-twentieth-century English novelist tradition. Clearly the sheer brute force of its language has a delayed cathartic effect upon the narrator's newly awakened poetics. He is, however, partial in his reading, referring mainly to Miller's *Tropic of Cancer* (1934) with its deliberately provocative introduction of shock-value language from the very first pages - 'O Tania, where now is that warm cunt of yours ...' (quoted, Pearson, *Obelisk*, p.456) - whilst ignoring *Tropic of Capricorn* (1964). The latter is of far greater relevance to his social and professional position. But he fares little better with Lawrence: 'he tried and he could convince  but even he could be worrying' (*TD*, p.50). 'Worrying' presumably because of his use of 'fuck', a word the narrator painfully self-consciously forces himself to use/print, but then suffers the guilt of unbidden emission: 'I have soiled the pages, stained the script' (*TD*, p.52).

Bragg encourages his narrator to express himself in explicitly Lawrentian terms of '[k]nowing beyond talk; knowing in my blood' (*TD*, p.126) whilst, unsurprisingly given his background, he is unable to construct a new public language of sexuality. He fails to persuade Bernadette to readily adopt this desired frankness of linguistic sexual exchange, In one of her letters she admits finding it impossible to commit the word 'fuck' to paper, even though she yelled it aloud in the throes of sex: 'I do remember calling out the word, the D.H. Lawrence word, the real word I suppose, the word paperback novelists throw around like navvies' (*TD*, p.215). Tellingly, it is to Jane Austen that Bernadette turns in her final letter, expressing a desire to 'be like one of her heroines ... someone as *true* as her heroines' (*TD*, p.215). True is itself a slippery four-letter word open to several meanings and Bernadette's italicising should alert the reader not only to the fictional/untrue context in which she uses it, but also to an unconscious wish to return to precisely that historic period of patriarchal hegemony that brought such grief to Sarah Walker.

Whereas Lawrence argues in *A Propos of 'Lady Chatterley's Lover'* for a 'phallic language' potentially capable of solving the difficulties of the relationship between language, writing and sex, Bragg's narrator always feels more comfortable with Biblical language:

> What happened was like a religious revelation. I saw the light and the light was you and you were the light. But the light shone elsewhere. It showed me, as it shows me, that nothing can ever be as important as the twinned redeemers love and sex. The planet lives through love. And sex. You cannot leave out that tormented and eroded three letter word but if you are human you must bind it to love ... The only force which will take us forward is love.
>
> But who can preach it? Who would dare to? It is a message that has been abused from the beginning. It evaporates on the tongue. The secret is to keep it to yourself. (*TD*, p.123)

This retreat to the private - the same sense of the primacy and fixity of the private as evoked in Austen's largely closed socio-political world represents an unacknowledged abandonment of Lawrence's phallocentric structures and, paradoxically, an inclination towards the female texts which Bernadette's letter takes as models for sexual consciousness. Published one year before pirated editions of *Lady Chatterley's Lover*, Virginia Woolf's *To the Lighthouse* celebrated a feminist intimate textual space that Bragg's narrator appears to replicate.

> She imagined how in the chambers of the mind and heart of the woman who was, physically, touching her, were stood like the treasures in the tombs of kings, tablets bearing sacred inscriptions, which if one could spell them out would teach everything, but they would never be offered openly, never be made public. What art was there, known to love or cunning, by which one pressed through into those secret chambers? What device for becoming, like waters poured into one jar, inextricably the same, one with the object one adored?
> (*Lighthouse*, p.70)

The narrator's radical credo of a (re)new(ed) linguistic sexual aesthetic is superseded by a turn to the feminine, written in the exile of a shabby room of his own, where his memoir (or 'secret chamber') is validated by love, not sex. His narrative attempt to forge a language to both reflect and enable the construction of an aesthetic of identity through sex may remain highly problematic, but by the text's conclusion he has moved a great distance from Hazlitt's final dismissal of Sarah Walker as a 'hapless weed' (*TD*, p.108).

The narrator's self-imposed exile at the novel's end not only mirrors his wife's, Angela, retreat to the isolation of her sickroom but also serves as a reminder of another sub-textual element of transgression involved in his adulterous betrayal of Angela. As Peter Preston sympathetically explains: 'Angela is an off-stage figure for much of the novel: ill, a voice calling from upstairs, conveniently and maybe contrivedly out of the way while the narrator pursues the affair. When her voice is heard, [it is] very affecting for she too has a narrative of love to set beside Bernadette's.'[5] Angela occupies an uncomfortable liminal space in the novel, situated midway between that of Charlotte Brontë's supposedly madwoman (Bertha Mason) in the attic and Coventry Patmore's Angel in the House.[6] Whilst it would have been convenient for the narrator to consign her to the former status, his inclusion of her letter in his memoir presents her as a late-twentieth century avatar of Patmore's Angel, both by nomenclature and by domestic practice. She remains deeply in love with her husband despite the increasingly one-sided nature of the relationship as she retires upstairs to her sickroom - and Bragg inserts a deft intratextual epistolary comment on the fears of gender age difference by having Angela muse upon the consequences of her being six years older than her husband (*TD*, p.157).

Angela too has felt the pull of obsessional love: 'I worshipped you, I know it's blasphemous as well as unhealthy to worship a human being but there we are' (*TD*, p.159). She ends her letter with a deeply moving admission of the loss of sexual attractiveness - '... I am old before my time sixty years can be young for some these days: not for me. I feel old and I look old ...' (*TD*, p.171) - coupled with her willingness to free her husband to find love elsewhere. Bragg accounts in part for Angela's liberal outlook

5.  Preston to Shapcott, email, 2 February 2011.

6.  Published between 1854 and 1861 Patmore's sequence of poems extolling married life, *The Angel in the House,* presented an ideal and sentimental image of the Victorian married couple.

by a metafictional comment on the state of the contemporary novel applicable to the direction of his own text: '... equally from novels I [Angela] know about the rise and fall of love affairs. I know that people seem much more outspoken now - *if novels are anything to go by* - and much less inhibited about everything' (italics added, *TD*, p.170). In effect, Angela's long-goodbye letter serves to bind her husband to her during the final months of illness: '... there was still that sweetness and innocence I had once loved so much. I knew I could never leave her. She needed to be taken care of' (*TD*, p.171). This final act of devotion represents a long overdue balancing of the marital books inasmuch as Angela's money has provided the bedrock of their security and which her husband has successfully invested without realising that Angela would have preferred to 'do something mad like fly to Venice or - best of all - go on safari. You thought it would be too showy' (*TD*, p.167). Whereas money serves to liberate Bernadette from the moment she wins the Rotary prize and makes her own decisions about how to spend it, it imprisons Angela who, despite her awareness of her legacy's corrosive influence on the marriage, lacks a strong enough personality to counter her husband's parsimonious sense of financial pride. Simon J. James's observation that 'money remains the site where realism and romance frequently compete' (*Unsettled Accounts*, p.3) can be seen as central to shaping moral and sexual exchange values in *A Time to Dance*.

Bragg's narrator is unable to escape the limitations of his puritanical psycho-sexual upbringing and it is predominantly the retentive technical language of money and banking rather than that of sex that shapes his use of literary language and metaphor. Money features every bit as much as the *deus ex machina* in Bragg's novel as it does in so much of Victorian literature, where plot is dependent upon its circulation for its imaginative functioning. In *A Time to Dance* money is highly visible throughout. It establishes Bernadette's cultural, rather than sexual, value when she is awarded the local Rotary Club's essay prize money and later confirms her worth, with interest, when she is given a large capital sum in the narrator's closing pages. The narrator's banking career is significant in giving shape to the compositional style of his confession, and for providing him with the comfort of a familiar aesthetic form in monitoring his reactions to the unexpected entry of sexual love on to the balance sheet. Throughout his *account* of the affair Bernadette is seen to accrue additional value both by virtue of demonstrating literary knowledge acquired against great domestic odds and by providing sexual capital for the narrator to draw upon. In banking parlance she not only retains her initial value but substantially enhances it so that by the story's end her lover/accountant feels able to provide her, and the reader, with a correct valuation. In reshaping *Liber Amoris* for the late twentieth century Bragg necessarily shifts financial capital from old male to young female ownership, leaving Bernadette in a much securer financial position to control her destiny than was the real-life Sarah Walker.

Banking metaphors proliferate throughout Bragg's novel and are embedded in its emotional fabric to an extent that it becomes impossible to ignore or forget the significance of the narrator's career. From the start of the affair he self-consciously acknowledges his blinkered sense of vision in reducing his feelings to entries in a ledger of balanced 'GAINS' and 'LOSSES', an accountancy 'love letter of a man cemented in his banks of sad and compromised certainties' (*TD*, p.35). In retrospect, he regrets the headlong rush to sex without what he regarded as the socially prescribed 'period of courtship' (*TD*, p.65) allowing him the time and space in which 'all the pros and cons, the debits and credits, the reds and blacks, the advantages and disadvantages, the plusses and minuses were calculated and double checked' (*TD*, pp.65-66). By mid-novel the language of banking is in danger of dominating and supplanting the love discourse. Chapter 10 begins with cold objective reflections upon the monetary consequences of divorce: 'I worked out the financial equation which could result from a divorce and a remarriage' (*TD*, p.95). It moves on to express regret at not having converted an intimate declaration of love into a financial statement: 'Why did I not sweep you away then and there and give you the talk I had prepared - complete with Debit and Credit, with Long-Term Prospects, and Short-Term Losses, a declaration of love as near an annual report as makes no matter?' (*TD*, p.96). He then writes an extraordinary passage in which sex and money become synonymous in a Freudian display of release and *double entendre*:

> I know that any suggestion of a relationship between
> love and money will make you taunt me again about
> my bank manager's view of life, but money began to
> represent uncalculated enjoyment. It gushed out with
> an eagerness which insisted it convert itself into life.
> Love was an unlimited account, endless credit, an
> interest-free loan for life. And this happened at the

same time as I fell so completely in love with you. You are too young to remember a slang word they used to have in the town, one which amused me very much when I arrived here more than thirty years ago: it was 'mint'. It was used for a woman's vagina. It was money.'  (*TD*, p.98)

The substitution of 'mint' for 'cunt' marks the moment of the removal of Lawrentian sexual language from the narrator's expressive range, replacing it with a financially inflected slang term rooted in the folk culture of Cumbria to which Bragg is so devoted.

The figure of Bragg, the disembodied author, glides in and out of the narrator's story, allowing a double consciousness to invade the text at culturally crucial moments. This is nowhere more apparent than when Bragg directs the reader to interpret his narrator's character, behaviour and background by referencing another banker, T.S. Eliot. From 1917 to 1925 Eliot held a day-time job at Lloyds Bank during which period he wrote his epic *The Waste Land* (1922), followed by *The Hollow Men* (1925). Bragg's 'I was a grey man. I was an empty man' (*TD*, p.105) echoes Eliot's 'We are the hollow men/We are the stuffed men' (p.89) and 'Of death's twilight kingdom/The hope only/Of *empty men*' (italics added, *Collected Poems*, p.91). Bragg's deep-rooted interest in the history of the Border Reivers is analogous to Eliot's interest in anthropology in *The Waste Land* and to that poem's sense of waiting for the world to end: 'We were in the land of Roman milecastles and bloody border wars - where the Kennedys came from - *wastelands, debatable lands, and the sea ready to take away the dead as it had done for years*' (italics added, *TD*, pp.201-202). Intertextually interesting, in the context of dance and time, the lost souls of Eliot's poem shuffle around rhythmically in meaningless rituals -

> *Here we go round the prickly pear*
> *Prickly pear prickly pear*
> *Here we go round the prickly pear*
> *At five o'clock in the morning.*
> (*Collected Poems*, p.91)

- long denuded of their original mythic meaning.

Bragg's narrator claims to have read Henry Miller's *Tropic of Cancer* and *Tropic of Capricorn* when young, but because he does so in the context of struggling to find an appropriate linguistic form to talk about all aspects of sex it is easy to assume that the *Cancer* novel is the more important formative model. In fact, his constant return to a narrative dependent upon, and controlled by, monetary metaphors, terms and structures nominates *Capricorn* as the more influential of the two texts, There is an uncanny sense in which the anomie of Eliot's poetry and the financial-beatific dialectic of Miller's prose converge to provide the narrator with an unexpected textual hermeneutic. To read Bragg through Miller is to understand the hollowness of a life defined by monetary necessity and the concomitant difficulty of rejecting its social invasiveness so as to 'have the ability and the patience to formulate what is not contained in the language of our time, for what is now intelligible is meaningless' (*Capricorn*, p.111). A fairly representative *Capricorn* passage illustrates the degree to which Miller's monetary and dance images may have lodged in the narrator's subconscious:

> To walk in money through the night crowd, protected by money, lulled by money, dulled by money, the crowd itself a money, the breath money, no least single object anywhere that is not money, money, money everywhere and still not enough, and then no money or a little money or less money or more money, but money, always money, and if you have money or you don't have money it is the money that counts and money makes money, *but what makes money make money?*
>
> Again the dance hall, the money rhythm, the love that comes over the radio, the impersonal, wingless touch of the crowd. A despair that reaches down to the very soles of the boots, an ennui, a desperation. ... to dance without joy, to be so desperately alone, to be almost inhuman because you are human. ... This is the dance of ice-cold life in the hollow of an atom, and the more we dance the colder it gets.
>
> (*Capricorn*, p.109)

Clearly there is a high level of sophisticated intertextuality at play in *A Time to Dance* here, but it forms and arises from the landscape of Bragg's youthful reading, making greater demands upon the reader's interpretative powers than the narrator is able to realise.

Hazlitt's essay 'On the Knowledge of Character' affirms that 'I do not think that what is called *Love at first sight* is so great an absurdity as it is sometimes imagined to be' ('Knowledge' p.172). Written while in Scotland waiting for his divorce from Sarah Stoddart, Hazlitt claims that such a phenomenon is predetermined, beyond self-control, and the physical manifestation of an image created in the mind: 'The idol we fall down and worship is an image familiar to our minds. It has been present to our waking thoughts, it has haunted us in our dreams, like some fairy vision' (ibid.). This belief is consistent with his 1812 lecture on Berkley's *Principles of Human Knowledge,* in which he insists that 'all ideas [ - and this would include the beatification of a woman - ] imply at least a power of "comprehension and abstraction" in the mind's activity' (*Quarrel,* p.148). Bragg's narrator is eventually drawn to read these essays and to internalise many of Hazlitt's views as his own. Bragg himself came early to an appreciation of Hazlitt's prose, first encountering him as a schoolboy, 'at one stage [he] knew chunks of a dozen or so essays off by heart and still sentences come back ...' ('In Our Time', subscribers' email letter, 8 April 2010). This admission of literary 'love at first sight' is germane to reading the novel's key set-piece of a Hazlitt lecture at the 1989 William Wordsworth Conference, an annual gathering at Grasmere sometimes attended by Bragg.

In the context of the Conference Bragg introduces an outline of *Liber Amoris* as a revelatory text for his narrator, forcing him to re-evaluate his own obsessive love through the lens of Hazlitt's experience and cries of anguished betrayal. But first he has to overcome a sense of intellectual inadequacy before he feels sufficiently relaxed to join the audience:

> There was a lecture advertised, open to the public, in what was described as the Conference Room in the hotel's basement. This lecture was part of a Wordsworth Summer Conference and normally I would have thought it a little above me. But we had been reading some of our Lakeland Romantics and the speaker was a literary politician whom I had often seen and generally enjoyed on television. The good weather appeared to have broken. I had no urge to go out to a pub without you. I was looking for something to fill in the time and as this promised to last no more than an hour and a half I felt I could risk it. Besides, the title beguiled me. 'Hazlitt In Love'. Of Hazlitt I had only a rather vague notion: but

anyone 'in love' intrigued me.

I paid my £2.50 and went in. When I came out, our lives had changed utterly: ruined.

*(TD*, p. 131)

At this point the autobiographical and the fictive become entangled, leaving the reader wondering to what degree the subsequent reading of *Liber Amoris* is Bragg's interpretation as opposed to the narrator's fictive response. Writing in 2010 Bragg says that 'some years ago he wanted to write a modern version of "Liber Amoris" ...' ('In Our Time', subscribers email letter, 8 April 2010). Indeed, his personal commitment to Hazlitt's work extends beyond the text to include a relationship with other Hazlitt devotees. The 'literary politician', for example, is a thinly disguised Michael Foot, an ardent admirer of Hazlitt who seldom missed the Grasmere Conference. As Jones comments, 'Michael did not attend merely as a listener, but always prepared a contribution to Wordsworthian studies' (*Hazlitt*, p.533). Foot became a close personal friend of Bragg's, appearing in his television programmes, as well as jointly hosting a traditional General Election-night party at the Bragg's North London home. This autobiographical sub-text suggests an authorial knowingness about the strengths and weaknesses of Foot's ideologically driven agenda in supporting the more questionable aspects of Hazlitt's life-style that would not have been available to his narrator. In Foot's 1989 review of Stanley Jones's Hazlitt biography - the same year as his fictional appearance in Bragg's novel - he argues 'the need for a vigorous defence given that *Liber Amoris* was regarded as a lewd and loathsome production' (*Uncollected*, p.153).[7] At the same time, however, his unsubstantiated description of Hazlitt's marriage to Sarah Stoddart as 'an absurd marriage which was doomed before it started' (*Uncollected*, p.152) raises the prospect of a prejudicial reading likely to mislead Bragg's narrator entering the Conference room without having read Hazlitt and unaware of Foot's literary-political radical agenda.

In the event, Foot's lecture inspires the narrator to immediately purchase both *Liber Amoris* and a recently published Hazlitt biography, retire to his room, and immerse himself in text and commentary. Central

7. Tom Paulin, who considers Hazlitt to be one of the greatest of all English critics and essayists makes an exception of *Liber Amoris*: 'Like a type of postmodernist writing, there is a nihilistic, self-flagellating desperation, a having-it-all-ways irony, a masturbatory, taut flaccidity, in the recycled clichés which comprise *Liber Amoris*' (p.45).

to his initial intoxication with what he reads is a growing realisation of the parallels between his and Hazlitt's circumstances and, in particular, the justification for a belief in the romantic concept of 'love at first sight'. Ironically this is precisely the phrase that Bragg will reprise in a letter from his seriously ill wife, Angela, anxious to express her love: 'Because you know I fell in love with you at first sight. People can. I did' *(TD*, p.158). The narrator appears wilfully ignorant of his wife's level of devotion. As he reads Hazlitt, euphoria turns to despair as he begins to equate Hazlitt's denunciation of Sarah Walker with a growing suspicion that Bernadette may have deceived him. Hazlitt offers little meaningful evidence for his accusations and even his later attempts to deliberately entrap Sarah are negotiated with the nimbleness of Samuel Richardson's *Pamela* - and in any case, it may be argued that her flirtatious behaviour is no more than the standard acceptable level of room-service by landladies and their daughters anxious to retain their male lodgers in a highly competitive market-place. But for Bragg's narrator, ignorant of the nuances of socio-economic history, and now highly susceptible to psychological authorial identification, mention of the term betrayal has done its damage and, like Hazlitt, he positively searches for reasons to doubt Bernadette's constancy.

Neither Bragg's narrator, nor Hazlitt, includes Jane Austen on their reading list. The former restricts himself almost exclusively to male writers with a Lake District connection: 'Hutchinson, Otley, Gilpin, West - and decent selections of the Wordsworths, Coleridge, De Quincey' *(TD*, p.18). Hazlitt's omission of Austen is something of a mystery, especially as she was discussed and admired within his circle of friends, and given his enjoyment of other female writers such as Mrs Inchbald and Mrs Radcliffe. Grayling believes that Hazlitt's reaction to Austen's novels would be instructive, 'all the more so as their moral outlooks are surprisingly similar' (*Quarrel*, p.232). In particular, an acquaintance with *Persuasion* (1817) might have persuaded Hazlitt and Bragg's narrator to reflect upon the heroine's discussion with Captain Harville of a contentious aspect of gender and sexuality central to their concerns, namely the relative constancy in love of men and women. (It is worth recalling that Bernadette references Austen's novels as models for her own future conduct.) Captain Harville's comments are proleptic of Bragg's narrator's response to *Liber Amoris:* '"I do not think I ever opened a book in my life which had not something to say upon woman's inconstancy"'. To which Anne replies '"... if you please, no references to examples in books. Men have every advantage of us in telling their own story. Education has been theirs in so much higher a degree; the pen has been in their hands. I will not allow books to prove any thing'" (*Persuasion*, pp.220-1). Bragg mimetically reproduces Hazlitt's educated male text representing a masculine view of women's cultural and social position. All the major female players in both their books are shown to have internalised the gendered discourse of their narrators, even though the narratives of inconstancy and betrayal are rightly the property of the male narrators, both of whom expose the objects of their obsessive gaze to the social condemnation of their peers and readers. Sarah Walker's future marriage prospects are severely curtailed by accusations of sexual lewdness, whilst Bernadette's abortion might be read as either a marker of sexual indiscretion or a lack of feminine independence at a time when the stigma of single motherhood was in fast decline. Anne Haverty's retelling of *Liber Amoris* in the first-person autobiographical voice of Sarah Walker in *The Far Side of a Kiss* provides a feminist corrective to the culturally dominant male representation of gender and sexuality. In her concluding paragraph Haverty's Sarah questions the veracity of the autobiographical text, equating the pen and the penis for the irretrievable damage they can do to female reputations:

> ... I conjure up fancies of a world without books. For I despise them and think they were better never to be invented. What are they but instruments that writers use to dupe us? On account of them, we have no knowledge of our own, nor way of our own for seeing the world. It is the writers who dazzle us by telling us what we are like, and what we should be like. I know now they write nothing but lies. And on account of them there is no more innocence in the world, nor free conduct, nor any more independence.

> (*Far Side*, p.241)

In his reframing of *Liber Amoris* Bragg provides a platform for the formerly marginalised female voice, recognising an ethic of authorial accountability absent from Hazlitt's methodology. Bernadette commands a significant textual space with a 14 page letter in the course of which Bragg goes some way to ameliorate the disparities and distortions of

Hazlitt's confusion of economically determined sexual harassment and romantic ideology. Whereas Sarah's voice is largely inaudible, Bernadette is able to delineate the limitations of the social and cultural situations within which she is forced to operate. There is a significant shift in the representation of feminine erotics between the two texts, in which *A Time to Dance* offers a form of cultural conversation between equals that promises a more honest and equal narrative of sexual relations. Nowhere is this more apparent than in the differing approaches to seduction and the shadowy presence of rape. Hazlitt's text offers little contradiction in its representation of Sarah as an economically motivated scheming seductress and himself as the innocent victim of her technique:

> Am I to suppose, then, that you are acting a part, a vile part, all this time, and that you come up here, and stay as long as I like, that you sit on my knee and put your arms around my neck, and feed me with kisses, and let me take other liberties with you, and that for a year together; and that you do all this not out of love, or liking, or regard, but go through your regular task, like some young witch, without one natural feeling, to show your cleverness, and get a few presents out of me ...
>
> (*Liber*, p.49)

If Sarah were acting a part it is odd that the country's foremost dramatic critic could neither discern the actress in his room nor deconstruct her role. She is there at his invitation and given her family's reliance on their lodger's rent it is not altogether surprising that Hazlitt's undefined sexual liberties are licensed as part of a delicately balanced economic nexus, immune to personal sexual attraction. There is no recognition of the slippery concept of seduction that Sarah must negotiate, along similar lines to Samuel Richardson's lower class servant Pamela, who resists advances from her employer's son before finally compelling him to marry her. Leslie Fielder labels *Pamela, or, Virtue Rewarded* (1740-1741) the 'first success story of the female bourgeois world, at once practical, prurient and edifying - a thoroughgoing piece of almost unconscious duplicity, though quite charming all the same' (*Love and Death*, p.60). Hazlitt echoes Richardson's sentiments in his essay 'Hot and Cold', affirming that the 'truest virtue is that which is least susceptible of contamination from its opposite' (in edited, Paulin, p.258). Yet he seems incapable of recognising the patriarchal power he is wielding to 'contaminate' Sarah's virtue, or of the physical and moral consequences, should she submit to more than sitting on his knee as he fumbles through her clothes for satisfaction.

Bragg's updating of this encounter tracks the initial premises of the original text - '... when he said "Sit on my knee" I did. He used to give me a pound. When he asked me to kiss him I didn't want to but my mother got hold of me ... and gave me a hammering. It was five pounds I got for a kiss' (*TD*, p.80) - but engages in a process of contesting the false premises and categories behind Hazlitt's logic. He recognises the internal family politico-economic power structure that might operate to coerce acts of sexual submissiveness, not only to maintain current income but potentially to access new forms of capital through marriage. When Bernadette tries to tell her mother that their lodger had moved beyond kisses - 'He started to play with me' (ibid.) - her mercenary reaction is to say 'I should be so lucky because he wanted to marry me ... and we would all be rich' (*TD*, p.81). While women have many common causes in gender issues, Bragg is too honest a writer not to acknowledge that they are sometimes painfully differentiated by life experiences which inform their perceptions. Mrs Kennedy represents a powerful feminine, not feminist, voice that aligns her with Richardson's Lovelace: 'I wanted to run away but she had thought of that and told the boys to keep an eye on me' (*TD*, p.81).

Hazlitt textually infects Sarah with the gross language of pollution - 'wert thou a wretched wanderer in the street, covered with rags, disease and infamy, I'd clasp thee to my bosom, and live and die with thee, my love, kiss me, thou little sorceress!' (*Liber*, p.52) Sarah's capitalised 'NEVER!' is a sufficiently shrill response to effect her escape. Bragg's intertextual response to Hazlitt's linguistic fore-play is a rather more squalid and violent plot driven episode of rape by a farmer lodger, deluded in his belief that Bernadette has led him on. From this moment of crisis Bragg is able to construct a narrative of physical and mental recovery and feminine advancement to rival that of his narrator's slow rehabilitation from the toxicity of his mis-reading of Hazlitt's text. There exists, of course, a constant risk of reinstating the norms of Hazlitt's masculine discourse within an intertextual contestation as the narrator is seduced by the ancestral power of a freely chosen, and in many ways admired, dominant discourse. Bragg succeeds in preventing his countertext from surreptitiously colluding with Hazlitt's ideological master text by admitting Bernadette's voice into the narrative on a near equal epistolary footing so as to highlight the on-going limited nature of cultural roles available to working-class girls, together with the risk of a persistent male dominated convergent culture, silencing any confident opposing voice questioning the authenticity of its version of reality. The various textual echoes are never quite the same as their original source and are sometimes, as in the discussion above, re-articulated in a feminine voice writing from a very different perspective. Overall, the epistolary duality of equality in Bragg's novel provides a partial feminisation of the text capable of commenting upon Hazlitt's original master narrative.

Bragg turns literally to the feminine in placing his narrator in a long tradition of representing nature as a woman. His deepening sexual relationship with Bernadette is celebrated in a precisely plotted number of Lake District locations - Ireby, Keswick, the Western Fells, the outer Northern Fells, Ullswater, Blake, Ennerdale, Borrowdale, Crummock, Bassenthwaite Lake, Grasmere - that chart the identification of person with place. The metaphoric form of this identity is the construction of a woman-nature affinity that propels the narrator into a re-evaluation of the Lakes from that of a geographical site to be explored with the aid of guide books and seen through the lens of literary representations to one of psychic healing and sensual nourishment experienced as erotic delight. The address to the feminine foregrounds a metaphysically sexualised reading of nature that both idealises the Lake District landscape as a place of female enchantment and seduction whilst carrying an undercurrent of male sexual violation. Given that Bernadette's voice remains silent in the use of nature-female metaphor, the reader might be inclined to question the extent to which, in such anatomical descriptive passages as the following, landscape aesthetics become complicit with (male) social power: 'The soft round fells were breasts, the broad valleys cleavages, the deep cuts vaginas, the warm cropped turf lay back in the sun like your bare pelt waiting to be disturbed' (*TD*, p.121). Kate Soper reads this coding of nature as feminine, deeply entrenched in Western thought, and 'allegorised as either a powerful maternal force, the womb of all human production or as the site of sexual enticement and ultimate seduction ... Nature as physical territory is also presented as a source of erotic delight, and sometimes of overwhelming provocation to her masculine voyeur-violator' ('Naturalized Woman', p.141). Very much attuned to Soper's imagery, Bragg also writes that 'the Lake District then to me was like the great egg of myth[8], the Garden of Eden, the original African woman-mother of humankind' (*TD*, p.122). The reproductive and the provocative co-exist in Bragg's association of the Lake District landscape with the female anatomy, described in physiological terms that read uncannily like a catalogue entry to accompany Gustave Courbet's 1866 painting *The Origin of the World* in which his passion for anthropomorphic landscape is fully exposed. It is an explicit painting of female pudenda cropped, like Bragg's prose description of Bernadette's body, to exclude the face as the eye is directed to gaze on the site of penetration and reproduction. Bragg's 'place of fecundity' finds its visual equivalent in Courbet's painting.

Deconstructing a popular novel to demonstrate the connection of its literary allusions with the painter's canvas expands the generally accepted limitations and restrictions of such novels to provide a technical bridge spanning the literary/historical gap between them and the canonical modernists. As with Bragg's encoded reference to Eliot's *The Hollow Men*, the critical exploration of literary and art allusion discloses interwoven themes encouraging a deeper reading of popular texts. The structural allusion to Courbet and art is necessarily mine, but once directed to Courbet's male gaze at the female as a depersonalised anthropomorphic landscape or eroticised desire as complementary to Bragg's prose, readers might be tempted to explore further the affinity between writing, painting and the semantics of representation.

Let me develop a little further this suggested critical reassessment of Bragg's work in the light of his own interest in the visual arts. Whilst Bragg is clearly not a modernist as the term is generally understood, he nevertheless readily engages in depicting cultural continuity, calling upon various cultural fragments, from Shakespeare to Eliot and beyond, to reassemble a late-twentieth century world illuminated by their presence. My reference to Courbet's painting as reverberating art allusion informing Bragg's use of the woman as landscape metaphor should be

---

8. In his essay 'D.H. Lawrence and the Dance' Mark Kinkead-Weekes writes of Lawrence's 'last perhaps greatest response to dancing' when he visited the Etruscan tombs in Tarquinia where there 'were wonderful lines of dancers that seemed to him to embody all the old pagan wisdom ... In the very place of death the Etruscans reaffirmed the vivid energy and continuity of life in a living cosmos ... So the dead man is seen feasting with his friend and his lover, holding between finger and thumb *the egg that speaks of life renewed*, beginning all over again' (italics added, 'Lawrence and Dance', p.59).

considered in the context of his narrator's claim to have access to an appreciation of a wide range of art, and in particular, paintings of the nude figure:

> I began to look in books of art and soon became absorbed by the nudes. ... Where did I read that Renoir said "I paint with my penis!"? Looking at some of his rather plump and fudged ladies, you can begin to believe it. But the others - Venus, Olympia, the monumental nudes of Géricault, David's perfect figures, Cézanne's solid flesh, Lautrec's diseased flesh, Rubens' too much flesh, Expressionist and Weimar crudities, Judith, the stones and stones of marbled late-Renaissance breast and thigh, how many? - none like you.
>
> (*TD*, p.58)

Here Bragg's narrator assumes the character of Hazlitt as renowned art critic but behind this display of apparent erudition is the repeated pattern of autobiographical content and the studied conflation of author and character. Bragg has interviewed, filmed and written about the world of art with an insider's knowledge - his 1983 book *Land of the Lakes*, includes, for example, a chapter on paintings of the Lakes, and his transcription of a 1985 *South Bank Show*'s profile of Francis Bacon contains the throwaway line 'And then we talked of Ingres, Michelangelo, flesh and sexuality' (*SBS*, p.109). More recently, Bragg's catalogue 'Introduction' to an exhibition of Cumbrian artist Julian Cooper's Lake District cave and rock mountain paintings, *Natural Forces*, describes looking for 'the skull beneath the skin of the landscape' (p.8). It is Bragg, not the narrator, whose wide knowledge of art and ready command of critical language annexes the painter's canvas to his metaphorical hinterland, inviting the reader to probe beneath the seemingly simple surface of his prose to uncover a more exacting world of structural allusions.

Bragg's metaphorical hinterland is firmly grounded in a closely observed and transcribed sense of place. The most explicit detailed description of all the novel's locations is that of the narrator's home town of Wigton. It is here that the story starts and ends and in which the supporting cast of players - Angela, bank work colleagues, the Kennedy family - appear, and never stray. Yet this is the one site that refuses to admit its identity. Hazlitt's close contemporaries were never in any doubt of his factual identity hiding behind the fictional persona 'H' and the Prefatory 'native of North Britain, who left his own country early in life, in consequence of political animosities and an ill-advised marriage' (*Liber*, p.41). The seemingly self-destructive inclusion of 'political animosities' and an 'ill-advised marriage' attach themselves to widely advertised aspects of Hazlitt's public and private life.

Bragg also makes little determined effort to either disguise or hide the clues to the narrator's home-town's identity, and it might be argued that this refusal to acknowledge the obvious actually calls attention to what has been suppressed in the blurring of fact and fiction. In presenting the town as something of a hybrid construction, Bragg is able to sidestep the epistemological question of the relation between literary discourse and the reality of the transparently autobiographical. For the reader concentrating on the pleasure of the plot, the biographical and historical criteria necessary for an audit of verifiability may well not be readily to hand, allowing the novel to blur the fine boundary between fact and fiction. Yet from the outset when Bernadette and the narrator leave the Crown public house to 'set off through the empty town, past St. Mary's Church, Fox the butcher's, the unisex hairdresser, the new children's clothes shop', and we are told that the population is calculated at 'five thousand souls' (*TD*, p.28), all the clues are provided for the detection of the factual Wigton. Indeed, the literary tourist following up on the many buildings and streets named in the novel might be gladdened to discover that despite Wigton being no more immune to the closure of small businesses in the face of supermarket competition, the firm of J.H. & J. Fox, family butchers, still trades at 55 High Street, Wigton.

Angela's letter to her husband gives a nostalgic historical perspective on Wigton: 'It was the last time things were nice, the end of the Fifties ... They hadn't knocked down half the town to build a car park ... no supermarkets so shops were shops and not warehouses ... You could pick strawberries in hedges that ran into the town and there were still horses about and men who knew about them' (*TD*, p.158). (The horse as an index of tradition's refusal to surrender to modernity is here, as elsewhere in Bragg's novels, an important and recurring trope linked to personal experience.) *A Time to Dance* is not an overtly political novel but in Angela's memory of Wigton's past there is a sense of something vital lost at the local level as national and international politics and economics enforce greater homogeneity. This yearning for a supposed Arcadian past has its programmatic counterpart in the environmental politics of the 1980s and Angela is 'especially taken by the progress of the Greens' (*TD*, p.183) as reported in the newspapers she so avidly reads. 1989 was in fact the year that ecology issues were foregrounded in the European Union elections and Green MEPs were returned to Brussels.

In a very real sense Angela's memories are also Bragg's memories. He was born in Wigton in 1939 and raised and educated there before gaining a place at Oxford University. As he recounts in his 1976 documentary study *Speak for England*, he later found himself drawn back to the town: 'When my first wife died I found that one of the courses of action I eventually took was to bring my daughter back to the place where I was born. For better or worse I wanted to root her into a part of the world and a family of relationships I knew' (*SE*, p.1). To have named Wigton in the novel would have meant creating a signifier pointing clearly at Bragg as the signified with the concomitant risk of unsettling the central fictional narrative of sexual self-discovery. Even so, Amanda Thursfield's on-line profile of Bragg cannot resist questioning the level of authorial involvement in the central character's dilemma and making *a priori* assumptions about his motivation: 'Unusually for Bragg this novel is written in the first person, and one cannot help speculating as to what events in the author's life seem to have turned him from humane but detached chronicler, as in the Cumbrian books, back into a writer who is closer and more personally and psychologically involved with his character ...' ('Melvyn Bragg', p.3).

In my reading of the novel, character development and personality is conditioned by a sense of place as a historical and socio-cultural reality as a base for dialectical engagement between the present and a specific period of English late-Romanticism and the literature of the Lake District. This narrative connection is made within an interpretative frame that references *Liber Amoris* both directly and indirectly throughout the text. Fiona Stafford describes the Romantic period as contributing a 'defining moment in literary history, when local detail ceased to be regarded as transient, irrelevant, or restrictive, and began to seem essential to art with any pretension to permanence' (*Local Attachments*, p.30). In a short but crucial passage Bragg names the small market town of Ireby as the location for a metafictional moment of past and present dialogue, intertwining literary poetic history with social history:

I drove you into the Northern Fells to a pub called The

Sun in Ireby and made a vow on the way not to tell you what Keats had written about the place. I did not then want to be the new Pygmalion. The saloon bar was empty at that early hour ...

I talked about Keats and the others who had turned the Lake District into a literary monument. It proved a good choice. Your teachers had not exaggerated. You knew your stuff ... this thoughtful young woman talking about Michael and eighteenth-century shepherds and how they were much worse off than the Wordsworth hero ...

(TD, p.47)

The reference to the narrator's claim that he did not want 'to be the new Pygmalion' appears somewhat disingenuous, considering that from the outset of their relationship he sketched out tentative plans for Bernadette 'to type up my articles, help with the filing, come on occasional field trips' (*TD*, p.37). His version of unfolding events might therefore be as unreliable as sections of Hazlitt's self-justificatory retrospective account of events. Bragg, however, is certainly anticipating his narrator's catastrophic literary engagement with Hazlitt when he makes his ironic reference to *Liber Amoris*'s sub-title, *The New Pygmalion*.

More importantly, it is the reference to John Keats that provides the clue to the novel's aesthetic form and a notion of Englishness, traditionally rooted in the countryside, with Ireby symbolically linking localised rural place and national poetics. The sequence is exemplary in its binding popular culture in times past to a sense of place that sets off a ripple of resonances spreading from the text to images of dance and their place in modernist literature. In June 1818 the twenty-two year old Keats, together with his friend Charles Brown, visited Ireby during a walking tour through Northern England, Ireland and Scotland. Writing to his brother Tom on 1 July 1818 Keats reports:

> After Skiddaw, we walked to Ireby the oldest market town in Cumberland where we were greatly amused by a country dancing school, holden at the Sun, it was indeed "no new cotillion fresh from France". No they kickit & jumpit with mettle extraordinary, & whiskit, & fleckit, & toe'd it, & go'd it, & twirled it, & wheel'd it, & stampt it, & sweated it, tattooing it the floor like mad.

The difference between our country dances & these scotch figures, is about the same as leisurely stirring a cup o'Tea & beating up a batter pudding. I was extremely gratified to think, that if I had pleasures they knew nothing of, they had also some into which I could not possibly enter. I hope I shall not return without having got the Highland fling, there was a fine a row of boys & girls as you ever saw, some beautiful faces, & one exquisite mouth. I never felt so near the glory of Patriotism, the glory of making by any means a country happier. This is what I like better than scenery.

(quoted in Walker, *Walking North*, p.159)

His companion is not quite so complimentary about Ireby but he too is caught up in the energy and transformative power of dance:

Ireby is said to be the oldest market town in the county - with not much of a market. It is a dull, beggarly looking place. Our inn was remarkably clean and neat, and the old host and hostess were very civil and prepossessing - but, heyday! What were those obstreperous doings over head? It was a dancing school under the tuition of a travelling master!

(quoted in Walker, *Walking North*, p.234)

For Keats, if not for Brown, the unexpected encounter with dance marks Ireby as an identity shaping place on the personal level and as a persisting cultural artefact on the national historical level. The visit to the Lakes convinced Keats that books were a poor substitute for direct physical and sensory contact with the natural environment. Bragg's narrator too must map out a personal trajectory away from reliance on printed knowledge to the epiphanal experience of physical and spiritual contact and revelation where flesh and Nature merge.

Bernadette's critical class inflected reference to Wordsworth's 'Michael', published in the 1800 edition of *Lyrical Ballads*, is textually relevant in the context of localism, place and national politics. Michael's cottage is far from London and the governing elite's concerns with 1893 French revolutionary radicalism destabilising British society, yet Greenhead Ghyll is central to Wordsworth's perception of a new sensibility. By the stage of his tour when Keats wrote about his stay in

Ireby he had shrugged off his metropolitan expectations of Wordsworth's Lake District, substituting his own visual and physical sensations for those described in the Lake poetry guide books. His Ireby experience appears to trigger an immediate and intense involvement with place and people, mirroring the life-changing journey awaiting Bragg's narrator.

In summoning the spirit of Keats, and traditional dance, Bragg is covertly celebrating his own joy of dwelling in a distinct local place - High Ireby - at the same time as realising the ancillary socio-poetic function for literary criticism of recording the transformative history of place, enabling future readers/visitors to map the changing landscape. The American academic Carol Kyros Walker's immensely attractive 1992 literary travel book *Walking North With Keats* follows this tradition of ecopoetics as she travels in Keats's footsteps, photographing and recording the natural scenery and man-made structures as near as possible to how they would have appeared to Keats. Her five pages of pictures of Ireby show the town looking much the same as when I first visited it in the autumn of 2010, except that the intervening years have seen The Sun transformed from community public house to private dwelling. Walker's evocative photographs of its dining room and the very entrance to Keats's dancing hall are now a valuable historic record of time past where today's readers can no longer visit. Maureen Allen's 2004 guide to the history of Ireby records that forty years after Keats's visit there were four public Houses in Ireby, but that by 2004 the 'Sun Inn and the Lion ... are now the only public houses which remain in Ireby' (*Ireby*, p.25). Taking the most recent *Rough Guide to the Lake District* with me on my visit I was assured that the traveller 'can eat well in the venerable beam-and-nook *Sun Inn*, whose small beer garden is a restful spot on a sunny day' (*Rough Guide*, p.177). Not any longer. What I stood outside was once clearly a pub, but now converted into a luxury home and on the market for £660,000. Thanks, however, to Keats and Bragg I was able to enjoy a historical sense of place by recovering a poetic/literary layer of tourism, memory and poetic significance, and superimpose it upon the two-dimensional map of the average tourist guide book to Ireby and the Lakes. The Sun Inn remains just visible as a part of social history but as it changes use it is the work of the poet/novelist whose act of naming keeps it in view, leaving a legacy of cultural preservation.

Texts, too, need their cultural custodians. Bragg's re-invention of

*Liber Amoris* is only one strand of what is revealed on close inspection to be an elaborate web of transtextual references skilfully encoded within the narrative of *A Time to Dance*. These encoded texts suggest possibilities beyond the master narrative, allowing the reader, for example, to hypothesise about alternative closures beyond the open-ended conclusion of Bragg's 'Will you [return]? Darling. Bernadette' (*TD*, p.220). Bernadette's turn to Jane Austen in her final letter is a reminder that, as Marilyn Butler puts it, Austen's plots 'rebuke individualistic female initiatives and imply that the consummation of a woman's life lies in marriage to a commanding man' (*Romantics*, p.98). Encoded within Bernadette's Austen reference is a shadow narrative of future marriage to the narrator, a man beginning to regain a measure of self-'command' as his memoir closes.

Bragg smuggles another submerged referential voice into the narrative by reprising a key moment from an exceptionally emotional and powerfully driven novel - Charlotte Brontë's *Jane Eyre* (1847):

> ... but I heard a voice somewhere cry
> 'Jane! Jane! Jane!' Nothing more.
> 'Oh God! What is it?' I gasped.
> ... And it was the voice of a human being - a known, loved,
> well-remembered voice - that of Edward Fairfax Rochester;
> and it spoke in pain and woe - wildly, eerily urgent.
> 'I am coming!' I cried. 'Wait for me! Oh I will come.'
> (*Jane Eyre*, p.442)

Less melodramatically, but with an equally powerful force of telepathic communication, Bragg's narrator's cry is answered by the life-line of a letter from Bernadette:

> Part of me regressed to primitivism, helplessly believing
> that wanting hard enough, becoming a want, a shout, a
> cry for you would bring you back. *You could hear my cry.*
> (italics added, *TD*, p.79)

Resistant to disclosure at a first reading, the array of intertextual discourse and agendas beyond the dominant one of *Liber Amoris* become an important part of Bragg's aesthetic, infusing the historical and physical reality of the Lake District with a sense of poetic myth and rhetoric. This is nowhere better illustrated than with the recalling of Keats's visit to Ireby. But Keats is only one of a number of historical, literary and cultural ghosts inhabiting the text. Through literary, landscape, and disguised autobiographical referents *A Time to Dance* re-writes the Romantic text in its own time, whilst in conversation with other texts and writers. It clearly writes back to Hazlitt's emergent canonical book, *Liber Amoris*, restoring and re-invigorating its potency in the Lake District setting. At the same time as inviting a reappraisal of a classic text it also draws intertextual[9] attention to a range of writers and artists from the Romantic to the modernist. Often revealing unexpected meanings, Bragg's literary interests and personal commitment to the Lake District combine in a search to bridge the epistemological gap between the recording observer and the central importance of place.

9.   Epigraphs are by nature intertextual and, if well chosen, part of the much larger conversation with which the novel is concerned. Ecclesiastes and Alexander Pope provide the aesthetic frame for *A Time to Dance*, offering clues to its mode of interrogation. The over-riding pessimistic tone of the *Book of Ecclesiastes* does not bode well for any optimistic interpretation of the novel's open ending, whilst its sense of the continuous and inevitable repetition of life events helps link the text to that of Hazlitt. It is also worth noting the self-referential link to the concluding chorus of W.H. Auden's poem 'Death's Echo' (*Collected Shorter Poems 1927-1957*, p.103) - 'Dance, dance, till you drop' - that prefaces Part III of Bragg's 1968 novel *Without a City Wall*. Intriguingly, Bragg turns to Alexander Pope rather than Hazlitt for his second epigraph with a quotation from his *Moral Essays* indicative of the reason / passion binary that is tested to destruction in the novel.

A Son of War

MELVYN BRAGG

# TEN

## SPEAK FOR WIGTON
### *THE SOLDIER'S RETURN*
### *A SON OF WAR*
### *CROSSING THE LINES*

With the publication of *The Soldier's Return* in 1999 Bragg initiated a trilogy of novels that would capture the specificity of a named factual place in Cumbria, namely his native Wigton, together with the lives of its inhabitants, chronicling how their individual and community shared forms of consciousness would develop and change across the generational fault lines from parents to children. In 2000 *The Soldier's Return* won the W H Smith Literary Award, prompting Professor John Carey, chair of the judging panel, to comment, 'This restrained but compelling novel is both an intimate social documentary and a moving human story'. The juxtaposition of 'social documentary' and 'human story' is particularly apposite in a novel which is also the starting point of Bragg's most closely and accurately recorded inspired semi-autobiographical fictional journey in which his alter ego, Joe Richardson, mirrors and comments upon Bragg's own early childhood and adolescent years, steeped in the small-town atmosphere of Wigton.[1]

The Wigton Trilogy contains within a deceptively straightforward structured narrative a variety of ways of writing - autobiography, cultural analysis, political comment, symbolic representation, psychological investigation, group dynamics - that transgress generic boundaries. Bragg develops a vivid picture of the sensibility and mentality of a varied cast of inter-related Wigton characters whose inner-most feelings and social situations become representative of the culture of England at large in the immediate post-War years.

Reading the Trilogy it is difficult to escape the conclusion that in many respects the story of Joe Richardson is, in essence, the story of Melvyn Bragg: both were brought up by loving working-class parents in

---

1. A fourth Joe Richardson novel, *Remember Me ...*, published in 2008, takes Joe/Bragg away from Wigton to Oxford and beyond, and swirls around a bleakly honest recollection of a particularly traumatic episode in Bragg's life that, as alluded to in Chapter 6 of this study, he first allows to surface in *A Silken Net*.

a Wigton pub, both were deeply rooted in the life of the town, both had a socially divisive upwardly-mobile grammar school education, both suffered from bouts of crippling depression, both had a culturally embedded but increasingly ambivalent relationship with Christianity and the Church, both had to confront the necessity to leave Wigton if their full creative potential was to be realised. For me, there is a vivid personal sense of recognition in Bragg's honest exploration of the deeply unsettling emotional tensions that inevitably accompany the contradictory material and emotional realities of a working-class child on a post-1945 educational trajectory from working-class popular culture to the more intellectually demanding, in terms of detailed study and argument, middle-class interests[2]. Bragg has publically stated on more than one occasion, his lack of interest in writing a conventional autobiography. But perhaps any interest in such a work is redundant, since he has often been writing about himself all along, beginning with his first published novel in 1965, *For Want of a Nail*, and nowhere more openly than in the Wigton Trilogy.

Fiction, according to Paul Eakin, is an 'inevitable and even essential ingredient of autobiography, generated as much by the unconscious workings of memory as it is by the conscious agency of imagination' (*Fictions in Autobiography*, p.17). Contrariwise, autobiography is an 'essential ingredient' of the Wigton Trilogy, offering readers the kind of close engagement with the inner workings of a developing fictional personality that Randall Stevenson claims to find lacking in the contemporary English novel. Bragg's novel sequence satisfies Stevenson's yearning for the lost values of the Bildungsroman, providing readers with 'a satisfying sense of the self ,continuing to present character as destiny, and usually finding psychological, or just logical, explanations for the development and nature of individual lives' (*Last of England?* p. 440). The Trilogy also shares some of the characteristics of the roman à clef in its purest form, in which only the names of the characters have been changed, whilst the back-bone of the plot weaves in and out of a real story, combining invented material with authorial recall of actual events and personal feelings.

2. Katie Wales's 'The Anxiety of Influence: Hoggart, Liminality and Melvyn Bragg's *Crossing the Lines'* looks at similarities between Richard Hoggart's *Uses of Literacy* and Bragg's *Crossing the Lines*, detailing their shared interest in questions of linguistic identity in the lives of educational and social boundary-crossing working-class grammar school children.

In the case of the Trilogy, the notion of identity between author and central protagonist is made all the more overt by the naming and loving depiction of Wigton as the real-life setting where Bragg's/ Joe Richardson's life unfolds. This is not to claim that the artistic process of turning his early life into narrative ensures a verifiably reliable and truthfully remembered fictionalisation of experiences inevitably coloured by the passage of time. Nevertheless, the creation of Joe Richardson in Bragg's shadow, and his subsequent fictional development, challenges the relationship between fact and fiction, truth and imagination, autobiography and the novel. Bragg himself accepts that memories are not a reliably accurate window into the past, preferring to describe his semi-autobiographical fiction as, in the case of his father's/ Sam Richardson's return home from war, 'misremembering', in which a distortion occurs as seminal events in life are reconstructed.

There is little room for doubt that the parallels between the fictional Richardson family and the factual Bragg family provide a convincing argument for the fruitful potential of a biographical reading of the Trilogy. The subtle introduction of similar factual/fictional names, unlikely to be readily identified by readers not familiar with Bragg's early upbringing, is one covert clue to the autobiographical aspect of the novel sequence. A telling example from *Crossing the Lines* (2003) will illustrate the point, demonstrating how Bragg artfully inserts a distortion of the lived experience into the fictional text. In the novel, Joe's English teacher is a Mr Tillotson, and it is Tillotson who advises him to read *Jude the Obscure* and *Barchester Towers* in preparation for his forthcoming Wadham College interview. At age thirteen Bragg went to Wigton's Nelson-Tomlinson Grammar School where he encountered the charismatic English teacher Arthur Tillotson Blacker. Bragg's fictional appropriation of his teacher's middle name is clearly something more than coincidence between the names of characters and of real personalities. But there is more than simply the transference of a name involved here, for the Mr Tillotson of fiction shares personality traits with his factual counterpart, and both play an important role in introducing Joe/ Bragg to the sheer joy of reading widely in English and American literature. In an article on 'Melvyn's schooldays' for the *Cumbria Life Magazine* in 1995, Alan Hanson gives a vivid sketch of the

> Relaxed and unconventional [Arthur Tillotson Blacker,
> who] would get the syllabus out of the way in the

opening weeks of term, then abandon himself and the class to an orgy of reading from the great works of English literature - drama, poetry, prose. It all had to be read aloud, relished for the music as well as the meaning.

(p.37)

This is the same fictional Tillotson who advises Joe to read as widely as possible before Oxford, 'While you still have time!' (*CL* p.294).But the parallels extend further, into Joe's/Bragg's introduction to dramatic performance and the world of theatre. It was under the tutelage of Mr Blacker that Bragg 'discovered that he had a natural feeling for words and a natural aptitude as a performer. He was a fluent and articulate debater. He played the lead role in the school play *Our Town*' (*CL* p.37). Likewise, in *Crossing the Lines*, we find Joe throwing himself enthusiastically into a school production of *Our Town*:

> 'There's no need for an American accent, Richardson.'
> 'It's an American play, Mr. Tillotson.'
> 'Standard English can cope.'
> 'I've been practising Mr. Tillotson' Joe could tease the teacher now.
> 'Unfortunately it shows.'
> 'But it won't make sense. I know it's called *Our Town* but it isn't. It's an American town.'
> 'It's an archetypical small town, Richardson. It's just as much English as American. It could even be Australian. As a matter of fact, I have a hunch Thornton Wilder pinched the graveyard scene from Thomas Hardy. Ideas move around Richardson, so can places, and the same notion can address superficially different circumstances. This is a small town in America which is much like a small town in England which is one of the reasons I chose it.'
>
> (*CL*, pp.307-8)

Rather than referencing Bragg's biographical details to help explain or justify their surfacing in his published fiction, I prefer to emphasise the skill with which he has reworked and stylised personal experience in writing it. In having Tillotson draw attention to Hardy and to Australia, Bragg imbues a minor theatrical production with significant cultural and sociological continuities, linking the small town of Wigton with the allure of Australia as a potential Richardson home in *The Soldier's Return* and with small-town America, further making the case, as argued in Chapter 8, for a re-appraisal of the Cumbrian regional novel in a trans-Atlantic context. In remembering Wilder's piece of nostalgic Americana, widely regarded as the play of the year in 1938, Bragg makes an artful American connection with an earlier event in Joe's life. The film of the year in 1938 was Walt Disney's *Snow White and the Seven Dwarfs*, a film featured in *A Son of War* (2001), and one that introduces the reader to a very young Joe as a budding enthusiastic performer. The adolescent Joe who 'hurled himself into this first rehearsal [of *Our Town*], gabbling, over-emphasising, over-dramatising, acting like mad' (*CL* p.308) has his beginnings in the young boy who 'knew all the songs [from *Snow White*] by heart and the film had possessed him. He went down to his aunt Gracie's house singing "Heigh-ho, heigh-ho" at the top of his voice and entertained them with three of the songs... Such force of happiness' (*SW* p.153). Here we have the presentation of a single consciousness tracking freely across memory to create a sense of growing intimacy between character and reader. Looked at in this broader context the Trilogy is seen to share a generic connection with the Romantic autobiographers, such as Bragg's revered Wordsworth, and with the great Romantic tradition of identifying poetry with truth and literary confession.

The character of Sam Richardson is based on that of Bragg's father, Stanley Bragg, whose death at the age of 82 was the genesis for *The Soldier's Return*. Bragg admits to being 'completely shaken by it' (*Writers at Warwick Archive*)[3] and of having 'a tremendous admiration' (ibid.) for his father. Stanley served in the air force, not the army, and whilst this is one of several differences between the factual and fictional fathers, such divergences cannot disguise that 'fiction is very good about emotional truth' (ibid.). Confession does not come easily to Sam Richardson, returning home after four and a half years of fighting the Japanese in Burma, and now bearing the psychological war wounds inflicted by witnessing mind-numbing atrocities committed by the Japanese army, and being forced to confront the often painful deaths of comrades. Back among family and friends Sam finds himself unable to articulate his deepest thoughts, feelings and fears, repressing memory at the expense of emotional security and stability. Bragg selects the Kohima epigraph -

3. The quotations are taken from Bragg's talk about *The Soldier's Return* at Warwick University in 1999. The full recording can be accessed at www.warwick.ac.uk

'When you go home, tell them of us and say/ For your tomorrow we gave our today' - both to preface *The Soldier's Return* and to mark a cathartic moment towards its conclusion. He demonstrates throughout the novel, and in its sequel *A Son of War*, just how difficult it was for Sam, and for thousands of other war-scarred veterans, to even begin to tell their story to a civilian population. Given the thankless task of writing letters of condolence to the families of fallen comrades 'Sam would stop now and then to brush aside memories too savage to be sent into any home' (*SR* p.34). It is only when the Burma veterans gather for a regimental reunion in Carlisle that they are able to talk openly of their shared experiences. As if to show the bursting of the floodgates of memory Bragg reprises the *Kohima epigraph*, quoting it in full, as Colonel Oliphant calls for a minute's silence in memory of their fallen comrades. Standing in 'instant massed silence (*SR* p.258) their repressed '[m]emories rose up in prayer' (ibid.).

The Colonel goes on to complete memory's textual circle by echoing the novel's opening reference to the 'Allied army in Burma described by Churchill (Sam had written it down) as "an army the like of which had not been seen since Xerses crossed the Hellespont"' (*SR* p.34). Having left school at fourteen, Sam has to ask Mr Kneale, a schoolteacher lodging with the family, to explain Churchill's classical allusion. Sam might have felt equally puzzled had anyone told him that his return from war after a long absence had its classical counterpart in that of Odysseus's return to his beloved Ithaca after twenty years. It is a measure of Bragg's ambition that he encodes Homer's epic into the opening pages of his narrative, referring to a train rather than a ship 'crammed with soldiers on the last lap of their odyssey' (*SR* p.6). They are returning to the women left 'to weave the days, waiting at home' (*SR* p.2) in the tradition of Penelope's weaving a shroud and every night unravelling what had been woven in the daytime.

Alan Sillitoe's *Guardian* review of *The Soldier's Return*, 'Odysseus in Wigton' identifies the parallel with Homer, praising Bragg's transition from the classical to the ordinary life of Everyman, so that 'if anyone now or in the future wants to know what it was like to live in a place like Wigton at that time, *The Soldier's Return* will tell them'. The Homer theme is also elaborated upon in Professor Sara Martin Alegre's substantial and impressively original academic paper *Odysseus's Unease: The Post-War Crisis of Masculinity in Melvyn Bragg's 'The Soldier's Return' and 'A Son of*

*War'*. Alegre employs a range of feminist theory to present a questioning analysis of post-war definitions of masculinity, emphasising that the 'important point that Bragg misses is that, unlike what might be supposed within a patriarchal masculinity, combat experience does not help father and son relate' (p.137). Alegre too, reads Sam's wife, Ellen, as a modern day Penelope, only she is 'no longer a meek Penelope' (p.142) but is ready to pursue her own 'wishes for a new kind of life arising from the altered gender roles brought on by the war' (ibid.).

Demobilisation presented returning soldiers with difficult gender role readjustments, appropriate to peacetime conditions in which many women had become necessarily accustomed to a greater degree of independence in the home and at work. They also needed to reconnect with their young children, who, for the duration of the war, may only have known their fathers as a photograph on the mantelpiece.[4] For Sam, the provision of a comparatively generously cut high-quality demob suit only serves to provide the material means to continue thinking back to Burma, rather than forward to a new start in Wigton, as he puts a pad for drafting letters of condolence 'in one of the capacious pockets of his suit, the envelopes in the other' (*SR* p.33). Closer to home, re-occupation of the marital bed becomes a problem requiring subtler psychological skills than letter writing. Many children became used to sleeping with their mother during the war, partly as a practical matter of economy since blankets and linens were scarce, and coal for winter warmth tightly rationed, but more significantly as a means of consolation for lonely mothers and children.

The shared bed becomes a symbol of the strong emotional attachment between Joe and his mother, a relationship that is emphasised on the very eve of Sam's return: 'The child had been uneasy all through the night; twice he had called out and prodded her with small fists' (*SR* p.5) before he 'nuzzled his face between her shoulder blades' (ibid.), then 'rolled over leaving a narrow channel between them - a sword's width' (ibid.). The military image of the sword is highly symbolic in the context of the looming battle for ownership of the bed as emotional territory. It is always in the background as Sam tries to re-establish a relationship with his son. Bragg

4. The difficulties faced by demobbed soldiers re-integrating into family and civilian life are fully documented in Chapter Two, 'So You're Back Then', in Alan Allport's 2009 study *Demobbed. Coming Home After the Second Word War* (Harvard and London: Yale U.P.) It is also instructive to read the extent to which so many of Sam Richardson's post-war problems are anticipated in J.B. Priestley's 1945 novel *Three Men in New Suits* , dealing with the difficult return to civilian life of three army veterans.

charts the difficulties of this domestic campaign over some 60 pages, in the course of which he enlists the reader's sympathy for the new parental role the demobbed Sam must now negotiate. At first, Sam is too exhausted to even realise that there is a problem, as Joe 'clambered over his father, transfixed in profound sleep, and took up his usual place alongside his mother'(*SR* p.40). Soon, however, Sam is compelled to take definite steps to stop Joe sleeping with them. Enlisting Ellen as a reluctant ally:

> He dumped the boy on the narrow little camp bed which practically filled the cubby hole.
> 'I want to sleep with Mammy.' 'This is where you sleep now.'
> Joe sniffed. He did not like the smell that came off his father.
> 'Why can't I sleep with Mammy?'
> 'Don't be such a baby.'
> ....Joe made a move but Sam put out a rather too heavy hand, pressing him down.
> 'Joe stops here.'
> 'Mammy?'
> Ellen tried not to pause.
> 'Do as your Daddy says. You're a big boy now.'
>
> (*SR* p.48-9)

Finally, Sam makes it clear that 'You've been in mammy's bed for the last time, Joe. That's final... The very last' (*SR* p.64), whilst combining firmness with a touching tenderness as he whispers a bedtime story. He is not so convinced of victory, however, that he does not fail to remind 'himself that he must fit a bolt to the door of his own bedroom' (*SR* p.65). This scene marks a new beginning for the father-son relationship and is significant as being the last occasion on which Joe kisses his father's photograph before bed. Bragg sensitively captures the moment of replacing the wartime iconic relationship with that of the peacetime real.

Sam's difficulty in communicating with his son, Joe, is but one symptom of the larger consequences of the psychological trauma of war interfering with his intellectual and emotional capacity to fully comprehend and articulate for a domestic Wigton audience the horror of the scenes he has been forced to witness in Burma. Such a failure to connect is at the centre of Rebecca West's 1918 novel, *The Return of the Soldier*, a work that is surely intended to be referenced by Bragg's choice of echoing title, *The Soldier's Return*. West wrote one of the first psychologically accurate representations of war trauma, and whilst there are certain similarities with Bragg's return to the subject in the context of the Second World War, there are also significant differences, particularly in the recognition of a sense of place. West ignores the interests of society at large, restricting her sphere of action to the secluded life of a house in the Thames Valley, summoning none of the presence of landscape and the passage of time that makes Bragg's Wigton a generically universal small town. There is also a tantalising blank space in *The Return of the Soldier* where the central protagonist's numbing war experience refuses to reveal the original source of the traumatic wound. This, according to Rob Hawkes, 'constitutes the central enigma of the novel, a hermeneutic gap which the novel's narrator is unable to close'(*Ford Madox Ford*, p.154). By way of contrast, while words continue to fail Sam when it comes to a language of description, Bragg, as narrator, is able to provide an explicit and accurate account of the atrocity at the white pagoda that continues to haunt Sam and his comrades.

Once home, Sam experiences a constant tension between the peace and quiet of the familiar countryside around Wigton and memories of the horrors of the Burmese jungle, a kind of dialectic of temporal states of being. Bragg deals with the problem of wartime epistemology by invoking the lingering presence of wartime memories within a particular Cumbrian landscape. Escaping to the countryside, Sam experiences the 'run of the small stream [as] the drum of monsoon...The hedgerow [as] jungle to be hacked through' (*SR* p.33). Within this objectively peaceful retreat Bragg diverts the 'soft gurgle of the stream' to morph in Sam's mind into a 'puddle of brains seeping out of the skull' (*SR* p.35) of a fallen comrade. Displaced topographical description gives voice to Sam's trauma and its reverberating aftermath.

Bragg makes Sam representative of tens of thousands of war veterans thought to be permanently scarred by the literally unspeakable horrors of war. Writing in the *Journal of Medical Science* in the immediate aftermath of demobilisation, Thomas Mann reckoned that as many as a quarter of otherwise healthy demobilised men were finding it difficult to reintegrate into peacetime civilian life. 'They must be regarded as a sociological as well as a medical problem, an incubus on the mental health of the nation' (quoted in Allport p.196). Bragg documents the case of another Burmese veteran, Jackie, as an extreme, but not unique, example of the long-lasting consequences of post-traumatic stress disorder resulting in the total alienation of the individual from society[5]. Asked as a friend to visit to visit Jackie, Sam finds him squatting immobile in a corner of his family's slum property. 'He's given up talking. He can go crazy halfway through the night, running about shouting' (*SR* p.68). Haunted by images of Japanese soldiers invading his domestic space and night-time dreams Jackie is eventually institionalised, but to no long-term healing effect. In *A Son of War* he takes to the road, leaving Wigton for Scotland. Rather than condemn the desertion of his family as irresponsible, Sam 'was amazed not that Jackie was doing this but that many more of those thousands [of damaged veterans] were not with him, walking without order, walking into neither fire nor lead, but going back beyond civilised war to the scavenging of time past' (*SW* p.128). Jackie leaves Wigton in the hope that geographical distance and a new landscape will help remove him from the contamination of persistent spectres from the past. An otherwise marginal scene in the Trilogy becomes charged with the tensions and ruptures in the social fabric of everyday life, and it is aesthetically significant that with Jackie's disappearance from Wigton and the text Bragg signals closure on the discourse of war trauma.

Running parallel to the narrative of Jackie's mental and physical breakdown is Bragg's account of Sam's more determined struggle back to normality under the constant fear that 'Burma would ambush him, shell him down, take him back there and abandon him unless he beat it down' (*SR* p.34). Throughout *The Soldier's Return* Sam exhibits classic symptoms of post-traumatic stress disorder, ranging from disturbed sleep to ready loss of temper, culminating in his raising his hand against his wife and son.

The issues Bragg raises in the context of Wigton are ones that frequently feature in American fiction's use of the Odyssey trope of soldiers returning home to small, often rural, places after the experience of war. *The Soldier's Return* and *A Son of War* visit the concerns of many post-Vietnam American era novels which look upon home as a place with the potential for healing the psychic scars of the hero(es), but with the proviso that it remains the individual's responsibility to make the transition effective.[6] Bragg puts this notion into practice through the

5. The character Jackie is loosely based on Bragg's recall of one of his father's pub regulars, George Greenham, who returned from service in Burma with an uncontrollable shake which Bragg attributes to the unspoken horrors of the jungle campaign (*Writers at Warwick Archive*).

6. Examples of such novels include N. Scott Momaday's *House Made of Dawn* (1968), Leslie Marmon Silko's *Ceremony* (1977), Louise Edrich's *Love Medicine* (1984), and Madison Smart Bell's *Soldier's Joy* (1989). Perhaps the best known recent novel about a soldier's return is, thanks in part to a successful film adaptation, is Charles Frazier's *Cold Mountain* (1997).

device of a doubling motif of two mentally scared veterans, Jackie and Sam, returning to the same place, Wigton, where their different ways of trying to cope are contrastingly played out. Freud's belief that whatever is repressed in a person's memory or past must inevitably resurface as anxiety is particularly relevant here, together with the allied observation that a return to the place of one's past, the place of one's birth, implies not only the possibility of new beginnings but also a kind of death. *The Soldier's Return* offers an extended meditation on both the strength and limitations of native place, Wigton, as a site of sanctuary, as Jackie and Sam respectively fail and learn to define home as a place of familiarity and safety. The crucial difference between Jackie and Sam that accounts for the latter's steady re-integration into his native Wigton and surrounding district is that Sam carries a topography of home in his head that allows him to meld himself back into the local landscape in memory and in actual sight. Bragg writes of a powerful physical pull between person, place, and family as Sam feels 'as if he were being reeled in, furiously, down past St Cuthbert's church, over the bridge at Burnfoot, across Market Hill and there, the early sun flat on the whole terrace of tall houses, there at last and for sure would also be his wife and son, waiting for him' (*SR* p.10). In the following extended passage Wigton become a character in its own right, playing a part in all that has happened to Sam, and offering within itself a network of relationships with other inhabitants and with the environment, holding out a tantalising promise of happiness in a 'place of peace' often imagined during the Burma campaign:

> The place pushed at him, wave after wave of his old life, his lives, all but stopping him in his tracks, the names themselves almost suffocating him with memories. On the right side Plasket's Lane where John Willy Stewart kept his ponies and sometimes let boys have a free ride. Tickle's Lane teeming with cottages where as a boy a friend had shown him, proudly, a floor carpeted in cockroaches. Station Road, New Street, Meeting House Lane: the weight and detail of the past seemed to press physically on his neck, bearing him down as the town had always threatened to do after the birth of Joe: most possibilities tested, life just begun. Soon the first of the pubs, the Blue Bell big

as a railway station, then the narrow, sly Vaults, the Vic, the dominating King's Arms. Nineteen pubs and pothouses in the town. In Burma he had totted them up more than once. And those small-paned windows in the same old shops, one or two with awnings out against the unseasonal sun; and faces all of which, it seemed, he recognised. When the first one or two stopped to say hello or waved 'Hiya Sam', then everyone appeared to notice him, 'How do, Sam?', and it was like pushing up against an Everest of the past, grand, dislocating, stirring and somehow new, bewildering, this place of peace.

(*CL* p.23)

There are similar passages of emotional and aesthetic bonding between person and place in the Trilogy, but none more powerful in their confident suggestion of how the meaning of place itself as a source of cultural and spiritual significance is generated in an individual consciousness.

There exists an aesthetic conspiracy between Sam's inability to publicly disclose the moment of his severe trauma and the text's own determination to remain silent. It is only when a cathartic domestic act of violence catapults the horror to the forefront of Sam's consciousness that the reader is finally granted access to the inner tumult of Sam's repressed memories. Stung by his son's rejection into physical violence against both mother and son Sam is instantly shocked by his actions, aware that '[h]is violence had recoiled on him and finally there was no escape from that unimaginable darkness beside the white pagoda in Burma' (*SR* p.294). In what follows in Chapter 26's cinematic extended visual flashback Bragg traces the effect of past horrors on the haunting of present consciousness, referring back to an event that has lodged itself deep in the inner recesses of Sam's mind as the secret material of a prolonged war elegy.

Toward the end of the Burma campaign Sam's company enter a recently abandoned settlement where the only sound is that of madly barking dogs near an innocent-looking white pagoda. 'They were lucky, Sam thought, white pagodas.' (*SR* p.302) So beyond evil is the cause of the dogs' barking that the only response open to Sam and his comrades is to retreat into silence, future sanity betrayed by the violated sacredness of the pagoda:

The Japanese had taken, when they were all accounted for, eleven young children, some very young, boys and girls. They had tied them to trees with barbed wire and then bayoneted them to death.

Not long since.

There they hung.[7]

Eleven trees. The children naked; ripped open, dead.

Perfectly still, save sometimes for blood which was driving the pariah dogs into a frenzy of leaping and scrabbling at the trunks, but they would catch their paws on the barbs and fall back.

(*CL* p.303)

Bragg writes a graphic tableau of shock and horror, depicting the world as a bleak, brutal place of unspeakable sadistic acts. Once the reader is aware of the crime, Sam's, and Jackie's, retreat into silence, whilst threatening their sanity, becomes a totally understandable response.

Were the story of the white pagoda to end in Burma it would simply underline the Conradian horrors of darkness that pursue Sam throughout *A Soldier's Return*. In the Trilogy, what one novel begins, another continues, so that the white pagoda becomes an intertextual international canopy, covering Burma, England, and, in *A Son of War*, Australia and Scotland. In the novel, Sam's wartime comrade Ian has emigrated to Australia, from where he sends a letter in which he tells how on the voyage out, in the midst of innocence, the spectre of evil retains a powerfully disturbing force:

One thing that happened on the ship I just want to tell you. None of us will forget the children the Japs had bayoneted and tied to trees with barbed wire. You made us bury them. Even though we should have pressed on. I never admired you more - even the time you saved my stupid life. You never referred to it.

7. Crucifixion was a punishment, torture and/or execution sometimes used by the Japanese military. Herbert James Edwards (1913-2000) was an Australian prisoner of war who survived being crucified for 63 hours by the Japanese soldiers overseeing the construction of the Burma railroad. He became the inspiration for the character of Joe Harman in Nevil Shute's 1950 novel *A Town Like Alice*. Shute, like Bragg's character Ian, was an emigrant to Australia. Ian's letter holds between its lines an intriguing intertextual link between Wigton/ England, and Alice/ Australia.

> That scene came back to haunt me. There were dozens
> of children on the ship. Some of the men rigged up a sort
> of gym-playground with ropes and you would see them
> hanging there - semi-naked like the little Burmese kids. I
> had nightmares for days. (*SW* p.28)

This letter becomes the catalyst that sets Sam free from his nightmarish private psychological prison. He shows the letter to Ellen who, when she reads it, 'fully realis[es] for the first time the narrowness of [Sam's] victory and the strength of the enemy' (*SW* p.30). From here on wartime memories begin to fade from the Trilogy, their shadows only apparent to the next generation in isolated incidents, such as that which a twelve year old Joe is suddenly aware of as he cycles to visit a girlfriend: 'The worst [incline] was a stretch alongside Brayton woods in which a man had recently been found hanged. He had used his army belt' (*SW* p.330). In the *Odyssey*, Odysseus openly grieves at the memory of fallen comrades at Troy, and when later a guest of the Phaecians he confronts his demons by asking the bard Democodus to sing about all that they suffered and soldiered through. Ian's letter performs the more prosaic but equally imperative task of storytelling, making public private grief, and easing a twentieth-century's soldier's return.

When it comes to the specifics of the Burma campaign Bragg moves from classical allusion to adapting passages from George Macdonald Fraser's *Quartered Safe Out Here. A Recollection of the War in Burma* (1994) in which the author describes his involvement in the campaign fought by Nine Section, made up largely of Cumbrian men.[8] Fraser's factual memoir provides Bragg's fictional portrayal with an element of realism and authenticity that lends credibility to what might otherwise, at times, read as exaggerated sensationalism. Turning to Fraser proves to be an inspired choice as his pages are saturated with precisely that unique sense of Cumbrian identity at loose in the world that Bragg's regional fiction so often engages with. Fraser's transcriptions of Cumbrian troop language, mixing dialect with newly assimilated Eastern words - '"Git hired Jock! Ye've bin on night patrol - if some booger challenges from underfoot, ye're liable to do 'm! Ah want to die me own fookin' way, not with a kukri up me gunga!"'(p.47)

---

8. Bragg drew my attention to the importance of Fraser's book as source material for the Burma sections of the novel in the course of a private conversation.

- also takes the reader back to the humiliation of the hiring scene in *A Hired Man*.

Names and events migrate from Fraser's facts to Bragg's fiction so that, for example, in both books we meet the Cumbrian Corporal Little, 'known inevitably as "Titch"...lean, dark, wiry, speaking seldom and then usually in the harsh derisive fashion of the Border' (p.12). In *A Soldier's Return* Titch takes 'off his boots to reveal his large white spongy feet, the soles devoid of all feeling... As he talked, Titch pinched and kneaded the spongy substance with his fubsy[9] fingers' (*SR* p.297). As source material, Fraser's informative foot/note describes how his 'soles, by the end of the campaign, were white, spongy, and entirely devoid of feeling' (p.56). In Fraser, the musketry instructors tell their recruits to look upon their Lee Enfield rifles as 'your wife... Treat her right and she'll give you full satisfaction' (p.20). When, in *The Soldier's Return*, Doug is given a Lee Enfield rifle, he 'thought it was the most beautiful thing he had ever beheld and when the sergeant had said, "She's your wife, treat her right and she won't let you down", Doug had muttered, "I'll treat her a bloody sight better than that"'(*SR* p.297). One last example of fictional borrowing provides an understated but telling detail of the stark reality of physical combat and the ability of human flesh to bend steel if sufficient aggression is employed. Fraser remembers watching an officer, 'a wild cat in action and a gentleman out of it... coming out of the dark with that bent bayonet on his rifle'(p.109). In *The Soldier's Return*, the similarly gentle Ian bayonets a 'Japanese with such force that the bayonet when pulled out was bent almost at a right angle' (*SR* p.112). It is clear from these examples that in writing about the Burma campaign Bragg's fiction draws on Fraser's factual material, but at the same time using a novelist's empathic techniques, be they characterisation, description, symbol or metaphor, to establish a clear distinction between the memoir and the novel.

Whilst neither *Quartered Safe Out Here* nor *The Soldier's Return* are overtly political works, in his closing pages Fraser begins a debate about the morality of dropping the atomic bomb on Hiroshima. He concludes that in order to save the lives of his comrades, and to have

9. In Cumbrian dialect 'fubsy' means chubby, plump, short. It remains very much in use, the most recent example I could find at the time of writing being in the *Cumbrian News & Star* newspaper for 9 September 2013 in an article 'Cat and Mouse Game comes to a Sticky End'.

the chance to become a grandfather, he 'would pull the plug on the whole Japanese nation and never blink' (p.220) whilst simultaneously condemning the act as barbaric. Bragg develops exactly this quality of ethical confusion, extending the debate across the generations[10], so that in *A Son of War* Joe is given nightmares by the history teacher, Mr Kneale's, prediction that the H-bomb will inevitably be deployed and that 'nobody would be left. Except primitive tribes in remote continents or archipelagos' (*SW* p.358). Sam discusses the nature of future potential conflict with his friend Alex Metcalfe, who muses that the dropping of the bomb may have put a stop to war: '"It's over though, isn't it, surely, war? The bombs have done for it, don't you think?"' Sam is not convinced: '"Not so long as there is something to be gained by it"'. To which Alex offers the zero sum equation of contemporary nuclear thinking: '"Who wins when atom bombs wipe everybody out?"'(*SW* p.265).

Sam and Alex are talking in 1946. Exactly the same sort of philosophical debate, questioning President Harry Truman's decision to deploy the atomic bomb was going on in America at this time. Published in 1946, Hermann Hagedorn's *The Bomb That Fell On America*, for example, explores the dialectic conundrum in which the 'beginning of international order' is threatened by 'the end of Western civilization' and the 'dawn of the greatest era in history' occurs during 'the world's all-time high in headaches'( Hagedorn p.32). Bragg effectively short-circuits the debate by relocating the universal to the regional and framing time-future in time-past as Alex concludes: 'But one thing is for sure  since those shivering Romans were stationed on [Hadrian's ] wall, war hasn't changed a lot' (*SW* p.264). Such seemingly casual remarks are symptomatic of the way in which a regional landscape is both an ambient backdrop and a way of relating it to larger concerns of universal significance.

Time-past and time-present collide when Sam persuades a reluctant Ellen to help him take on the tenancy of the Black-a-Moor pub on Market Hill in the heart of the local community. This is where autobiography and fiction merge since, when Bragg was eight years old, his father Stanley persuaded an equally reluctant Ethel to agree to take

10. A similar, but more politically focused discussion occurs in Bragg's earlier novel, *Without A City Wall* - see in particular, for example, page 246 - and a discussion of Labour Party policy on nuclear disarmament.

on the tenancy of the Black-a Moor on Market Hill[11]. Both the fictional and factual pubs share similar architectural features and history:

> At the back there was a small yard, raked, showing the slope of the hill, with lavatories for the men. The women came upstairs and used the bathroom of the house. There were stables in the yard, above which was a good dry loft that Mr Hewson had once thought of turning into a workshop. The backyard was permanently gloomy. A very high wall hid the garden of what had once been the old grammar school, next door, now occupied by two maiden sisters. (*SW* p.242)

In *A Son of War* the retiring landlady, Mrs Hewson, takes a macabre delight in telling the impressionable Joe the tale of how the pub acquired its name .In real life it was the site of bull-baiting and, when that became illegal, bruising prize-fighting. This factual legacy of violent physical activity carries over into Mrs Hewson's story of the death of a little black pot boy, of Joe's age, who was subjected to constant mental torment and physical abuse at the hands of the pub's patrons. The stables were in use then and 'one wet night, a bad night, a fella came on a black stallion, a terrible size and temper on it' (*SW* p.250) and for sport the pot boy was locked in its stable. His screaming and shouting only served to further unsettle the horse which, in a frenzy kicked him to death. And now, she gleefully informs Joe, his ghost can still be heard '"running about under the roof at night"' (ibid.). Joe is visibly shaken by the story - 'Poor little black boy he thought. Poor little boy. He could hear his screams' (*SW* p.251) - which sinks deep into his subconscious, only to emerge at moments of night-time crisis.

Time and again Joe's bedroom becomes the site of a haunting

11. The present-day Black-a-Moor Hotel and its neighbour, the former free grammar school, are pictured in Grahamslaw's *Wigton Through Time* ( p.60). It also features on a literary connection website (homesteadbb.free-online.co.uk) where it is described as 'still very much a working man's pub, friendly but basic'. There is also a most interesting and informative interview about Stanley Bragg and the pub in *Speak for England* which includes: 'Your father was in the Black-a-Moor then of course. It more or less became the centre [for hound trailing[. Your dad was interested in hound trailing and with him having the facilities of a room where we could meet, I think gradually the lads from other pubs that were hound trailers used to come down to the Black-a-Moor and it was then decided that we would form a club..... And we got up to somewhere about a hundred and fifty, two hundred membership... your dad was the Secretary, we had a committee and we did things right .I think this was a big boost for Wigton' (SE p.398).

described in realistically terrifying terms: 'Red. Dark. The noise growing. A funny sound? The little black boy. Say it often enough and it will go away, his daddy had told him when he had winkled out of him the root of his fear of the loft. But he was there, the little blackamoor. Joe had heard him call out. He had heard him cry' (*SW* p.266). Bragg hints at a gothic haunting of Joe's bedroom by connecting his fear at bedtime with his empathetic reading of *Jane Eyre*, in which Jane's experience in the red-room, described by Sandra M Gilbert and Susan Gubar as 'probably the most metaphorically vibrant of all her early experiences' (*Madwoman* p.340), effectively locks her into a deeply problematic introspection: '[Joe] had wanted to sob while he was reading *Jane Eyre*' (SW p.382). Marilyn Chandler's *Dwelling in the Text* argues that:

> Houses... reflect not only the psychological structure of the main character or the social structures in which he is entrapped but the structure of the text itself, thereby setting up a four-way, and ultimately self-referential analogy among writer, text, character, and house. The same architectural habit of mind that designs and builds a house both to reflect patterns within it and to configure life in certain patterns may design a narrative to reflect and recast what the author conceives to be the essential patterns of our lives. (p.3)

A self-referential analogy between Bragg, text, Joe, and the Black-a-Moor pub could hardly be clearer. The black boy's cry not only echoes the Gothic tradition in English literature but, more significantly, invokes the ever present power of childhood ghosts nightly resurrected through the active exercise of imagination in sensitive children such as Joe/Bragg.

Bragg makes no secret of his own childhood terrors lurking in the dark recesses of his pub bedroom. Recalling his ordeal in a *Daily Telegraph* interview (22 October 2011) Bragg tells how:

> It started in bed. I had this little bedroom, a bit like a narrow cell, and something that was inside my head left my head and drifted across the room and was in the top right hand corner of the room.
> It was something like a light but I knew that it was me and I didn't know what this was. I was frozen. It got to be chronic and my school results went plunging and I got

really physically frightened.

And there was absolutely nobody on Earth I could tell. I couldn't even hint it to anybody because I'm finding it hard enough to talk about it now.

The reader will recall that Joe's 'bedroom resembled a cell' (*SW* p.383). Joe's 'cell' also takes on the colouring of Jane's red-room. And, in a fascinating intertextual reference taking us back to my discussion of entrapment in *The Silken Net*, it also acquires the colouring of Charlotte Perkins Gillman's story 'The Yellow-Wallpaper': 'The floor was lino-red and yellow squares. The curtains yellow and flowery. The wallpaper was also ornamental with [yellow] flowers' (*SW* p.383). Joe attempts to exorcise the black boy's ghost by confronting it head on, not in his bedroom but in the stables where the crime was committed. Wearing his boxing gloves he attacks the stable wall with frenzied blows, accompanied by 'the little black boy screaming in his head, in his sights ...bang, bang, screaming from the horse's hoofs' (*SW* p.336). Then, in a quick cinematic cut, Bragg switches the action outdoors to Joe being taken for a ride on his uncle Colin's motorbike/stallion: 'Joe got on the pillion rather gingerly' (*SW* p.337), whilst all the time 'the boy's screaming was still in his head' (ibid.).

Joe, like Bragg, learns to face and partially defeat his adolescent fears alone. We are given an insight into the healing process as Joe symbolically turns to the heritage of the black boy's descendants, and the music that grew out of slavery, discovering the great American blues and jazz singers. 'They told him something nothing else could and in their blackness he found hope. Big Bill Broonzy, Leadbelly, Memphis Slim, Billie Holiday[12], there could never be enough; there never was' (*SW* p.401). Bragg references the American blues tradition in other novels, notably *Without a City Wall*, but here it is in tune with the inner soundtrack of Joe's mind, making an entirely logical, if unexpected, leap from *Jane Eyre* to Billie Holiday. Such challenging cultural pairings are

12. Given that Joe's disturbed state of mind is triggered by the historic death of a black boy at white hands it would appear likely that he would discovered Billie Holiday's classic 1939 recording of *Strange Fruit*, confronting the lynching of black men in the deep South: 'Southern trees bare a strange fruit./ Blood on the leaves and blood at the root,/ Black bodies swinging in the Southern breeze,/ Strange fruit hanging from the poplar trees.' The complete lyric and the history of song's genesis can be found in Donald Clarke's *Wishing on the Moon. The Life and Times of Billie Holiday* (1994) pp.163-170. In *Crossing the Lines* Joe Richardson gets to hear his boyhood hero Memphis Slim play piano at a jazz club in Paris.

part of what makes Bragg's work so refreshing, allowing Wigton to speak for a wide cultural constituency.

Both *The Soldier's Return* and *A Son of War* feature gift giving within the extended Richardson family. Ellen is puzzled by her husband's home-coming present of a traditional Indian sari - '"What are they for?"' (*SW* p.20) - but the reader is invited to decode the choice through Sam's eyes and is thus able to appreciate its symbolic subtext of pent-up longing and sexual urgency encoded in the garment. Explaining how '"Indian women wrap them around themselves for dresses" [Sam] saw their bodies undulating and he remembered the time of his longing for his wife' (ibid.). For Sam, the sexual idea lurking in the garment fetishises it as an erotically charged gift, whereas for Ellen it carries the fear of foreign infidelity. Asked how he knows they wrap themselves in the garment, Sam's reply 'Guesswork' invokes in Ellen a sense of relief that 'he had kept away from all that' (ibid.). The language here is conservative, logical, and it's restrained euphemistic 'all that', offering a narrow interpretation upon a whole world of sexual possibilities, is true to the character of husband and wife. The coda to the terse exchanges is that, in her relief at Sam's faithfulness, Ellen flings the unfolded saris into the air filling the relative drabness of a room in Wigton with an adjectival rainbow of bright colours which, as with previous examples of Bragg's connective windows, link the provincial to far-flung peoples, places and practices.

Sam's present of a small wooden train set for Joe is an instant unqualified success. The toy train then becomes a metaphor for the real as trains underpin important moments in the text, from Sam's first leaving the troop train to walk home, to his Conradian leap/push from a departing train at the start of a journey to Australia at the end of *A Soldier's Return*, and, in mid-text, to a moment of father-son bonding when Sam rescues Joe from a precarious climb onto the ledge of a railway bridge. This later incident of childhood bravura occurs soon after Sam begins to teach Joe to box in response to the wanton destruction of the toy train by a gang of older boys. Boxing, and boxing gloves, are the textual legacy of the wooden train and will continue to feature throughout the following two novels in the Trilogy.

The railway also becomes the site for the creation of a legend. In *A Son of War* Bragg introduces a modern Wigton folk hero in the person of the teenage gang-leader Speed, a son of the traumatised Jackie, who is dismissed from the army post he loves because he refuses to betray his personal code of honour, and who assumes the role of Western hero to avenge the rape of the girl he will then marry and protect. Speed's response to social difficulties is usually extreme, primitive, and almost atavistic - his behaviour is at the mercy of instinctual appetites. His appeal is that of the knightly, chivalrous, if violent, hero of epic, who's negative and destructive qualities are more than compensated for by an intensity and excitement for life that endears him to his friends. For Joe, the moment of transcendence from mere mortal to legendary figure occurs when Speed fearlessly lies between railway tracks, 'his arms flat out, press[ing] his face down between two sleepers' (*SW* p.130) while an express train hurtles over him. Images of masculinity, action, and adventure are linked by the engines 'heroic plume' of steam and the carriage wheels which 'outcharioted those vehicles of war' (ibid.). Joe instinctively knows, but cannot explain, that 'something unmistakable had happened. He knew but could not explain it. Speed had passed over into legend' (*SW* p.131). Joe experiences a track-side epiphany, becoming aware of the promise and wonder of a possible future existence, one that he will pursue by the markedly different route of educational upward mobility.

It is worth a brief aside to consider the extent of Bragg's railway metaphoric span to include the, albeit textually asymmetrical, consideration of the feminine. Taking advantage of Sam visiting his father, Ellen slips into Carlisle to see David Lean's 1945 film *Brief Encounter.* Set in a railway station in the winter of 1938-9, the film stars Ellen's idol Celia Johnson as the conventional housewife Laura, married to a dull but reliable husband. Laura is tempted by the prospect of romance after a chance encounter with a handsome doctor, played by Trevor Howard. As her husband Fred completes his crossword puzzle Laura conjures up an image of the doctor against the soaring strains of Rachmaninoff which colour her fantasy life and hint at the pent-up frustration of a monochrome existence across the same metaphoric dimension as the flung saris' suggestion of an alternative sexual existence. In David Kynaston's summary the film concludes as 'a vindication of restraint, domesticity and pre-war values' (*Austerity Britain* p. 99). The railway as a metaphor of escape runs up against the buffers for both Sam and Ellen, and it is left to their son to make the distancing rail journey to Oxford in *Crossing the Lines.*

Chapter One of *A Son of War* features images of masculinity closely linked to the aggressive instinct. They occur in another scene of gift giving by Sam, this time of a pair of 'big boxing gloves [laid out] like a bouquet on the table' (*SW* p.3). Bragg demonstrates an artful lexical organising with the inclusion of the noun bouquet conveying a feminist interest in the male gloves as soft defensive attire. Perceptively, Emma Tristram, in her *Times Literary Supplement* review of the novel's opening refers to 'scenes which are garlanded with symbols'. The boxing gloves are afforded anthropomorphic properties, coming 'almost alive' and reminding Sam 'of new pups'. The text colludes with the puppy-like nature of the gloves in referring to Joe's hands as paws - 'the cavernous gloves were on Joe's seven-year-old-paws' (*SW* p.4) - whilst anticipating their physical use when we remember that south-paw is a technical boxing term.

The choice of boxing gloves as gift is one moment in an on-going sequence that acquires ramifications and meanings well into *Crossing the Lines*. From the outset Bragg produces a schematic symbolic picture of the masculine-feminine binary in the Richardson family, when describing the boxing gloves as 'redder and bloodier [than berries, speaking] for a power beyond the holly' (*SW* p.3) which Ellen picks, 'feeding the fire with the richly ruby-berried holly' (*SW* p.7). For Ellen, the 'leaf, the berry and the thorn' recall the recent pleasure of consensual sex, totally devoid of force.

Bragg uses metonymy to govern the narrative structure of the boxing gloves as representative of masculinity and evocative of father-son bonding. This is seen in action when Sam takes Joe to Carlisle's Covered Market to watch the fight between Jackie Tempest of Lancaster and the local light-weight contestant Jackie Moran. The fight is reported in naturalistically brutal terms which carry a textual memory of the Neate-Hackman fight in Hazlitt's celebrated essay 'The Fight', including shared references to sledge-hammer blows. In Hazlitt:

> [Neate] held out both his arms at full length straight before him, like two sledge-hammers, and raised his left an inch or two higher. [Hickman] could not get over this guard - they struck mutually and fell, but without advantage on either side ... Neate then made a tremendous lunge at him, and hit him full in the face ... he hung suspended for a second or two and then fell back, throwing his hands into the air, and with his face lifted to the sky, I never saw any thing more terrific than his aspect

before he fell. All traces of life, of natural expression, were gone from him. His face was like a human skull, a death's head, spouting blood, the mouth gaped blood

('The Fight' p.151-2)

In *A Son of War*:

But Tempest suddenly hit home with one of his right swinging punches and Moran stopped stock still, and as his supporters held their breath, Tempest landed what was later described as a 'sledgehammer blow', which caught the local man on the right temple and shuddered his skull, blanked his brain, his body keeled, no brake, slam into the canvas, he did not hear the count, he did not know that even now the crowd, his crowd, tried to lift him, he had to be carried to his corner...

(*SW* p.237-8)

Hazlitt's mouth gaping blood seeps into Bragg's concluding 'whirlpool of blows and punches and brave blood' (*SW* p.241).

Hazlitt as a divisive figure has, of course, already featured large in *A Time to Dance*, but in *Crossing the Lines* his essay becomes the occasion of a father-son bonding. In a scene that provides an intensely aesthetically satisfying sense of closure, 'The Fight' becomes the object of gift-reversal allowing the son to treat his father as an equal inside his own literary ring. Returning home from the sixth form, where his parents are helping him stay on, Joe 'fumbled in his school bag and pulled out *A Selection of Essays* by William Hazlitt. "There is a really smashing piece on boxing." "I've not read many good books about boxing." Sam took it. "Thanks."' (*CL* p.204) One word, 'Thanks', is here used with rigour and tied convincingly to Sam's character, a man of few emotive words and considerable self-discipline, to modify the father-son relationship to one of equality. Something similar happens when Joe bumps into Speed for the last time. Speed's parting words are '"Still got those boxing gloves?" Joe shook his head. "See you Joe." And Speed was gone.' (*CL* p.229) The absent gloves break the last link in the chain linking Speed and past violence to Joe's present academic aspirations. Closure is as abrupt and as sudden as a knock-out punch, demonstrating again Bragg's restrained use of adjectives and adverbs when in pursuit of the speed of cinematic editing.

Bragg's investment in pictorial and cinematically generated

imagery is evidenced by the striking regularity of his turn to cinematic references to provide visual metaphors for his textual action. His first published novel, *For Want of a Nail*, introduces the reader to the childhood delights of the Saturday matinée at Wigton's cinema, a youthful cinema habit that is apparent in many of the subsequent novels. As a child in Wigton Bragg saw an 'average of two [films] a week between the ages of five and eighteen; that would be about 1,300 films' (*SBS* p.36). In emphasising the role of film in Bragg's novels, both as metaphor and as editing model, it is worth noting that an early unpublished novel, *Mirrors and Wire*, takes less than ten pages before introducing a character by reference to his iconic film star looks: '"What's he like"... Oh, nice... More a young Cary Grant than a Brando; but delicious"'(*MW* p.9). By his own account, for the young Bragg, 'the cinema was a wonder. It brought us people and stories we did not quite dare to believe were true or in any way part of the real business of life, which was the factory, the pub, the washing on a wet day, the grim emptiness of Sunday, the repressed words flaring up into Saturday-night brawls' (*SS* p.14). And best of all were the 'musicals where people lived in an impossible way - singing and dancing all the time' (ibid.). Joe's fascination with Disney's *Snow White* is his gateway into this magical world of singing and dancing, with its boldly coloured forms and freewheeling movements. Disney's influence may be detected in, for example, the colour symbolism and kinetic visual exuberance of the sari scene in *The Soldier's Return* when Ellen flings the garments 'like streamers over the room, their colours gorgeous, high yellows, Prussian blues, green, orange, burnt-oak reds, a swirl of colours like her dreams' (*SR* p.20). Disney was also giving his youthful admirer an entertaining but instructive cartoon lesson in symbolism with such songs as *Whistle While You Work*: 'And as you sweep the room/Imagine that the broom is someone that you love/ and soon you'll be dancing to the tune'. Certainly the Oxford educated Joe/Bragg would surely applaud Eleanor Byrne and Martin McQuillan's exegesis that the 'broom both marks the absence of the mother and the re-imagining of her, through a domestic action' (*Deconstructing Disney* p.62). Bragg brings a similar level of astute interpretation to an extended reference to Ingmar Bergman's 1953 film *Summer with Monika* to effectively provide an extra-diegetic soundtrack to the break-up of Joe's romance with Rachel in the closing pages of *Crossing the Lines*.

In the autumn of 1958 Bragg, like Joe, was at Oxford University, missing his home and the distinctive landscape of the North, and separated from his girlfriend. Bragg finds himself walking down Oxford's Walton Street when he sees a poster outside the Scala Cinema advertising *Summer with Monika*. He is immediately struck by the fact that '[t[he girl on the poster was near twin to the girl I'd left behind' (*SBS* p.36). Initially drawn in by Harriet Anderson's (Monika) face - 'Our work begins with the human face... The possibility of drawing near to the human face is the primary originality and the distinctive quality of the cinema' (Bergman, quoted in Deleuze, *Cinema* p.99) - Bragg soon discovers that the film 'spoke to the condition of many adolescents in the 50s: it could have been my story or that of thousands of others' (*SS* p.17). Indeed. 'Harriet Anderson could have stepped out of the screen and into the streets of Wigton any day' (ibid.).This sense of personal involvement is augmented by a unity between the Scandinavian and Lake District landscapes: '...the vast grey sky, the occasional release of a short summer' (*SS* p.18). Once in possession of these published biographical details, albeit strictly film related, it is difficult not to read sections of *Crossing the Lines* as a surrogate autobiography. In the following passage for example, autobiography and fiction become sutured to the extent that Joe/Bragg appear as undivided selves:

> She looked so like her. Had he carried on down Walton Street and just glanced quickly at the photographs outside the Scala Cinema he would have sworn they were of Rachel. The film was called *Summer with Monika*. The photographs of the star drew him into the cinema. He rearranged his timetable as he bought the afternoon ticket. He had not been to this or any art cinema before.
>
> (*CL*, p.461)

Joe is unnerved by Monika's self-regard and rejection of her boyfriend, Harry, and although he reassures himself of Rachel's faithfulness, Bergman's ending will prove proleptic of Bragg's. Writing enthusiastically about the film to Rachel, Joe concludes his letter by saying 'I won't spoil the story for you. You have to see it' (*CL* p.463). But Rachel never gets to see *Summer with Monika* and it is she who, in mirroring Monika's behaviour, spoils Joe's story. In the novel Bragg's art borrows from Bergman's as film informs a partial reflection in the novel; Monika becomes pregnant and Harry accepts responsibility in marrying her; Joe promises to marry Rachel if their fears of a pregnancy prove founded. The influence of film, and of Bergman in particular, shapes this concluding sequence in *Crossing the Lines* such that 'Summer with Rachel' reads as Bragg's Lake District homage to Bergman.

In his 'Introduction' to *Speak for England* Bragg advances the sociological and historical case 'to substantiate the claim that Wigton can be described as a representative setting for a book on England' (*SE* p.4). His postscript concludes that '[w[hat emerges most strongly ... is the richness of character and interest within this cross-section of people... in a small town which would not claim to be much out of the ordinary' (*SE* p.478). In the fictional Trilogy Bragg sets himself the task of fleshing out the richness of communal life in an otherwise unremarkable setting by bringing the privileged insights of a native son to co-ordinate the details of provincial life so as to position and understand them in a broader national as well as a regional perspective. Part of Wigton's claim to representative status is achieved by right/accident of geography: 'Wigton is in the northern part of Cumberland, on the border with Scotland, geographically about the middle of the British Isles' (*SE* p.5). Comparisons with Arnold Bennett again come to mind as Bragg's argument reprises that of Bennett's attribution of essential qualities of Englishness to the Five Towns of the Potteries, in his *The Old Wives' Tale* (1908), on the basis of geographical centrality, achieved by omitting the other home nations: 'It is England in little, lost in the midst of England, unsung by searchers after the extreme; perhaps occasionally somewhat sore at their neglect, but how proud in their instinctive cognizance of its representative features and traits' (p.3). Bragg is heir to this tradition of universality in the provincial; both writers construct a detailed topography of their home town, in which buildings, transport, open spaces, streets and private dwellings all become part of a closely observed external world impinging on the everyday behaviour and psychology of individual inhabitants. Indeed, Bennett's view of the well-written regional novel, outlined in his *The Author's Craft*, holds true for Bragg one hundred years later:

> Every street is a mirror, an illustration, an exposition, an explanation of the human beings who live in it. Nothing in it is to be neglected. Everything in it is valuable, if the perspective is maintained. Nevertheless, in the narrow individualistic novels of English literature - and in some of the best - you will find a domestic organism described as

> though it existed in a vacuum. As though it reacted on
> nothing and was reacted on by nothing; and as though it
> could be adequately rendered without reference to
> anything exterior to itself.                    (p.24)

Bennett's point is well met by Bragg's effective portrayal of the interconnectedness of external and internal worlds, the importance of the Black-a-Moor pub in explaining the motivation and psychology of Richardson family being a prime example. Bragg selects specific images, such as that of the black pot boy, that locate character in Wigton so as to determine, reveal, and reflect human psychology. Writing about the imagined town, Robert Squillace regrets that 'one of the most chaffing restrictions of inhabiting an area perceived as provincial is the extent to which that identity is imposed from outside. Such images prove stubbornly immune to alteration' (p.1). Bennett and Bragg share a common preoccupation with shaping the perception of regional native place as being more vibrant, complex, full of lively personalities, and historically interesting than the cosmopolitan outsider's limited caricature of provincial place.

One of the more important influences on the shaping of Joe's/Bragg's life is the Church, as both a social as well as a religious institution. Early in *A Son of War* Bragg has Ellen conduct the reader on a bustling cinematic tracking shot of Wigton's seven religious sects and twelve churches. They are precisely placed within the town's geography so as to juxtapose the co-existence of the sacred and the secular in a demonstration of the authenticity of the variety of life within Wigton's boundaries: the Primitive Methodists by the police station, the Mission between a factory and stables, the Congregationalists beside the pig auction, the Methodists by the girls' grammar school. Amongst this microcosmic test-case for urban ecological investigation stands St. Mary's, solid and traditional, Ellen's 'own church... where she had sent Joe to be in the choir in response to a call for trebles' (*SW* p.32), and located 'beside the market-place, still used seven hundred years on' (ibid.). Later, Joe, like his secular creator, begins to adopt an ambivalent cultural rather than a spiritual relationship towards organised religion. This gradual disenchantment is a thread running through *A Son of War*, presenting the reader with tantalising autobiographical glimpses, camouflaged only by fictional details while significant shared life events remain the same. One example: it was Bragg's uncles, not his mother who 'hauled [him] into the choir of St. Mary's' (*BB* p.345). But in all essentials,

Bragg's factual recounting of the central importance of St. Mary's in his early years provides the blue-print for Joe's formative experiences:

> The church was a strong strand in my childhood. Choir meant regular attendance at the choir practice, church services, Sunday school, the church youth club...debates, outings, games and dances in the Parish Rooms. The Bible came into the school in morning assemblies, prayers, hymns and lessons called Religious Instruction. I was caught up in it, doused in it, bound in it, and then, in the heady liberation of adolescence, unbound. But there has continued to be a residue, stronger than a 'trace memory', but much less ...than the total Christian demand on a believer. (*BB* pp.346-7)

All this is important in the context of the Trilogy because Bragg, whatever his religious doubts, continues to regard the Church as providing society with purpose and coherence, developed through generations and firmly rooted in and attached to place. There is a wider argument to be had in the national context that if regional writing is losing its importance this is in part linked to the churches losing their own sense of identity at the heart of local culture.

Bragg has made a practical gesture to stem any such local decline by bringing his family and his books into direct contact with St. Mary's with the gift of three stained glass windows[13] 'as a tribute to my parents and family and as a thanksgiving to the church for what I had got out of it' (*BB* p.346). They tell the story of Wigton, bringing the secular sites adjoining the town's churches inside the body of the church itself: not only 'the church itself, but the factory, the cattle auction, the rivers, the once prosperous now obsolete mills, the streets, terraced houses, the special features of the place and the people' (*BB* p.346-7). The Bragg family windows are a visual response not only to a sense of place but also to time, depicting the same cultural values as those promoted in the Trilogy. Brian Campbell's design brief catches the essence of Bragg's novels: 'the spirit of the project, commingling Wigton with history, commerce and culture with the parish church's spiritual and pastoral role

---

13. There is an informative booklet produced by Wigton P.C.C., *The Bragg Family Windows*, giving a detailed, and well-illustrated, account of the windows commissioning, design and manufacture. Grahamslaw's *Wigton Through Time* also includes a photograph of a Bragg window showing the church 'as a beacon in the twilight Wigton landscape' (p.35).

in the community' (*Bragg Family Windows* p.14). Visiting Wigton on a dull Saturday afternoon on October, the sight of these windows brought the town to life, reminding me of just how organically Bragg's fiction has grown from the local whilst going on to remake the landscape, for readers, in its image. They make a fitting visual coda to the Trilogy, suggestive to writers and readers of Vaughan Williams's advice to young composers; 'If the roots of your art are firmly planted in your own soil and that soil has anything individual to give you, you may still gain the whole world and not lose your soul' (quoted in Harris, *Romantic Moderns* p.159).

Given Bragg's oft repeated declaration that he has no intention of ever writing his autobiography, in large part because he distrusts the objectivity of memory's recall together with the all too human tendency to suppress the darker recesses of recall, the Richardson sequence of novels is likely to remain the nearest we will get to reading an aesthetic text revealing the interiority of Bragg's autobiographical consciousness. As I have shown, there is a frequent almost documentary reconstruction of aspects of Bragg's youthful life that, whatever the author's disclaimers, make it inevitable that Joe Richardson's story will be read as the story of Melvyn Bragg, albeit one cloaked in the classic nineteenth-century Bildungsroman trajectory of the hero in the act of becoming. Joe's story is inextricably linked to that of many of his generation who are part of a post-War historical epoch fashioned by increasing State intervention, especially in education, and by the politics of the Cold War. Bragg's achievement is to sketch this wider picture whilst keeping the roots of his art 'firmly planted in [Wigton's] soil' so as to create a satisfying account of the developing significance of self in close interaction with the lovingly delineated environment of his youth. Describing an interview with a film director he knew well and much admired, Bragg quotes David Lean's guiding principle for the construction of an epic: 'You have to be terribly careful not to let the landscape swamp the people. It is a fine line' (*SBS* p.117). Landscape and character share star billing in the Richardson novels, so that in 'exploring his own soil' Bragg realises his expressed ambition of writing ' an Everyman epic, paired down... to make ordinary language speak the way I wanted it to'(*Writers at Warwick Archive*). To speak for Wigton.

Grace and Mary

MELVYN BRAGG

'Quite simply one of the best writers we have'
*Sunday Telegraph*

# ELEVEN

# DANCING IN THE DARK
## GRACE AND MARY

After *Remember Me...*, the sequel to *Crossing the Lines*, was published in 2008 Bragg confesses, in his own words, to feeling 'totally depleted'[1] and consequently unable to find either the inspiration or energy to begin another work of fiction. Determined, however, not to lose the habit of writing, he produced three non-fiction works in each of the next three years, editing *In Our Time* (2009), compiling *The South Bank Show: Final Cut* (2010), and researching and writing *The Book of Books: The Radical Impact of the King James Bible 1611-2011* (2011). The latter volume is very much a labour of love and a testament to Bragg's reverence for biblical history and scholarship, together with an awareness of Christianity's continuing influence on the social, political and artistic life of contemporary society. Describing his state of emotional exhaustion at the March 2011 Keswick Literary Festival, 'Words by the Water'[2], Bragg also gave an optimistic hint that his fictional hiatus might be coming to an end, telling his audience that he had an idea for a novel fermenting somewhere at the back of his mind. He mused about a possible Cumbrian tale spanning a century and featuring an, as yet, unknown woman who had nevertheless set two possible titles buzzing in his brain - 'The Woman Who Walked Away' and 'The Woman Who Walked Alone'. His novelist's imagination was already at work to the extent that 'I know something about her... and I think it's a wonderful story if only I could find it' (Keswick). In the event he found two women who became the eponymous heroines of *Grace and Mary* (2013), a miniature Cumbrian epic written in the shape-shifting form of a fictional memoir. It is a novel of personal and communal history, of memory and

1. All direct quotes in this opening paragraph are taken from my transcription of Bragg's talk, 'Back Then - Remembrance of Times Past in Wigton', given at the Keswick Literary Festival on 5 March, 2011.I am grateful to Melvyn Bragg and to the Festival organisers for permission to record and reproduce excerpts from the talk. Where further Keswick festival quotes appear in this chapter they are identified by appending Keswick in brackets.
2. Melvyn Bragg is the President of 'Words by the Water'. His 'Foreword' to the 2011 programme is typically celebratory of the Cumbrian landscape and writers that are to the fore in his novels: '...I look forward to coming out of the theatre and seeing that Skiddaw is still safely there and just as Coleridge described it. While on the left Wordsworth's jewel of a lake will be - turbulent? Mirror pond? It will always be an exhilaration to see it and to wander down to it and perhaps throw in a pebble'.

loss, but above all an affirmation that what will survive of us is love.

   *Grace and Mary* complements and completes the sequence of Joe Richardson novels discussed in my previous chapter. For Joe we now read John, a successful London-based historical and biographical writer and for Ellen, Mary, the latter now an elderly dementia patient in her nineties, and largely confined to a nursing home on the Cumbrian coast. Mary is illegitimate and now too old and amnesiac to tell John the truth about his grandmother, Grace.  As Mary's grip on the past loosens, John claims the author's freedom to imagine and rearrange the past to create a family history out of lost and half-forgotten fragments.  Wigton, however, remains a constant, and Bragg invests one very specific year, 1947 - when the strong bonds of local community, conservative family values, and religious institutions still commanded respect and adherence - with the power to engender a fiction of the future. In telling the two women's story Bragg weaves his own biography - a post-War childhood in Wigton, the town's characters, recollected incidents and emotions - into the fabric of a fictional memoir that is coherent, believable, emotionally honest, and ultimately, very moving. Reviewing the novel in the *Times Literary Supplement* (12 July, 2013) Clare Morgan  emphasises the high degree of artistic control exercised by Bragg in combining everyday mundane scenes with those moments of existential intensity that go to shape the personality:

> That Melvyn Bragg can speak unselfconsciously of 'the soul' attests to *Grace and Mary*'s preoccupation with the sort of existential questions a more faint-hearted novelist might be reluctant to address. Is life in the mind, or in the moment? Does knowledge lie in the scientific discussion of cause and effect, or in the visceral connections of human emotions? Is poetry a more lasting discourse than religion? And how can a person come to terms with the transience of life, and the swift hand that dispenses change?
>
> (p.21)

In attempting to find provisional answers to these fundamental questions Bragg dispenses with the traditional standard chronological structure of the memoir/biography so as to permit the past to collide with and include the present, allowing his narrator to create a history that is as subject to alteration as is the fictional consciousness that writes it.

   It is worth recalling that the publication of *Grace and Mary* brings to eight the number of semi-autobiographical novels containing what Bragg refers to as 'misrememberings' - the others being *The Cumbrian Trilogy* and the four Joe Richardson novels. Written at different times between 1969 and 2013 the forty-four year time span sees the author growing older and increasingly able to appraise his material from varying vantage points, whether positive or negative, as he himself inevitably ages. *The Cumbrian Trilogy* is the most polemical of the books, reading as much as a political position statement or manifesto as a personal narrative attempting to fictionally rescue the unrecorded history of Bragg's ancestors. The trilogy is expansive and discursive, focusing equally on social and political arguments, at the same time as chronicling family history. The Richardson novels build on and develop the seminal events of Joe's early childhood. In both sets of novels the geographical setting and the pivotal moments remain very much the same, as does Bragg's implied interpretation of their meaning, although the later novels contain more overtly biographical material. *Grace and Mary*'s perspective, however, is somewhat different. The novel covers a far greater time span, encompassing three generations within its relatively short 249 pages. It is of necessity paired down to essentials, and narrated with a rapid cinematic crosscutting forward momentum. Even so, Bragg's Cumbrian story remains remarkably stable across the different texts, with Wigton as the repository and custodian of family history, culminating with *Grace and Mary* as the summation of a cohesive personal story in which the free play of events, imagined and real, explores and interrogates the personalities of three very different linked generations.

At the risk of repetition, it should be obvious as this study draws to an end that Bragg's fiction will inevitably continue to attract autobiographical exegesis if only because the public persona of the author as a media personality is now too well-known to avoid reading the public face into the fictional character. A significant part, therefore, of the meaning of his novels consists of a sophisticated transaction between the reconstructed subjectivity of the writer's memory and its active interrogation by the informed reader, although where the two meet remains contested territory. The psychologist Susan Engel, in her aptly named study *Context is Everything: The Nature of Memory* writes that the author's past is constructed through the very act of writing:

> Writers...want to justify, and use the past to explain who
> they are...If you take a literary approach to thinking about
> memory, you are more likely to find idiosyncrasy rather

than pattern, individuality rather than generalizations. The writer and the literary critic, in other words want the past to entertain, engage, and perhaps illuminate the narrator, and by extension or identification, the reader.

(p.83)

The critic might also wish to comment upon salient biographical details in order to illuminate the narrator's story. These, in the case of *Grace and Mary,* might provide clues to understanding the moments and patterns of personal significance that anchor the novelist to the experience of the text. Bragg was 73 when the novel was published, completing it just before his mother, Mary Ethel Bragg, died in 2012. The decisive role played by memory and biography in Bragg's fictional re-creation of his mother's life, coupled with the novelist's prerogative of imaginative empathy in restoring the life of his grandmother, brings out once again his affinity with Wordsworth's biographical writerly qualities, not least 'the spontaneous overflow of powerful feelings [channelled into] emotion recollected in tranquillity' (*Lyrical Ballads,*p.21). Looking back from the early twenty-first century to the beginning of the twentieth, Bragg is well able to reflect on the characters, scenes, images, places, all of which might appear arbitrary in isolation and at the moment of first encounter but which are now revealed as part of a larger and significant pattern.

Two of Wigton's more colourful characters reappear in *Grace and Mary* to take their place as part of the town's significant but unofficially recognised and unrecorded alternative history. Kettler and Diddler exist on the margins of Wigton society, offering a radically different life-style choice to that sanctioned by the dominant culture. Both characters have appeared in earlier novels in their role as societal outsiders bringing colour, comedy, and humanity to an otherwise strictly regulated and rationed wartime and post-War economy. We first meet them in *The Soldier's Return* where they are living on Vinegar Hill, the poorest and most deprived area of Wigton, but one where Sam Richardson enjoyed his childhood upbringing:

> The ponies were tethered in the field that muddied around it and there were two donkeys apparently leaning against a wall. Dogs scavenged everywhere. Mongrels and lurchers they always kept. Children war-whooped and next to the building was a fire, the men and the older boys

sitting around it, as Sam remembered them doing since
his childhood.
'Sit down, Sam. We've some spuds in that fire. They'll be
out in no time.'
Diddler, the oldest of the men, extended the welcome.
Kettler was also there, quite drunk, lolling like a lord on
the mat of coats and old carpet they had put down for
comfort. Diddler's was the full tinker look, the wide-
gashed mouth, the high cheekbones, broad forehead,
narrow-socketed blue eyes, long tangled hair.

(SR, p.330)

Vinegar Hill is depicted as an important cultural space for redescription
and difference as an integral part of the town's memory, an area which
Mary would have known well. Diddler's outsider status is emphasised in
*A Son of War* where he is described as 'a horse trader and general dealer,
a rogue rover, and the leader of a pack bypassed by history, outside the
mechanism of society, harking back to the days before the town was
settled' (*SW* p.100). This is a profile privileging longevity and survival
over contemporary mores and one that Mary would have been
sympathetic to. But by the conclusion of *Crossing the Lines* '[t]hey were
pulling down Vinegar Hill. The council had declared it unsafe and unfit
for human habitation' (*CL*, p.488).

Bragg has clearly retained and cherished vivid memories of
Kettler and Diddler, memories of real inhabitants of Wigton which he has
delighted in recounting in print and in public appearances over the years
so that they have come to constitute an important part of his remembered
self. As a result of Bragg's literary intervention they are now part of the
folk history of Wigton. Knowing just how much 'Mary loved stories
about Wigton [,t]he place, the community, the people [who] had grafted
themselves onto her mind since childhood' (*GM* ,pp.102-3) John/Bragg
resurrects these two lords of misrule to entertain his mother with 'what
she knew and had forgotten about Kettler' (ibid.) and Diddler:

When he had left school Kettler had worked in the coal
mines a few miles from Wigton and from there gone on to
the land as a labourer and had eventually been netted for
the war, though not without two years of a masterful
evasive strategy. He'd landed up in uniform, in France,
which he hated, and in battle, which he hated. When he

came back he settled in Wigton, signed on for the dole, vowed to dedicate himself to drink and work as little as possible within the bounds of survival. He gathered around him a small but loyal posse of equally dedicated men, one of whom, Diddler, had inherited a couple of houses, better described as hovels, from a father who was a rag-and-bone, scrap-iron, move-anything merchant. Diddler's father, his flat cart and his grey pony combed the streets and the countryside daily and he had snapped up or, some said, just snaffled enough to invest in the hovels. Kettler had a room in one of them and promised to pay the rent one day. (*GM*, p.103)

Here Bragg restructures and polishes the rehearsed narrative of the three Richardson novels to shape memory recall and in so doing offers Mary a tentative grasp on known, satisfying and stable stories from her past. Bragg's choice of two liminal[3] characters for the trigger most likely to awaken Mary's memory of, and delight in, Wigton's past is significant, as they are textually defined as representing 'an openness as opposed to a closedness in morality' (Swartz, p.99), a positioning sympathetic with her own family history.

Bragg then embarks on the story of Kettler's riotous behaviour as ringmaster, with Diddler costumed as a wild bear, disrupting the town's annual carnival and thus entering into folk myth. In *Speak for England* Bragg interviews Joe Bill Lightfoot (born 1908) who recounts his version of Kettler and the bear. In introducing his interviewee Bragg makes the interesting proleptic aside that in doing full justice to Lightfoot's voice, 'fiction would be better'. Lightfoot tells how:

He had him dressed up as a bear. And a great chain around him. So like after the carnival was finished, plain as a pikestaff, here's old Tomboy [Diddler] with his great lang chain. It was a plough chain, that's what it was. He gets the plough chain, he fastens it around the lamppost

3. Sarah Gilead's discussion of liminality in her 'Liminality, Anti-Liminality, and the Victorian Novel' (1988) suggests that the existence of characters such as Kettler and Diddler help the general populace to reconcile themselves to society's rules and regulations, particularly at a time of change such as existed in post-War Britain: 'Seeming to be outside the group, the liminal figure is actually its moral representative and, in fact, exists to serve the social structure from which he seems to have been separated. The liminal figure provides for his audience a vicarious experience that offers a kind of safety valve for the hostility or frustration engendered by the limitations of structured life' (quoted in Omar Swartz *The View from On the Road*, p.98).

at this side, at this end, he locks it, but you see they would be half drunk before they went to the carnival. So he looks at Nimble, he says, Where the hell's thou going? He says I'se gaan for a drink. He says, What about me? Oh, he says, bears can't drink. No, all ever Kettler lived for was tricks and money.                    (*SE*, p.170)

Bragg fictionalises the story thus:

When the carnival reached the middle of the town, it had swung off west at the fountain to go down a road of bungalows to the park recently opened, built about half a mile from the old town centre. That was where the sports were held and the floats and the costumes judged. Kettler and Diddler wanted none of that. The fountain was a large memorial to the wife of a local man who, generations before, had gone to London, found it paved with gold, come back, restored a castle and on the death of his wife, commissioned a central monument in the town to her memory... Kettler and his friends adopted it as the forum for their daily chronicling of the town. Black railings protected it and it was to these railings that Kettler padlocked his good friend Diddler while he strolled across to the Kings Arms. The howls of the bear were heard throughout the streets... When asked in the pub why he had padlocked his friend, Kettler said, 'Bears dissent drink'. It became a catchphrase and for years Kettler dragged it round the pubs like a tin can tied to a dog's tail. 'Bears dissent drink, Diddler, remember?'    (*GM*, p.105)

The basic facts remain the same but Bragg also finds space to include a fragment of local history as an additional anchor for Mary's memory in space and time. A reading of the two versions makes possible an appreciation of Bragg's skill in blending the factual and the literary, shaping regional fiction with the authority of local reality.

Such escapades as the above are in the anarchic anti-establishment tradition of Shakespeare's Falstaff and his drinking cronies in *Henry IV Part 1*. Kettler is no mere figment of Bragg's imagination but rather a larger than life personality awaiting fictional rebirth: 'Kettler had been in the First World War. He came to our pub a lot. He decided the thing to do was drink, and to work as little as possible. He had a nose so bulbous that only Rembrandt could do it justice, so colourful that even Turner would have had to join in'(Keswick). The comparison with Bardolph is plain to see - 'as thou art our admiral, thou bearest the lantern of the poop, but 'tis the nose of thee. Thou art the knight o the burning lamp'( Act 111, Scene 3) - but the literary echo extends further and is interesting in terms of memory's ability to recall the more unpleasant aspects of the past alongside its pleasurable moments. We know that in *Henry V* Nym and Bardolph are hanged while Pistol is left alive to return to England as a robber. At the conclusion of John's amusing Kettler stories his mother's sole recollection is that '"Kettler would torture things - at school. Frogs." "I didn't know that," said John. And he laughed. Sometimes what else could you do?' (*GM*, p.106). Age is now teaching John something that he will have to incorporate into his previously largely positive memories of Kettler. His nervous laughter, however, is very much in line with the response his mother has been forced to adopt to the stigma of illegitimacy, described by Bragg as 'a scar visible to so many who knew "the truth" in that little gossiping town' (*Daily Mail*, 27 April 2013, p.40). The conflict in values exemplified here is a reminder of the legacy of cruelty and intolerance that lingered on in Wigton's social landscape in the inter-war years, mirroring prevailing universal social attitudes.

One of the more endearing, and biographically true, of Kettler's exploits concerns his recycling of the same prodded rug as a raffle prize around the local pubs. When asked who had won, he always he claimed the winning ticket belonged to some stranger from a suitably distant location:

> Well what they used to do like in them days they had what they called a hearthrug. So they used to make a raffle a week and then, of a Saturday night, the fun of the fair they had  Tomboy and Nimble and Kettler. But never no bugger ever won this raffle. Never. They used the same mat. They only had one mat but nobody won it. Of course they would start it up at the Highland Laddie, up where Bell's cut meat up at. Well they used to start there, all tickets. The whole hearthrug wasn't wrapped up, just underneath the arm, took it out, all the colours of the rainbow, beautiful. Then they would come down into the Crown and Mitre into the Kildare, across to the Half Moon, Lion and Lamb, and that went all the way round the pubs. As drunk as jinny owlets.

And then when they got bloody tired they would throw
the mat to Kettle and it was put out of the way. And that
went on for weeks.                                    (*SE*, p.170)

In *Grace and Mary* Bragg recycles the rug story as part of a by now
recognisable mythic form of semi-autobiographical fiction dedicated to
celebrating the perennially complementary relations between individuals
and Wigton's cultural history:

> 'Kettler and Diddler would go into the pubs on a Saturday
> night.' With this prodded rug. John told his mother the story as
> once she had told stories to him.
> 'It was a very fine prodded rug. They held a raffle for it. Tickets
> threepence each, six tickets for a shilling and round the pubs
> they went on Saturday night. Everybody joined in... There
> were about fourteen pubs in those days... And the rug raffle
> thrived. Every Sunday and Monday people would say, "Who
> won it?" "Oh," Kettler would say," a couple from Carlisle."
> The next week, "Who won it?" "Oh, a lad from Fletchertown,
> I forget his name." And again "Who won it...?" They kept it
> going for about a month and then people started to notice that
> it was always the same prodded rug, a fine rug, and they
> began to say it was strange that no one they knew ever won it.
> People were getting very upset and just at that moment Kettler
> announced, in the bar of the Lion and Lamb, that they were
> out of prodded rugs and there would be no more raffles. "All
> over!"'                                           (*GM*, p.105-6)

Bragg clothes eternal principles of behaviour in the guise of specific
characters and their actions in the course of objectifying and universalising
the affectionate interest he feels for his part in Wigton's history. And it is
affectionate, for as he remembers, even when the rug ruse was exposed,
Kettler's reputation as a lovable rogue and local character saved him from
any punishment beyond laughter.

Prodded rugs were something of a prized local possession and
were one of two gifts offered to the women employees at Redmayne's[4],
Wigton's clothing factory, when they left. Mary/Mrs Bragg, however,

4. Samuel Redmayne began The Wigton Clothing Company, a made to measure gentlemens
tailor, in 1868, in what was then known as Jonahs Brewery, before opening a factory on
Station Road in 1875. In the 1950s the business was ay its height with twenty-four branch
shops and three factories. Business then steadily declined and the Station Road factory was
demolished in 1987 to make way for houses and a supermarket.

chose the fish knives. Fish knives might appear largely inconsequential, and even beyond close interpretation, but in *Grace and Mary* they become a socially complex and legible sign that helps to explain Mary's/Mrs Bragg's personality. Their recall by John enables the text to recover their contribution to the psychological construction of meaning:

> John remembered those knives and forks. He had first come across them when he was four or five. They were tucked away at the bottom of a bed-linen chest he was excavating at the time. He pulled out the green case as if he had stumbled into Ali Baba's cave... Six forks, very thin but exotic, and six things that looked like knives but had no real blade and were very easy to bend. Silver, he was sure of that... His mother told him that they were fish knives and that they were special... From then on and as the years passed he kept encountering them... The last time he had seen them was when he was in the bathroom looking for a razor blade in the old chest of drawers to which everything which might come in helpful in the future had was condemned...The knives and forks had fallen on hard times. The damp of the bathroom had rusted them, the velvet was faded, the little snip catches were broken. They were of no further use.
>
> They had never once been put on the table.
>
> The only fish he could remember them eating in his childhood had come from the fish-and-chip shop and was so coated in an armour of batter that the puny forks would have buckled in any attempt to break through to the cod. (*GM*, p.78-9)

As Bragg recalls from his own childhood, 'The only fish we really had came from the Spanish fish-and-chip shop next to the fountain. And the batter was very hard, it would have bent the knives' (Keswick). John/Bragg sees the knives as a way into the past, an object on which both he and his mother can focus in common as a vehicle for transferring memory from Mary's consciousness into the time frame of the present.[5] They function as

5. There remains to be written a critical interpretation of objects such as Mary's fish knives in terms of what Marx refers to as social hieroglyphics, a complex sign of the hinterland behind the object. At the very moment of their gifting to Mary the history of cutlery manufacture in England was about to undergo a radical change, presaging a decline in its future production indicative of a general decline in British manufacturing output. Prior to World War 11 cutlery was made mainly in Birmingham and Sheffield but the wartime government ordered Birminghams metal industries to concentrate on war production, leaving Sheffield as the centre of cutlery manufacture. With Sheffield's late twentieth-century decline, Mary's fish knives represent an important moment of British industry on the cusp of decline. Today, however, they serve as a memory trigger to a lost heritage, appearing on, for instance, eBay where their exchange value far exceeds their use value.

intercorporeal objects of intersection enabling Mary to look back over a time-span of some fifty years. When John persists in questioning her unlikely choice, '[s]uddenly, she smiled and swung her head, with a gesture that was both young and old, and said, 'Swank! Just swank!' (*GM*, p.80).

Mary's uncharacteristic outburst of 'Swank' and her subsequent hiding of the cutlery travels back in time to allow the text to move from the present consciousness of a daughter to the past consciousness of a mother, with fish knives acting as the point of intersection between generations. Both Grace and Mary are innately unswanky, reserved, even, at times, self-effacing women in whom a continuity of personality traits is demonstrated as fish knives and dolls become vehicles, metaphors, that slip the moorings of their original material function, becoming recoded to record a moment at which time present and time past converge to reveal an essential connectivity between mother and daughter. Thus, when Mary exclaims 'Swank', the word becomes a link to the past narrative of Grace and the tender moment when she buys 'a doll in Victorian dress' for Mary's fourth birthday. It may have been an extravagant purchase in the context of Grace's precarious economic position but, significantly, it was definitely 'not swanky' (*GM*, p.211). The textual repetition of 'swank' binds together narrative moments at the same time as emphasising what are seen as life-turning episodes for both women.

The one location in Wigton where an ostentatious display of swank is socially acceptable, even encouraged and envied, is on the dance floor. In *Grace and Mary*, music, song, and above all, dance, provide their own independent commentary able to conjure up the ghosts of memory. Chapter Five of the novel is a loving recreation of dance at a time of economic hardship acting as a potent symbol of survival and community togetherness. It is set in the harsh winter of 1947 [6]. The vitality of dance in 'the bare Congregational Hall in Water Street' (*GM*, p.43) brings recollections of childhood happiness, a sensory fullness, an overflowing abundance of the pure joy of being such that John's hope is that these primal joys revisited will unlock his mother's memory of her love of dance and its associated good companions, music and laughter. His wish is to prompt a positive response to the question 'Do you remember when we danced the Valeta?' (*GM*, p.47). Bragg retains a vivid recollection of dancing the Valeta, seeing it as an epiphany moment in his childhood, a

6. The extreme early winter months of 1947's big freeze are vividly brought to life in the vernacularly titled chapter 8 of David Kynaston's *Austerity Britain 1945-51*, 'Christ It's Bleeding Cold'.

key to interpreting the values of post-War Wigton society and a metaphor for social cohesion. This is a weighty responsibility for dance to assume but in this Bragg again shows himself to be as much an heir to Bennett as to Hardy and Lawrence. The parallels repay close attention, especially in the way that both writers respond to dance as a rite of passage and as a post-war phenomenon. The liberatory rhythms of dance are responsible for opening Edwin Clayhanger's adolescent eyes in Bennett's 1910 novel *Clayhanger* when he is intoxicated by the sensuality of Florence Simcox's clog dancing at the Dragon/George Hotel in the tightly knit community of Bursley/Burslem. Edwin is ravished by a union of matter and spirit, the memory of which haunts him at key moments throughout the rest of his life. Patricia Alden interprets Bennett's clog-dancing scene as showing that 'art is connected with freedom, and the entire scene celebrates a cultural form which is democratic rather than elitist' (*Social Mobility*, p.83). Her statement might also serve to describe dancing the Valeta in another parochial setting at the heart of a small town community, namely Wigton. One further example from Bennett, this time from his none-fiction essays, must suffice to show the aesthetic link between his response to World War 1 and Bragg's representation of the Congregational Hall and the spirit of 1947 in the wake of World War II. Bennett believed that the generation that had survived the carnage of war had;

> ...rediscovered, or is rediscovering the great secrets - lost since the Elizabethan Age - that the chief thing in life is to feel that you are fully alive, that continued repression is absurd, that dullness is a social crime, that the present is quite as important as the future, that life oughtn't to be a straight line but a series of ups and downs, and that moments of ecstasy are the finest moments and the summits of existence. ('Dancing', pp.109-10).

These are sweeping assertions to make in any context but Bennett does little to mitigate the shock of the new when he privileges dance as the social art form best able to capture and represent a new beginning: ' Now the most spectacular symptom of the new spirit is the the revival and the full democratisation of dancing'(ibid.). Bragg repositions the spirit of dance and its associated set of signs, signals, gestures and messages to identify post-World War II Wigton, and English society, in much the same way as Bennett co-opted the culturally quotidian performative art of dance as an important element in the reconstruction of popular culture after an earlier conflict.' Dancing' was published just after the end of the Great War; John's memories of similar 'finest moments and the summits of existence' are very precisely dated just two years after the end of World War II. Bragg selects the 'chaos of that winter [quite deliberately] partly because of the snow which was bound around [and] which seemed to epitomise a kind of pacification and settlement... and something God sent to say after those two World Wars what it is to be still; let's have a quietness... snow on snow, in the bleak midwinter' (Keswick). Amidst this quietness and isolation Bragg speaks of a society 'bankrupted by two World Wars' and of a town which was still suffering from 'the open wounds of war' (ibid.) but which felt able to turn to dance that winter as 'a modest but perfect act of defiance and coming through' (ibid.). As if subconsciously reverting to the Victorian world of Bennett's *Clayhanger*, Bragg eulogises the gathering in the Congregational Hall: 'Our little huddle was a Victorian huddle in Wigton... it was basically an endangered species... not unlike some of the tribes in the Amazon jungle. It's gone now. It was a different place...Wigton was a constricted place, the smallest place that dragged all the biggest things to it. And we were IT' (ibid.). Such a succinct, clear, and proud statement of the centrality of local place, the 'IT' at the centre of the universe, is what links Wigton to the aesthetic of Bennett's Bursley', reading as the marmoreal credo of regional novelists searching to discover their 'World in a Grain of Sand'.

Dance is embedded in Bragg's story-line and illustrates the potential for astonishing transformations, as feelings and emotions difficult to articulate in the course of ordinary conversation are acted out in the flow of the dance, momentarily expunging the reality of a pinched, anxious and weary post-War society. The already blurred and disputed border separating fact from fiction now becomes unpoliced and porous as Bragg's power of recall, along with an associated near overwhelming sense of emotion-laden nostalgia, dictates the text's structure. Entering Wigton's Congregational Hall, readers encounter characters who, far from being even thinly veiled members of the local community, are undisguised and celebrated members of it. Chapter Five approaches prose fiction as a continual shifting of textual form between the autobiographical memoir and the imaginative novel, conflating subjectivity and objectivity, as the centripetal pull of the dance floor negates literary difference. Such a conflation is central to this, and to the other semi-autobiographical novels previously discussed, as an aesthetically important component of Bragg's artful search for objectivity from a near perfect honest fidelity to subjectivity. His recording eye resembles that of a child, the eight-year old Bragg, but it is allied to the shaping adult intelligence capable of linking Wigton's past to Mary's present. It might be argued that such intensity of sensual cognition is the prized prerogative of childhood, and just as the child cannot easily dissemble so the ageing writer finds it incumbent to write a literary memoir linking real remembered people to an equally real sense of place. By this stage of Bragg's writing, the factual truths of *Speak for England* and the fictional verities of *Grace and Mary* deftly intersect each other to create the literary legend of Wigton.

Bragg is able to cast his mind back over 65 years to speak passionately and movingly of childhood time and place. Remembering the Congregational Hall dances in front a Keswick audience he tells how:

> The star of this ballroom, this bleak empty room with a piano, a little stage, and a coal fire so small that it needn't have been there, but it was, the star of this show was Mrs Studholme, or Queenie, a wonderful dancer, a woman of a certain size. But not only was she a wonderful dancer, but she had sons, three or four, who were also wonderful dancers, who worked in a factory.
>
> (Keswick)

In the novel a 'two-bar electric fire [which] made a doomed attempt to warm the room' (*GM* ,p. 37) replaces the remembered coal fire, but the very real animated presence of Queenie and her boys undergoes no such fictional displacement:

> John knew that for dancing he had to look at the Studholme boys and copy them. Queenie's boys. There were only three that night, one in his last year at school, one well into his apprenticeship, the other on leave from his National Service. All suited. Queenie never took off her coat... Mary loved watching those boys... Dancing defined them... They whirled and whooped the Gay Gordons round the room, which was losing the final pockets of gloom and warming by the minute with the rising body heat... the room was alive with the joy of it.
>
> (*GM*, p.39)

Leaving aside the highly unlikely threat of a libel case, what would be the literary purpose in allocating such memorable and sympathetically remembered characters fictionally disguised names? Why change the setting, construct an entirely imagined scene, fabricate an action so sharply recalled in all its joy? To evade the tradition of Romantic confession and autobiographically inflected texts might well be seen as a betrayal of those boyhood figures whose textual reincarnation has helped turn Wigton into a lasting theatre of memory. Figures such as Fred Ingrams and Tommy Jackson, both of whom keep their real names and activities in the novel, as the band the Two Wigton Mashers, Tommy laying down 'a good beat' on drums while Fred's trumpet calls 'out the troops, summoning the game and the lame, its brass perfection ringing with magisterial exhilaration in the heads of the lucky dancers' (*GM*, p.41). The highlight occurs when the Valeta is announced - 'Fred Ingrams picked up his trumpet and wetted his lips. Tommy Jackson nodded' (*GM*, p. 43) - and 'for Mary, John would come to think, the glory was the communion of two circles, and its imitative, gentle parody of distant, unobtainable privilege taken over by ordinary people and made into their own with a smile at the ease of it' (*GM*, p.42). The memory comes full-circle in the nursing home as Mary suddenly and unexpectedly begins to sing the Hokey-cokey, inspiring her fellow residents to join in to recreate a sedentary shadow of the Valeta from the static circle of their chairs. Phenomenologically, for Mary, and for the watching and remembering John, space and time are momentarily detached from their fixed trajectory of rational sequential stages, liberating Mary from her sensory prison and bending time to her consciousness.

Likewise, the poetry of dreams has the potential to betray time with sudden sweeps from ecstatic joy to overwhelming sadness. When the convalescent World War I soldier, Alan, recites from memory W B Yeats's 'He Wishes For The Cloths Of Heaven' to John's grandmother, Grace, the 'words wove into her soul' (*GM*, p.137). If, as in Freud's analysis, art and dreams share a common endgame of metaphorically revealing the contents of the subconscious mind, then Alan's is simultaneously revealing of his self-convinced love for Grace whilst being dissembling not only to her but also to his own deeper reality. The irony of the poem's final line - 'Tread softly because you tread on my dreams' - is that when Alan returns to his first love, abandoning a pregnant Grace, he destroys Grace's dream of happiness. 'He Wishes for the Cloths of Heaven' was included in Yeats's love poems to Maud Gonne published in *The Wind Among the Reeds* (1899) and is described by O B Duanne as 'a beautifully sculpted, richly imagined expression of a devotion that is not entirely without hope' (*Yeats*, p. 10). But, as Christopher Ricks somewhat cynically observes, 'when artists have a dream, it is not of being famous but of being believed... an artist is someone who is especially good at, generous about, imagining beliefs that he or she doesn't hold' (*Dylan's Visions*, p. 377). Perhaps Grace would have been well advised to have turned to and heeded the earlier poems in Yeats's collection, such as, for example, 'The Hosting of the Sidhe' with its warning to 'Empty your heart of its mortal dream' as the faeries threaten to ' *come between him and the hope of his heart*' (*Yeats Selected Poetry*, p.24). Rather, when Grace takes the train from Carlisle to Birmingham in the vain hope of seeing Alan at his parents' house, she continues to emotionally invest in the recited poem 'which she now knew off by heart', using her book of Yeats's poems as a barrier 'in case anyone threatened to intrude' (*GM*, p. 190). Years later, visiting Mrs Johnson who has unofficially adopted her daughter, the memory of Alan's voice and Yeats's words still retain the power to haunt and distress Grace, reminding her of her crushed dreams. Here Bragg's story artfully and insistently returns to the cluster of brief narratives related to Yeats's poetry and the world of unfulfilled dreams, to, in Robert Creeley's words 'summon characters and occasions, which must always implicate far more than we know literally, or can in any sense finally imagine' ('Introduction' *Book of Dreams*, p.ix). In a poignant passage, Grace buys her daughter a Victorian doll for her fourth birthday, and then suffers pangs of memory when she hears Mary ask Mrs Johnson: '"Can I call [my doll] Sally?" "Yes. I think Sally's just right. Sally. Where does Sally come from?" Suddenly Grace was all but crushed with the voice of Alan reciting "Down by the sally gardens, my love and I did meet..." She breathed in deeply' (*GM*, pp.212). At which point Bragg dispels any lingering Celtic twilight to give the doll 'a local habitation and a name' (*GM*, p. 52) in the life of Wigton: '"Sally army," said Mary. "I take her to watch them play at the end of Water Street at the end of a Saturday afternoon," said Mrs Johnson, again proprietorially...' (*GM*, p.213).

Poetry/song lyrics and the world of dreams link past to present, Grace to Mary, Mary to John, as Bragg moves effortlessly between the world of Irish poetic mythology and the contemporary world of popular culture. Watching his mother asleep in the nursing home, John recalls the words of Peter Sarsted's 1968 hit single, 'Where Do You Go To My Lovely', with its frustrated desire to unlock the secrets of the beloved's dream world: 'And was this sleep a dreamless deadness. She never mentioned her dreams. She never talked of a nightmare. Was she lucky in that or did the forgetfulness strike so deeply that the unconscious regurgitation of the day which flashed up on the screens of sleep was also beyond memory?' (*GM*, p.49). Bragg's choice of song has a wider resonance in connecting with his and Mary's love of dance, including as it does a reference to the French ballerina Zizi Jeanmaire, and all set to a faux European waltz tune, the forerunner to the Valeta. In addition, there is an important textual sense in which the reference to contemporary pop lyrics is a variation on the earlier habit of learning poetry by heart. Alan's ability to recite Yeats would not have been seen as something exceptional in the early 1900s, whereas by the end of the century it would be regarded as idiosyncratic and elitist. Bragg understands and incorporates this cultural shift into the historical sequencing of the novel. In a *New Statesman* article, with a title that could well serve as an epigraph to *Grace and Mary* - '"Shame is a revolutionary emotion" On culture and progress' (12-25 April, 2013, pp.147-51) - Bragg responds to the playwright David Hare's 'existentialist anxiety about the consumer society' with:

> Alongside the developments we've been discussing there's pop culture. Ask anyone brought up in the late Fifties or early Sixties how many lines of contemporary poetry they can remember, and there'll be silence after a short time. But ask them how many lyrics from pop songs they can remember and you'd be here all night. They'd not only sing them, they'd tell you where and when they heard them for the first time. I don't think it's quite sunk in yet how much it's now part of the culture.

The pop lyric, now digitally retrievable with ease, has supplanted literary poetry as popular culture's commentary of choice on the world of our dreams. Bragg's textual leap from Yeats to Sarsted reads as an entirely natural, if initially unsettling, cultural linking of three generations via the poetic soundtrack of their lives.

*Grace and Mary* also owes allegiance to the dream factory of the 1930s classical Hollywood musicals, in which the act of dancing becomes a populist defiant gesture against the politics of despair and the economics of adversity. When Tommy Jackson and Fred Ingrams hit their stride they provide the soundtrack for a group transformation in Wigton as astonishing as anything in a Fred Astaire and Ginger Rogers movie. Even their singing suggests an unstoppable life-force mix of insouciance, energy and friendship:

> Oh we dance and we sing
> And we don't care a jot
> We're a jolly fine lot
> We're all right, when we're tight
> And we're jolly good company...          (*GM*, p.41)

Dancing the Valeta becomes a metaphor for 'jolly good company', performance as a symbol of group consciousness, with the unlooked for bonus of granting Mary a vision of justified swank and elegance inherited from the ballrooms of the Hapsburg Empire as 'working men unselfconsciously put hand on hip and swung their legs in an elegant arc as if showing off a well-bred leg' (*GM*, p.42). With the novel's concluding paragraph past and present merge as fragments of history coalesce into a single now, a collapsed chronology of the memories of characters and those of their author. Tommy and Fred's music plays on uninterrupted, spilling out over the page and across time to forge a narrative circle in which the novel's opening statement of intent to rescue the secrets of a 'disintegrating memory' before life 'enters into darkness' (*GM*, p.1), is creatively realised as the dance begins again and time collapses in a small northern town at the epicentre of Bragg's own memory:

> And then Fred Ingrams on the trumpet wet his lips and Tommy Jackson hit the drums and all of them, the Studholme boys and Queenie, Kettler and other people from the town out for an evening's celebration, Grace and Mary and himself, all of them formed up in the twin circles, and the music started up and they moved left to right, and they danced, one last time, and how magnificently they danced, when they danced the Valeta!

> *Eternity in an Hour*

# AFTERWORD
## Melvyn Bragg

The line pursued most steadily in John's book is that of emphasising the consistency of autobiography in my fiction. Not only facts or incidents from my own life but also those from my immediate family - my grandfather, father and mother, the people I knew in the town of Wigton in which I lived until I was twenty, friends, local histories and sometimes the larger histories on which we surf and not least the landscape of that area of north Cumbria. There is a chronicling strand there as well, reclamation. Everything that encases the work could be seen as 'clearly' autobiographical. Its interiority is a different matter.

Autobiographically based fiction whose practitioners to name just a quintet include early Tolstoy, Proust, D.H. Lawrence, James Joyce, Philip Roth (to take some of the best), and whose other disciples, clothed in varying levels of disguise orchestrate a fair amount of the fiction we read, is too close to memoir for the taste of some. Too close to fact to be fiction. It is, in my view, as valid in this 'loose and baggy monster' we call a novel as any of the other varieties.

What the autobiographical base gives to this author is a feeling of authenticity, of a planting of the work in known ground, place and time. For reasons that may range from a life still umbilically tied to childhood and youth, to a conviction that a deeper strength of a novel can be plumbed by founding it on what was and is known of an external world in an intimate, tactile and historically enriched way, it is part of the palette, there to hand. Other novelists have other methods every bit as valid, often opposed to mine, but this is what I do. The prime ambition of a novel is to say what the author can uniquely say, whatever the weather of fashion, theory and commerce.

Charles Darwin went to North Wales to study geology before setting off for the Galapagos Islands. On that trip he was looking for confirmation of what he had seen in Wales - the gradual evolution of rocks, a completely new way of dating and comprehending the world. But, a classically cautious man, he needed more proof. He found it in the finch. He collected many specimens including the finch and encouraged the sailors to collect for him and so we have a set of finches. The finch on island number one, wind assisted across the ocean to another island, is different, but not much. On the next island, it is even more different, but undoubtedly related to the finch on island number one. And so it goes on across several islands until we encounter a bird which is finch-like and related but so essentially different that it cannot even mate with finch one. Evolution in action. And that as far as I am concerned is autobiographical fiction.

Mary, for example, in *Grace and Mary*, is based on my own mother during the five years in which she suffered increasingly from dementia. In the short novel, in which she occupies about half, we see her in the 'present' - that is in her last few years at the beginning of the 21st century. But we also see her as a child, as a young woman, and a married woman.

I was very close to my mother, like many children born (1939) at the start of World War Two. I lacked a father, who was in the forces. As in most working class homes I slept in my mother's bed for the first few years. She cleaned houses and I was bundled along with her until I went to primary school. As an only child I must have become very dependent but she was a most independently minded woman. To be brief, she was for a while my whole world. She was illegitimate - as in *Grace and Mary* - and fostered from birth in the town of Wigton which branded with shame and blame such mothers and children in those days. My mother's reaction was to embrace the town, to adopt it and to love it with unspoken intensity. She passed that on to me. To put the volumes of that unconscious transaction within a few pages must in itself have been an exercise in editing that re-made a woman out of what she was. But more than that, something else happened as it always does when I base a fictional character on someone I know. Like the finch, they change essentially.

The act of writing fiction takes the writer and the reader into a world provoked by the imagination. There is a ruthlessness in autobiographical fiction: you take what you need and use that as the catalyst for the character. Again and again I could itemise in *Grace and Mary* that Mary was not 'like that', did not 'do that', would never have 'said that' - and on it goes. It is as if there is something chemical about it. You take one substance, dip it into a test tube and because of what is in that tube - in this case the solutions of fiction - it can change colour, odour, shape, taste and essence. Readers sense that every bit as much as writers. Borges wrote that sometimes readers find more in a book than the author thinks has been put into it. Mary is my mother in fiction and had you met her, having read the book, I hope that there would be recognition but the realities are different and distinctive.

Because of imagination. And that is why I think that fiction can be such an overwhelmingly successful means of understanding and keying into the human condition. Because of imagination.

We are supposed to use only about 5% of our minds. The going view was that the other 95% was unknowable or junk. Oddly, we are supposed to know only about 5% of the universe. Until recently the rest was thought to be as empty as it was dark. Now we know that the dark teems with Dark Energy - it is a galactic Ali Baba's cave just waiting for the key to understanding. The brain is more complex than the universe and I think that soon we will find that the vast currently unknown domain will be every bit as full of something as the universe itself. Knowledge of the Unconscious has taken us some of the way. Dreams swirl up out of that darkness as do inexplicable impulses and sensations, and the often inexplicable nature - evil, altruism, courage, psychopathic violence ...

Down there, I think, are networks and interchanges which consume most of the interstices of our lives. In that den lurks Imagination, called by Einstein the most essential quality in all knowledge seeking. Evoked by Shakespeare in *A Midsummer Night's Dream*

> As Imagination bodies forth
> The form of things unknown
> The poet's pen turns them to shapes
> And gives to airy nothings a local habitation and a name

Newton imagined gravity. Michelangelo imagined David and Rembrandt imagined himself again and again. It is a faculty across all human endeavour, which I have heard called a knack, that everyone possesses and some choose to use more intensively than others. Like many other writers, I find myself writing scenes I have neither planned nor dreamed but out they come and seem as natural as the description of a cloud.

Grace, the mother of Mary, is wholly invented and imagined. I met her twice, both times I was about ten or eleven, and never for more than half an hour. And yet 'seeing her' in a unique half-waking dream when my mother was entering dementia and was asking for her mother (which one, I thought, the biological or the foster?) set in motion the novel, which spans a century.

There are those who think that imagination is at its mightiest in great fantasy novels or magical realism or roaring adventures which defy belief or any number of genres, and without doubt imagination is there. But no less, I think, and no less remarkable in what can be called naturalistic or realistic fiction. The flights of James Joyce fly as high as any space story; the affinities of Lawrence are as vertiginous as any magical realism. My aim is to create credible characters and to follow their path by going as deeply into their feelings as I can without cheating or exaggerating. Keeping close to the truth of my observation and of my memory and experience and letting imagination flesh them out so that others can know them through this common bond.

Experience is a pillar in the structure of our thought. We are not only what we have done or not done but what we have read, felt, learned: we are all encyclopaedias of the multiple lives and thoughts through which we travel daily. We are the world in our grain of mind. Writers have produced books about places they have never visited, of people they have never met, of people who never existed and imagination can make them real to the reader. My world seems more limited but it is not. It is the world itself. It is the circumference which appears limited. But that is an illusion. All human life is in the mind of a man or a woman. And other versions are in other minds. That is all.

Finally, there is memory. The idea of this, like imagination, is explored in *Grace and Mary*. It is as infinite as our future is finite. Memory shifts its materials to match the occasion. It is not a rock quarry but a network of rivers and pools, waterfalls and reservoirs, ready to serve the purpose which can alter from moment to moment. It is unreliable, powerful, trivial, our closest companion, our changing character, our hold sometimes on consistency, our so far best way of meeting the world. Extended now by technology, served by dazzling developments in computer science but still there, deep in the mind, at the heart of things.

For me, it is misremembering what I have found most fertile. When I began *The Soldier's Return* with the image of the man coming back from the war into the council house yard to be met by his wife and son, I did not know that I was completely wrong about that image. An image I could have sworn to the truth of. But it was not like that. Yet because I selected that, and believed that, I could write a novel, not a memoir, of a man, my father, whose death in the mid 1990s had lit the fuse of the novel. A girl I knew and on whom I based a character in a novel told me 'it didn't happen like that'. And I was pleased. Because for me it worked for the novel.

Letting memory dance is one of the profound, almost visceral pleasures in the act of writing. And having it dance and roam in a time and a place, in a landscape and among a people I also knew in their other non-fictional life, is like communicating with the dead, with ghosts, with the glittering fugitive reality of what we might be, what it is like to live.

Melvyn Bragg
12 February 2014

# BIBLIOGRAPHY

Alden, Patricia. *Social Mobility in the English Bildungsroman.*
New York: Edwin Mellen Press, 1979.

Alegre, Sarah Martin. *Odysseus's Unease; The Post-War Crises of Masculinity in Melvyn Bragg's 'The Soldier's Return' & 'A Son of War'.*
www.ual.es/Odisea09_MartinAlegra.pdf, 2008.

Allen, Maureen. *Ireby.* Caldbeck: Maureen Allen, 2004

Allport, Alan. *Demobbed: Coming Home After the Second World War.*
New Haven & London: Yale U.P., 2009.

Armbruster, Karla. 'Creating the world we must save: the paradox of television documentaries' in Neil Campbell. *The Culture of the American New West.*
Edinburgh: Edinburgh U.P., 2000.

Armstrong, Isobel. *Victorian Poetry. Poetry, Poetics and Politics.*
London: Macmillan, 1978.

Arthur, Jason. 'The Chinatown and the City'. *Modern Fiction Studies, Vol. 58, No. 2.*
Baltimore: John Hopkins U.P., 2012.

Auden, W. H. *Collected Shorter Poems: 1927-1957.* London:
Faber & Faber, 1966.

Auerbach, Nina. *Woman and the Demon: The Life of a Victorian Myth.*
Cambridge, Mass.: Harvard U.P., 1984.

Austen, Jane. *Persuasion.* Oxford: Oxford U.P., 1990.

Bachelard, Gaston. *The Poetics of Space,* translated Maria Jolas.
Boston: Beacon Press, 1994.

Bate, Jonathan. *The Cure for Love.* London: Picador, 1998.
*The Song of the Earth,* London: Picador, 2000.

Benn, Tony. *Arguments for Socialism.* London: Jonathan Cape, 1979.

Bennett, Arnold. *The Old Wives' Tale.* London: Chapman & Hall, 1908.
*Paris Nights.* London: Hodder & Stoughton,1914.
*The Author's Craft.* London: Hodder & Stoughton,1914.
*Books and Persons.* London: Chatto & Windus, 1917.

Bentley, Phyllis. *The English Regional Novel.* Woking: Allen & Unwin, 1941.

Blake, William. Edited Geoffrey Keynes. *Complete Writings.*
London: Oxford U.P., 1969.

Bordwell, David, Janet Staigner & Kristin Thompson.
*The Classical Hollywood Cinema; Film Style & Modes of Production.*
London: Routledge, 1988.

Bourne, George. *Memoirs of a Surrey Labourer.* Stroud: Amberley Publishing, 2010.

Bragg, Melvyn. *For Want of a Nail.* London: Hodder & Stoughton, 1990 [1965].
*The Second Inheritance.* London: Hodder & Stoughton, 1989 [1966].
*Without a City Wall.* London: Secker & Warburg, 1968.
*The Hired Man.* London: Secker & Warburg, 1969.
*A Place in England.* London: Secker & Warburg, 1970.
*The Nerve.* London: Secker & Warburg, 1971.

*Josh Lawton*. London: Secker & Warburg, 1972.

*The Silken Net*. London:Secker & Warburg, 1974.

*Speak for England*. London: Secker & Warburg, 1976.

*Autumn Manoeuvres*. London: Secker & Warburg, 1978.

*Kingdom Come*. London: Secker & Warburg, 1980.

*My Favourite Stories of Lakeland*. Guildford: Lutterworth Press, 1981.

*Land of the Lakes*. London: Secker & Warburg, 1983.

*Cumbria in Verse*. London:  Secker & Warburg. 1984.

*Laurence Olivier*. London: Hutchinson, 1984.

*The Hired Man: A Musical*, ( Music & Lyrics by Howard Goodall). London: Samuel French, 1986.

*The Maid of Buttermere*. London: Hodder & Stoughton, 1987.

*Rich. The Life of Richard Burton*. London: Hodder & Stoughton, 1988.

*A Time to Dance*. London: Hodder & Stoughton, 1990.

*A Time to Dance: the Screenplay*. London:  Sceptre, 1992.

'Introduction' *The Parish of Lamplugh*, edited Ann Lister & Betty Marshall: Lamplugh District Council, 1993.

*The Seventh Seal*. London: Palgrave Macmillan (BFI), 1993.

*The Soldier's Return*. London: Sceptre, 1999.

*A Son of War*. London: Sceptre, 2001.

*Crossing the Lines*. London: Sceptre, 2003.

*The Adventure of English*. London: Hodder & Stoughton, 2003.

 'Introduction', *D H Lawrence. The Prussian Officer & Other Stories*. London: Panther Books, 1985.

'Foreword', Sid Chaplin. *The Watchers and the Watched*. Hexham: Flambard Press, 2004.

*The Bragg Family Windows*. Wigton P.C.C.

*Remember Me...* London: Sceptre, 2008.

*In Our Time*. London: Hodder & Stoughton, 2009.

*The South Bank Show*. London: Hodder & Stoughton, 2010.

*The Book of Books: The Radical Impact of the King James Bible 1611-2011*. London: Hodder & Stoughton, 2011.

'Shame is a Revolutionary Emotion'. *New Statesman*. London, April 12-25, 2013.

*Grace and Mary*. London: Sceptre, 2013.

'Introduction', *Julian Cooper. Natural Forces. Paintings 2014*. London: Michael Richardson Contemporary Art, Art Space Gallery, 2014.

Brontë, Charlotte. *Jane Eyre*. Oxford: Oxford U.P., 1993.

Brook, Peter. *The Empty Space*. Middlesex: Pelican, 1972.

Brown, Jules. edt. *The Rough Guide to The Lake District.* Rough Guides, 2010.

Butler, Marilyn. *Romantics, Rebels & Reactionaries*. Oxford: Oxford U. P., 1981.

Byrne, Eleanor & Martin McQuillan. *Deconstructing Disney.* London: Pluto Press. 1999.

Cameron, Sharon. *Writing Nature: Henry Thoreau's Journal.* Oxford: Oxford U.P.,1985.

Campbell, Neil. *The Culture of the American New West.*
        Edinburgh: Edinburgh U.P., 2000

Carey, John. *The Intellectuals and the Masses.* London: Faber & Faber, 1992.

Carric T W. *The History of Wigton.* Carlisle: Bookcase, 1992.

Cavaliero, Glen. *The Rural Tradition in the English Novel: 1900-1939.*
        London: Macmillan, 1977.

Chandler, Marilyn. *Dwelling in the Text: Houses in American Fiction.*
        Berkeley: California U.P., 1991.

Chatwin, Bruce. *The Songlines.* London: Jonathan Cape, 1987.

Clark, Anna. *The Struggle for the Breeches.* Berkeley: Cakifornia U.P., 1997.

Clarke, Donald. *Wishing on the Moon: The Life & Times of Billie Holiday.*
        London: Viking, 1994.

Claudel, Paul. *Strasbourg.* Edtd. Anthony Hartley, *The Penguin Book of French Verse. 4.*
        London: Penguin, 1966.

Coe, Jonathan. *The Rotters Club.* London: Viking, 2001

Coleridge, Samuel Taylor. *Biographia Literaria,* edited George Watson.
        London: Dent, 1975.

Cook, Jon. *Hazlitt in Love.* London: Short Books, 2007

Coupe, Laurence, edited. *The Green Studies Reader.* London: Routledge, 2000.

Creech, Robert. *Closet Writing/Gay Reading: The Case of Melville's Pierre.*
        Chicago: Chicago U.P.,1993.

Creeley, Robert. 'Introduction', Jack Kerouac. *Book of Dreams.*
        San Francisco: City Lights Books, 2001.

Davies, Philip. *Memory and Writing. From Wordsworth to Lawrence.*
        Liverpool: Liverpool U.P.,1983.

Deleuze, Gilles. *Cinema. The Movement Image,* translated Hugh Tomlinson &
        Barbara Habberjam. London; The Atlantic Press, 1966.

De Quincey, Thomas. *Confessions of an English Opium Eater.* Ware: Wordsworth, 2009.

Dickens, Charles. *Oliver Twist.* London: Collins, 1964.
                *Pickwick Papers.* London: Penguin, 1972.

Drabble, Margaret. *The Ice Age.* London: Weidenfeld & Nicolson, 1977.
        Edited, *The English Companion to English Literature.* Oxford: Oxford U.P., 2006.

Duanne, O.B., edited. *Yeats. Romantic Visionary.* London: Brockhampton Press, 1966.

Eakin, Paul John. *Fictions in Autobiography: Studies in the Art of Self-Invention.*
        Princeton: Princeton U.P., 1985.

Eliot, George. *Adam Bede.* London: Zodiac Press, 1952
                *Middlemarch.* New York: Norton, 1977.

Eliot, T S. *Collected Poems 1909-1963.* London: Faber & Faber, 1963.

Ellison, Ralph. *Invisible Man.* London: Penguin, 1965.

Engel, Susan. *Context is Everything. The Nature of Memory.*
        New York: Freeman, 1999.

Evernden, Neil. 'Beyond Ecology: Self, Place and the Pathetic Fallacy'
        in edited, Glotfelty, Cheryll & Harold Fromm. *Ecocriticism Reader.*
        Athens, Georgia: Georgia U. P., 1996.

Fiedler, Leslie A. *Love and Death in the American Novel.* London: Paladin, 1970.

Foot, Michael, edited Brian Brivati. *The Uncollected Michael Foot.*
    London: Politico's, 2004.

Ford, Ford Madox. *Parade's End.* London: Random House, 1992.

Foucault, Michel. *Aesthetics.The Essential Works 2.* London: Allen Lane, 1998.

Fowles, John. *The French Lieutenant's Woman.* London: Jonathan Cape, 1969.

Fraser, George MacDonald. *Quartered Safe Out Here. A Recollection of the War in
    Burma.* London: Harvill, 1992.

Fulford, Tim. *Landscape, Liberty and Authority.* New York: Cambridge U.P., 1996.

Garber, Majorie. *Vested Interests:Cross-Dressing and Cultural Anxiety.*
    New York: Harper Collins,1992.

Genett, Gérard. *Paratexts Thresholds of Interpretation,* translated by Jane E. Lewin.
    Cambridge: Cambridge U.P., 1997.

Gervais, David. *Literary Englands. Versions of 'Englishnes' in modern writing.*
    Cambridge: Cambridge U.P., 1993.

Giddens, Anthony. *The Consequences of Modernity.* Stanford: Stanford U.P.,1990.

Gilbert, Sandra M & Susan Gubar. *The Madwoman in the Attic.*
    New Haven & London: Yale U.P., 1984.

Gilman, Charlotte Perkins: *The Yellow Wall-Paper & Other Stories.*
    Oxford: Oxford U. P.,1995.

Godden, Richard. *Fictions of Labour.* New York: Cambridge U.P.,1997.

Goffman, Erving. *The Presentation of Self in Everyday Life.*
    London: Allen Lane, 1969.

Goodway, David. *Anarchist Seeds beneath the Snow.* Liverpool: Liverpool U.P.. 2006,

Goodwin, John, edited. *Peter Hall's Diaries. The Story of a Dramatic Battle.*
    London: Hamish Hamilton, 1983.

Grahamslaw, Trevor. *Wigton Through Time.* Stroud: Amberly, 2010.

Gray, Timothy. *Gary Snyder & the Pacific Rim: Creating Counter Cultural Community.*
    Iowa City: Iowa U.P., 2006.

Grayling, A C. *The Quarrel of the Age.* London: Weidenfeld & Nicolson, 2000.

Gubar, Susan. 'This is my rifle, this is my gun' in  Margaret R Higonnet edited,
    *Behind the Lines.* New Haven: Yale U.P., 1987.

Haggard, Henry Rider. *King Solomon's Mines.* London: Collins, 1955.

Hagedorn, Hermann. *The Bomb that Fell on America.*
    Santa Barbara: Pacific Coast Publishing,1946.

Hall, Sarah. *The Carhullan Army.* London: Faber & Faber, 2007.

Hammond, Paul. *Love Between Men in English Literature.*
    New York: St.Martin's Press, 1996.

Hampl, W S 'Desires Deferred: Homosexuals & Queer Reprentations in the
    Novels of Iris Murdoch'. *Modern Fiction Studies, Vol.47, No.3.*
    Baltimore: John Hopkins U.P., 2001.

Hankinson, Alan. 'Melvyn's schooldays'.
    Carlisle: *Cumbria Life Magazine,* Christmas 1995.

Hanna, Stephen P & Vincent J Del Casino. *Mapping Tourism.*
        Minneapolis: Minnesota U.P., 2003.
Harding, Brian. 'Comparative Metafictions of History', in edited Ann Massa &
        Alistair Stead. *Forked Tongues?* London: Longman, 1994.
Hardy, Thomas. 'General Preface to the Wessex Edition of 1912',
        *Desperate Remedies.* London: Macmillan, 1962.
        *Jude the Obscure.* Oxford: Oxford U.P., 1985.
Harris, Alexandra. *Romantic Moderns.* London: Thames & Hudson, 2010.
Harris, Oliver. *William Burroughs & the Secret of Fascination.*
        Carbondale: Southern Illinois U.P., 2003.
Harrison, Martin. 'Television & Radio', D E Butler and Anthony King.
        *The British General Election of 1966.* London: Macmillan, 1966.
Harvey, David. *Spaces of Hope.* Edinburgh: Edinburgh U.P., 2000.
Harvie, Christopher. *The Centre of Things.* London: Routledge, 1991.
Haste, Cate. *Sheila Fell: A Passion for Paint.* Farnham: Lund Humphries, 2010.
Haverty, Anne. *The Far Side of a Kiss.* London: Chatto & Windus, 2000.
Hawkes, Rob. *Ford Madox Ford & the Misfit Moderns: Edwardian Fiction and
        the First World War.* Basingstoke: Palgrave Macmillan, 2012.
Hawthorne, Nathanial. *The House of the Seven Gables.* New York: Penguin, 1986.
        'The Custom House' in *The Scarlet Letter.* New York: Norton, 1988.
Hazlitt, William. *Liber Amoris,* edited Gregory Dart. Manchester: Carcenet, 2008.
        *The Fight & Other Writings*, edited Tom Paulin & David Chandler.
        London: Penguin, 2000.
Heaney, Seamus. *Preoccupations.* London: Faber & Faber, 1980.
Hennessy, Peter. *Having It So Good: Britain in the Fifties.* London: Penguin, 2007.
Hess, Scott. *William Wordsworth & the Ecology of Authorship.*
        Virginia: Virginia U.P., 2012.
Hoggart, Richard. *The Uses of Literacy.* Harmondsworth: Pelican, 1958.
Holme, Constance. *The Lonely Plough.* London: Oxford U.P., 1943.
Holmes, Richard. *Coleridge. Early Visions.* London; Penguin, 1989.
Humble, Nicola. 'The Queer Pleasure of Reading'. Working Papers on the Web.
Jacobs, Lewis. *The Rise of American Film.* New York: Harcourt, Brace & Co. 1939.
James, David. *Contemporary British Fiction & the Artistry of Space.*
        London: Continuum , 2008.
James, Simon J. *Unsettled Accounts.* London: Anthem Press, 2003.
Jenkins, Roy. *A Life at the Centre.* London: Macmillan, 1991.
Jones, Stanley. *William Hazlitt.* Oxford: Oxford, 1989.
Kalliney, Peter J. *Cities of Affluence and Anger: A Literary Geography of Modern England.*
        Charlottesville: Virginia U.P., 2007.
Keith, W J. *Regions of the Imagination.* Toronto: Toronto U.P., 1988.
Kelly, Oliver. *Witnessing: Beyond Recognition*. Minneapolis: Minnesota U.P., 2001.
Kermode, Frank. *Concerning E M Forster.* London: Weidenfeld & Nicolson, 2009.
Kerouac, Jack. *On the Road.* London: Penguin, 1991.

Kinkead-Weekes, Mark. 'D H Lawrence & the Dance', in edited Peter Preston. *DH Lawrence. The Journal of the D H Lawrence Society.* Nottingham: D H Lawrence Society. 1993.

Kitson, Peter J. 'Political Thinker', in edited Lucy Newlyn, *The Cambridge Companion to Coleridge.* Cambridge: Cambridge, 2002.

Krakauer, Jon. *Into the Wild.* London: Pan, 1998.

Kynaston, David. *Austerity Britain. 1945-51.* London: Bloomsbury, 2007.

Laing, R. D. *The Politics of Experience.* New York: Pantheon Books, 1967. *The Divided Self.* London: Penguin, 1990.

Larabee, Mark D. *Front Lines of Modernism: Remapping the Great War in British Fiction.* New York: Palgrave Macmillan, 2011.

Larkin, Philip. *Collected Poems.*London: The Marvell Press and Faber & Faber, 1988.

Lawrence, D H. *Women in Love.* Middlesex: Penguin, 1960.

Leeming, Glenda. *Margaret Drabble.* Tavistock: Nothcote House Publishers, 2006.

Low, Gail Ching-Liang. *White Skins/Black Masks.* London: Routledge, 1996.

Massingham, H. J. *Remembrance: An Autobiography.* London: Batsford, 1942.

McCutheon, Mark. 'Liber Amoris and the Lineaments of Hazlitt's Desire' in *Texas Studies in Literature and Language, Vol.46,* No.4. Austen, USA: Texas U.P., 2004.

McKenzie, D F. 'Typography & Meaning: The Case of William Congreve' in edited Peter D MacDonald & Michael F Suarez. *Making Meaning. 'Patterns of the Mind' & Other Essays.* Boston: Massachusetts U.P., 2002.

McKenzie, Robert & Allan Silver. *Angels in Marble.* London: Heinemann 1968.

Meinig, D. W. 'The Beholding Eye' in edited, Meinig. *The Interpretation of Ordinary Landscapes.* Oxford: Oxford U.P., 1979

Milder, Robert. 'Introduction', Herman Melville. *Billy Budd, Sailor.* Oxford: Oxford U.P.,1997.

Miller, Henry. *Tropic of Capricorn.* London: John Calder, 1964.

Milton, John. Edited Merritt Y Hughes, *John Milton: Complete Poems & Major Prose.* London: Odyssey, 1957.

Mitchell, Lee Clark. *Westerns. Making the Man in Fiction & Film.* Chicago U.P.,1996.

Monsman, Gerald. 'H Rider Haggard's Nada the Lily: A Triumph of Translation' in *English Literature in Translation 1880-1920, Vol.47, No.4.* Greensboro, USA: Carolina U.P., 2004.

Oliver, Kelly. *Witnessing Beyond Recognition.* Minneapolis:Minnesota U.P., 1966.

Opie, Iona & Peter Opie. Edited, *The Oxford Book of Children's Verse.* London: Oxford U.P., 1960.

Pace, Joe. 'Emotion and Cognition in The Prelude', *Romanticism on the Net.* www.erudt.org

Paglia, Camille. *Sexual Personae.* London & New Haven: Yale U.P., 1990.

Paulin, Tom. *The Day-Star of Liberty.* London: Faber & Faber, 1998.

Pearson, Neil. *Obelisk: A History of Jack Kahane and the Obelisk Press.* Liverpool: Liverpool U.P.,2007.

Pinkney, Tony. *Raymond Williams.* Bridgend: Seren Books, 1991.

Plotz, John. 'Can the Sofa Speak? A Look at Critical Theory' in *Criticism Vol.47, No.1.* Detroit: Wayne State U.P., 2005.

Ricks, Christopher. *Dylan's Vision of Sin.* London: Viking, 2003.

Robinson, Daniel. 'Taking "Other Liberties" with Hazlitt's Liber Amoris' in *Studies in Short Fiction No. 34* . Newberry College, 1997.

Robinson, Paul A. *The Sexual Radicals.* London: Paladin, 1970.

Russett, Margaret. *Fictions and Fakes: Forging Romantic Authenticity, 1760-1845.* New York: Cambridge U.P.,2006.

Sagar, Keith. 'D H Lawrence: Dramatist' in *The D H Lawrence Review.* Nottingham: D H Lawrence Society, 1978.

Said, Edward W, *Culture & Imperialism.* London: Chatto & Windus, 1993.

Sandbrook, Dominic. *Seasons in the Sun.* London: Allen Lane, 2012.

Saunders, Max. *Self Impression.* Oxford: Oxford U.P., 2010.

Scott, J. *Piranesi.* London: Academy Editions, 1975. www.britishmuseum.org

Scott, Walter. *Ivanhoe.* London: Collins, 1954.

Scruggs, Charles. 'Jean Toomer & Kenneth Burke and The Persistance of the Past'. *American Literary History Vol.13, No.1.* Oxford: Oxford U.P.,2001.

Showalter, Elaine. *Sister's Choice.* Oxford: Oxford U.P. ,1991.

Sillitoe, Alan. *Mountains and Caverns.* London: W H Allen, 1975.
'Odysseus in Wigton'. London: *Guardian,* 28 August 1999.

Silverman, Kaja. *Male Subjectivity at the Margins.* London: Routledge, 1992.

Snell, K D M. Edited, *The Regional novel in Britain and Ireland: 1800-1990* . Cambridge: Cambridge U.P.,1998.

Sontag, Susan. *Illness as Metaphor.* New York: Farrer, Straus & Giroux, 1978.

Soper, Kate. 'Naturalized Woman & Feminized Nature' in edited Laurence Coupe. *The Green Studies Reader.* London: Routledge, 2000.

Spicer, Jack. Edited Robin Blazer. *The Collected Books of Jack Spicer.* Los Angeles: Black Sparrow Press.

Squillace, Robert. 'The Imagined Town and the Unknowable City' in edited, John Shapcott. *Bennett and his Contemporaries Write the Town and the City.* Stoke-on Trent: Arnold Bennett Society, 2008.

Stafford, Fiona. *Local Attachments.* New York: Oxford U.P., 2010.

Stephenson, Randall. *The Last of England?* New York: Oxford U.P., 2004.

Swartz, Omar. *The View from On the Road.* Carbondale, USA: Southern Illinois U.P.,1999.

Taylor, D J. *After the War.* London: Flamingo, 1994.

Taylor, Richard H. edited, *The Personal Notebooks of Thomas Hardy.* London: Macmillan, 1978.

Thompson, E P. *The Making of the English Working Class.* London: Penguin, 1968.

Thompson, Flora. *Lark Rise to Candleford.* Middlesex: Penguin, 1973.

Thompson, Ian. *The English Lakes.* London: Bloomsbury, 2010.

Thoreau, Henry David. *Walden.* Oxford: Oxford U.P., 1997.

Thursfield, Amanda. *Melvyn Bragg.* www. contemporarywriters.com, 2003.

Tillyard, E M W. *The Epic Strain in the English Novel.* London: Chatto & Windus, 1967.

Toft, John. 'Midland Voices' in edited, Alan Pedley. *The Arnold Bennett Society Newsletter, Vol.4,* No.18. Ross-on-Wye, Winter 2011-12.

Turnbull, Ronald. *Blencathra. Portrait of a Mountain.* London: Francis Lincoln, 2010.

Valéry, Paul. *The Graveyard by the Sea.* Edited Anthony Hartley, *The Penguin Book of French Verse. 4.* Middlesex: Penguin, 1996.

Wales, Katie. ' The Anxiety of Influence: Hoggart, Liminality and Melvyn Bragg's *Crossing the Lines* 'in edited Sue Owen. *Re-Reading Richard Hoggart.* Cambridge: Cambridge Scholars Publishing, 2008.

Walker, Carol Kyros, *Walking North With Keats.* New Haven & London: Yale U.P., 1992.

Welch, Lew. *I remain: The Letters of Lew Welch & The Correspondence of his Friends. Volume Two: 1960 -1971.* Bolinas, California: Grey Fox Press.

Wendt, Kerry Higgins. *The Epigraphic Character: Fiction & Metafiction in the Twentieth-Century Novel.* Unpublished thesis, Emory University, USA, 2011.

West, Rebecca. *The Return of the Soldier.* London: Penguin, 1988.

Wharton, Edith. *The Writing of Fiction.* New York: Touchstone, 1997.

White, Hayden. *Tropics of Discourse: Essays & Cultural Criticism.* Baltimore: The John Hopkins U.P., 1985.

Williams W M. *The Sociology of an English Village: Gosforth.* London: Routledge & Kegan Paul, 1956.

Williams, Raymond. *Border Country.* London: Hogarth Press, 1960.
*Keywords.* London: Fontana, 1976.
*The Country and The City.* New York: Oxford U.P., 1975.
Politics and letters. London: Verso, 1981.

Wister,Owen. *The Virginian.* Lincoln, USA: Nebraska U.P. (Bison Books), 1992.

Withey, Lynne. *Grand Tours & Cook's Tours: A History of Leisure Travel, 1750 to 1950.* London: Aurum,1997.

Wolfe, Tom.'Introduction',*The New Journalism,* edited Wolfe & E W Johnson. London: Picador, 1975.

Woolf, Virginia. *To The Lighthouse.* London: Hogarth Press, 1982.

Wordsworth, William. *The Prelude,* edited Jonathan Wordsworth. London: Penguin, 1995.
*A Guide Through the District of the Lakes In the North of England.* London: Rupert Hart-Davis, 1951.

Wordsworth, William & Coleridge, Samuel Taylor. *Lyrical Ballads & Other Poems.* Ware: Wordsworth Editions, 2003.

Wu, Duncan. *William Hazlitt: The First Modern Man.* New York: Oxford U.P., 2008.

Yeats, W B. Edited A Norman Jeffares. *Selected Poetry.* London: Macmillan, 1972.

Zang, Tianying. *D H Lawrence's Philosophy of Nature - An Eastern View.* Bloomington: Trafford, 2006

# INDEX